Calling the Horses

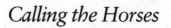

Calling the Horses

A RACING AUTOBIOGRAPHY

Peter O'Sullevan

STANLEY PAUL

London Sydney Auckland Johannesburg

Stanley Paul and Co. Ltd

An imprint of Century Hutchinson

Brookmount House, 62–65 Chandos Place,
Covent Garden, London WC2N 4NW

Century Hutchinson Australia (Pty) Ltd
20 Alfred Street, Milson's Point, Sydney 2061

Century Hutchinson New Zealand Limited
191 Archers Road, PO Box 40–086, Glenfield, Auckland 10

Century Hutchinson South Africa (Pty) Ltd
PO Box 337, Bergvlei 2012, South Africa

First published 1989
Reprinted 1989 (four times)

Set by Tek Art Limited

Printed and bound in Great Britain by Butler and Tanner Ltd, Frome and London

British Library Cataloguing in Publication Data

O'Sullevan, Peter
Calling the horses: a racing autobiography.
1. Racehorses. Racing. Biographies
I. Title
798.4'0092'4

ISBN 0 09 173714 1

Contents

Photographic acknowledgement

The author and publishers would like to thank the following for permission to reproduce their copyright photographs: *Daily Express*, Popperfoto, Sport & General Press Agency, Central Press and Gerry Cranham.

CHAPTER 1

Never Look Behind

When Fairy and I galloped round Tattenham Corner some three months before the 1925 Derby winner, Manna, I had the sure conviction of a seven-year-old that I would be a jockey. Fairy was stuck with being a chestnut Welsh pony with a flaxen mane and tail and a distinctly incongruous name. Between us there was a complete understanding. Could be, given the opportunity, an only child develops a closer affinity with animals.

By the time Fairy came into my life my dear, volatile English mother and contrastingly tranquil, idolized, Irish father had discovered that they were irreconcilably incompatible and I was being indulgently 'brought up' by my mother's parents, Sir John and Lady Henry, in a rambling country house in the vast, unspoiled Surrey acreage of Gatton Park, near Reigate.

It was the promise of my grandmother's head groom, Truelove (I never did known his Christian name), of a ride round Epsom racecourse that made me overcome my aversion to dressing up as a Red Indian and taking part in a Reigate parade in which Truelove was a Canadian Mountie. Pattenden, the splendid chauffeur who taught me to drive before I was ten, wore Latin-American gear suited to leading Peru, the llama; and Boris, the Russian chef, appeared as a Cossack. I remember being desperately embarrassed, but Fairy, who could show a fair expanse of white in the eye if anything displeased him, positively lapped it up.

Truelove appeared a little evasive when I broached the fulfilment of his promise, and advised me not to mention it to Her Ladyship. I didn't – before or after. He was, he explained, waiting to hear from a friend who worked for Mr Nightingall, the trainer, what would be the best time to avoid racehorses at exercise.

We started early on 'the day' and didn't even pause at the lodge gate, where there was a lady who used to claim Truelove's close attention. He was riding a good hunter and point-to-point horse with a wild eye called Machiavelli, who struck sparks from the tarmac as we crossed the only traffic-bearing road. As instructed, I'd got a penny gripped between knee and saddle both sides. If you dropped one you had to forfeit it. They went back into my pocket as we neared the Downs and I took my leathers up three holes.

Mr Truelove never spoke much, which was nice; just smoked, looking sharply left and right before striking a match as if an invisible sniper might get him, and whistled whenever he saw a young lady.

The nearer we got to the white rails by the six-furlong chute, the more fidgety he and 'Machi' became. Fairy, who snorted and shied as a lark got up from under his feet, felt ready for anything.

There were a couple of horses on the inside of the course by the 1½-mile start and a man with a lurcher at the top of Tattenham Hill. 'I'll wait here,' said Mr T. 'You trot over to the far rail, Master Peter, then you can canter down the hill and along to the grandstands; but pull up as soon as you come to the first building, turn round and come back the same way – here.' He didn't look very happy.

Fairy wasn't convinced we ought to leave him, but, once on our way, he flew down the hill – it didn't seem very steep – and into the straight. He had a semaphore system with his ears: the offside usually pricked and the near turned back to listen for communication. Both were flattened as we reached the stands and I shouted excitedly, 'We've won' and 'Steady', and he eased up. I knew how Steve Donoghue must feel.

When we turned, puffing, Fairy took hold of his bit again and indicated gameness for another gallop back to our mentor. Just as I reached him a man appeared from nowhere and shouted. Mr Truelove didn't seem to hear him. He just said, 'We'd best trot on', adding the only philosophical aside I ever heard him utter, 'A good soldier never looks behind.'

I was longing to tell somebody about the exploit – especially a very pretty housemaid who would sometimes warn me if my delightful, though totally unpredictable, grandmother, a brave and wonderful horsewoman until well into her seventieth year, was in a 'mood'. But I didn't. Then one day she said, knowingly, 'I've been hearing stories about you, Master Peter.' That Truelove, he certainly got around.

Association with Fairy was interrupted after I had been taught to use the clippers on him. These were powered by twin cogs and a starting handle like the hare on an unlicensed dog track. In order to make certain that they caused him no discomfort I tried them on my index finger and severed the top. Pattenden drove me on a rather noisy journey to Redhill hospital to have the remains sewn back, untidily.

The finger turned septic and the asthma, which was to plague me for another decade and beyond, began to tighten its grip and create the strain with which every acute sufferer will be familiar. Among areas of ill health that both GPs and so-called specialists seemed powerless to cope with effectively were respiratory problems and dermatology.

There may have been marginal progress in the former category, but my regrettably extensive experience among skin specialists of six nationalities has led me to the unavoidable conclusion that they are frequently insensitive and as helpful as a welshing bookmaker. Following a visiting medic's diagnosis that horse contact was respons- ible for my asthma, I learned the shattering news that Fairy had been sold. Too late the hospital tests, which could discern no allergy whatever.

His 'replacement' – as if Fairy could be replaced – was lethal both ends and packed the buck of a bronco without the stimulus of those nauseating aids, a cinch applied to a horse's most delicate region, employed by 'brave' US cowboys. When unshipped by Tartar, as he was revealingly named, I had to pay Truelove half a crown to buy the piece of ground I'd fallen on. Given the deeds every time, I'd have become one of the biggest landowners in Surrey. But at least Tartar taught me to sit tight.

A further dimension was added to my ambitions – which already included reporting in the caring manner of the *Sunday Express*'s Geoffrey Gilbey – when on 25 March 1927 the man on the wireless said that there would shortly take place the first action commentary on the Grand National from Aintree. Against a noisy background Meyrick Good announced the thirty-seven runners and riders and discussed the regrettably misty scene with his assistant, George Allison, who revealed that they were speaking from 'Mr E.C. Topham's private stand'.

Meyrick had been 'Man on the Spot' for the *Sporting Life* for many years and was an expert race-reader. Ever since 1921, when Lord Derby invited him to his box to 'read' the race to King George V, this had become established practice. Despite this new responsibility, the monarch still stood on his right by the open microphone – with Allison, whose job was to provide the 'colour' – on his other side. The Man on the Spot sure must have employed a good agent, or dealt with a magnanimous Corporation negotiator, for his share of the £254 13s 4d cost of the broadcast was – believe it or not, latter-day twentieth-century sports commentators – 100 guineas!

Even at the birth of outside sportscasting the BBC's ambivalent attitude to the sport of kings was evident. Meyrick complained that, having been told to prepare comment on all the leading candidates for pre-race transmission, it was cancelled at the eleventh hour.

Certainly no one who backed Sprig (personally I was 'on' Bovril III) could complain of neglect. The commentator had both tipped and backed the ten-year-old, who was trained by his life-long friend Tom Leader and ridden by Tom's son Ted.

These details may not have been totally unconnected with his temporary departure from complete impartiality in the closing stages, when he not only yelled, 'Come on, Ted, you'll win,' but in the ensuing excitement omitted to announce the official placings: first Sprig, second Bovril III, third Bright's Boy, and fourth Drinmond. Distances one length, same.

Meyrick received some flattering mail after the event, but this did not include a letter bearing the BBC cipher, and the following year the Corporation booked Geoffrey Gilbey assisted by Bill Hobbiss. At the same time outlay on the broadcast was reduced sharply to £173 12s, with Geoffrey, who devoted much of his time to prison visiting and supporting those less fortunate than himself, allocated 50 guineas. Bill Hobbiss, a somewhat irascible character, was for many years both the gifted assessor for *Raceform*'s renowned Private Handicap Book and adviser to immensely likeable Sam Armstrong (father of Newmarket trainer Robert, and of Susan Piggott).

As far as I was concerned, the 1928 Grand National broadcast was a great improvement on its predecessor. Memorable, despite an unpromising start to the day. Pattenden had been expecting to drive my grandfather to Croydon Airport in the Minerva in the morning, but the arrangements had been cancelled. Truelove and I had written out our slips, money folded inside, when Pattenden came into the yard, having already collected from four other members of the staff, to explain the problem. The horses had already been exercised and, because of asthma, my bicycle was taboo. But I was breathing well at that moment, and if I took the back drive and the long way round through the park I shouldn't be spotted. 'Don't get caught,' was my fellow conspirators' only instruction.

Off-course betting was very furtive in those days, and when I delivered the envelope to the butcher where the bookie's runner called, all he said, in a rather unnaturally loud voice for the benefit of other customers in the sawdust-laid shop, was, 'The order will be attended to, young man.'

My first commission coincided with my first touch – sixpence each-way on 100/1 chance Tipperary Tim. Who knows what might have happened that year had not Easter Hero decimated the forty-two-horse field when getting lodged on top of the Canal Turn fence, or if Great Span's saddle had not slipped, or if Billy Barton had not fallen when upsides my hero at the last fence, by which time they were the only two left in the race. To me, as to the winner, amateur Bill Dutton's tubed partner, who was also breathing freely this day, these were merely questions of academic interest.

Come to think of it, but for personal oxygen shortage I'd have still been at Hawtreys Preparatory School, Westgate-on-Sea, on National day – Friday, 30 March. I'd moved on from Mr and Mrs Bull's cosy nearby day school to become an unwilling resident of Francis Cautley's spartan academy on 25 January 1928. The area was reputed to be particularly healthy; to me the invariably arctic chill made Cheltenham's National Hunt Festival at its iciest seem Riviera-like by comparison.

I was returned before term's end, studies and – far more importantly – football interrupted by bronchial pneumonia. My father was directed to 'see he takes his medicine' when it was time for the eagerly awaited annual week's holiday with him at Phyllis Court Club, Henley-on-Thames, where he taught me to row and we would ride in the morning and race in the afternoon.

In citations I was to read later in life, Colonel John Joseph O'Sullevan DSO was described by a trio of lords field-marshal as coolly gallant and without fear; and by Cork Judge Hynes as 'totally fearless and impartial in the performance of his difficult duties' as County Kerry resident magistrate from 1918 to 1922. But he became uncharacteristically fearful and affected by his powerlessness to help when asthma attacked me while we were together. Sadly, although he never suffered from it personally until he was in his fifties, he was suddenly stricken in 1936 and died within a day of our last meeting in Zurich. He had flown there for treatment from Antigua, where he'd settled with my stepmother five years before.

Meanwhile my academic qualifications did not, regrettably, extend to passing the Common Entrance exam to Charterhouse. Paradoxically – since I had no difficulty in calculating the returns on a winning 1s each-way double at 11/4 and 9/2 – it was mathematics, notably algebra, that proved furthest from my comprehension. Generously, the Hawtreys headmaster wrote to his public school counterpart reporting that I had topped the 1931 First XI bowling averages – in a season when the team was unbeaten – and further could be guaranteed to make the Charterhouse Football First XI. His assurance was accepted and, thankfully, justified; though I doubt whether Francis Cautley would have fully approved the precedence I accorded race meetings (both horse and greyhound) over devotional attendance.

				HAWTREYS 1st XI
	BOWLING FOR 1931			
NAME	OVERS	RUNS	WICKETS	AVERAGE PER WICKET
1 P. O'SULLEVAN	38	60	10	6·00
2 I.K. WHITE-SMITH	18	53	7	7·57
3 C.D. EARLE	3	8	1	8·00
4 E.R. YATES	107	161	20	8·05
5 A.H. CAMPBELL	130	285	23	10·22
6 I.C.S. MUNRO	57	142	8	17·75
7 HON: O.R. BECKETT	3	26	1	26·00

My mother had married again in 1928 – happily another like my father for whom horses were high priority. Strangely, although she raced regularly with my stepfather at Lingfield, Sandown, Lewes, Gatwick and Hurst Park as well as Ascot and Goodwood, and ensured that my column had at least one reader when I joined the *Daily Express* in 1950, I don't think she ever really got around to distinguishing between two-year-olds and their elders, or handicaps and conditions races etc. – but she still loved it.

I spent holidays with her and my stepfather, Colonel Bertram Pott, at their house in Kent in the early thirties when Cinders was the near-white Arab pony in my life who sustained my unwarranted dreams of riding glory. It was a period of very 'live' information. Haslar, the butler, had formerly been in the employ of the Lambourn trainer Captain Ossie Bell, with whose head lad he prudently remained in close contact. I doubt whether the stable's principal patron, Sir Hugo Cunliffe-Owen, was better informed or whether my bicycle was ever employed to better purpose.

Bertie Pott, or the 'Governor' as I called him, was nearly thirty years my mother's senior and a truly sweet man. His family had a long association with Kent. He was for years Lord of the Manor of Southborough. He'd commanded a squadron of the West Kent Yeomanry in both the Boer and 1914–18 wars; had ridden numerous point-to-point winners; and, before his fortunes were traumatically affected by the 1927 collapse of rubber in the USA, shared a Scottish shoot with Kentish neighbours Lords Camden and Abergavenny. He was anxious that I should learn to shoot, and regular instruction followed.

In the gun room at Paddock Wood an illustrated rhyme gave cautionary warning:

> Never, never let your gun
> Pointed be at anyone.
> That it may unloaded be
> Matters not the least to me . . .

and ended with the thought that:

> All the pheasants ever bred
> Won't repay for one man dead.

Frankly, I was not at all sure about that one.

My first day out with the Governor's syndicate filled him with pride. I shot everything within range and returned home to eat dinner in silence. I cleaned my gun that evening, put it away and never took it out again.

CHAPTER 2

Finding the Key

Asthma apart, my biggest handicap at Charterhouse was John Alexander Sutton, who had a hot line to the powerful Wroughton stable of Ivor Anthony. A nephew of Aubrey Hastings, from whom Ivor took over in 1929, John was two years and eight months my senior, long in the leg and greyhound-swift at getting to the school library's only copy of the *Sporting Life* before me. This major inconvenience was greatly alleviated in 1933 when he offered the advice that the Wroughton horse Kellsborough Jack (25/1, what a beauty!) should not be excluded from my Grand National calculations.

Thanks be, I paid less attention fifteen years later when we met on the lawn at Ascot before the 1948 running of the Clarence House Stakes. John, whose frequent encounters with adversity left his faith in the next 'good thing' touchingly unimpaired, had, he said, just 'pinched' a grand (£1000). Gordon Richards, who rode so many winners for John's stepfather, Herbert Blagrave, had told him that Royal Forest – winner of his only two previous races, including the Coventry – was both a very good two-year-old and improving all the time. The three-horse opposition included two apparently modest youngsters and an unraced colt, Burpham, who was considered just about ready for a run and that's all.

Jack Burns, William Hill, Hector Macdonald, Maxie Parker and Laurie Wallis were betting on the rails at that time, and John had no difficulty in betting a total of £18,000 to £1000 on. 'If you want to get the day's expenses, there's no harm in laying £1000 to £50 on, or you might do even better,' he counselled, adding, 'It's only a question of going down and coming back.'

Royal Forest, who started 25/1 on, managed that part. But not before being stung by a wasp, which was accounted the reason for his half-length defeat by 33/1 newcomer Burpham.

The Sutton cattle had long since changed hands at Swindon market when Royal Forest met Burpham in the Dewhurst and beat him five and a half lengths – on the bit.

As for personal 'results', an unwelcome double – double pneumonia – ended my stay at Charterhouse: a Harley Street specialist prescribed my urgent exit to the mountain air of Switzerland. It was particularly charitable of my housemaster, the Rev Lancelot Allen, to write to my stepfather expressing such embarrassing-to-repeat comments as 'Peter's sustained and courageous battle against his delicacy has been the admiration of us all', when I had, on occasion, fled the sanatorium to encourage a greyhound at Aldershot with wheezy enthusiasm.

Cosmopolitan Alpine College at Arveyes was, in many ways, a great bonus. But the assumption that the magnificent mountains radiate health-promoting properties is difficult to sustain in a country whose chemists appear as extensively patronized as British betting shops. And possibly to no greater advantage. As far as I was concerned, reversion to asthma would have been 21 lb preferable to the skin problems which replaced it. James and Cecily Barnard, who ran the College with skill and sensitivity, ultimately had to write to England in a similar vein to the Rev Allen before them.

A room in the Woolavington Wing of the Middlesex Hospital became my new home. Here, having taken a correspondence course in journalism with the Regent Institute, I began, in between treatment, to accumulate enough rejection slips to paper the Rowley Mile – double thickness. Admittedly my subjects were not all that mirth-making. Public apathy towards the plight of two million sufferers from leprosy in the British Empire was one; another was inspired by Professor J. B. S. Haldane's *Inequality of Man*, in which he wrote that 'If any newspaper were to publish a daily warning of the early signs of cancer of the womb, it would save many lives, but would certainly lose in circulation and probably be prosecuted for indecency.' (At least I got that one printed as a letter to 'The First British News Magazine' – *News Review.*) Interspersed between these admonitory salvos were enthusiastic racing articles directed at weeklies and provincials which overlooked horse-racing. I have to report that they continued to do so.

On my seventeenth birthday my customarily careful but sometimes impulsively generous grandmother had given me an undreamed-of passport to freedom in the form of the ignition key to a shining new, sealing-wax red 8 hp Morris coupé – RD 6647: 1935 list price, believe it or not, £100! After three months 'inside', emboldened by daytime use of a medicated mask through which I could see and not be seen, and encouraged by my delicious blue-eyed brunette nurse and friend, Vivien, I began night-time sorties in the car. Later I made a comprehensive tour of Britain, visiting the Silver Rings or open course at nearly every circuit in England and Scotland.

Bed and breakfast in a modest hotel in the thirties varied between 5s 6d and 10s (27½p and 50p), and I have the bills to prove it! It was similar throughout Europe, where in early 1938 I drove through ten countries, racing in France, Italy, Hungary (a wonderful ride here along Lake Balaton), Austria and Belgium, returning sadly convinced by the arrogant German demeanour that war was imminent. Back in England, I tried a sulphur cure in Harrogate where Prime Minister Neville Chamberlain was 'taking the waters' – hopefully to better advantage.

Reflecting on the power of the horse to influence the direction of human lives, I posted three 5s each-way doubles and an each-way treble to the Scottish bookmaker I mostly bet with while at Charterhouse. Two obliged; the third was placed. Having already built up a credit with the Harrogate firm of Eastwood and Wray, I collected it and sent flowers to my grandmother together with the information that I was bound for Iceland. After paying my fare (steerage) to the Iceland Steamship Co. Ltd, I sailed aboard the *Bruarfoss* on the four-day voyage from Leith with a sizeable bankroll of £22. It was like tackling the Bay of Biscay in a rowing boat. I'd barely moved from what passed for a bunk in two days when an Icelandic sailor brought tidings that the wireless operator had been alerted to receive an urgent telegram for passenger O'Sullevan. To my eternal embarrassment it read, bless her,

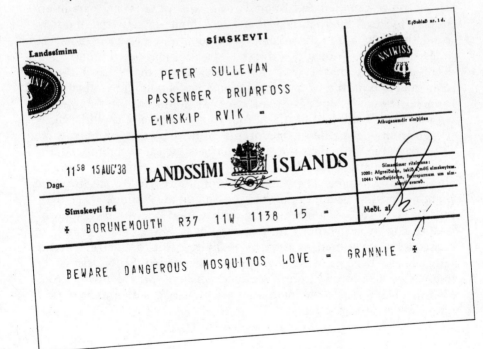

The warning was justified, though they only occurred in a certain part of Iceland, which has a larger surface area than Ireland and, at that time, had a population smaller than that of Brighton.

I came to an arrangement to take over a cabin for 2s 6d a night while the ship was in port at Reykjavik. I bathed in and drank sulphur (really nasty); visited a leper colony supervised by a memorably dedicated director; emptied the contents of my suitcase into a sack, hired two ponies – one to carry the rented tent – and rode into the interior, living rough for a week; and went racing. It was Tote only, a dirt surface and smashing, sturdy, well-kept ponies who were not abused and appeared to relish competition. The longest race was 350 metres!

From Iceland I got a passage to Bergen, the vessel stopping off at the Faroe Islands to pick up whalemeat for the silver fox farms in Norway. On via the twelve-hour scenic rail route to Oslo and thence to Sweden's striking capital, Stockholm, built on twelve islands – a blend of old and new. Some good pictures here – notably in the National Museum – and excellent trotting. A happy feature of Scandinavian racing is that the authorities have for long taken a firm view regarding use of the whip and imposed proper restrictions on its employment.

It was after returning to Stockholm forty-one years later in the cheerful company of Willie Carson, Paul Cook, Pat Eddery, Lester Piggott, Steve Cauthen and Brian Taylor, who were taking part in an All-Star Jockeys' International, that I flew home in reflective mood – wondering how best to put across the Scandinavian message. On a level of lesser concern, I noted that the small pack of marinated salmon and dill (Gravadlax) that I took home cost more than the 370-mile steamboat trip on the Göta Canal linking Stockholm and Gothenburg, from where I got a ship to Newcastle in 1938. Returning after six weeks, with a beard, I still had nearly £2 out of the original £22 with which to get from Newcastle – one of the principal areas of harrowing malnutrition in those days – to Leith, retrieve the car and return south.

As my generation was being called up, in preparation for the war ahead, I sought a medical examination with, it occurred to me, as much chance of passing as a pit pony had of winning the National. 'I certify', read Dr Hartigan's uncompromising verdict, 'that Peter John O'Sullevan is suffering from chronic furunculosis of a severe nature and in consequence is unfitted to serve as a soldier.' Not for the first time I retreated to the peace of the sparsely populated Scilly Isles and, following a £34 'draw' from three successful each-way doubles, wrote offering my services to the International Council of Labour as a courier, ultimately eliciting the reply:

Telegraphic Address: "LABREPCOM, SOWEST, LONDON."

Telephone: VICTORIA 9434 (8 lines)

THE LABOUR PARTY

TRANSPORT HOUSE (South Block), SMITH SQUARE, LONDON, S.W.1

Hon. Treasurer:
GEORGE LATHAN, M.P.

Secretary:
J. S. MIDDLETON

National Agent:
GEORGE R. SHEPHERD

July 13, 1939

Mr. P.J O'Sullivan,
St. Mary's,
Isles of S cilly.

Dear Sir,

I have received your letter of July 3, and I am also informed by Mr. Francis Williams, editor of the "Daily Herald", that you would like copies of the Message to the German People for distribution in Germany at your own risk and expense. How many copies shall I send you?

I would warn you, however, that distribution of this leaflet in Germany is fraught with very grave risk to you. If you accept such a responsibi ity, it must be understood that it is done not only at your own risk, but also on your _own_ responsibility. I would not dare to invite you to take such risks.

Yours sincerely,

William Gillie

WILLIAM GILLIES
Secretary,
International Department

Read the "DAILY HERALD" every day and "LABOUR" and "THE LABOUR WOMAN" every month

A Penzance garage had contrived a secret compartment in the car; the five hundred leaflets I'd requested and been sent for distribution to the German people were stowed; and I was ready and waiting in Chelsea for the 'off', when travel facilities to Germany were withdrawn.

The next day a Charterhouse friend, John Hayne, with whom I'd shared a greyhound and several narrow escapes at termtime race meetings and who was now assistant/pupil trainer with Jack (J. C.) Waugh at Chilton, called with an urgent request. He'd been summoned for a month's military course just after being appointed racing correspondent on the *Reading Gazette*; he rented a 7s 6d a week thatched cottage in Chilton which he didn't want to leave empty, and he had a young Airedale who needed feeding and exercise. Could I take over job, cottage and dog? I could and did.

Well, you know the way fortune runs in cycles in the racing game. Whether training, riding, betting, tipping – whatever – there are times when everything goes right, and if you're not careful you can begin to kid yourself you've found the key. There are others (a lot more frequent) when everything goes so wrong you begin to despair of ever getting it right again.

I worked hard on the book and got in touch with what contacts I had – and a few I hadn't. The Aston Tirrold trainer John Bisgood (a wartime naval commander, he was thereafter referred to irreverently as the man who sank the *Ark Royal*) was in the latter category. He couldn't have been more polite and helpful when I phoned about his runners – in contrast to the occasion when a verdict was given against him at Wolverhampton and he was fined for inquiring of the judge somewhat forcefully whether that official had mislaid his white stick, guide dog, or both.

I went racing every day (for me this has always been a vital ingredient in finding winners) and, mercifully, it all went right. The cottage wasn't on the phone, but whenever I saw Jack Waugh he reported that John had called to say, 'Tell Peter fantastic – I hope he's backing them.' Frankly, apart from two (Maggie, who won at 11/2, and a loser) I wasn't, being too afraid it would stop the winning streak. But it was really something to drive round Reading and see socking great placards – 'Twenty-two winners in five days'.

Not that either of us made imperishable names for ourselves; as war got nearer than settling day the paper folded. It was the closest I got to being a racing journalist for five years.

The day war was declared – confounding a firm rumour in Chelsea that Gracie Fields had persuaded Mussolini to intercede successfully with Hitler – old Bill Surrey, newsvendor and bookie's runner, stood at his pitch opposite Chelsea Town Hall using an *Evening News* poster as an apron. It read in bold black four-inch letters:

KEEP CALM – AND DIG

This exhortation highlighted the general air of unreality.

Bill looked dead worried. 'You've got a few bob to come, haven't you?' he asked, accepting a penny and handing me a paper in one deft movement.

I said I had, but I'd rather have two or three of those posters.

'You're on,' he said. And, compulsive collector of inconsequential memorabilia, I have them still.

Poor Bill's turned-in feet gave him a lot of trouble. As he once observed, slightly ambiguously, 'If I'd gone into the sales ring with them as a yearling, there wouldn't have been no bid.'

He shuffled to his box to get more papers, beckoning me over. 'They won't put a block on the horses and dogs on account of this lot, will they?' he asked.

I said I didn't think so. They'd be sure to want to maintain the bloodstock industry and provide entertainment if possible.

He cheered up a bit, explaining he'd got a treble running on Blue Peter (winner of the 2000 Guineas and the Derby) in the Leger. It was the only classic lost in the five years of the war.

London was emptying as fast as the stands after the favourite's got beat in the last. I joined the Town Hall as a volunteer, changed the car for a four-seater and helped evacuate families to the country and distribute supplies. When funds ran low I signed up with the Chelsea Civil Defence Rescue Service at the unextravagant rate of £4 12s 6d a week – which left £2 4s 6d after paying the rent on my Britten Street flat. Mr Tuson's pawn shop in the King's Road never had a more regular customer. My late father's gold cigarette case with the family crest – a dove bearing an olive branch perched on a crown (all Irishmen are descended from the Kings of Ireland) and the legend in Gaelic 'The hand that will do no harm' – was in and out like the cuckoo on a Swiss clock. Punting needed to be selective, and profitable.

It was in this unpromising financial climate that I learned of my uncle's intention to disperse his horses – three hunters and a very interesting young prospect, half-brother to the 1938 Cheltenham Gold Cup winner Morse Code – to the army. It was a period when many were putting down their pets to spare them the fate with which we were threatened. I hurried to Richmond Park, where trenches were being dug both to provide cover for the defence and to inhibit the progress of German tanks when, as expected, they were dropped by parachute, to learn the cost of livery at the Robin Hood Gate Stables.

Not unnaturally, perhaps, my uncle was initially unresponsive to my plea on behalf of Morse Code's relative (I'd thought to call him SO'S) on the grounds that a small Chelsea flat, on the second floor at that, would be unsuitable accommodation. I explained that I had viewed the premises in Richmond Park (£2 10s per week or £1 10s half livery) and they were fine. I understood him to have relented, and alerted the head porter that I was expecting a horse – a precaution in case SO'S was delivered during a duty period (alternate twenty-four hours) and needed to be re-routed to the Civil Defence Depot.

We were a motley crew based at Carlyle Square: there were two artists, an accountant, a builder, a butler, a carpenter, a chauffeur, an engineer, a greengrocer, a mechanic, a professional thief, a schoolmaster, a spiv, a window cleaner and more. Not that the peacetime thief revealed this detail in his job description. 'I put myself down as a handyman,' he told me once, adding, 'I didn't say handy at shinning up drainpipes.'

The spiv – best snooker player and best company in the depot – was officially a promoter. One of his most fruitful civilian activities involved employing all the girls who worked in a large laundry near Wimbledon to queue for tickets during the tennis championships. 'I bought them all gloves,' he related, 'so that they looked the part. That was their whack. They'd queue all night for those gloves.'

We were assembled in squads of five with the driver (me) of the stretcher party vehicle sharing responsibilities on arrival at an 'incident'. Thus, while others were either performing or preparing for more heroic contribution to the war effort, we placed the lives of the local citizenry in greater peril than the enemy had yet achieved by speeding through the Royal Borough on interminable exercises. Horizontal in simulated rubble, brave volunteers wore labels indicating the injuries to which we were required to apply first aid.

One of the first civilian casualties in Chelsea was an unfortunate lady who, according to label, had suffered a severed artery, requiring the application of a tourniquet. The crew concerned did a good job up to the moment of placing her on a stretcher. Then, in their anxiety to deliver the mock invalid to a waiting ambulance with maximum speed, they stumbled and tipped her out so that she broke a leg.

To the dismay of the rodent population, we dressed in yellow oilskins and shinned down metal ladders into the sewers to receive instruction in decontamination following a gas attack. It wasn't one of my favourite exercises. Back at the flat after one of these excursions I was savouring a particularly welcome bath when the doorbell rang and a man called through the letterbox, 'I've got a horse downstairs for a Mr O'Sullevan.'

Rumours of imminent air attack were intensifying and the carrier was obviously keen to return to the quiet Suffolk countryside as soon as possible. He had a bridle in the box but no saddle. Neither had I.

Morse Code's half-brother eyed his unfamiliar surroundings with keen interest. A bright chestnut, he stood about 16.2 on good clean limbs with a girth that clearly indicated he'd been unaffected by food rationing.

The driver gave me a leg up and wished me luck. 'First stop Richmond Park,' I called out and a moment later we were grazing a headstone in St Luke's churchyard. An oncoming motorist obviously hadn't appreciated the impermanence of the partnership between horse and man when the latter is both riding bareback and without great skill. Back on course down the perilous King's Road route almost every object encountered – sandbags and buses in particular – represented a new experience in the hitherto sheltered life of my partner, occasioning abrupt evasive action. By the time we reached the World's End landmark, the Nell Gwynn, I was reflecting that, under similar circumstances, Charles II's mistress would have found the monarch a disappointing guest. Putney Bridge twice threatened an unscheduled water jump. Ultimate arrival was effected with exuberant panache by one; exhausted relief by the other. No need for identification.

I knew of an Epsom trainer who was particularly jumping orientated, so I rang him – only to learn that he had joined the RAF. But his head lad, Charlie Bell, had taken over and would be happy to see me. So I cycled to Treadwell House Stables, Epsom, to extol the merit of this well-bred horse with whose half-brother Mr Bell was naturally familiar. Several of the lads had worked for that martinet of a stableman, Stanley Wootton, from whom the yard was leased, and this was reflected in its immaculate appearance.

After going round the horses, most of which were known to me on the racecourse, we cycled down to Albert Road where Charlie lived with his sister Mary. Over a cup of tea he revealed his terms – £4 a week. This was going to impose a severe strain on my resources, but I knew I had to go ahead.

I said I'd ride the horse to the stables the day after tomorrow. And after Mary had insisted on a tot of whisky for the road – there wasn't a great deal of resistance – and Charlie had supplemented it, I pedalled back to Chelsea convinced beyond doubt that a new 'chasing phenomenon was about to be introduced to an incredulous public. On my return I opened a letter from Weatherby and Sons of 15 Cavendish Square, dated 23 August 1940: 'With reference to your call at this office, we beg to advise you that the colours "Black, yellow crossbelts, with a yellow cap" are available for registration under National Hunt Rules.'

CHAPTER 3

A Pocketful of Readies

Within a week the Chelsea Civil Defence was in action for real. The first body I helped carry from an air-raid shelter which had received a direct hit was a young girl whose right hand showed that she had one finger left to varnish when the bomb struck. Among all the 'incidents' (as they were euphemistically termed) which were to follow, this one became printed indelibly on my memory – a symbol of the obscenity of war.

The bombing resulted in renewed exodus from London, and to supplement my income I drove a local firm's furniture van on my off-duty days, ferrying household contents to Wales (mostly) and the West Country. It was no sinecure. All signposts and road markings had been removed in order to confuse the enemy (there were no motorways, needless to say) and there was an instruction to be wary of giving directions for fear of assisting the Fifth Column.

Meanwhile Charlie Bell reported the stable's latest acquisition: a very good jumper but, as far as he could determine to date, 'without a great turn of foot'. I was surprised by the latter observation, I told him, because he had seemed to show plenty of speed in Richmond Park. Equipped with a saddle, he'd been a lovely ride, showing great élan in jumping the trenches.

'Aye,' said Bradford-born Charlie, 'they all run fast passing trees.'

In any event we would need full details of his pedigree for registration before entries could be made. So I wrote to my uncle for the appropriate information, only to receive the devastating reply, 'I don't know what gave you the idea that I'd sent you the half-brother to Morse Code. I sent you my old hunter, Hawthorn, and I do hope you are not trying to turn him into a racehorse . . .'

Charlie reacted to my apology with the contention that it would be all the more creditable to win a race with him. Hawthorn, by Sprig o' Mint (by Spearmint) – dam's pedigree unknown – was registered as Wild Thyme II and made his debut in the two-mile Coventry Novices' Steeplechase at Cheltenham on 6 November 1940. On the strength of word in the weighing-room that he was a sound jumper, Wild Thyme was selected as the one to give them a 'lead', so that he was ahead of the field over the first three fences. From there on my massive 33/1 wager (£50 to 30s) looked less secure. And after he'd made a mistake at the water and begun to get in serious arrears, partner Wally Crump wisely pulled up.

Craving, like all owners, a word of encouragement to sustain hope for the future, I was entranced by Wally's firm assertion that 'he'll be much better for that.' He explained that he had feared the horse might have hurt his back at the water, which was why he had eased him. 'He'd have gone close otherwise,' he insisted, adding, 'and he pulled up sound as a bell.'

By the time I reached London Wild Thyme had become a winner without a penalty. It was merely a matter of selecting an engagement which coincided, once again, with an off-duty day. The chosen target was Nottingham on Monday, 25 November.

The conditions of the Wilford Steeplechase of 100 sovereigns (the second to receive 10 sovereigns and the third 5 sovereigns out of the Plate) provided for a 10 lb allowance to maidens of six years old and upwards. Surely only enemy intervention could keep W.T. out of the first three?

The racecard carried a police air-raid notice which read: 'In the event of an air-raid warning racing will be postponed until the "raiders passed" signal is given. The public are advised to scatter and lie down. If possible, the car park should be avoided on account of the danger of splintering glass.' The sirens did sound once during the programme, prompting a Tattersall's bookmaker to raise his umbrella, but it was the intervention of the water jump, again, rather than the malevolent Luftwaffe, that was accounted the reason for W.T.'s failure to take advantage of the concessionary poundage. Not that he fell at or in it. He just took rather a long while deciding how best to handle it, and by the time the crossing had been effected most of the others had gone beyond recall. Wally Crump kindly put it down to the sun shining on the water, which underlined the capriciousness of the November climate, for it certainly wasn't shining anywhere else on the Colwick circuit.

Failure must have gone to my head. A horse I'd always liked, Sundange, was given to Charlie, so I leased him – with an option to purchase – in December 1940. Frenchie Nicholson, who shared a jump jockeys' title with Fred Rimell and later became a noted creator of jockeys (Pat Eddery, Walter Swinburn, Paul Cook, Tony Murray, Richard Fox and Roger Wernham were among his pupils) rode him at Cheltenham where on 11 December he ran a respectable fifth of twenty-one. Good to fast ground was essential and thereafter wherever we went it rained – bombs or just rain.

I'd been wasting in order to ride Wild Thyme in a Plumpton Novices in February 1941. Our last 'school' over fences (more for my benefit than his) was in company with an old horse of Nat Smyth's called Lemon Cheese and one of Jack Reardon's ridden by the Belgian jockey 'Nobby' Sawers, whom Charlie had befriended and recommended to his often dyspeptic Epsom colleague Jack.

It was a foggy morning; I was in a cold sweat with flu, and after six months in racing stables Wild Thyme seemed to have developed a mouth of iron. Charlie's head lad, Wally Green, who very helpfully kept me informed regarding the aspirations of local stables, confided discouragingly, 'He'd pull over a Sherman tank now.'

It took us a while to find the first fence, which looked about as inviting as the Berlin Wall. We hacked back fifty yards or so and set off together. W.T. held his head so low he might have been questing for truffles. That he took off and landed accurately owed nothing to communication from his passenger.

There was a rending crash and thud at the third, where Reardon's horse hit the ground with the finality of an unopened parachute. As soon as it could be arranged I pulled up and returned to the scene of disaster. 'Nobby' was lying, chalk-white and unconscious, when Jack Reardon loomed up, regarded the prone form with utter contempt, shouted at Charlie, 'I thought you said this bugger could ride', then turned and galloped off to look for his horse. This is a tough game all right, I thought.

Our Belgian friend spoke very little English and currently didn't look like speaking a lot of any language. I laid my jacket over him and waited while Charlie rode off to summon help. 'Nobby' just about came to in the ambulance but was detained in hospital. I checked in at the Civil Defence sick bay before reporting for duty and was similarly detained – developing pneumonia. So Frenchie Nicholson took over on Wild Thyme in the Worthing Novices' Chase (£70 first; £5 second; £3 third) at Plumpton and got a right dressing-down in the process.

The Duchess of Norfolk's Ticca Gari, ridden by six times champion Gerry Wilson, won; Ron Smyth, who rode three Champion Hurdle winners, was second on Lemon Cheese; and that fine amateur, author and later breeder of Brigadier Gerard, Captain John Hislop, third on Birnam. Perhaps not unreasonably, Frenchie pulled up W.T. in front of the stands to avoid the imminent probability of being lapped, a tactic which Wally Green interpreted as an act of gross treason. By way of demonstrating his displeasure Charlie's head lad dashed on to the course

– showing speed which W.T. would have been hard pressed to match – to shower him with forcefully expressed abuse.

'You ought to bloody well be paid in white feathers for that ride,' fumed Wally. 'He was just getting his second wind.'

To which Frenchie responded gently, 'It would need to have been a lot better than the first one.'

That was Wild Thyme's last racecourse appearance, though he enjoyed many years of retirement.

Sundange looked to have a very good chance at Plumpton on 8 March, though Frenchie, who rode first jockey for Reg Hobbs, insisted he wouldn't beat his partner, Medoc II, at a difference of 14 lb. Sundange started favourite and Medoc II hacked up.

We kidded ourselves that the track hadn't suited ours, but when the pair met at Cheltenham twelve days later in the Seven Springs Handicap, Lord Sefton's seven-year-old gave us 20 lb and a further comprehensive beating. The following year Medoc won the Gold Cup by eight lengths.

'Nobby' Sawers had ridden Sundange a few times, and it was after his latest run that he inquired whether I would be at Ludlow in two days' time. My petrol ration was running low, so I thought it doubtful. He said, speaking confidentially and in French, 'I have been assured I will ride the winner of the Selling Handicap Hurdle there. So perhaps you should have a few *sous* on it. He is called Niersteiner.'

I'd had a little 'touch' about two months earlier and, tipped off by a fellow worker in the Rescue Service that a friend wanted to sell a 15 hp Flying Standard saloon in immaculate condition for £50, I bought it and leased it to the Council for £2 a week on the basis of withdrawal at twenty-four hours' notice on either side. On the way back to London from Cheltenham on 20 March I stopped at the garage at Barrington (next to the Inn for all Seasons) which had become a regular staging post and asked the patron what he'd give me for a 1937 Standard. He reckoned that, provided it fulfilled all the usual credentials of a second-hand car – showroom condition, low mileage, original tyres, chauffeur-driven for an elderly person who hardly ever went out, etc. – it could be up to £60. I said I would deliver it the day after tomorrow.

I collected the car on the evening of the 21st. It wasn't taxed because the Council ran it on an official permit, so I wrote 'licence applied for' on a circular cut-out the size of a Road Fund disc and stuck it on the windscreen. If I was going to be at Barrington, twenty miles the London side of Cheltenham, sell the car and reach Ludlow by 2 p.m., I'd have to leave Chelsea before my duty ended at nine o'clock.

There was a very nice elderly Scot, a chauffeur in peacetime, who worked on the opposite shift. Would there ever (I was inclined to lapse into stage Irish in times of stress), would there ever be a chance of him covering for me from 6 a.m. the next day? He'd bandaged a nasty cut for me once after I'd been blown off my bike by bomb blast in Belgrave Square. I'd been cycling back to the depot one night after visiting a girlfriend.

'I suppose,' he reacted drily, 'you'll be wanting to make sure no bombs have fallen in Pembroke Close.'

I explained the different nature of this situation.

He would not only be pleased to co-operate, but he produced a 10s note for investment on the 'good thing', who was trained in Shropshire in the small yard of his owner, Percy Arm, an enthusiast who combined skilful preparation of a few generally modest horses with running a garage business.

My 'relief' was right on time the next morning. He helped push the car out of the depot yard so that no one was alerted by the engine, then assisted for a fraught half-hour in overcoming its reluctance to start.

Detours for craters and unexploded bombs slowed my exit from London. A blasted shop front in Shepherds Bush bore a placard 'NO BUSINESS AS USUAL'. I drove slowly to conserve petrol, anxious that there might not be enough in the tank to complete the necessary eighty miles.

Shortly before Northolt Aerodome I was thumbed for a lift by an airman. He'd heard that the Cheltenham road was impassable at High Wycombe. There was no shortage of rumour. Three miles after setting him down, a motorcycle police cop waved me into the side. Bored by the pace, or lack of it, I had been giving a little attention to the *Racing Calendar* which was draped across my knees and, after parking his machine very deliberately, he asked whether I always read a paper while driving.

I thought of replying, 'Only the *Racing Calendar*', but it occurred to me that flippancy might be inappropriate to present circumstances.

He didn't look as if he indulged in anything so trivial as playing the horses, but you never know. Mutual interest in the vagaries of the racing horse had been known, like wine, to undermine disharmony in human relations. I said I had been verifying the name of a horse which was expected to win that afternoon.

He noted that the tax disc on the car was home-made, and asked to see my identity card and driving licence. These, at least, were in order.

'I suggest, sir,' he commented, 'that in future you confine study of the horses to such times as you are stationary.'

I assured him of my compliance. He took a couple of paces towards his bike, then turned and inquired, 'Did you mention the name of that horse?'

'Niersteiner,' I told him.

'Good luck,' he said, and was gone.

By the time I reached Barrington the needle on the petrol gauge had long ceased flickering. There wasn't enough left to fill my cigarette lighter. With a pocketful of readies and around ninety miles cross-country travel ahead, I set off towards Northleach. All the indications were that Niersteiner would be a very fair price – especially in view of his rider's relative obscurity. I would probably have £25 on the boards and £20 at Tote odds – keeping £15 in case of the unthinkable.

I hadn't been walking for more than ten minutes when a car responded to my wave. As every motorist knows, up to 80 per cent of hitch-hikers are 'on the tap'. The driver leaned across his lady passenger and said, 'If you just want a lift, get in. If you want to borrow money, don't.'

I leaped in, assuring my benefactor, idiotically, that I'd just sold my car and had plenty of money.

A sales rep and his girlfriend, their destination was Cheltenham, where I bought them a drink and, on the advice of the landlord, caught a bus to Gloucester. It was no use trying to get a lift in a town unless you were in forces uniform (half price at race meetings), so I walked for an hour out of Gloucester before getting a short ride with a farmer and six pigs. I was drifting right off any semblance of a main thoroughfare and time was running out. Chances of making Ludlow for the two o'clock were now all of 50/1 and the odds a place. It became a matter of getting to a telephone and ringing William Hill, with whom I'd opened an account on 3 July 1939, and whose terms included an additional 10 per cent on all Tote commissions.

A tractor-borne farmer reckoned that my best bet was to make for the village of Bredwardine, but if I'd like to come with him, he was going back to the farm about two miles away and I could use his phone. I'd brought several packets of cigarettes for acknowledging assistance and he was delighted with one of them.

Unfortunately his phone was out of order and his wife was out with the car. Fortified by a pint of home-made cider with the near-potency of Calvados, I ran a good three miles before finding a cottage which announced: 'Cream teas with strawberry jam 2s 6d'. It was just about post time. The charming lady who answered my knock would be delighted to serve me, but she regretted she was not on the phone. What the hell! Cream was unheard of in London, and jam was severely rationed – so was tea, come to that.

After lovely hot scones I picked up a lift in a lorry just outside Hereford. He was going to a transport café west of Whitney where I might well find a truck bound for London. He was right. Further, for the £3 proffered, the driver of a massive Leyland would also buy me the best breakfast to be had in Hammersmith. We steamed into the Broadway at 6 a.m. and while my friend ordered tea, toast and dripping, fried spam and egg (powder), I walked to the Underground to buy a paper. Under the Ludlow results, I read:

2.0 NIERSTEINER (N. Sawers) 20/1
    Portpatrick (T. Isaac) 20/1
    Caravan Girl (C. Mitchell) 10/1

Winner trained P. J. Arm.
Tote dividends £4 11s 6d (2s unit) places £1 4s 3d; 14s, 6s 6d.
Distances: 2 Lengths, 3. No bid for winner. 23 ran.

When I paid out the £10 10s due to my Scottish friend Bernie, who had kindly stood in for me at the depot, he said, 'Well done, but what a pity you didn't have it on the Tote!'

CHAPTER 4

Rosebud

'You like greyhounds, don't you?' The questioner was a tall, reserved, red-haired, fellow Rescue Service worker named Bravington – a member of the jewellery family whose advertising slogan was: 'Buy her a Bravington ring and she's yours'. As we were on the same shift, and since I spent every Stamford Bridge race day scorching up and down the Fulham Road in between bomb alerts, it was a fair assumption.

When I replied in the affirmative, he said, in a matter-of-fact manner, 'I've got a greyhound, but his trainer who has him in Devon is joining up, so he's got to be put down.' From his battledress he produced a photograph.

It was like being shown a photo of Nijinsky as a two-year-old and learning that he was to be destroyed. He was perfection. Light fawn with pale points, he had a fine, intelligent head, large, bold eyes set well apart, deep brisket, quarters combining grace and power, and a hind leg like an ideal thoroughbred.

I said, 'You can't really be serious.' Surely it would be possible to find someone in the country who would give him a home?

He explained that greyhounds who were accustomed to kennel life were consequently untrained domestically as well as being expensive to keep.

I envisaged the flat being dismantled. 'Give him to me,' I suggested.

He would do so very willingly, provided he hadn't been put down already.

The alert had sounded ten minutes earlier. There was the whine of a bomb and a crump as it landed not far away. My squad was the next out and I had to start the Humber's engine. 'For God's sake ring your man,' I called as I left him.

By evening he had done so and the dog was still there, but John Skeaping, the artist, who had him, would like me to ring personally. The first animal picture I ever owned was a treasured Skeaping print of a reed buck, published by the Medici Gallery. John, who was to become a firm friend for the remaining thirty-nine years of his colourful life, thought I should know that 'Bim' Bravington's greyhound – who had only met his master once or twice – was a sweet dog but very sensitive, so he could be a problem, especially in London.

'He's not very interested in racing,' reported John, 'but he loves picking blackberries.'

Slim arrived at Paddington Station wide-eyed as a startled rabbit and wild as a mountain fox. An accomplished thief, escapologist and demolition expert, he would not consider performing outside any function that could be fulfilled at home.

The first fortnight was a nightmare, but let no one pursuade you that a greyhound is either unintelligent or domestically untrainable. Slim was brilliant. Within a month he was not only house-trained but would trot alongside my bicycle no more than a yard away, though I never risked him off the lead in heavy traffic or after an alert, because he was terrified during an air raid. He'd sleep peacefully at the foot of the bed or alongside my bunk at the depot, but once the siren sounded there was a stealthy movement and his head would be on the pillow. He was always ravenously hungry or greedy, yet after two months together he would sit indefinitely at any distance from his feed bowl until called.

Sundange had a lucky escape from serious injury one night when a bomb blew most of the roof off his box at Treadwell House. When I took Slim to see him he travelled in the sidecar of a BSA combination which I'd bought for a tenner. He loved the sidecar and waited obediently in it on arrival.

A fortnight later we went back to Epsom to see the horses, only this time I called in first for a cup of tea with Charlie Bell and Mary in Albert Road. It was only three-quarters of a mile to the stable, through a fairly complicated built-up area, but a little more comfortable for Charlie in the sidecar without Slim. So I left the dog in the house, warning Mary that he could give 21 lb to Houdini and lose him.

Ten minutes later there was a panic message to the yard. Mary had opened the door 'a couple of inches' to a caller and Slim had got out and flown. He'd gone missing from the depot before now when I had been out on a call, but he'd turned up at the flat. This was different. I told Charlie I was just going to ride around and ask anyone I met if they'd seen him.

As I ran across the yard one of the lads came out of the tack room. 'Your greyhound'll make himself ill, Mr Peter,' he said.

I asked what he meant.

'He popped into the yard a few moments back, clocked you, and went straight into the feed house.'

And there was Slim in the bath, hock deep in hot mash, bran and linseed all over his chops, looking sheepish. He'd only ever been to the yard once before, and by a different route.

'You wicked dog,' I said sternly. I could have wept with relief.

Charlie Bell, possibly the only licensed trainer to have travelled from Epsom to Cheltenham and back in a sidecar shared with a greyhound, was not going too well. One of the stable's pre-war owners, a widow, had just married again and wanted to buy a horse. Provided I would forgo my lease, Charlie would like to sell her Sundange. Formalities completed, Mrs Grace Nicholson renamed him Myowne. He soon met up with his old adversary Medoc II, and in Cheltenham's Painswick Chase on 22 November, receiving 2 stone this time, beat him three lengths into third place, winning handsomely at 7/1. 'CHANGE OF NAME BRINGS LUCK' was the caption over the *Evening News* story, which recorded that 'his former owner always thought he would make a top-class chaser'.

Back at Cheltenham for the Winchcombe Handicap Chase on 6 December, the son of Sundari won 'in the smoothest possible manner' (*Evening Star*). An 8/1 chance this time, he gave 9 lb to the two lengths runner-up, with Medoc II (conceding 21 lb) third. These were achievements which none of the assorted hopefuls John Skeaping and I shared in the stable – Light Rescue, Headley Boy, Smiling Sambo, Shy Torb – was able to emulate.

John, who as a young man won every significant scholarship for sculpture, including the British Institution, the Royal Academy Gold Medal and the Prix de Rome, did his army training in Oxford. He moved on to the Intelligence Service, and would invariably come to the depot or flat when he was in town. Impressed with Slim's condition and happy outlook, he used him as a model for the fine greyhound 'stills' which feature, along with the O'Sullevan poodle, Pucci, as the frontispiece in his 1961 classic Studio Books publication *Drawing Dogs*. Since first seeing them I had coveted a set of five all-action greyhound drawings which had never been reproduced. Over a fish-and-chip supper in Shepherds Bush, after we'd shared a less than entirely successful evening's punting at the White City, a rough audit of our resources revealed John's total assets to be 16s and mine a relatively plutocratic £18.

'You know those bloody drawings,' said John. 'I don't know why the hell you want them, but you can have them for a tenner if you like.'

I said I'd give him £15 for them.

'You're mad,' he said. 'I'd want a couple of Leonardos thrown in for that.'

There was a pub in Britten Street, the Builders Arms, which Slim would not pass without crossing to the opposite side of the road. He was terrified of small dogs and a terrier had once bitten him on the behind there, while, to add injury to insult, a cat who was lurking in the doorway caught him on the nose as he towed me out.

There was also a shop which he preferred not to pass at all. No. 34 King's Road (currently a shoe shop) had a frontage of porcelain tiles embossed, simply 'Grant – Butcher'. Here Reginald Frampton, the manager, who was not just a greyhound fancier but a greyhound fanatic, dispensed the prescribed meat rations with smiling impartiality to each of his queuing customers – save one. The four-legged exception was beckoned into the back of the shop from which he would emerge, following a delay which was sometimes viewed with tepid enthusiasm by the less favoured, lipsmacking his appreciation.

There was a fair straight on grass in Carlyle Square and, fixing my bicycle upside down at one end of the garden, I used a pedal shaft to tow a lure consisting of a rabbit skin with a small piece of beef inside. Slim thought this was a terrific game and he seemed to me to be very fast. But, of course, I had formed a similar impression in respect of Wild Thyme. When Reg and I took him to Staines for a trial behind a sleigh hare, however, his 17.43 over the 300-yard circuit wasn't bad at all. He needed a racing name so I called him Rosebud, after the enigmatic deathbed word in *Citizen Kane*. He now had regular exercise and massage, regular feed (assured by Grant – Butcher and the delicatessens of Peterkin on Chelsea Green and Boris opposite Carlyle Square). Third time out he skated up. He was also a good winner at a far less organized flapping track, Loudwater, where the hare was driven on the Carlyle Square principle. The gaffer was the most uncanny handicapper in my experience. He would receive dogs from all over the country, many of them 'borrowed' for the day from top London and provincial stadia and so impermanently disguised that, on a wet day, the complexion of the competitors could change dramatically. When they were presented for grading, the boss would just run his hands over each dog like a faith healer and say 'Third race', 'Fifth' or whatever. And although there was only one easy bend to be negotiated, limiting scope for hard luck stories, they'd invariably finish *dans un mouchoir* as the French say.

Less successful was our single excursion to Southall where there was an electric hare. Slim regarded this device with contemptuous disdain and disgraced both of us by ignoring the absurdity and jumping the rails to greet me.

But at Staines, where Brian Swift's father, Jack, was a leading bookmaker for several years, Slim was an acknowledged and dependable regular until a sad day in August 1942.

Charlie and I had been to Newmarket to back Dancing Light each-way (fourth, of course) in the Tuddenham Handicap; Reg had taken Slim, and my commission, to Staines. Midway between Royston and

Baldock, on a return journey elongated by failure, we were lucky to survive a front tyre burst on the motorbike. So we got back late and Slim was waiting in the flat for hours. As he ran to the door he left a trail of blood. He'd won his race but had taken fright as Reg put him down at the foot of the moving staircase in the Underground, whipped round and got a foot lacerated in the escalator. He'd been bandaged and thought to be OK, but when I rushed him to a top Wimbledon vet, he said he'd have to amputate two toes. It was wretched leaving him at the clinic, where he became so frantic when I visited him that my sustained absence for ten days was politely but firmly requested.

'Rosebud' was a very faded rose when I finally collected him in a Model T Ford saloon I'd bought for £15 from a trader in Warren Street (there was a regular kerbside trade here for many years) so that he could lie in full-length comfort when we were both at the depot. He had been prescribed a sedentary life until he got stronger; I was lucky, therefore, to get a job in between Rescue Depot shifts in the production department of the publisher John Lane–The Bodley Head in Blooms- bury. 'Your hours', read the letter of appointment, 'will be from 11 a.m. until 5.30 p.m. every other day excluding Saturdays.' It also confirmed, 'The salary will be 30s. [£1.50] per week.'

It wasn't a lot, but probably more than I was worth. There was an unwritten understanding that, granted immaculate behaviour, Slim could be accommodated, and that there would be additional pay for reading and reporting on manuscripts out of hours. So such duty-time diversions as greyhound racing, snooker, football, dismantling and rebuilding petrol engines and even giving talks to indulgent fellow workers on the neat New England poet, T. S. Eliot, were placed in abeyance.

The managing director, Cecil Greenwood, was a delightful man to work for; I met most of the firm's authors, including the greatly admired Rex Warner who added to my growing list of signed first editions. A munificent Christmas bonus helped, though not substantially, to support my racehorse-of-the-moment, Knight of the Garden.

The Knight's nearest claim to fame was recorded at Southwell where, after falling at an early stage of a novices' chase, he showed greater aptitude for scaling the adjacent railway embankment than the fences, and gave serious competition to a goods train for all of six furlongs. It was probably the best race he ran. I could only hope that one of the objects of my ante-post attention would perform with even greater distinction.

As a life-long collector of vouchers associated with future events, I believe this form of speculation to be outstandingly the most entertain- ing and potentially rewarding. It is no accident that the specialist horse-

JOHN LANE THE BODLEY HEAD LIMITED
EIGHT BURY PLACE LONDON W.C.1

Directors
STANLEY UNWIN
G. WREN HOWARD
W. G. TAYLOR

Manager
C. J. GREENWOOD

Telephone
HOLBORN 9596-7

Telegrams and Cables
BODLEIAN
WESTCENT LONDON

All communications to be addressed to the Company

WJE/CRH   21st December, 1942.

Dear *Mr. O'Sullevan*

        I have been instructed by the Directors to hand
you £ 2/-/- as a Bonus, <u>Tax Free</u>.

        Of course you will have to include this in your
Return next year as a <u>Bonus Tax Free</u> so that the Tax
Commissioners can collect the necessary amount of Tax
from the Company.

        With best wishes.

                        Yours sincerely,
                for JOHN LANE THE BODLEY HEAD LTD.

                                    [signature]
                                        Secretary.

Mr. D. J. O'Sullevan

racing dailies in every country where bookmakers form a futures market are more forward-looking, informative and vital than elsewhere. A French racegoer with the foresight to select a two-year-old to win the following year's Prix du Jockey Club (French Derby) has no means of expressing his opinion in terms of odds. Even on the day of the event, an absurdly outmoded system of coupling horses for betting purposes, if the owner of one has just a minor share in another, inhibits freedom of choice.

Win or lose, every punter recalls with relish the occasions on which he beat the market through observation, information, intuition, luck or whatever. There was a faint element of the first ingredient, more of the second, in the inspiration for my tenner on Tropical Sun 'invested' six weeks or so prior to the 1943 Oaks and before she had made a seasonal reappearance. Although unsuccessful in her three outings as a two-year-old, I'd seen the daughter of that marvellous little horse Hyperion run very respectably. She'd been given a modest 7.13 in the Free Handicap, 22 lb below the top-rated filly, so would clearly need to improve. The whisper was that she had not only progressed but was Beckhampton's best. Although Tropical Sun's name did not figure in the published lists this was no guarantee that astronomical odds would be available. George Ward, who operated Chelsea's premier credit business (J. Osborne & Co.) at 35 Smith Street, was an unpredictable layer – even when his tape machine hadn't just been blown out of order by bomb blast. Sometimes he would be delighted to get the outsiders in the book; at others he'd prefer to have them run for the firm. I hoped for 100/1; would be happy with fifties.

George studied handicapper Arthur Fawcett's assessment and came up with 66/1. He didn't fancy £1000–£15 but would do £660–£10. And a playful £1675–£1 double with Epsom's Derby outsider Straight Deal.

Slim was walking from Chelsea to Bloomsbury and back every other day by now, his injury long forgotten. He was so fit that I dropped him off at 'Grant – Butcher' one morning – having placed the Underground out of bounds – so that his friend, Reg Frampton, could take him back to Staines for a trial. His time was slower than formerly, but he showed great zest and returned to fly in on 1 May.

Three weeks later Tropical Sun met eighteen opponents in a mile maiden at Salisbury and won comfortably by four lengths. The following month at Windsor, over one and a quarter miles, she was even more impressive.

Thirteen days to the Oaks, with Tropical Sun challenging Ribbon for favouritism, and I have to go down with jaundice. It was no time to turn yellow as my complexion but, forty-five years on, I would have done what I did on the day – hedged my bet. Apart from the fact that at that time £660 would have bought you a nomination to any stallion standing in Britain and still left enough to celebrate with ten cases of vintage Dom Pérignon, I think it's a bit daft to forgo the opportunity of turning foresight to profitable account.

I say this in the sure knowledge that if I had never hedged any one of around ten thousand (yes, ten thousand) vouchers accumulated over the years, I would, *on paper*, be better off. But paper profits may be furlongs short of reality. Betting is an emotional as well as a cerebral activity, in which a punter's pride operates to the bookmaker's advantage quite as potently as any horse bearing the *Timeform* symbol for unreliability. Hedging may limit profit potential, but it reduces frustration – the element which breeds temptation to chase losses.

Holding a hospital phone in a clammy hand at 1.40 p.m. on Friday, 18 June 1943, five minutes before the 'off' for the Oaks, I learned that

Tropical Sun was a firm 7/4 favourite. I laid £360–£160 (9/4) against her, so that if she won I'd got £300 to come and if she was beaten £150. In that rare situation I figured I could afford a 'pony' (£25) each-way; they went 20/1 bar four, Why Hurry at 7/1.

These traditional Epsom classics were run during the war at Newmarket. In his usual skilful manner, BBC radio commentator Raymond Glendenning had already started to set the scene at 1.35, announcing the runners, jockeys and the draw, but withholding information regarding either the going or the weather, which might have assisted the enemy, and overlooking any evidence of pecuniary transactions, news of which was expressly forbidden by the Corporation. It was not until 1958 that the BBC took cognizance of the existence of betting on horse races and permitted reference to starting prices. It was a further three years before BBC TV or radio commentators were allowed to report pre-race odds.

Just before the 'off' Raymond handed over to Frank More O'Ferrall (the charming, urbane founder of the Anglo-Irish Bloodstock Agency) who was to cover the start and early running from the Devil's Dyke. As the tapes rose Frank related that two of the thirteen starters were very slowly away. Sam Wragg's partner Noontide had whipped round and severely hampered Eph Smith on the strongly fancied Ribbon.

Outsiders Tidworth and Solesa were early leaders, Michael Beary on the latter (by a Leger winner, Solario, out of an Oaks third, Mesa) determined to ensure a test of stamina. With experienced race reader Wilf Taylor picking them out for him, Raymond took up the commentary soon after they passed under the five-furlong gate.

Tidworth and Solesa were still taking them along. Ribbon had made up lost ground. The field was bunching – it looked a wide open race. Running down into the dip Gordon hit the front on Tropical Sun. The early leaders had fallen right away. Tropical Sun was clear but Why Hurry was challenging. Ribbon was coming there too and Herringbone . . . and Cincture also. 'It's anybody's race,' called Raymond and – would you believe it? – there was a power cut.

Hospitals had emergency generators – conceivably for more vital purposes – and life was soon restored to the crackling headphones. But by then the BBC was well into *Junior Stars* with Deanna Durbin.

I've got a hang-up that it's unlucky to ask in a direct manner for a result – like telephoning a bookmaker and inquiring what won the 1.45 at Newmarket. I guess it's a lot to do with sustaining hope. Let's face it, on the majority of occasions the direct answer will be unfavourable. On the other hand, ask for the winning Tote dividend on the race and, whatever the answer, almost, hope remains permissible. Admittedly, few favourites pay ten points over the odds, but it's possible. Equally, if you've backed a probable 7/1 chance and the 'divi' represents 3/1, you're still in with a chance. A good one. The danger about inquiring along these lines is that the over-helpful response may be, 'Oh yes, that was X's race', and the pleasure of anticipation is abruptly terminated.

A favoured ploy, impractical under my circumstances of the moment, was to take an upstairs seat in a bus (Slim was not permitted downstairs anyway) and attempt to read another passenger's evening paper. A headline 'Favourites routed at Stockton' would promote extravagant dreams on an afternoon when the components of an each-way yankee were all long-odds chances. A desperate resort was actually to purchase a late edition, fold it with eyes averted, and read the text from the bottom – upside-down.

On this occasion there was no opportunity to prolong suspense. When I woke from a nap, there on the bed was the *Evening Standard* and a caption which left little to the imagination: 'WHY HURRY WINS THE OAKS FROM RIBBON AND TROPICAL SUN'. It would have been exciting had Tropical Sun been able to initiate that £1675–£1 double with Straight Deal (who won the next day's Derby at 100/6, carrying a small consolatory investment), but I would never have backed Why Hurry excepting the hedging opportunity, and the Oaks profit was still a very handy £368 15s.

So when a week's convalescence was prescribed, I took the train via Ruabon to the mountains of north-west Wales and the sybaritic comfort of Portmeirion – the bizarre cluster of immaculately equipped Italianate cottages created by architect Clough Williams-Ellis along the sheltered estuary of Cardigan Bay to resemble Sorrento in Snowdonia. Here binoculars were for studying both the colourful variety of wildfowl, who enjoyed unaccustomed tranquillity while man was otherwise preoccupied, and the general birdlife whose habitat had not yet been violated by modern farming. Poultry was still reared naturally, animals also, in an era so soon to be tarnished by conveyor-belt production and its attendant horrors which the organization Compassion in World Farming strives so hard to alleviate.

CHAPTER 5

Printing the Chaff

In 1944, while German scientists were refining the flying bombs and rockets which were already menacing London, Matt Peacock, a dour, affectionately regarded Yorkshireman, was cultivating a rather more wholesome 'flier' in the shapely form of a two-year-old by Nearco out of Rosy Legend named Dante. Well before his first public appearance (at Stockton on 10 April 1944) it was being said that anyone who backed him to win the following year's Derby need have only one concern – survival.

My personal odds were not improved in this respect on 23 February (a bad month for 'incidents') when four bombs struck World's End at 10.30 p.m. and the busted water and gas mains meant all-night work in very damp conditions. As appropriate to us, maybe, as the RAF's motto, 'Per Ardua Ad Astra', would have been 'Per Ardua Ad Sciatica'. Antibiotics were just coming into use, but pneumonia was still viewed with far more seriousness than today, so for me there was no escaping from the Cadogan Square nursing home after examination there a couple of days later.

Only rumour travelled faster than flying bombs at this time. One of them was that the PACs (pilotless aircraft), as they were known to air-raid wardens – there were other less genteel descriptions – were in fact guided by a suicide pilot. Some claimed to have seen a 'little man' inside the missile as it sped by at window level before exploding – evidence which gave rise to a belief that the Germans were employing millions of Japanese kamikaze pilots.

More implausible, maybe, was the rumour circulating at Pontefract on Saturday, 22 April after the two-year-old Timanova, trained by Matt Peacock and ridden by Willie Nevett, had made a winning debut in the nineteen-runner Castle Plate – beating his nearest pursuer by six lengths. Here the legend was being freely touted by men of sober demeanour, if not inclination, that the Yorkshire missile Dante, who had trotted up twelve days earlier, was 21 lb superior to his stable companion.

38

Certainly Private Nevett of the Royal Army Ordnance Corps, who had by this time ridden more than a thousand winners, finished second to Sir Gordon Richards in the championship four times, won a wartime Derby (Owen Tudor) and been 'Cock of the North' for many years, never collected his winning riding fee (£5 5s) with less effort, excepting official walk-overs, than on Dante's second appearance.

Starting 6/1 on in Stockton's Linthorpe Stakes on 29 April, he was under restraint throughout. *Raceform* barely acknowledged the presence of his seven rivals, including the second and third among those who 'also ran' behind the winner, who had 'an exercise gallop'. A month later he disposed of the useful Langton Abbot (1946 Lincoln winner) by six lengths.

Even so, when it came to the Coventry Stakes on 17 June, ten days after the Normandy landings, there were few southerners to heed the sage of Halifax, Phil Bull's, monstrous assertion that Lord Derby's High Peak 'wouldn't be within hail of Dante' at Newmarket. They were inseparable in the betting at 11/8. But they were separated by six lengths in the race – in Dante's favour.

While Sir Eric Ohlson's colt was proving himself to be that rare phenomenon, a horse capable of matching strides with his home reputation, the flying bombs were similarly sustaining their momentum. It was rush hour traffic over London in early summer when one of the worst 'incidents' I was called to was created by a buzz bomb exploding in Turk's Row, off Lower Sloane Street, between two blocks of buildings which included a hostel for US servicemen, among whom there were heavy casualties. Between the missile's engine cutting out and its plunge to earth there was an interval of approximately ten seconds. When the lunch hour became a popular time for dispatching the eerie destroyer office workers would watch from rooftops, scattering for cover when the engine stopped. Most animals' hearing being much more acute than ours, poor Slim knew when a bomb was approaching from the Kent coast. Immediately he crept into the shoe cupboard, you could bet there'd soon be a roar overhead. Above the cupboard was a placard rescued from an isolated door after a row of houses had been dismembered off Sydney Street. It read:

BUZZ BOMB NOTICE
Away for week-end – try next door

And scribbled underneath it: 'Thanks very much – next door'.

The pressure was maintained throughout July 1944, when Home Secretary Herbert Morrison sent a message to the Rescue Services praising their stoicism, and for most of August. But come September, with Dante retaining his unbeaten sequence in the Middle Park Stakes, the pace slackened. And Duncan Sandys, Chairman of the Flying-Bomb Counter-Measures Committee, announced: 'Except for a few last shots, the Battle of London is ended'.

As I was nurturing a personal time bomb, University College Hospital kindly arranged appendix removal, after which the Civil Defence medic concluded that my release from the casualty service might be effected without undue hindrance to the war effort. There was an advert in the *Sporting Life* for a racing sub. Bodley Head boss Cecil Greenwood had already committed perjury by giving me a smashing reference. It was worth a try. Fred Harrison, racing editor of the Press Association, replied to my letter and proposed an interview.

Regrettably, my brief attendance at Pitman's Secretarial College in Southampton Row had resulted in my teacher, Elizabeth Collinson, being converted to racing before she had converted me to shorthand. As a result my 'speed' was 50 per cent slower than longhand and 75 per cent untranscribable. My typing standard was, if anything, inferior. Mr Harrison, whose authoritarian predecessor had worn a starched wing collar and frock coat, was contrastingly self-effacing, mild-mannered and instantly likeable. Fingering the Bodley Head production manager's generous interpretation of my limited skills – 'Excellent editorial work . . . outstandingly well written reports on MSS . . . great loss to publishing' – he inquired why I should want to forgo such prospects for journalism.

The horses, I explained.

He pointed out that the PA (an agency whose purpose is to gather news and service national and provincial newspapers) was seeking an office man as much as an outside reporter, and it might be a while before an opportunity to work on the course occurred.

Then it came, the question. Did I take notes in shorthand?

In the time it takes Dante to run five furlongs I could, I claimed, just about write 'They're off', and even read back the message. But fluent I was not.

Happily this deficiency was overlooked. Journalists, like politicians, are not required to hold qualifications.

There were several applicants for the job and Fred Harrison requested me to write three to four hundred words on the end-of-week programme at Ascot on 7 October, to be delivered the previous day.

'Snowy' Parker, who shared with George Todd a gift for repairing and maintaining unsound horses, was confident that he'd win the Ascot Cesarewitch with The Towkay – provided he kept sound. A greyhound enthusiast, Snowy, who trained near Charlie Bell at Epsom, invited me to view his big handicap hope in an insubstantial yard which, in the wake of bomb blast, appeared unlikely to survive the onslaught of a gentle summer breeze. The Towkay, whose immediate box neighbours were a litter of greyhound whelps on one side and the chickens which laid the eggs which supplemented the horses' diet on the other, looked in good shape after a couple of preparatory outings.

'If his old pins stand up, he'll be back before blackout, I'll guarantee you that,' said Snowy.

Vic Smyth appeared to have a 'good thing' in Jack Hylton's Elysium, who'd been runner-up to Court Martial last time out, and Johnnie Dines, who didn't drive and would welcome a lift to Ascot on Saturday, said Gordon thought he'd win the Cambridgeshire (the autumn double took place on the same day) on Fun Fair.

My good friend and lightweight, Midge Richardson, had been impressed by his previous partnership of the modest Grand Opera in a nursery and thought she'd have a good chance in a maiden. Her trainer, Michael Blackmore, was similarly optimistic. So I made her a selection – each-way because there was an automatic short-priced one of Dorothy Paget's in the race.

When delivering my hopeful offering to Fred Harrison, I mentioned Johnnie Dines, the very successful lightweight and 'job' jockey of the twenties and thirties, who was now training at Epsom. I couldn't have dropped a better name. Henri de Montherlant, wasn't it, who claimed that the only occasion on which man assumes an ethereal expression is in recollection or contemplation of financial gain. The name Dines recalled for Fred Harrison the memory of a series of blissfully rewarding wagers. Sitting back in his editorial chair, placing his fingertips together, eyes half closed behind steel-rimmed spectacles, he reverently recited a litany of his benefactor's achievements. They included: Chester Cup (twice), Ebor (twice), Northumberland Plate, Victoria Cup, Cambridgeshire and Cesarewitch, Liverpool Autumn, Summer and Spring Cups, Manchester Cup, Newbury Autumn and Summer Cups, Esher Cup, etc. etc. I don't know if he backed them all, but I do know that, to live reasonably on a PA salary in those days, it was desirable to back a few winners.

Sadly The Towkay, backed from 100/6 to 7/1 third favourite, broke down. Not seriously – he was still winning races for Snowy's yard three years later – but there was enough of an 'if' for Eph Smith wisely to pull him up. Elysium (4/6) won well, and Fun Fair (13/2) and Gordon Richards resisted Dennis Dillon's mount Giraud (receiving over 2 stone) by a fast-shrinking head in the Ascot Cambridgeshire. Then, amazingly, another narrow verdict went my way when the ninth and last race favourite, Game Shot colt (two-year-olds didn't have to be named at that time), just failed to catch 20/1 outsider Grand Opera. £1 each way on the Tote paid over £70.

It's a funny game, this tipping. I received a letter from Fred Harrison saying I would be hearing from him in due course, adding, 'What a pity you didn't tell me to *back* Grand Opera!'

A fortnight later, by which time I reckoned to be a 100/8 chance and no takers, I was offered a 'trial' which would lead to a contract if satisfactory. A sub's job is to tidy up or emasculate the outside man's 'copy'. Or, as it is widely expressed, to sift the wheat from the chaff – and print the chaff.

There wasn't a lot of racing at the time, so one of my principal tasks was to write obituaries in readiness for the demise of prominent owners and breeders. An unexhilarating exercise, though not without its lighter moments. Carried away by the authenticity of an emotional and comprehensive obit I had written on Lord Rosebery one morning, I almost fainted at the sight of the 6th Earl's resurrection in the paddock that afternoon.

The 'trial' was punctuated by a spell of bronchitis and several days' obligatory absence. When Freddy Harrison said the editor-in-chief would like to see me, I feared the worst.

Henry Martin, austere boss of the Press Association, had no personal interest in racing, nor, I suspected, did it meet with his unqualified approval. Had I enjoyed being in the office?

I wouldn't have taken 50/1 about getting the job by this time, especially after admitting that an office held little appeal for me as I wished to be out reporting racing.

'Well,' he said, 'Mr Harrison has given you the highest possible commendation, and I am sure there will be opportunities.'

If he'd said I'd won first dividend on the pools, I'd have been less surprised. The letter of appointment, dated 4 December 1944 at a salary of £9 9s a week plus 17s 6d a week temporary war bonus, was subject to four weeks' notice on either side.

I celebrated by 'investing' in three ante-post vouchers with J. Osborne of 35 Smith Street: £475–£100 Dante to win the 1945 2000 Guineas; £450–£50 Dante to win the '45 Derby and £70–£2 to complete the double. The best horse to be trained in the north in my time – and, more significantly in Phil Bull's time, as he confirmed to me at the 1987 Gimcrack Dinner – he was beaten once in nine races: in the 2000 Guineas for which he started even money.

A few days before the Guineas, which was run on the July course at Newmarket, Dante's near-side vision gave grounds for concern. It was thought that his eye had been struck by a flint. Drawn 20, on the stands side, he may never have seen Court Martial (drawn 10) who, despite shortening his stride in the closing stages, held on, gamely, by a neck.

Dante's eyesight continued to be a source of worry and rumour. In the Derby he momentarily drifted off a true line, as though losing his way, before running on to win comfortably. It was a marvellous performance by a handsome horse of outstanding class, understandably rated by his equally popular northern partner, Willie Nevett, for whom he was a third Derby winner, 'the best I ever rode'. The Leger appeared a foregone conclusion.

But in the month before Dante's full brother was sold for 28,000 guineas – then a world record for a yearling – dark rumours gathered momentum. Behind the unacceptable curtain of secrecy which surrounded his Middleham stable, the fine horse's horizon was shrinking fast. By mid-August bookmakers in general were convinced that the Yorkshire crowd would not be seeing their hero on the Knavesmire – setting for the 1945 final classic – on 5 September.

It is widely accepted that the bookmakers' intelligence service is a highly efficient operation. Less generally acknowledged is the detail that punters are the chief source of information. Thus were bookmakers alerted when 'informed' ante-post backers, who would not normally be expected to oppose Dante, started to support his distant Derby victims, Chamossaire and Rising Light.

On 25 August, three days after the PA had issued a communiqué from the stable declaring detrimental rumours to be unfounded, Dante was scratched from the St Leger. During his races he seldom saw another horse. Now, tragically, he would never see one clearly again. The pride of Yorkshire, whose younger brother, Sayajirao, went on to win the 1947 St Leger, was almost totally blind.

CHAPTER 6

Assigned to the Course

Most sports departments employ a general factotum to fulfil various duties under differing titles. The PA incumbent at this time, Harry Mordecai, who had joined the agency as a lift boy before the war and who was, like most cockneys, a keen and sardonic observer of the *comédie humaine*, now operated officially for 'dispatch'. Whatever his tasks on non-race days, Harry left the clear impression that, when either the horses or the dogs were running, it was his firm duty to stand permanent guard over the tape machine from which vantage point, as a fellow punter, he would recount, in discreet tic-tac, the day's disasters as they unfolded. He was the obvious one to question as to the best method of approach to the esteemed racing editor in order to obtain leave to accompany Slim, alias Rosebud, my greyhound, on his forthcoming visit to Staines.

My counsellor warned that he had already exploited the frailty of his own grandmother and offered the novel suggestion that I employ the unvarnished truth. 'The old man loves a gamble,' said Harry. 'He'll probably want to be "on" with you.' He did. Extracting a pound note from his wallet, Freddy Harrison requested: 'Please invest this for me.' And I don't think he was all that dismayed when Harry's grandmother suffered one of her 'turns', necessitating the simultaneous absence of her solicitous grandson.

Expectation increased when Slim drew trap 6, because he'd tended to be a wide runner ever since losing those two toes. He knew when success was particularly desirable. We had 5/2 to our money and returned the boss 5/1. Slim had Steak Chateaubriand for dinner. The passport to Staines was secured for the future.

In between times, office life was more tolerable than agreeable, until the short, thick-set figure of Captain John de Moraville MC, formerly of the 4th Hussars, stomped up to the racing desk, surveyed the scene with an air of benevolent defiance and, in consequence of an earlier interview, presented himself for his 'trial'. He had been a prisoner-of-war with, among others, the amateur rider Dicky Black (who achieved a career highlight when winning the 1947 Cheltenham Gold Cup on Fortina), and the three of us were to form a bond which would have been easier to interrupt than the headlong flight of a runaway horse.

For a time Johnnie and I were office colleagues, which certainly brightened the lunch hour. Then I was lucky enough to get a 'break' outside, at Windsor, on a day when friends such as Jakie Astor (who referred to me as 'Peter O'Socialist') and Johnnie Hislop, as well as members of the Crazy Gang – Bud Flanagan and Chesney Allen – were around and there seemed plenty to report, as you'd expect with an eleven-race programme. From then on I was assigned to the course on race days – which were still acutely rationed.

Jumping had ceased in March 1942 and only resumed, on a restricted scale, in the 1944–5 season, during which twenty-eight days were scheduled on four allocated courses – Catterick and Wetherby in the north, Cheltenham and Windsor for the south. However, because of unfavourable weather only seventeen programmes survived. The total prize winnings of the top owner, Frances Blakeney, whose Brains Trust won the Champion Hurdle and three more races, were £770.

On the Flat twelve courses were in use in 1945, with regionalized racing continuing, apart from prescribed events, until 1 August. So it was southern area horses which competed for the ten races on the opening day of the season at Ascot on 2 April, when a pretty stable 'lass', Diana Byrom, attracted as much attention as her Johnnie Dines-trained winner, Prawn Curry. Northern trainers had Pontefract to themselves the following day, and the locals won Newmarket's opening programme, which featured the first major shock of the season.

Charlie Elliott, maybe the most instinctive, natural jockey in all my experience, had told me about this two-year-old three days earlier at Salisbury. We'd been chatting about the French racing scene, with which Charlie was very familiar. He had lived in Paris between 1931 and 1939, during which time he rode four French Derby winners in the orange and grey colours of Marcel Boussac. Still in touch with his cross-Channel associates, he was convinced that successful Gallic raids were imminent.

'Their horses have had the best there is and racing's hardly been touched by the war,' he insisted. 'Come over at the weekend – you'll see.'

It was an idea which I wasn't slow to follow.

Not that the 'good thing' at Newmarket was going to be any great assistance. 'It's called Goodasgold,' said Charlie, 'and it should win from here to there' – he pointed to the distant spire of Salisbury Cathedral – 'but the "dogs" have been barking it for a fortnight, so it won't be backable.'

Just as well. Supported, nevertheless, by the intrepid, from 3/1 on to 5/1 on, the inappropriately named 'flier' cruised upsides generally unfancied rivals (they went 10/1 bar one) until two furlongs out, where he took an abrupt right turn and left the course. A fortnight later odds layers still went in with their heads down (5/2 on to 3/1 on), and Goodasgold returned with his head up.

I suppose it's something to do with age, but I can still see that race, the Barrow Maiden Stakes (Div 1), as if it were on video. Goodasgold sauntered into the dip with Charlie kidding to him, as he could do so artistically, and the colt returning the compliment. Meantime Gordon Richards seemed to be getting into an amazing tangle, as if he had dropped his knitting, on the Aga Khan's powerfully challenging filly Leventina. Goodasgold looked positively astonished as Leventina ranged alongside. Such exertion was clearly not for him and, head carried in the lofty posture signifying oxygen shortage or irresolution, he saw them by. Gordon's acrobatics had been prompted by a seriously slipping saddle. It was an effort worthy of rather more appreciative acknowledgement than the overheard comment, 'That Gordon bloody nearly fell off.'

Goodasgold, incidentally, was runner-up again, with Charlie Elliott aboard, next time out; responded similarly when hot favourite in the tenderly persuasive hands of Michael Beary; and, after six months' rest, reappeared at odds-on to convey five times champion Doug Smith into the second stall at Lincoln. He had worked brilliantly with senior stable companion Langton Abbot. But that didn't stop the latter winning the Handicap the next day for Teddy Lambton, who did not run Goodasgold again.

In the aftermath of the war there was a faint undercurrent of tension between men whose duties had separated them from the sport and those who, through whatever circumstances, had been able to sustain their involvement; while, because of the occupation, the French racing world was more overtly divided by the taint of collaboration. But the appeal of the horse, uncontaminated by human trivia and with his graceful capacity for impartial redistribution of wealth between the post-war credited, and sometimes less creditable, resulted in packed grand-stands.

In May 1945 the PA editor-in-chief kindly wrote to say that the board of directors had accepted 'the joint recommendation of the general manager and myself' to increase my basic salary from £9 9s to £10 10s. Expense allowance was 10s a day for all metropolitan meetings, including Brighton (£1 if staying overnight), and first-class rail fares or the equivalent if using one's own car. But sorties to Chantilly, whither I could catch a late sleeper from Victoria and arrive in good time to watch morning work, had to be self-funded. And my hopes of interpreting racing action over the airwaves were no nearer fulfilment.

At least I was getting plenty of practice, as one of my duties was to 'read' each race to a colleague who had to translate the comments into the PA 'Description'. In a letter dated 4 June 1945, Freddy Harrison wrote, 'In addition to the Description and Gossip on Oaks and Derby day, please cover the course road and station scenes after racing is over. Mr Morris is to telephone it direct to Editorial.' Neither Sun Stream nor Dante had done me any harm in their respective classics, and the approval with which the 'copy' was received in London doubtless owed more to its interpretation by my friend Ted Morris, following a possibly over-swift infusion of champagne at its point of transmission, Newmarket station, than to any contribution of mine.

One of the 'scenes' had been inspired by racing enthusiast Chick Wilson, a casually assembled one-time music hall artiste, who had forsaken such relatively facile pursuits as sawing ladies in two for the entertainment of patrons of the Chiswick Empire in favour of the most ambitious trick of all, trying to part bookmakers from their money. Chick was no more built for speed than he was given to backing the winner of the last. So he would wait by a taxi while the final race was being run, learn the worst from exiting patrons, and then get aboard. On this rare occasion he was reliably informed that the horse he had supported, Golden Cloud, had obliged.

The unexpected necessity to return and claim his money had made him late. He was confronted by a unique situation, the sight of the Liverpool Street train packed to capacity – no room for a jockey, still less for his bulky frame. An accomplished ventriloquist, Chick had a voice by comparison with which the MGM lion sounded as if it had laryngitis. Requesting an intending fellow traveller to engage the nearest railway official in urgent conversation, he shuffled along the platform to the third-class section and boomed in *basso profundo*: 'Fast train for London approaching platform two. London passengers platform two. Hurry along please over the bridge. The London train is now running from platform two.'

Angry first-class passengers banged on doors and windows (they were usually locked in until moments before departure, after showing the appropriate ticket), and while they were being pacified the other carriages emptied. As passengers ran round, like chickens disturbed by a fox, Chick went into his barking routine. He'd backed a winner and was having the time of his life. By the time a leisurely goods train had sauntered past platform two and the chaos had been reduced, he was innocently occupying a corner seat on the now refilling London train and, between canine growls and barks, assuring the ticket inspector that only one of his invisible dogs was savage and that he would do his best to restrain him.

PA reporters had what one might term modest status vis-à-vis their national newspaper colleagues at this time. In 1947, for example, when another excellent and supportive Racing Editor, Jack Garland, succeeded Freddy Harrison, he wrote me saying, 'The invitation you have received to the St Leger Dinner is a great honour and the first time one has been issued to a member of the PA racing team. Please send an account of the proceedings and I will credit you with a guinea!'

In the interim an invitation was issued by *The Times* in October 1945 requesting applications for the position of racing correspondent. The PA job offered security, anonymity and infinitely less pressure than a daily; but correspondingly less opportunity for self-expression and less than extravagant remuneration. I had as much chance of getting it as my current filly, Queen Penguin, had of winning the Oaks, and she wasn't even entered. But I couldn't resist having a go.

Loyally, my ex-boss at the Bodley Head, Cecil Greenwood, weighed in with another commendation, this time addressed to 'W. F. Casey Esq., Assistant Editor, *The Times*', in which he again cast me in the improbable role of one whose 'obvious obsession for sport has robbed publishing of his lively intelligence, culture, and uncommon ability to express himself in good English prose . . . etc.'. He must have made considerable impact because, from among forty-six applicants, I was actually short-listed. Very short. In fact, excepting the emergence of a surprise runner, in the person of an infinitely better qualified candidate, Francis (Frank) Byrne, the pattern of my racing life would have taken very different shape.

Frank, eight years my senior, and raised among horses in Ireland, had been up at Cambridge at the same time as the former *Times* racing correspondent, Noel Carlile, who had died in September 1945. Despite paying closer attention to action at nearby Newmarket than to his Labour MP tutor, the younger son of Tipperary surgeon Patrick Byrne still achieved a science degree and qualified as a lawyer. It was a Cambridge associate who prompted the astute and civilized *Times* sports editor, Oliver Beaumont, to contact F. Byrne, then racing writer for the *Evening News*. When he did so, Frank invited Oliver to his club, the Junior Carlton, and there, three very dry martinis later, the *Times* secured one of its best interpreters of the racing scene in the paper's distinguished history.

Frank, who shares with me a love of wine as well as horses – he gave Pat and me a magnum of 1929 Château Pétrus when we were married – insists to this day that in winning the *Times* contract (£1100 per annum, rising to £2000 twenty years later) he did me as great a service as Be Friendly and Attivo. Well, nearly!

'It would never have suited you,' says he. 'To begin with, the money would hardly have helped you stay at the Ritz in Paris on your French visits, and, more importantly, they would never have let you broadcast as you have.'

The Times insisted that Frank's services were devoted exclusively to the paper. During his early years he had no back-up and few holidays until Jimmy Snow was employed, largely to cover the north, in 1954. 'Still,' he says, 'it was a great paper to work for during the sports editorship of Oliver Beaumont. Then, when he died, it became horrible.'

Just as it is easier to adjust a betting forecast than to compile one, so is it easier to alter copy than to originate it. To his dismay and discomfort, Frank found that under the subsequent incumbent, John Hennessey ('The only no-star Hennessey in my experience,' says Jimmy Snow, with uncharacteristic asperity), his 'copy' 'was not only undergoing a re-write, but having up to five or six mistakes inserted into it daily'. Such situations, originating partly through a conflict in 'style', are not unique, but none the less painful to the writer who is misrepresented. Although only fifty-five, Frank, whose occasional 'confident selections' had for twenty years proved a punters' lifeline (*The Times* did not lower itself to nominating a nap, any more than the BBC recognized betting), decided there was only one course open to him. He quit.

In 1973 my late great colleague, Clive Graham, and I were to encounter the identical predicament.

CHAPTER 7

Chance Meeting

Frost, winter racing's perennial adversary, disrupted programmes in the early part of 1946, frustrating all connected with the sport and severely limiting the pleasure of a stableman's life. Clerks of the course were less than wholly communicative in those days, and it was the responsibility of the PA duty reporters to be on site by 6.30 to 7 a.m. to telephone London regarding 'prospects' and the outcome of any inspection.

Johnnie de Moraville and I were working together by this time. Racing was scheduled at Wincanton the following day, 28 February, and I had driven overnight to Johnnie's house at Childrey in Berkshire – the construction of which had been accelerated by his not entirely unexpected success aboard 33/1 winner Wise Man at Warwick in a seven-horse field in 1934 – so that we could share transport the next morning. The roads were icebound, but the temperature was expected to rise in the night. As we prepared to leave at 4 a.m. there was the solemn hush which follows a heavy fall of snow, or the fall of the favourite at the first. The cross-country route was charted by abandoned cars. After two and a half hours in and out of ditches there were still fifteen miles to go when the outline of a phone box caught our attention. Employing the overworked shovel to obtain entry, I rang the office and left a message with the switchboard: 'Wincanton racing prospects nil. More follows.'

Then I thought, that's pretty feeble. What's the point in being on the spot, almost, if you can't be more informative than that? I dialled 0 again and asked for another transfer-charge call to London Central 7440. 'Wincanton racing has been abandoned,' I said, adding confidently, 'quote from the clerk of the course to follow.'

'I've told them it's off,' I reported, returning numb to the car.

'My dear fellow,' reacted my colleague, 'I should think so too. Let's go and find a cup of coffee before we die of frostbite.'

We drove into Mere, seven miles from the Somerset course, and the road was clear. There was no snow on the rooftops. As we hopefully approached the Old Ship Hotel, the joint-service boys (who worked for the Tape and whom we were supposed to beat with the news on such occasions, and vice versa) were tumbling out into their car. Coffee would have to wait. Johnnie broke into his second twenty-pack of the day, handed me one, lit up, and we proceeded in silence. Fast. There was green grass in a valley to the south.

Except when suffering pre-commentary nerves or running a temperature, I've never hoped for an abandonment. But this was different. The PA snap would have gone to all subscribers, BBC included, and all trainers and other inquirers would have been relayed the news. To survive in racing it is advisable to give precedence to the favourable portents. Passing through a village well below the level of the exposed racecourse, I noted, gratefully, that unclaimed milk bottles were frozen on the doorsteps. But as we swung into the car park, there, of all unwelcome sights, was a racehorse. The only one present, as it turned out. Exhaling puffs of steam into the ice-cold air, he was walking from the direction of the frost-white circuit. 'What's it like?' I asked his lad, nervously. He'd driven his burly partner down from Neville Crump's Middleham stable the previous day and could envisage little profit from the voyage.

'You'd need ten pickaxes to bury your mother-in-law out there,' he offered, 'and you still wouldn't get the job done. It's hard as rock cakes in t'canteen.' The joint-service team turned up as the clerk of the course appeared and revealed that he was awaiting his steward. Abandonment, he reckoned, was 'a mere formality'.

The senior member of the 'opposition' directed a fellow workman towards a phone to await a signal just as a Land Rover delivered the steward. After a brief exchange with the clerk, the only man who wasn't being paid for his presence that morning strode on to what should have been the field of action, followed, lethargically, by a black labrador, to whom the sight of his master without a gun had all the appeal of a meatless bone. After conscientiously prodding wide areas of the unyielding surface, the steward strode back towards us and inquired in a tone which matched the temperature, 'Are you the press?'

We nodded, acknowledging our collective shame, and he pronounced, 'The meeting is abandoned.' He looked at his watch, 'At 7.45.'

The joint-service leader made the appropriate sign, but his confederate had left the phone and was returning from his post. He had called the office, he explained, and been informed that the PA had issued news of Wincanton's abandonment more than one hour previously – and where the hell had they been?

'Isn't it time we had that coffee?' suggested Johnnie. It was. And, assured it would be laced with brandy, the 'opposition' agreed to join us. That was the first and last time I anticipated the outcome of an inspection.

In the same month the local weather prompted a more rewarding excursion to report the Gold Cup prep race of the celebrated Prince Regent at Baldoyle, the seaside circuit north of Dublin which used to feature both jumping and the opening of the Flat. Alas, it is no longer a racecourse. One of the two best horses to have competed unsuccessfully in the Grand National in my time (the other is Crisp), Prince Regent was Ireland's outstanding 'chaser of the war years.

He had won the Irish National in 1942, and his first post-war visit to England was to collect a £100 'chase at Wetherby, for which he started 10/1 on, on 15 December 1945. A powerful son of My Prince, with great depth of girth, he was so superior to the majority of his contemporaries that, on this chilly February afternoon, he was required to concede 3 stone (and five years) to his principal Baldoyle rival, Dorothy Paget's progressive young four-race winner Loyal King.

Tom Dreaper, an infinitely patient and gentle man, who was later to handle one of jumping's immortals, Arkle, had a very special affection for Prince Regent, who was his last winning ride in a 'bumper'. 'You couldn't say he did badly,' he murmured, almost to himself, while the vast crowd's hero was returning through a sea of admirers after less than half-length defeat by a horse who, in his next race, ridiculed the opposition under 11 stone 12 lb in the Grand Annual at the Cheltenham National Hunt Festival.

As a postscript to my 'copy', telephoned from the old Shelbourne Hotel in Dublin, I added, 'If Prince Regent gets beat in the Gold Cup I'll go to work for a living.' The Prince himself may not have been in his prime at eleven, but he still won the Gold Cup without any bother, beating ex-Irish Poor Flame – who had passed the post first in each of his five previous outings that season – by five lengths, and then running a magnificent race under 12 stone 5 lb to be third in the National. Just as Crisp was to do twenty-seven years later, he led over the last, only for the prodigious weight concession to turn the tide against him on the run in. He ran an honourable fourth under 12 stone 7 lb the following year and, in association with another grand old veteran, Jack Moloney, won his last race (by ten lengths under 12.5!) as a fourteen-year-old at Lingfield on 14 January 1949.

I remember Rae Johnstone telling me at the time I was ghosting his life story in 1958 that old Jack, who wasn't too hot at the reading stakes, would pass the morning paper which he had been studying earnestly to his neighbour in the Turkish baths, explaining that he had left his glasses with his clothes, and asking, 'Would you ever tell me what it says here?' Rae was always much too considerate to let on that Jack had been holding the paper upside down.

'Le Crocodile', as the french *turfistes* knew Rae Johnstone – because of his habit of waiting, Harry Wragg-like, to gobble up the opposition – was the first of the great international jockeys. Born on 13 April 1905 in New South Wales, Australia, he won thirty classics; rode more than two thousand winners in nine countries; was no stranger to adversity and in all innocence might have got us both warned off in 1956. I first met him in early March 1946. All the evidence supported Charlie Elliott's view that wartime racing and breeding schedules in England and France would reflect favourably on French horses. The vast bloodstock enterprise of the textile magnate Marcel Boussac, who had won seven French Derbys by 1945 and was to win another five, was virtually unaffected; whereas most English studs had been converted, partly or wholly, to agricultural needs, and competition restricted.

As a tenuous ability to communicate in French was one of my only qualifications, it seemed a pity not to exercise it. More in optimism than in expectation of a favourable reaction, I wrote to Monsieur Boussac in January seeking an interview. Several weeks later the request was granted for the beginning of March, provided a list of questions was submitted in advance. Freddy Harrison would need to obtain the authority of 'management' before sanctioning this 'unprecedented departure'. It was granted with, apparently, well-contained enthusiasm and the proviso that expense was carefully controlled.

A few days before I flew to Paris Epsom-based bookmaker Charlie Hunter Simmonds, who had a horse with Charlie Bell and who knew I went to France occasionally, asked if I'd do him a favour on my next trip. Through an intermediary, he'd been approached by a French trainer who, with his owners, wished to place commissions on the stable's intended runners in England. The difficulty was that neither spoke the other's language. Would I interpret?

The Boussac interview seemed to go OK, especially since the 'Patron', as he was widely known, suggested that I contact his manager, the charming Comte François de Brignac, and ask him to show me the horses at Villa Pharis and Villa Djebel at Chantilly. More immediately, I met Charlie Simmonds and the Maisons-Laffitte trainer, Joseph Lieux, in the bar of the Hôtel George V. If the horse we were principally discussing turned out to be half as good as he sounded towards the end of an excellent dinner, the Royal Mint was going to have to step up production. Early next morning I took my hangover to Maisons to meet him.

It was said that, when the Russian crowds saw Trotsky astride a ceremonial horse, they exclaimed, 'What a man!', but when Lenin was similarly positioned they noted, 'What a horse!' Here was a duo who perfectly complemented each other: Rae Johnstone, with his indolent, natural grace, and the heavily built Sayani, who was paradoxically so feather-light in his flowing action. When he arrived in the yard as a youngster, Sayani had evoked from the head lad the comment to Mme Lieux: 'The master has bought a young ox among the yearlings this year.'

The toast that evening at dinner at Lapérouse was *'Sayani et, peut-être, le Cambridgeshire.'* He was a hell of a horse, especially once his astute handler had found the key to his optimum talent. This was, once fit, to ensure the very minimum exertion to sustain health and vigour. It was Joseph's firm adherence to this routine with the three-year-old, who would have to achieve a weight-carrying record to win the big Newmarket handicap under 9 stone 4 lb, that was the reason for the son of Fair Copy starting as high as 25/1 seventh favourite – despite considerable ante-post support – in the thirty-four-runner field.

Ten days before the race Sayani, who had won the prestigious Prix Jacques le Marois at Deauville, was sent to Jack Reardon's at Epsom whither his trainer flew over regularly 'just to look at him', as Jack put it, when insisting that it was out of the question for a horse to win the Cambridgeshire, 'or any other race', on such a preparation. Ken Gethin, who rode out on the downs regularly for his father-in-law Peter Thrale, Harold Wallington and others was just as emphatic: 'If you're on that, mate,' (I was), he told me, 'you've left your money behind.' On the day he said to Rae in the weighing-room that Sayani looked like a bullock – 'and he'll be just about as fit as one'.

It was an amazing race. I was getting the occasional race-reading job to the established broadcasters at this time, as well as sometimes receiving an unextravagant fee for inflicting my limited knowledge on listeners to the BBC Overseas Service. But I was uninvolved, apart from PA duties, for the race and had my binoculars focused on Sayani as the tapes whipped up nine furlongs down the course.

Co-favourites were the runaway Lincoln winner Langton Abbot, who met Sayani 8 lb better than weight-for-age, and Wayward Belle, a top-flight three-year-old filly who had won her last four, including the Nassau and Duke of York, who was receiving 13 lb from Sayani. Rae was drawn 14, towards the stands side of centre, Langton Abbot number 30, and Wayward Belle 21. Gordon Richards on the heavily backed Claro (receiving 15 lb), winner of the Irish 2000 Guineas and close second in the Irish Derby, lined up on the 'inner', number 3.

Horses jumped a lot less straight from behind the five-strand tape barrier than they do from stalls. Now as the starter, Hubert Allison, released the gate there was almost instant scrimmaging in the centre. It was difficult to tell from the stands how much ground Sayani had covered (150 yards was the post-race estimate) when he stumbled on to his nose and I lost him momentarily, as he would have lost a less accomplished horseman than Rae. Reidentified, he appeared 'out with the washing'. I was focusing on another even bigger French gamble (there were five Gallic challengers), Philadelphe II, when the binoculars revealed Sayani almost rejoining the pack. With two furlongs to run he could even make the first six – if he sprouted wings. He did. When Rae 'picked him up', taking a firmer hold and squeezing him but *not* administering a gratuitous striping, the Lieux family's 'young ox' devoured the hill as if it were the equine equivalent of caviare.

The judge posted the verdict: Sayani by a head from Claro, who beat Toronto (a northern-trained six-race-winner who was receiving 25 lb!) by the same margin, with Langton Abbot a further head away fourth. The handicapper could be as proud of his work as Joseph Lieux. Gordon, the first to congratulate Rae, remarked, 'That was some performance' – a detail fully acknowledged by the Newmarket race crowd, who gave the victorious duo a well-deserved ovation. Interestingly, the senior Jockey Club starter, who had the best view of Sayani's early difficulties, and who was not given to exaggeration, believed the winner to be 'possibly the best horse, up to one and a quarter miles, almost of the century'.

The wartime limitation of stamina tests, coupled with surviving breeders' commercial need to produce quick-maturing speed horses, left Britain particularly vulnerable at distances of a mile and beyond; especially coinciding with the sustained success of the Boussac in-breeding formula. Despite his 'dodgy' pins, that fine old bandaged stayer Marsyas won on five of his six visits, including the Queen Alexandra Stakes, Goodwood and Doncaster Cups. Another Boussac, Caracalla II, led a French 1, 2, 3 in the Gold Cup on the day before stable companion Priam II won the Hardwicke. With eight winners of twelve races, therefore, the emperor of the French turf finished second (£21,377) in the 1946 list of leading owners in Britain, £590 behind the Aga Khan, Prince Karim's grandfather.

Even more illustrative of the weakness of the home defence was the same year's King George VI Stakes, run at Ascot on 12 October. Only three of the eleven runners were trained in England, and when that ebullient character 'Lulu' Chataignoux's Souverain (11/2) fulfilled his owner's confident prediction, he beat the English Derby winner Airborne (4/5) by an extended five lengths. Yet when it came to the Gallic gamble of the year, at Manchester on 16 November, the overworked patron saint of bookmakers was on the alert.

'Keep it to yourself,' said Rae a fortnight before the race, 'but as long as it's soft on the day, a gun wouldn't stop this one.' And mud at Manchester in November was as sure as snow on Mont Blanc in January. Longtime compulsive gambler William Raphael Johnstone had

– like an alcoholic who has taken the cure – totally forsworn betting. Otherwise he would have mortgaged his and his blonde French wife Mary's Auteuil flat and all its contents for Dornot in the Manchester November Handicap.

By a French Derby winner out of a French '1000' winner, this four-year-old, on whom Rae had twice scored at Longchamp with plenty in hand, was no handicapper. Yet he'd been assessed to concede 1 lb to compatriot Quatrain, who would have needed a concession of 2 stone to match strides with him going to post. It had 'come up mud' such as could only be seen at Castle Irwell, and while others would be sunk without trace Dornot handled such circumstance as a hydrofoil on a benign sea.

I'd executed part of the commission, averaging 100/8; he was 5/1 favourite and should have been evens. Joseph Lieux had a well-fancied runner in the last, L'Oseille, and Charlie Bell figured he'd got a fair outside chance of winning the Nursery at Lingfield with Housey-Housey. I had three tenner doubles, or three weeks' wages, and stood by the 'Blower' boys in the Manchester stand to hear the result of the 1.30 down south. Housey-Housey won at 100/7 and I began to feel sorry for the bookmakers.

Forty-five minutes later, while Rae was hacking through the fog to the start, Charlie Smirke – who never missed much, if anything, and who was upsides on Star of Autumn – noted Dornot's action and called across, 'You'll win a hundred yards!' That's what was going through the mind of the favourite's partner during the race as he turned towards home, positively cantering, when he heard a snap. Poor Dornot had broken a fetlock. Mercifully the vet was swiftly on site and saw him into the float. Sedated and taken to Newmarket, he lived in slings until he was mended and able to fulfil a successful life at stud. If there was consolation for Rae, it was that the jockey from whom he learnt most about race-riding, Harry Wragg, won that 'November' on his last day before retirement.

Oh yes, and L'Oseille finished second! It wasn't the most successful afternoon of my undistinguished career, but it was a contrastingly happy evening.

In that era the Flat season opened on Lincoln's windswept Carholme and ended at Manchester with a series of farewell parties in the old Midland Hotel and dancing to the infectious rhythm of Joe Orlando, an inveterate punter to whom, regrettably, I had confided news of Dornot's imminent victory. During a brief interval the dapper band-leader, matinée idol of the local scene, joined me for a little consolatory refreshment. It wasn't in Joe's nature to be reproachful; rather was he concerned over the fate of the horse. 'You know', he reflected wistfully, in his Italo-Mancunian accent, 'owners they tell me when their horse is expected. The trainers they let me know when they have something special. Jockeys ring me with hot news. Father Ryan there,' – he nodded towards a Catholic priest – 'blesses my ventures. And when I lose, some bookmakers they will not even take my money. And still I cannot break even.'

Then, suddenly discarding defeatist meditation, he leaned forward as if about to give me a 'good thing' for Monday's jumping programme at Wolverhampton. But he raised his glass and, with a courtly bow across the table, said '*Saluté*', adding, 'The tall young lady you are dancing with is a beautiful girl, the most striking in the ballroom.'

Had Dornot won I would have flown back to Paris with the connections for a celebration dinner, returning on Sunday. And I would never have met Pat, my future wife.

CHAPTER 8

Alias Patrick Moore

The Racehorse, price threepence, which had closed at the outbreak of war, was revived by its proprietor, Roger de Wesselow, at the end of his service with SOE – Special Operations Executive. During the deep freeze in 1947, when there was no racing in England between 22 January and 13 March, Roger asked me if I'd care to do a bi-weekly column for them. I didn't much favour writing under a nom-de-plume, but PA staff were not permitted to contribute to any other organization under their own name. And if, as it seemed, I was to continue to own horses so resolutely unaddicted to success, a small income supplement would clearly be desirable. So with the Flat imminent, weather permitting, 'Patrick Moore' launched on 7 March with news, both exclusive and unhelpful, to the effect that Lincoln top-weight Vagabond II had been moved from the Paris area to the relative warmth of Bordeaux, where he was enjoying (I hoped) an uninterrupted preparation for his target on 26 March.

As soon as the frost, which caused the abandonment of the National Hunt Festival, had relaxed, extensive flooding followed, so that local training schedules remained severely restricted. I drove Cyril Luckman, the Scout of the *Daily Express*, to Lincoln on Sunday 23 March, and he told me that in all his forty-four years on the paper he had never seen such conditions. As we made detours to avoid swollen rivers, it seemed inconceivable for the meeting to open on time. Early next day, after a quick swim round the track, the stewards abandoned day one. The first few furlongs of the straight were still waterlogged on Tuesday, despite strong drying winds, so all races were run over the round course with six- and seven-furlong events started by flag. By big race time the following afternoon the round course still represented the only usable terrain – and only just, at that.

Soon after the start the biggest field of the season, forty-six, had to race into a left-hand bend which was churned into a sea of mud. Harry Carr, who was riding a 66/1 outsider and hoped to be partnering some more significant prospects during the ensuing eight months, advised,

58

'Anyone who wants to go the longest way round, follow me!' Vagabond II, sightless in his near eye since a yearling, had drawn far off the rails with thirty-three opponents on his blind side. In anticipation of fitness advantage, there were seven French challengers and an additional Gallic jockey in Paul Blanc, whom John Goldsmith had engaged for French-bred Querneuville – the subject of a serious gamble by his bookmaker owner, Percy Thompson, who had staked the pilot to a small fortune and told him so.

Vagabond II and Rae Johnstone were all but knocked over at the start, and by the time they reached the bend, behind a dark brown cloud of spray, the seven-year-old wasn't the only one of the duo to be partially sightless. They were never 'at the races' in an event summarized by Charlie Smirke as 'worse than the invasion of Sicily!'. One of the only riders whose colours were still identifiable at the finish was Ken Gethin, who had been in the front rank throughout on Persian Book. First he, then Querneuville, looked like winning until, well inside the last furlong, Blanc's feverish lunge for the line unbalanced Percy Thompson's horse, who ducked towards the stands. Eighteen-year-old Manny Mercer, for whom horses ran as for the amazing Bill Shoemaker, was sitting in behind, almost unnoticed, on 100/1 outsider Jockey Treble, when the daylight was offered and accepted – like a wild bird fleeing a wire cage. Official placings: Jockey Treble, Persian Book, Querneuville. Distances: neck, head. Bookmaker Syd Oxenham owned the winner. And he may not have been the only member of his profession to show a profit on the race. Now every time I see cheerful 'Popol' Blanc, who is employed by the Société d'Encouragement, at his weighing-room post at Longchamp, I wonder whether there would have been a different outcome to the 1947 Lincoln had he not been apprised of the 'fortune' awaiting him.

As the big meeting at Cheltenham in March had been abandoned, the Festival races were reopened. Willie Head took the opportunity to enter his son Alec's Le Paillon for the Champion Hurdle on Saturday, 12 April and give him an ideal preparatory run. Winner of seven in a row at Auteuil in the previous season, he had run a terrific race on 23 March when conceding massive weight, needing the run, and finishing very fast to be fourth. Bruce Hobbs told me that Willie Head wanted to know if I could put a bet on for him, and when I located him he reported that his cousin Vic Smyth rated National Spirit's chances highly, adding, 'I think he'll have to be pretty good to beat mine.' Willie would like a 'tenner' on him, if possible.

It was a sparkling contest with the exceptionally tall National Spirit holding the ultimate favourite, Le Paillon, throughout the run-in to win by a length. Obviously Alec was handicapped by lack of experience of a highly individual circuit, but National Spirit was a very good horse that day – he was no mug at any time – and I doubt whether excuses for Patrick Moore's 'best bet of the week' were all that in order. Anyway, Le Paillon found a nice little consolation race in the Arc de Triomphe.

The Gold Cup, run on the same afternoon, was won by Dicky Black, on Fortina, with whom he and his trainer, Hector Christie, were achieving an unprecedented double after victory in Manchester's prestigious Lancashire Chase. Dicky, who was to turn pro the following season, was so confident that he'd have gone very close to winning Caughoo's National the previous month on 66/1 chance Rowland Roy 'but for flicking the top of Becher's second time round' that Patrick Moore was persuaded to nominate the pair in the next issue of *The Racehorse* for the Scottish equivalent on 19 April, when they obliged by six lengths at 6/1.

A high percentage of the winners ridden by 'Mr R. Black' at this time were trained 'Capt. J. de Moraville', who left the PA at the end of May 1946 to build up a useful little team. The foundation member was his own King Penguin, who became a partnership horse when Johnnie forfeited two legs in the eight-year-old while playing poker in a PoW camp. Unaffected by this dismemberment, King Penguin won first time out at Ludlow on 3 October 1946, later collecting at both Birmingham and Manchester.

A little less successful was Bobsfel, who joined the stable in July 1946 after Johnnie Dines had recommended him as a potential National Hunt performer. A failure on the Flat, this son of Bobsleigh had the size and scope for jumping but was for sale because his owner did not favour the winter game. Bobsfel had always shown plenty of ability at home, and Johnnie Dines reckoned a change of environment and activity could encourage him to exercise his talent in public. Johnnie de Moraville, Tommy Clyde and I bought him in partnership and he 'ran' in my colours. Reaching the gallops from Frethorne House involved the occasional encounter with cars, a circumstance which, as a former resident of Epsom, held no terror for Bobsfel. But his first sight of a cow over a Berkshire hedgerow had him rooted to the ground with amazement.

As we were to discover, he tended to take root like a weed and with even less encouragement. Still his homework, when accomplished without interruption, was bright enough to inspire support on his hurdles debut at Wincanton on 16 November 1946. He sustained hope for half the journey, after which he appeared to take the view that some of the others were regarding the event far too seriously. With two to jump he had had enough and pulled himself up.

As we were all friends, Dicky Black was able to dispense with the routine assurances ('He'll be all the better for the experience; was "blinded" at the second last flight; didn't handle the going; would prefer a left-hand course etc. . . .') and express his authentic opinion, which was that he wouldn't be over-confident about him in a walk-over. Even proprietorial reluctance to accept the unfavourable had to be overcome after Bobsfel had repeated the performance in a Windsor 'seller'.

It is always disturbing for a trainer when a conspicuously unsuccessful performer is transformed on admission to another yard. Bobsfel seemed an unlikely source of embarrassment after reappearing for a new handler, Arthur Garnham, at Ludlow on 19 April 1947. Starting 25/1 others he made no more impact than at Towcester on 3 May or Newton Abbot a week later. Then on the afternoon of 28 May at Ludlow Dicky was astonished to hear a bookmaker calling 3/1 Bobsfel. Similar odds against naming the winners of the Derby, Oaks and Leger would not have appeared less generous. On enquiring the grounds for this parsimony he was told that there had been a lot of money for the five-year-old, and Dicky's offer to lay £50–£10 against him was unhesitatingly accepted. Whatever got into Bobsfel that day, Ken Mullins, his first-time rider, reported that he'd never experienced a more hairy ride than on the 100/30 second favourite, who barely took off at a hurdle while making all the running to win comfortably by four lengths – his partner's twentieth winner in thirty-five National Hunt rides since Easter Monday.

Anyone who assumed Bobsfel to be a reformed character received emphatic evidence to the contrary. Next time out, under Bob Turnell at Buckfastleigh, he made no show whatever; while, reunited with Ken Mullins on what turned out to be a final racecourse appearance in the eleven-runner Burpham Handicap Hurdle on 23 September 1947, he trailed home a distant last – nothing behind him but the green turf of Fontwell Park.

It was a situation which Dicky Black would have preferred to his own during the following race, the second division of the Singleton Novices' Hurdle. Here Johnnie de Moraville ran an ex-point-to-point horse, Scarlet Tecum, for whom he had plans which did not include an over-taxing initiation to National Hunt racing. Under the circumstances the owner, Sir Freddie Freake, was advised to forgo the journey since the 20/1 chance would be in need of a race. It turned out that he was not the only competitor in this condition, including the favourite, Maestro. After the latter had 'blown up' and the second favourite, Victory Salute, had fallen, hampering another fancied runner in the process, the initiative passed to the third favourite, Scone, who approached the first in the home straight with a commanding advantage over Scarlet Tecum. Unfortunately Scone made a comprehensive hash of the obstacle and, with Dicky Black sitting motionless as a wax effigy, Scarlet Tecum, who had been jumping immaculately in his own time throughout, sailed into the lead and returned to the silent welcome of an ocean liner berthing a day early. Johnnie was not very pleased and my endeavours, while conducting an interview for the PA, to persuade him to adopt an expression more suited to a winning trainer were only partially successful.

Unlike most horses who succeed when least required, Scarlet Tecum collected again under more acceptable circumstances; but my replacement for Bobsfel, the inappropriately named Mr Star, in whom Johnnie de M. took a half share, embraced failure with even greater persistence than his predecessor. Before the extent of his allergy to the winner's circle had been fully appreciated, Mr Star was even recommended on occasion to Patrick Moore's readers in *The Racehorse*. Fortunately, I had more helpful suggestions for them that year – notably for the autumn double, initiated by Whiteway's (100/8) runaway Cesarewitch victory and completed a fortnight later by Fairey Fulmar (28/1) in the Cambridgeshire.

One of the penalties of tipping for a living is that, whereas a travel writer's ill-chosen selections are seldom exposed, a doctor's incorrect diagnosis undiscovered, or a bureaucrat's miscalculation undetected, a horse race selector is open to instant judgement. (If 'selector' sounds like a pretentious euphemism for 'tipster', I use the former to distinguish between race writing and offering tips or information for sale.)

One of my longtime colleagues, Peter Scott (Hotspur of the *Daily Telegraph*), had a habit of investing a pound or two on what he considered to be the main danger to his newspaper selection, hoping thereby to 'stop' the threat, or achieve small consolation if he failed to do so. I wouldn't go quite as far as my one-time protégé, for whom, at the instigation of my mother, who was a friend of his parents, I obtained a first newspaper interview; but it often seemed to me over-extravagant to expect to win both glory and cash. So that after taking 25/1 about Whiteway (£50 each-way with Laurie Wallis) I feebly laid off all but a tenner's worth at 100/6, and not only overlooked personal interest in the double but, having been asked to place Cambridgeshire commissions on Vagabond II and Admiral's Yarn (both unplaced), even failed to invest a shilling on Fairey Fulmar on the day. Pathetic. Whiteway at least underwrote a drive to Italy – which included such gastro-highlights as Chez Point at Vienne and Mère Brazier at Lyon – to visit Signor Tesio's lovely Maggiore lakeside stud. I'd written to the great man before leaving England, asking if it would be possible to interview him at Dormello, the stud he had founded in 1898. When I reached the Grand Hotel, Menaggio, on Lake Como there was a letter saying he would be delighted and, if I liked, we could go on to Milan to see his racing stables.

'If you come here by train, get out at the station of Arona and a car will meet you. If you come by car, it is *before* reaching Arona but at less than two miles.'

I waste hours being over-punctual and, having located the house well in advance of schedule, drove to the nearest café. The *patron* was an authority on the man who has made the most significant impact on worldwide bloodstock breeding this century. He confirmed a story I had been told earlier – but for which I still cannot vouch – that the clairvoyant who bought the unprepossessing Catnip, granddam of the great Nearco, for seventy-five guineas at the Newmarket December Sales in 1945, developed his empathy with horses through sheer chance. While a serving cavalry officer, he responded to a dare by vaulting on to the hotel balcony of a lady's bedroom. The situation developed elements of farce which, in the contemporary moral climate, led to his dishonour and resignation from his regiment. Federico Tesio took off for South America and it was here, riding through regions populated by wild horses, that his appreciation and understanding of the race developed and crystallized into an obsession. By the year he died, 1954, he had won twenty-one Italian Derbys.

I was so intrigued by the stud I didn't ask him about early days; it would have seemed impertinent anyway. But there was no hesitation when he suggested moving on to Milan – he had a direct line to his stables fifty miles away – to see the horses in training. One, Tenerani, whose half sister Trevisana was a useful two-year-old this year (1947), he anticipated sending to England for a race or two the following season. He won both, the 1½ miles Queen Elizabeth Stakes at Ascot (beating Black Tarquin a short head) and the 2 mile 5 furlongs Goodwood Cup, in which poor Arbar broke down. Tenerani, whose dam, Tofanello, Signor Tesio had bought as a yearling at Doncaster for 140 guineas, was, of course, to become the sire of the horse of his era, Ribot – unbeaten in sixteen races. I had the privilege of commentating during his storming victories in the Arc de Triomphe, in one of which he was pulling Enrico Camici out of the saddle from start to finish, and the King George VI and Queen Elizabeth Diamond Stakes.

At this time, asked which was the best he ever bred and trained, Signor Tesio was in no doubt that Nearco ('a horse of great class'), unbeaten in fourteen races, surpassed all others. Both Nearco and Ribot won over distances from five to fifteen furlongs. Sadly, Signor Tesio did not live to see Ribot run, so we will never know how he would have assessed them in relation to each other.

Charming Donna Lydia Tesio was disinclined to make comparisons. With her unfailing courtesy she showed me the yearlings in the mid-fifties and we were in constant touch during the traumatic preliminaries to Botticelli's bid for glory in England. A big, strong horse by Blue Peter out of a Niccolo Dell'Arca mare, he had two dislikes, travel and mud. So when the poor lad was injured on exiting from a plane flying him to Ascot for the 1954 King George VI and Queen Elizabeth Diamond Stakes, for which the going was conservatively styled 'dead', it seemed prudent not to tip him. Under the circumstances he performed very respectably behind the Queen's splendid Aureole, whose maternal grandsire was the Tesio winner of eight of his nine races, Donatello II.

For his next attempt Botticelli was despatched by rail, only for a landslide to halt progress outside Milan. His target had been the 1955 Ascot Gold Cup, which was also delayed owing to a rail strike during the Royal Meeting. The Italian rail link having been re-established, the horse with an understandable antipathy to displacement was packed off again, with his personal supply of Italian spring water, on a journey which included a both unscheduled and unenjoyable ten-hour halt in a Paris railway siding and which lasted for three days. If he wasn't feeling like running 2½ miles in the deferred (to 13 July) Gold Cup, you couldn't blame him. But the surface was firm, the opposition unspectacular, and, under these circumstances, readers were invited to go nap. Backed from 3/1 to 9/4 second favourite to the Boussac horse Elpenor, he fairly bolted in. Donna Lydia was to have visited Newmarket for the first time since he won to see him take on Hafiz II in the Champion Stakes, but a slight injury prevented him running.

There are those in the world of racing who live more or less permanently on the fringe of disaster. Some of them are trainers. And my old friend Charlie Bell was one of them. Not that Charlie didn't know his job; far from it. Apprenticed to Fred Darling as a kid, he'd 'done' winners, ridden winners, knew about horses' legs, was acknowledged a very good feeder and became a top-class head lad. But there is a lot of difference between looking after a stable's horses, reporting on them to your governor – with whose decisions you might or might not agree – and making those decisions yourself. Charlie had training thrust upon him at the outbreak of World War II when his boss, who later became Group Captain Langlands, joined the RAF. They were difficult times even for firmly established trainers and, considering the material he had to work on, Charlie did marvellously. But, to understate his situation, it was a struggle. Or as John Skeaping, who used to ride out with me at Treadwell House when on leave from the army, put it, 'not so much a question of keeping the wolf from the door as of preventing it coming into the house and having pups'.

From his first year to his last – he joined Tom Jones at Newmarket in 1956 and reverted to being a head lad – I had a horse of sorts with Charlie: Wild Thyme II, Sundange, Headley Boy, Knight of the Garden, Smiling Sambo, Light Rescue, Shy Torb, Prickly Pear, Queen Penguin, Misconception, Iror, The Solid Man, Fidonia and Pretty Fair. The date of 11 March 1954 was a highlight when Pretty Fair, the only one of the lot to achieve a place while carrying my colours, won the Castle Hill Selling Hurdle at Windsor ridden by French jockey and friend René Emery. It was in the era before 'sellers' were needlessly emasculated and, according to current accepted practice, I was obliged to guarantee £50 to the representative (Paddy Brudenell-Bruce) of the owner of the runner-up (Squadron-Leader Stanhope Joel) to ensure he did not bid me up at the subsequent auction. The first prize money was £186; I'd had £20 on my benefactor at 7/2 and laid £11–£10 'in running' to Mickey Fingers at the final flight. With the entry, transport, riding fee and presents, which included cash and a framed photograph of our hero for Charlie, cash for the lad and an engraved Hermès pocket knife for René, £50 for Stan Joel and buying in the winner for 110 guineas, I only lost £14 on the race!

In the aftermath of victory trainer and owner reflected over a drink or two on their varying fortune over the years, inevitably recalling the traumatic afternoon of 17 November 1948 when Blakesley, ridden by Vince Mooney, ran for the stable at Chepstow in the Selling Handicap Chase.

At this time Johnnie de Moraville had a very useful French import called Rondo II. Like so many in France, he'd learned to jump in a loose school and did it for fun. After a smooth enough debut in a novices' at Worcester, where Dicky Black let him stride on after jumping the first flight, his target was Manchester's Hopeful Hurdle on 20 November. It was going to take a useful one to beat him. The son of Le Gosse was ideally suited to a partner with good hands who would leave him to make his own arrangements at the obstacles. Unfortunately Dicky was 'out' owing to a bad fall at Liverpool on 11 November, but gifted horseman Jack Moloney seemed an ideal substitute. I had a fair-sized commission to place for him and, deeply impressed by the Worcester performance, determined to add to it.

The Manchester meeting was scheduled to open on the 18th, so I drove up on the previous day accompanied by my PA working colleague Stanley ('Skimp') Langley, whose father was a respected professional work watcher at Newmarket. Although Skimp and I shared racing information fairly freely and I had suggested during the journey that there should be a bet at Manchester, I had made no reference to Blakesley's participation in the 1 o'clock at Chepstow that afternoon.

It was required procedure to ring into the Fleet Street office of the PA while *en route* to a major meeting to learn whether there were any stories to be followed up on arrival. By the time we reached Towcester it was getting near post time at Chepstow. So, pulling up at the Saracen's Head, I said I'd get the drinks if my colleague would call the racing desk. As an afterthought I added, 'While you're on, ask them what won the first at Chepstow.'

A few minutes later, he walked into the bar looking, I thought, a little hurt. 'Anything doing?' I asked. 'No, all quiet,' he answered 'and you know what won the 1 o'clock at Chepstow, don't you?' I didn't, I told him. 'Well,' he said, 'it was your stable, Charlie Bell, Blakesley.'

If I wasn't pale beforehand, I was now. Over the weekend Charlie had outlined his financial situation. It was not healthy; but he had the immediate means of urgent resuscitation if only I would help. The owner of Blakesley, he explained, insisted on him running the horse at Chepstow despite the fact that he'd had a setback and been in his box for a fortnight. He was perfectly sound but was nowhere near fit to run. He'd be near enough favourite. Could I get a bookmaker to lay him? I thought he should have another go at the owner. And he did. Mr Farmiloe, proprietor of the ten-year-old who had cost 85 guineas and had won at Wolverhampton the previous season, reiterated that as long as the horse was sound he'd come to no harm and the outing would benefit him in future handicaps. He positively wished him to run.

I pointed out to Charlie that I could only ask a bookmaker to lay Blakesley for a sum I'd be able to pay if he won. He insisted that the horse couldn't win were he to start overnight; there'd be no risk whatever in opposing him to lose a million. As my liquid assets were £999,650 short of this amount I had rung a bookmaker who bet at Chepstow and asked him to lay Blakesley to lose me £350 – several thousand pounds in contemporary values. Whatever the bet won I'd send on to Charlie.

Backed early on at 2/1, Blakesley drifted in the market to 5/1; he improved steadily in the straight and won readily by three lengths. My account with the Welsh bookmaker for the week ending read:

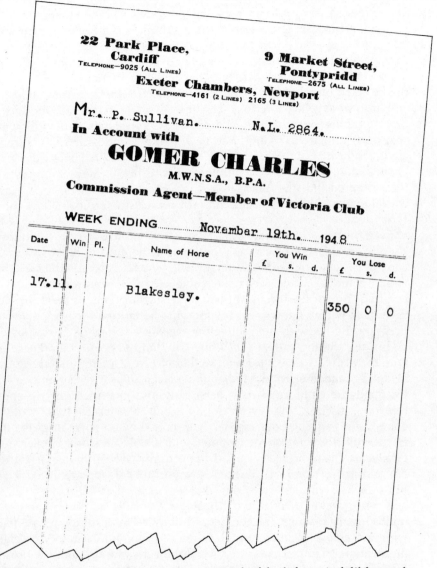

**22 Park Place,
Cardiff**
TELEPHONE—9025 (ALL LINES)

**9 Market Street,
Pontypridd**
TELEPHONE—2675 (ALL LINES)

Exeter Chambers, Newport
TELEPHONE—4161 (2 LINES) 2165 (3 LINES)

Mr. P. Sullivan. N.L. 2864.

In Account with

GOMER CHARLES

M.W.N.S.A., B.P.A.

Commission Agent—Member of Victoria Club

WEEK ENDING November 19th. 1948

Date	Win	Pl.	Name of Horse	You Win £ s. d.	You Lose £ s. d.
17.11.			Blakesley.		350 0 0

Maybe the race I didn't see, but certainly felt, left an indelible mark and accounts for my repeated TV commentary reference to 'Vince' Mooney (who had one of his easiest winning rides on Blakesley) instead of his contemporary namesake Kevin who featured, incidentally, in that memorable Whitbread Gold Cup finish on Queen Elizabeth the Queen Mother's Special Cargo in 1984.

The Rondo II commission averaged 7/2. He started 2/1 and made every yard of the running in the Hopeful Hurdle to win by three lengths.

Under the circumstances my personal interest was limited to ten shillings (50p). A great asset to his stable, Rondo II, like most horses – especially talented ones – had his individual characteristics: he relished front running and if he saw that a rival was struggling to get to him he'd make every effort to fight him off; but challenged by a runner who was 'on the bit' he'd dissolve faster than a bookmaker's early morning odds.

A lion among his inferiors, he jumped off and ran the opposition ragged in Lingfield's Hidden Mystery Chase at the turn of the following year on 1 January, carrying 12 stone 3 lb and giving 23 lb to the second whom he beat, easing up, by four lengths. Rondo II had enjoyed a little break before Lingfield and Johnnie, whose horses were in sparkling form, figured that the outing would have put him spot on for a clash with the outstanding two-mile chaser, Cool Customer, in six days' time at Sandown.

Even with a 5 lb penalty Rondo II would receive over a stone from 'Coolie', and Dicky Black could not believe there was a horse in Britain capable of such concession. William Hill, who had been on the receiving end of some recent de Moraville stable successes, was widely acknowledged as one of the foremost bookmakers of his time, or maybe of any time. Less widely known was the fact that he fancied turning punter on occasion. I'd bet with Bill Hill before the war at Northolt Park (ponies) and in the shilling ring at the White City, and first opened an account with the firm in 1939. We got on well (apart from a temporary hiccough in 1955), and he proposed that if I placed an entire commission in his hands he would add to it personally and guarantee the optimum return. I discussed this with Johnnie and we agreed that, without committing ourselves beyond one bet, there'd be no harm in giving it a try. Rondo II's Sandown encounter with Cool Customer in the Mole Handicap Chase seemed a good opportunity. The top weight started 5/4 favourite; Rondo II, backed down from 9/4, was returned 15/8. Bill's clerk, Bernie, 'showed out' that we were on at 5/2.

A good jockey makes it his business to know as much about the opposition as his own partner. Tim Molony wasn't champion five times without being a good jockey. Despite ex-Irish Cool Customer's weight disadvantage Tim decided to attack Rondo II's morale from the outset. He went with him, matching strides and leaps, so that the duo staged a memorable exhibition in their assault on the railway fences along the far side of one of the finest jumping courses in the world. Whether it was the tactic or whether the race came just too soon after Lingfield, where the nature of the soil places a premium on effort, or whether the ex-French horse was simply not feeling his very best, Rondo II was the first to crack. And that was that. Bill Hill wrote as follows:

William Hill (PARK LANE) *Ltd.*

TELEGRAMS:
HILHOUSE, TELEX, LONDON

CABLEGRAMS:
HILHOUSE, LONDON

TELEPHONES:
WHITEHALL 0981 (200 LINES)

DIRECTORS   WILLIAM HILL, I. M HILL

ESTABLISHED 25 YEARS   MEMBERS OF THE N.S.L., B.P.A. & T.G.S.

HILL HOUSE   ·   LONDON W.I.

26th January, 1949.

Reference   WH/IC

P.J. O'Sullevan, Esq.,
14 Beverley House,
Britten Street,
Chelsea,
LONDON, S.W.3.

Dear Peter,

Would you be kind enough to let me have your cheque for £1,000. in respect of the commission on RONDO at Sandown on Saturday last, the 22nd instant, made out to me personally. Perhaps you would be good enough to send it to my private address - 51 Albion Gate, W.2. As you may know, I had a substantial bet privately and included yours with mine.

Yours sincerely,

William Hill

The assumption that no horse could concede a stone to Rondo II over two miles of fences was justified later (19 March 1949), when the Mole Handicap Chase principals renewed rivalry over the same circuit in the Lilac Chase, with 'Coolie' (13/8 on) conceding 14 lb to Rondo II (4/1). Cool Customer barely saw which way Rondo II went. Regrettably, correct assumptions often yield the wrong result.

Peter Dimmock, wartime squadron-leader, peacetime opportunist, joined the PA Racing Section after being demobbed in 1946. Neither his comprehension of the subject nor his reverence for accuracy commended him as ideal material, and I could have believed more readily in my prospects of riding the Grand National winner than that, within three years, he would be my boss, or one of them. Restless, ambitious and not over-absorbed in the thoroughbred, Peter had been with the PA less than a month when he spotted an advertisement inviting application for the position of BBC television executive. 'Half the interview board were ex-RAF,' he recalled later, and within weeks he was installed at Alexandra Palace with the title of Assistant to the Outside Broadcasts Manager BBC TV, Ian (later Lord) Orr-Ewing. Soon he would not only succeed Ian as OB General Manager, but make the most significant contribution to outside broadcasting of his era. In the interim he became a racing commentator, compensating for any shortage of ability with unlimited confidence and employing me as race reader, both for radio and television. The PA was generously indulgent in allowing me to fulful this role, not only at obscure courses but from highly inconvenient vantage points for many major events.

In order to cover the early running of the 2¼ miles Cesarewitch for radio we would run down the course and stand atop the Devil's Dyke, prevailing wind permitting, from which point it was still impossible to distinguish the early running. As soon as I saw the white flag fall and called the 'off' to my colleague, he would begin an impressive quickfire recital of the order, reading from the bottom of the racecard to the top, on the assumption that the lightweights would make the early running. When the correct order became determinable and I began to call it, Peter would announce a series of dramatic changes before handing over to the Grandstand and Raymond Glendenning who, not to be outdone, would give the pack a further sharp shuffle before heeding the urgent correctives of his race reader and relaying a, hopefully, more accurate interpretation of the trend of events. Raymond could inject more suspense than Hitchcock into the closing stages of a race, and at the end of the Cambridgeshire, which Geoffrey Gilbey told the BBC in 1927 it would never be possible to broadcast, he was still indulging controlled hysteria long after the numbers had been placed in the frame and the winner was being led out of the unsaddling enclosure. Television was the death of histrionics.

Operating as a team, with Peter Dimmock doing the spieling, we had covered a variety of races for both sound and TV, when Peter, thoughtfully, sent a memo from Alexandra Palace to Broadcasting House and radio executive Geoffrey Peck, commending me as a prospective commentator. 'Peter O'Sullevan,' he wrote, 'is chief representative for the Press Association and is also their race reader for the race descriptions which appear in the leading sporting publications. His commentaries during our television rehearsals are very good indeed. In fact', he added generously, 'he is as good as I am bad. O'Sullevan is keen to have a crack at sound broadcasting. Perhaps you would get in touch with him direct.' Peter reported that Mr Peck had reacted by saying that their requirement was more for race readers than commentators (whom they would have to pay), but that he could arrange a trial.

Sports broadcasting had for long been largely the exclusive preserve of the professional BBC staff man, who was prompted throughout by a specialist. I didn't know whether this technique was feasible for other sports, but felt certain that, in order to keep pace with horseracing tempo, the race reader had to be the commentator.

Australian race callers operated thus – though clearly enjoying the bonus of relatively tight, flat circuits and prime vantage points – and Rae Johnstone had obtained records of their top men, like Ken Howard, for me to study. The event selected for my trial was to be the second following the day's 'live' transmission from Cheltenham. After I had researched it diligently and, hopefully, memorized the colours, this was changed during the afternoon to the race immediately after the 'big one', on the grounds that any further delay would interfere with dismantling the OB equipment. Few functions within the Corporation are performed with greater speed and dedication than the act of de-rigging. Remonstration would have been unproductive. I'd have felt more cheerful if the platform to which I was directed for the recording had been a scaffold. One of the runners was lathered with sweat but he was dry as a bone compared with the commentator. St Vitus himself would have held his raceglasses steadier and I couldn't, for the life of me, remember the name of the horse lying third; there's nothing like a microphone to promote instant amnesia. My voice seemed to have risen several octaves and I couldn't get it down. I distinctly remember taking time during running to reflect – maybe they've forgotten to record it. But they hadn't. It was a long while before I received the verdict. Dated 14 January 1948, with apologies for the lapse of time, Geoffrey Peck wrote to report that, 'As a result of listening to the recording, the Director of Outside Broadcasting asks me to say that although he would not enthuse, he feels that perhaps with a little more practice you would probably do a very much better job.'

Fortunately for me the TV bosses were more indulgent, and on 31 January 1948 I commentated the three TV races (fee 15 guineas) from Kempton, where Peter Dimmock was the producer. He was brilliant at the job (and was later to 'produce' the Coronation), but this did not alter the fact that involvement in TV racing in this era was, to me, as much a hideous nightmare as an exhilarating adventure.

Commentary boxes were non-existent; any semblance of shelter was the exception, and equipment malfunction the norm. While the commentator could receive the producer's directives through his headset, he had no means of response other than via the 'live' transmission. So that if the producer shouted (for example), 'Look at your monitor', the commentator had to overcome a powerful urge to react by yelling, 'The monitor isn't working.' It usually wasn't. On other occasions the shadowy black and white images that flitted across a sunlit or rainswept screen were as readily identifiable as white mice in a snowstorm or black mice in a coal mine. A (usually defective) harness was designed to hold the microphone tight against your upper lip. To look right or left it was necessary to turn the entire body to avoid loss of sound. On a good day, standing for two hours on an open scaffold at (say) Sedgefield, you could bring off the double – a stiff neck as well as pneumonia.

Worse was the requirement to undertake an 'in vision' scene set before racing. This involved perching on a sometimes gale-cooled grandstand roof reciting the day's menu into the cold eye of a camera, or standing on the water jump, waiting for the ice to break, while explaining why the programme had been abandoned. As I would as soon have jumped from the top of the Empire State Building wearing a pair of water wings as address a crowd of three, this was a daunting experience which was not improved by my mother's well-remembered comment: 'Darling, I saw you on television yesterday and you looked absolutely ghastly. I do hope you're never going to do that again.'

Only after calling the 'off' and settling into commentary was I happy. Though whether that happiness was widely shared remained open to question. There were complaints both within and without the Corporation that I spoke too quickly and became incoherently excited towards the finish; while a less than devoted anonymous fan from Hammersmith complained with regularity that the monotone of my delivery sent him to sleep faster than an anaesthetic. Doubtless they all had a point. What I do know is that the more I speeded up at the finish, the more the sound effects operator got to work raising the background volume. So that, in a race between us to the line, the decibel count tended to get a little out of hand. The most a racing commentator can hope for is to annoy as few people as possible. As an inevitable purveyor of unwelcome tidings, he is not only an intruder upon private grief but liable to be held partially accountable for it.

Come 1949 I'd covered a variety of courses for BBC TV, including the best I've ever worked at, Sandown, and the 'sound' organizers were so hard up for commentators to make up their four-man Grand National team that I was invited to the position of fence no. 1, which becomes no. 17 on the second circuit. In theory the principal broadcaster, Raymond Glendenning, who operated from the main site in the Grandstand, would hand over as the field crossed the Melling Road and galloped towards the first of the thirty fences. In fact Raymond, a charming man and a very good broadcaster, was as reluctant to hand over as a politician is to release a captive audience. You were liable to receive the 'office' to speak well after the first unfortunates had hit the deck. I looked forward to the day with all the keen anticipation of a visit to the dentist.

The previous year Clive Graham, delayed in Paris, had sent to the press room at Salisbury an urgent telegram reading:

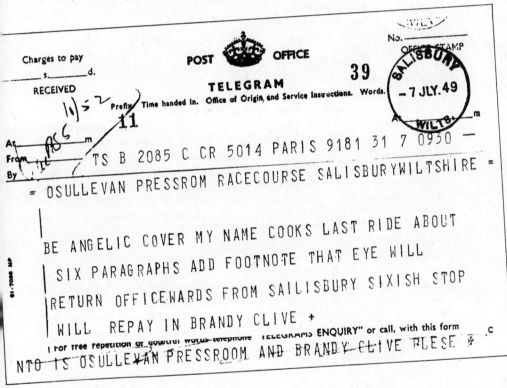

So I telephoned a column under his name to the *Daily Express*. It was the forerunner of several like occurrences and, I guess, the beginning of a partnership which was to endure until the day of his death from cancer on 20 August 1974. It was natural that, when requested by the BBC to name a race reader to share my ordeal in 1949, I should have turned to Clive – as related in a melancholy *Express* feature twenty-five years later:

My friend Clive
'His name will live as long as the sport which he illumined'

WHEN cancer finally extinguished the graceful wit of Robert Alexander Clive Graham, a great sport not only lost one of its greatest advocates, but a compassionate, understanding friend.

Clive knew he had the disease from which he died but was determined that others should be shielded from his knowledge.

He "knew" that, when he left his sick bed on July 27, 1974, to see the King George VI and Queen Elizabeth Stakes at Ascot, he would be seeing his last race "live".

To less than a handful who, unknown to Clive, were aware of his tragic circumstance, the 1974 Derby TV broadcast was an unforgettably poignant occasion.

The unnatural hesitancy of the BBC's long-time and irreplaceable paddock commentator revealed the effect of cerebral infection.

In his last remaining weeks Clive restlessly bombarded the racing authorities, as well as editors and Members of Parliament, with panaceas for the difficulties which beset the sport he loved and lived for – unmindful of his own condition.

Frankly we seldom agreed on racing policy and mutually relished our disagreement.

But nearly 30 years ago, at a time when the BBC insisted that a sound-radio commentator should work with a "race reader," it was Clive Graham whom I called on to assist me at the first fence in the Grand National broadcast.

In those days a commentator was expected to work from ground level, and, having persuaded Clive to climb on to the sloping tin roof of a latrine, I recall that his contribution to the action as the field crossed obstacle No. 1 was: "Help, I'm going to fall of the ———— roof."

Partners

We were broadcasting partners ever since. And in 1950 when the former "Scout" Cyril Luckman retired, it was Clive who proposed: "What about us joining forces in journalism?"

If circumstance had ever separated us, it could not have severed a friendship which could only end one way.

Now countless thousands will find it as hard as I do to realise that never again will they hear the warm, urbane voice which set so high a standard in his field of broadcasting or read the consistently outstanding column in racing journalism.

How ironical that as recently as July 24 I received a letter from Goodwood racecourse director Ralph Hubbard asking whether I thought Clive would like a race named after him at the 1975 May meeting.

"He has done so much more for racing than is generally appreciated," he wrote, adding: "I had the idea it's about time someone honoured the living for a change."

One thing is sure: the name Clive Graham will live as long as the sport which he illumined so eloquently remains one of the traditions of the country.

CHAPTER 9

Boarding the Express

When Cyril Luckman (The Scout) retired from his position on the *Daily Express* in January 1950, after nearly fifty years with the paper, I was invited to an interview with the Editor, Arthur Christiansen. Cyril, who was to be retained as racing consultant, had made several generous references to my 'scoops' for the Press Association while he was writing under the pseudonym 'Uncle Dudley' in *The Racehorse*, and he made a strong recommendation on my behalf. He and Clive Graham were not on particularly good terms and they had both made similar proposals without each other's knowledge. Clive told me, frankly, 'I think we would make a good team, if you take it on, and I'd just as soon not have you in opposition!'

Lord Beaverbrook's outstanding, volatile Editor laughed in his Cagney-like style and rasped, 'I am told that the terms will have to be sufficient to enable you to continue to stay at the Ritz in Paris.'

The location of my more salubrious lodgings owed a great deal more to the horses (like Derby winner Nimbus and stayer Vulgan in 1949) than to the PA. I didn't expect to be funded at the Ritz (where I stayed for twenty-five years, using a relatively modest and inexpensive room, except when Pat accompanied me, but enjoying the service of splendid personnel), but a more realistic approach to the cost of perpetual travel would be appreciated. I said that I was anxious to continue my endeavour to commentate, and Mr Christiansen responded by indicating that there should be no problem unless 'the boss' – who believed television to be the enemy of newspapers – intervened. The Company Secretary, James Hutchison, confirmed a proposal of £30 per week, plus an expense allowance of £12 per week and a further expense allowance of £4 per race meeting attended. It was a clear improvement on the PA salary rate, which had risen to £16 5s, plus £1 12s 6d overnight expenses, in December 1949.

On 1 February 1950 Arthur Christiansen wrote:

I went to see Cyril Luckman at his home last night, and told him that I had made you an offer to join the racing staff of the *Express* which I thought you would accept. He seemed very pleased that his advice had been accepted by me. The rules of the *Express* in regard to broadcasting have been rather rigid in the past. We take the view that a man's whole energies should be devoted to the service of this newspaper. However, I am not against our specialists doing an occasional broadcast, so long as it is not a regular assignment. I also like to be asked officially for permission to broadcast, so that I can keep this thing under proper control.

Three days later he followed up with:

I am very pleased to hear that you can start on March 1st, and I have notified the Cashiers to that effect. I have also notified Clive Graham of this arrangement.

It is OK on this occasion for you to go ahead with your television and broadcasting commitments, as outlined in your letter of February 2nd.

It occurred to me that the spoken and written word apropos broadcasting did not reflect one and the same attitude. I wondered if I'd done the right thing.

I decided to take a short holiday between jobs, and we were staying at the Reserve at Beaulieu (I still haven't found a much better hotel of its kind, worldwide) when an acutely embarrassing 'blurb' appeared in the *Express*. It heralded the paper's acquisition of a young fount of racing knowledge who had 'learnt the way of the world at Charterhouse', a phrase which both underlined the dearth of material available to the copywriter and suggested that I had been expelled for unsavoury activity.

Sports editors inspire varying reaction among those who work under their authority. The noted sports columnist Peter Wilson regarded the current *Express* incumbent, Harold Hardman, as 'a narrow-gutted, mean-spirited little man with no talent and still less milk of human kindness'. The description might have grossly flattered one of his successors but, personally, I found H.H. a model of his kind: appreciative of effort, responsive to suggestion and preferring encouragement to disparagement.

My first assignment was to follow the traditional pattern and produce a series of articles on individual stables and their prospects for the imminent Flat season. Among the disadvantages of this well-worn ritual were the limitation in scope of one stable per article and the obligation to one's host to mention a catalogue of hopefuls including unfurnished (and unfurnishable?) maidens whose slow-paying owners might be encouraged by a favourable word in print. I proposed covering the training centres regionally; Epsom, Lambourn, Newmarket and the North, incorporating the knowledge of local correspondents, like Bill Browning at Newmarket; condensing Ireland into one feature after visiting, essentially, the two men most directly responsible for putting Irish Bloodstock on the international map, Vincent O'Brien and Paddy Prendergast; and starting with a first-ever, comprehensive-as-possible, English review of French stables at Maisons-Laffitte and Chantilly. Harold Hardman acquiesced enthusiastically. The Foreign Department booked me a flight to Paris and a self-drive at Le Bourget. Rae and Mary Johnstone joined me at Taillevent for dinner and I left the Ritz at 5.45 a.m. the following day on the first of three early morning sorties which were to be repeated for twenty-three consecutive years.

If April is the 'cruellest month', when so many potential flyers are grounded in the heat of competition, March is the most exciting: the 'period of full illusion' as Percy Carter, the Chantilly trainer, used to call it. Percy was typical of so many trainers at Maisons and Chantilly. They would say, 'Give us a ring when you're coming. If you want to see first lot I'll be on the Piste des Reservoirs [or whatever]. If you want to see second lot join me later. If you want to see them in their boxes come round at so-and-so.' Very few French journalists (my friend Michel Bouchet became an exception) were interested in seeing the horses, and trainers, generally, were both naturally hospitable and flattered by overseas interest. Alec Head, like his splendid father Willie, was at Maisons at this time when more than three thousand horses were trained here, barely twelve miles from the Place de l'Etoile. He became a firm friend and we seemed to have a tacit understanding that I would refrain from allusion to his defeat on Le Paillon if he would conveniently forget the humiliating occasion at Maisons, when I was riding out with his string. My partner, Scribe, whipped round and neatly deposited me on the soft woodland soil in front of the twenty-five horse lot. Having done so he courteously waited to be remounted.

With similar Gallic *politesse* his owner sent the following telegram, stamped 23 March 1952:

POST OFFICE
OVERSEAS TELEGRAM

CR 2 PARIS 624027 35 22 2326 =

ELT = PETE O SULLIVAN DAILY EXPRESS LONDRES =

GLAD INFORM YOU THAT PROBABLY TUE TO YOUR EXPERT TRAINING MY TEN YEARS OLD SCRIBE RIDDEN BY MASSARD WON THIRD RACE SAINTCLOUD THIS AFTERNOON REGARDS =

PIERRE DU PASQUIER =

CT ELT PETE O

In 1951 Alec rang to say he'd got a problem, which he flew over to discuss. The Aga Khan had offered him a contract to become private trainer. It should represent an improvement in the quality of horses he was handling, but would, of course, mean the end of his association with loyal and highly satisfied owners like M. Paul Duboscq and all who had supported him from the outset. I said I thought it would be mad to do so.

Not long afterwards he rang and said, 'You'd better be first with the news, I've decided to take the Aga's horses.' In 1952 he won the Coronation Cup and Arc de Triomphe with near-black Nuccio, whom the Aga had bought at the end of his three-year-old career and whom Clive Graham described on TV as 'looking a little lonely without a hearse behind him'! And in October 1952, at the age of twenty-eight, Alec topped the list of winning trainers in France. So much for my brilliant advice. It was the beginning of a golden association which would even gather momentum when Aly Khan succeeded his father, and during which Alec, who developed a close friendship with his English counterpart, Sir Noel Murless, became one of the great trainers of his time.

Before leaving for Paris and that first French stable's tour, which, happily, pinpointed a winner or two for the coming season, I called up a valued contact in Steve Ahern and asked him to ferret out the names of a few of the two-year-old 'flying machines' at Epsom and elsewhere. Several bookmakers in my time have started with virtually nothing and ended up fairly wealthy men. Only one backer of my acquaintance has duplicated that achievement – Steve (christened Milne) Ahern.

Among bookmakers who have made it from scratch, one of the leading layers in the north of England started his working life as bobbin boy in a Lancashire mill. Appointed the factory 'runner', it didn't take him long to realize that the money he collected on behalf of his workmates from the bookmaker generally amounted to less than he had delivered. He began by sticking a few bets, and then the lot. It has worked for some, but not all.

When Milne Ahern ran away from home at fourteen and was befriended by Steve Donoghue (hence the nickname, which stuck for life), who found the lad on the doorstep of his Pall Mall apartment, he had nothing. The ten times champion jockey got him a job with the trainer Laing Ward at Foxhill, and when the patron of the yard, Jimmy White, committed suicide, young Ahern moved on to Edward Harper. Harper trained for the gambling confederacy, later known as the Hermits of Druid's Lodge, at East Everleigh where the lads' wages were two shillings (10p) per week. Here Ahern developed an eye for a horse, picked up a few punters and, more significantly, a lot of contacts. Syndicate members took a very unfavourable view of information leaks, and when Steve was caught seeking to improve his financial status by posting letter bets he prudently made a run for it. And that was the end of his life in stables. Twenty punting years later, a disciplined and selective professional bettor, he owned property in Majorca as well as in the UK; found difficulty in 'getting on'; and had learned by experience the proper evaluation of news from his multi-contacts. If I wanted to know before finalizing a selection whether a horse had eaten up and was in good heart, it was the exception for Steve to be unable to discover the answer. More immediately, the fruits of his research on my behalf were not universally welcomed. The Epsom jockey Ken Gethin reported, 'I thought my father-in-law [Peter Thrale] was going to have a heart attack at breakfast when he saw the names of his three two-year-olds you'd mentioned in the *Express*.'

Apparently when Peter met fellow trainer Tommy Carey on the Downs later and was complaining about the exposure of his best youngsters, Tommy said, 'The ——'s got mine too!' But they were fine when I met them afterwards. Peter Thrale said, 'That Tommy Carey was hopping mad that you named his best youngsters, but I told him nobody believes what they read in the paper anyway.' And Tommy said, 'Peter Thrale was doing his nut about you printing the names of his good two-year-olds, but I told him the only time to worry was if they got beat.'

Unwittingly I did Tommy a bad turn at Epsom four years later but a few good ones in the interim – notably in mid-April this 1950 season when asked to place a commission for the Alexandre Lieux-trained filly Camaree in the 1000 Guineas. Rated no better than 18 lb behind the best of her age in France, she'd impressed Rae Johnstone when overcoming the handicap of a slipping saddle on her seasonal debut, and he'd persuaded connections she was up to a crack at the classic. Since she was on offer at 20/1 I suggested Tommy take a small interest and, as the grey daughter of Maurepas was thought to be improving daily, kept plugging her prospects in the paper. Largely due to Charlie Smirke's encouragement I'd tipped the '2000' winner Palestine (4/1) and no sooner had Camaree (10/1) obliged in the fillies' race than Rae contended he'd win the Oaks too – not on Camaree, but on the Boussac daughter of Astronomie, Asmena. After readers had been advised to take the 16/1 about the sister to Gold Cup winner Arbar, her name was removed from advertised ante-post lists for ten days. Personal relations with William Hill, who knew this was one to keep on the right side, were temporarily strained after I had written (10 May 1950), 'It's about time that bookmakers betting on the race remembered there is no H in

Oaks and chalked up a price against Asmena – unquoted since 16/1 was offered last Monday week.'

I was 'on' at this rate, but without the remotest prospect of collecting, when the now second favourite for the Oaks turned at the end of the parade to canter past the Epsom stands on 25 May. I was standing next to Geoffrey Gilbey on the press balcony when he exclaimed, 'Good heavens, whatever's that?' That, I told him despondently, as poor Asmena winced her way down as if wearing invisible hobbles, was my misguided selection, adding, 'If you want £50–£1 about a 5/1 chance, I'd be happy to lay it.' Understandably he didn't. The filly had a rheumatic tendency and was so apprehensive on the, to her, unfamiliarly firm ground, that as they walked across the downs to the 1½ miles start Rae told Charlie Elliott (on third favourite Plume II) he'd have to pull her up after a quarter of a mile if she didn't use herself better.

Gordon Richards had taken over on 9/4 favourite Camaree, Asmena having drifted from an opening 7/2 on course to 5/1. In mid-division as the nineteen-runner field raced to the top of Tattenham Hill, Asmena was moving well and, stiffness forgotten, she made the descent smoothly about eight lengths behind Camaree, who went for home with three furlongs to run. Rae held on to the Boussac filly until halfway in the straight where Camaree faltered, faded, and Asmena took over. Plume II and Martin Molony-ridden Stella Polaris gave chase, but the chestnut leader had already lightly tossed her crutches over the bookmakers' rails and was heading for the winner's circle.

Victory left Rae Johnstone, who had been harshly criticized for his Derby defeat on non-staying Colombo twenty-six years earlier, with an English classics record of seven firsts, two seconds, three thirds and a fourth in twenty rides. Could he bring off the Oaks–Derby double in two days' time? Arthur Christiansen wrote:

Daily Express

LONDON EXPRESS NEWSPAPER LIMITED
FLEET STREET - LONDON
TELEPHONE
CENTRAL 8000

May 26th, 1950.

My dear O'Sullevan,

My congratulations to you on your successes in the Two Thousand, the One Thousand and the Oaks.

I pray that you will complete your success in the Derby tomorrow!

Yours sincerely,

Peter O'Sullevan, Esq.

Rae had long maintained that the training schedule of the Boussac horses was too severe. By the end of April Janus and Geraphar, two of the principal hopes of winning the boss his first Epsom Derby after nineteen years' endeavour, had succumbed to the strain. The team was so powerful, however, that whatever Rae rode in the orange and grey on Saturday, 27 May would be well backed and with good reason. He rang on 29 April to say that he now looked like being aboard Pardal or Galcador at Epsom and, yes, Asmena was fine but doing too much work. I hadn't had a Derby bet. Galcador (33/1) was twice Pardal's odds; he was unbeaten in two runs, once as a two-year-old, and was a compact, handy sort with a lovely Arab head. There is no more a course-proof Epsom type than there is a clear-cut Aintree ideal, but this chestnut son of four times French champion sire Djebel sure looked as if he'd act on the track. My ante-post voucher file confirms that I rang Conrad & Company and took £500–£35 Pardal and £500–£15 Galcador; James McLean, Glasgow, £1000–£30 Galcador; J. Osborne, £400–£12 Galcador; Lemon and Ross, 40 Sydney Street, SW3, £300–£9 Galcador.

After TV commentating at Kempton on 13 May I flew to Paris for the next afternoon's programme at Longchamp, where Rae won the local '1000' on the Boussac filly Corejada, and on Galcador was beaten half a length by Tantième in the colts' classic. The pair totally outclassed the remainder, and I was pleased to hear from François Mathet that he had a high opinion of the winner, who was later beaten a short head in the French Derby (by Johnstone-ridden Scratch II) and then won the Arc de Triomphe. With Pardal nominated for the Irish Derby, Galcador was routed to Epsom, along with four more Gallic challengers. The volume of the overseas challenge was accounted for by the apparent weakness of the home defence – with one exception, Prince Simon.

The 'talking horse' of 1949, the American-bred son of Princequillo, was a great big two-year-old whom Captain (later Sir) Cecil Boyd-Rochfort kept under wraps in his first season because of the persistently firm ground. By Wood Ditton Stakes day at Newmarket on 13 April 1950 Prince Simon was being spoken of as an assured successor to Pegasus. Treated with caution by the bookmakers and respect by the opposition, the 3/1 on chance won stylishly, finishing a conservative two lengths clear of his closest pursuer, Charlie Smirke-ridden Peter David. The general view was that racegoers had probably seen the 2000 Guineas winner and certainly had had a preview of the Derby winner. Prince Simon firmed as warm favourite for both events. 'Smirkie', who could invariably be relied upon to oppose popular assumption, doubted whether his Wood Ditton partner had the talent to win a crooked egg and spoon race, and questioned the Prince's ability to cope with the acceleration of a more experienced rival. It was the latter weakness that he exploited so brilliantly when getting first run on Palestine, winner of six of his seven races as a two-year-old in the Guineas. To me his exposure of the favourite's limitation at Newmarket increased the appeal of an each-way alternative at Epsom.

Among the home side the claims of Lord Rosebery's Castle Rock were being touted, following success in a conspicuously sub-standard Chester Vase, an invariably significant contest at the meeting which was summarily and indefensibly dropped from the BBC TV racing schedule in 1986. But it required a strong blend of imagination and patriotic fervour to envisage the son of Rockefella having enough class. He had run four times unplaced as a two-year-old before winning a Birmingham nursery under 8 stone.

Geoff Watson made a good case for Vieux Manoir, but insufficient to weaken personal resolve to side with Galcador or the Volterra hope L'Amiral, whom I had seen win over the full distance in the Prix Hocquart at Longchamp on 7 May. I reported then that, 'While immaculate Mme Suzy Volterra was rewarding L'Amiral with a tentative pat from a white-gloved hand, M. Boussac was standing in the background, forcing a wintry smile to conceal his perplexity.' For Pardal, until now rated by the Patron superior to Galcador, had finished more than four lengths adrift of the winner.

As D-Day drew closer I still, perversely, leant towards Galcador. Among the many strange facts of racing life is the apparent impossibility of discovering whether a three-year-old can truly stay the classic distance of 1½ miles – other than via a bona fide horse race. Of course he may be galloped twelve furlongs by a handler seeking the reassurance which may enable him to sleep at night. But the trainer not only runs the risk of overdoing the work, he is a long way from staging a rehearsal under competitive, public conditions. As that wise horsemaster Major Dick Hern says: 'You get very little time to learn about your classic three-year-olds before their testing time materializes, and you want them, above all, to enjoy their work. They have it hard enough on the course.' Aware of the tough prep that a long-term Boussac classic contender would likely undergo, I felt Galcador might be advantaged by having become a relatively late sub. Added to which, if he had class he could still get away with being a top-flight mile and a quarter horse. Others had, before and since.

'You're kidding yourself, Peter,' said Rae. 'You've cottoned on to the horse and you want to ride with your money. You know L'Amiral will stay and mine probably won't.' It was eighteen hours before I had to send in my 'copy', and a few of us were dining at Henri Sartori's excellent Le Coq d'Or in Stratton Street, including L'Amiral's rider,

Roger Poincelet, with whom I shared a birthday, 3 March. Entertaining and outgoing, Roger was a fine horseman – to see him hacking to post on an exaggeratedly long rein was a joy to watch – and a very fair judge. His horse had been held up in customs for three hours *en route* to Epsom, but 'If he's unaffected and his recent work with Amour Drake is right he must nearly win,' was the pilot's view. L'Amiral had lately gone six furlongs with the older horse and run all over him. 'It's not as if Amour Drake doesn't work at home,' enthused Roger. 'He's very *regulier*, so unless he's off colour, and we'll know that tomorrow, L'Amiral is good.'

I left Chelsea at 6 a.m. the next morning to see Epsom's overnight Derby lodgers exercise on the Downs, which were later preserved for posterity by Australian-born trainer Stanley Wootton whose benevolence was so shamefully unrecognized in his lifetime. For sheer quality there was no comparison between the symmetry of Galcador and the indifferently assembled frame of Admiral Drake's angular son, L'Amiral. But it had to be conceded that the latter did move with elastic action and appeared in very good spirits. His trainer Dick Carver, who had won the Derby two years earlier with My Love, admitted, 'If Amour Drake [second in the premier classic the previous year] puts up a good show this afternoon I'll have to fancy this fellow a lot.'

Among Amour Drake's Coronation Cup opponents were a former stable companion, Royal Drake (second in the 1948 Derby), who had just won Newmarket's March Stakes from another of today's runners, Flush Royal; also recent scorer Spy Legend and the Ormonde Stakes runner-up Iron Duke. If Amour Drake handled these as well as fellow French challenger Double Rose III, the tip for L'Amiral would be irresistible. Secretly I rather hoped he wouldn't and that shortly after 3.15 p.m. I could 'phone 'lead' number one: 'Go with Galcador to complete the Derby–Oaks double initiated by Asmena on Thursday . . .', rather than 'On the broad shoulders of dapper twenty-nine-year-old Roger Poincelet, five times champion jockey of France, and the less-impressive frame of L'Amiral rest my Derby hopes this afternoon.'

Well, Amour Drake didn't just win. Never off the bit, he cruised into the lead shortly after entering the straight and passed the post, cantering, five lengths clear of his nearest vain pursuer, Iron Duke.

'*Pas mauvais*, eh?' grinned Roger Poincelet, with a wink, as he carried his saddle into the weighing room. I left the course to phone the only possible 'lead' and returned after the last to meet the ace Australian commentator, Fred Tupper, who'd been sent over by his Melbourne radio station to broadcast the richest-ever Derby (£17,010 10s to the winner) to home listeners, and for whom I'd been booked to race-read.

Accustomed to the flat oval circuit of Flemington and the helpful

amenity of a purpose-built, properly located commentary box, Fred
viewed with dismay the prospect of working from the open rooftop of
the owners' and trainers' stand; as well as the disconcerting detail,
which I was obliged to point out as we walked the near-deserted track,
that on Derby Day (tomorrow) the crowds gathering at the top of
Tattenham Hill, 150 feet higher than the start, would obscure all but
the caps of the jockeys in that area, so that all twenty-five in this case
had to be learnt and distinguished. The programme would be
transmitted by radio telephone to Melbourne through Broadcasting
House and the plan was that when it began Fred would set the scene
and then hand over to me to read the runners and riders and give a
rundown of the contestants – accenting the chances of Australian
jockeys Rae Johnstone (Galcador), Scobie Breasley (Telegram II), Edgar
Britt (Rising Flame) and Tommy Burn (Babu's Pet). The question as to
whether actual odds might be mentioned was uncertain. While the BBC
mandarins did not acknowledge the existence of monetary transactions
in connection with horse races, they were aware that antipodean morals
were not similarly protected. It was proposed that an effects microphone, strategically placed adjacent to a Tattersall's bookmaker not
renowned for prolonged silences, might satisfy both honour and the
customers. After Fred Tupper had called the race and repeated the result
I was to give a brief summary before he handed back to the studio.

On a mercenary note I'd hedged the Galcador bets and stood to win
£1000 with no outlay. It would be a nice little 'touch', but to set up the
chance of going through the card in the classics had to be preferable.
And I still had a nagging feeling I'd done it all wrong. At the off they
bet 2/1 Prince Simon, 11/2 L'Amiral, 7/1 Vieux Manoir, 9/1 Castle
Rock, 100/9 Galcador and Khorossan, 25/1 Telegram II, 28/1 Napoleon
Bonaparte, 40/1 Persia and Double Eclipse, 50/1 Rising Flame and Port
O'Light and from 66/1 to 100/1 others.

Once in a while, to a commentator's relief, a race develops a 'pattern'
which eases the task of describing the action. Fred, who had been very
apprehensive in the unfamiliar environment before the off, happened on
one of those races. Invariably, in that era, a no-hoper or two would
confer fleeting distinction on a proud proprietor by briefly heading the
Derby field at an unsustainable gallop. Pewter Platter and Mattygainmal
were urged into this role at tapesrise, with Harry Carr and Prince Simon
predictably taking a prominent position along with the Scottish-trained
Persia, L'Amiral, Vieux Manoir and 'Smirkie' on the Dee Stakes winner
Khorossan. Having drawn number 1, Rae had to 'use' Galcador earlier
than he'd have liked to avoid being squeezed out at the initial elbow.
At the top of the hill, halfway, where Mattygainmal went into reverse,
Fred began to call the full order. I'd spent four hours digesting colours

the previous evening in the hope of justifying my contract fee (10 guineas to include all expenses) and as the names were fired at him my colleague wove them into his word picture. Rounding Tattenham Corner Pewter Platter rolled off the rail, tiring fast, and Prince Simon took over, followed by L'Amiral, still moving sweetly; Persia, Khorossan and Galcador came next. I remember thinking, Why the hell didn't you play safe? as Fred called: 'Prince Simon looks home and hosed.'

A quarter of a mile to run and the favourite was four lengths clear. In three strides L'Amiral went from going well to going nowhere. Rae, who had picked him to follow 'knowing' that, whatever else, he would stay, was left with no option but to ease out and launch his partner in pursuit – prematurely.

'Galcador,' I shouted at Fred. 'Galcador and Rae Johnstone challenging for Australia,' he called, 'getting ground with every stride. Prince Simon's only a length up, half a length . . . a hundred and fifty yards to go and Galcador's got him. He's taken a neck. He's taken a half . . . Prince Simon's fighting back . . . Galcador's hanging on. He's won it. Galcador's won it. Prince Simon came second, Double Eclipse came third and Telegram II, ridden by Scobie Breasley, fourth.' The official verdict was a head and four lengths. Fred handed the mike to me for a summary and, knowing that Rae's mother would be staying up listening, I told her that her son William Raphael had become the first jockey to complete the Oaks–Derby double at Epsom since William Bullock forty-two years before. And I thought, I hope he fares better than his predecessor – who was reputed to have received a present of a glass of wine and a cigar from Chevalier Ginistrelli after achieving the twosome on the remarkable owner–trainer's filly Signorinetta in 1908.

Fred and I retrieved our grey toppers, which we'd anchored under some sacking, and hurried down to the unsaddling enclosure. Walking towards us when we reached ground level was our BBC liaison, Ronnie Pantlin. Either he had backed Prince Simon or something was wrong. 'Sorry, boys,' he said, 'there's been a circuit problem. We don't know yet if you got through.' I usually didn't drink on a racecourse because I was supposed to be working. This was an exception. Ronnie would join us in the bar when he had further news.

Predictably, the riders in the stands were giving Harry Carr plenty of stick for getting beat on the favourite. And, predictably, Cecil Boyd-Rochfort loyally stood by his jockey, describing criticism as 'outrageous'. Seldom fully satisfied with his own performance, Rae felt that he had come too soon – otherwise he'd have won more easily. I quoted Harry later saying, 'No jockey begins to thrash his horse two furlongs from home.' (Amen to that.) 'Prince Simon was running on at the same pace and Galcador was faltering in the last few yards. Nothing will beat him over the Leger course and distance,' he added. Alas, long-time ante-post favourite for the final classic Prince Simon bruised a foot and was a late withdrawal. He'd been beaten a head, again, in the interim in the King Edward VII at Ascot in what turned out to be his final appearance. Cecil Boyd-Rochfort said of him, 'In forty years' experience I never had a nicer or more unlucky horse.'

I felt a right idiot for failing to tip Galcador. Worse when the cheques followed – with one bookmaker, Herky Ross, writing on the week's statement, 'Were you a member of the Maquis?!' As Leger time approached I began promoting Vieux Manoir if the going was heavy; otherwise Scratch II. Thanks to Rae I learned that the latter was being sent to York a few days before. So I went to see him work and as a result, despite persistent rain, advised 'Switch to Scratch'. Vieux Manoir had already proved his aptitude for the distance by winning the gruelling one mile seven furlongs Grand Prix de Paris at Longchamp on 25 June. The trip was too far too soon. Scratch, who came fourth, had a less arduous race in defeat.

As Lucien Robert, Baron Guy de Rothschild's manager, said over dinner at Doncaster, 'Vieux Manoir would be odds-on if the race were run in France.' But Jean Laumain had not ridden the Yorkshire track and it took knowing. Rae's experience could be a decisive factor. In the end it was. Not that Laumain was to blame; rather his intended pacemaker, Miel Rosa, who'd had a rough trip over, dropped out before the entrance to the long, daunting straight, leaving the 7/4 favourite out on his own and Rae nursing Scratch II, backed from 6/1 to 9/2, behind. He left Vieux Manoir to get lonely, refusing to be drawn until close to home, where a sharp forward thrust left him shooting into an open goal.

In a way, tipping four of the five classic winners made that Derby lapse all the more tiresome. The Epsom broadcast did get through to Australia after all, and the station even requested the BBC to arrange an encore for the same team from a provincial course. Whatever the wisdom of selecting now defunct Birmingham for this exercise, it was not an inspired decision to locate Fred Tupper and myself on the flat, low-slung roof of the weighing-room, from which it was possible to view no more than 60 per cent of the action. Since the winning post was admittedly within our sights the Midland Region programme assistant clearly felt remonstrance to be excessively pernickety. The broadcast, which owed more to improvisation than to accuracy, was received without complaint. But how sad, fourteen years later, when flying to Melbourne with Scobie Breasley for the Cup, to find Fred having to employ his microphone technique to describe the contents of a local store rather than one of nature's greater glories.

CHAPTER 10

Aim Him at the Wire, Sir

The qualities which characterize a top trainer – flair, an eye for detail and the ability to inspire the team under his authority – are those which distinguish an outstanding editor. Arthur Christiansen is still remembered not only as the foremost Editor in the lifetime of the *Daily Express*, but as one of the supreme practitioners of his profession. I was doubly lucky both to work under him and to enjoy his friendship. He took a keen interest in the sport which, in the context of life as a whole, has been defined as the 'great triviality'. Approving a light approach to the subject, Chris generously peppered the daily bulletins that were displayed in the newsroom with commendation of my modest offerings, which monotonously reflected the ornamental but otherwise unproductive attributes of the O'Sullevan horses of the moment – like Misconception, The Solid Man and the once-talented Fidonia.

Raced, to employ the verb loosely, in partnership with film actor and stylish amateur rider Teddy Underdown, Misconception made his two-year-old debut at Chepstow, ridden by the charming Australian Neville Sellwood, on the day Pat and I were married – 9 June 1951. Neville, who was tragically killed at Maisons-Laffitte eleven years later while employed as stable jockey to Alec Head, gave it as his unfailingly polite and encouraging opinion that there could well be a race to be won with the dish-backed son of Emir d'Iran whom I had bought for £25 as a yearling.

During the quest for the elusive race, Teddy, who featured prominently in such box office winners as *In Which We Serve* and *Beat the Devil*, was temporarily out of work and finding support for his half of Misconception rather burdensome. Charlie Bell was very anxious to retain the reluctant hero, so Teddy agreed we should give him to my friend Nick (Lord) Eliot with a proviso that the horse stayed in the yard at least until he won a race, and there would be a £50 contingency due over his first triumph. Relieved of the handicap of carrying my colours, Misconception shed his inertia like a lizard abandoning superfluous skin and won first time out for Nick (later Lord St Germans). Nick continued

87

to support Charlie with exemplary loyalty, installing him at Upavon, where Neville Crump once trained, when the lease of his Epsom yard expired.

Misconception was named after a series of cameos whose favourable acceptance owed much to the illustrations of Artie Jackson, and in the first of which I introduced a largely fictitious character, Bert at the garage, whose astringent comments on his creator became a long-running feature.

A Popular Misconception

PROBABLY the most wide-spread misconception entertained in racing is that the owner has a "touch" each time his horse wins.

The most normal sequence of events is as follows: H, being the horse, is well galloped at home. O, the owner, immediately informs all friends, including Bert at the garage, that H is a phenomenon.

T, the trainer, suggests that H (being super-H in embryo) be not fully exerted first time out. "Of course, he'll win if he can, but it would not do him any good to have a hard race."

O, being very wise (like all Os before they become desperate) agrees wholeheartedly, impressing trainer by adding that he abhors use of whip.

H, having been allowed to perform more or less at his leisure, runs very respectable race.

J, the jockey (fee five guineas for a ride, seven guineas for a winner) informs proud O that he "could easily have been nearer – would be delighted to ride next time."

O impresses friends – including Bert at the garage – by repeating J's remarks. Whispers name of course and date selected for next effort.

On "the day" T expresses confidence – with cagey proviso that H "will be even better next time, but is sure to be in first three."

H finishes fourth. J explains that course did not suit H, who "kept changing his legs" (not, unfortunately, with another H).

O forgives lapse, explains reason for defeat to disgruntled friends, also to Bert, who is received without enthusiasm in "local".

H is launched on course which all (excluding H) consider ideal, and O's remaining friends are tipped off.

H finishes third but, as there are only seven runners, each-way bets lose. (Bert looks forward to day when petrol rationing will be reinstituted, and hopes that O will try to get extra gallon out of him.)

J says altered going did not suit H, but stranger in Turkish baths tells O that J is crooked. H did not have chance from the start.

Friendless O changes J (also garage) and places extra large bets hoping to reimburse former friends with winnings. H runs worst race yet, and J says H is running over wrong distance.

Disgusted O changes T, and new T says no wonder H runs badly. Poor H is full of w. .ms.

H, who is not full of w. .ms, but

who is bored to death with New. .ar-ket (as any self-respecting H would be), runs again.

T says H is very well, but disgusted and impoverished O says that is not good enough. O will not bet again until H is certainty.

Unsupported save by J. Citizen, who has nasty suspicious mind and considers H has been "cheating" for months, and untipped save by corres-pondent who mistook H for H of same name who died 20 years ago. H wins at 100–6. O sells car.

The Roman conquerors, who had picked up the habit from the Greeks, are generally credited with having introduced horse-racing to England, where the Downs of Wiltshire were a favoured site. Maybe The Solid Man, who, whenever opportunity permitted, was my partner at Upavon, drew inspiration from history. Whatever, the springy turf acted as a trampoline to his spirits, making him deaf to the messages that my uncommunicative hands were supposed to transmit through the reins. After exuberant negotiation of the three schooling fences he tended to launch into a headlong, unguided tour of the region. On a July morning in 1951, with an intended race in the offing, a gallop over several miles did not feature in the curriculum for the 16.2 hands solid-from-the-feet-up The Solid Man. As, with a resigned shrug, I sped by the trainer's placid hack, Charlie pointed his crop to the west and delivered the valedictory counsel: 'Aim him at the wire, sir.'

Legacy of the war, there was a long stretch of giant barbed-wire coils sprouting wisps of greenery which made it resemble the Bullfinch at Auteuil. Like a vast tidal wave it swept closer. I barely had time to reflect, 'That's nice, we're going to take it on,' and to derive what comfort I could from the knowledge that he'd been round Aintree in the 1948 Molyneux Chase without touching a twig, when, grunting from the effort, The Solid Man went into orbit and we were flying over a minefield. There is nothing, I learned, like the sight of rolled barbed wire to secure a rider's seat. Although my partner sprawled on landing, coming to an involuntary halt, the association remained intact. We cantered back to rejoin Charlie who said 'Ee, that booger can jump.' He'd had the old horse for several years, winning six races with him, and I'd only come by him to prevent his sale out of the yard.

'We'll give him a good rest and go for a couple of them early races at Newton Abbot,' suggested Charlie, adding, 'He's best when fresh.' He was that all right.

I hoped Fred Winter would ride him on his first run in my seemingly blighted colours on 6 August 1951. The subsequent four times champion said, in his usual engaging way, that he'd be delighted. Then, two days before the race, on the opening day of the season, he broke a collarbone. The deputy I was lucky to book turned out to be another champion in embryo who, if he'd returned to the course thirty years later, would have been besieged by autograph hunters. His name – Dick Francis. The pair were bowling along up front ('Going easily', as *Chaseform* put it), looking good value for the 10/1 offered in the Plymouth Selling Handicap Chase, when The Solid Man hit the fifth fence about six inches from its base. He managed to reach the far side and, finding a 'spare leg', remained vertical. But Dick had preceded him and, unequipped with emergency landing gear, was horizontal. Happily there were no injuries and, as I wrote when telephoning copy during the long journey back to Chelsea (success turns miles into kilometres), 'Dick, being of a charitable disposition, was inclined to blame himself for severance of the partnership.'

Wounds heal quickly in racing. Jockeys heal quicker than the norm because they are the fittest long-serving athletes in action. Trainers heal quickly of necessity: it's bad for business to appear stricken. Owners must heal quickly to retain sanity, punters to retain credit and bookmakers to retain credibility. By two-thirds of the way home I was unreasonably convinced that The Solid Man had been an unlucky loser. He was normally nimble as Fred Astaire, so his unaccustomed lapse was surely due to carelessness because he was going *so* easily. Overlooking the minor detail that the field had not reached halfway at the time of the incident, I rated him a winner without a penalty. Grounds for celebration. I stopped and rang Pat, asking her to call our friend Mario at the Caprice and book for 8.30.

Redemption day was set for 18 August. Same course, same rider. Regrettably I would have to forgo the imminent triumph. I was working seven days a week, and holidays had to be planned well ahead. After writing copy on Friday, 17 August (for Saturday's paper), we were to catch the last car ferry to Dunkirk that evening.

Sometimes we took a leisurely route to Provence. This time, by driving through the night, we lunched in balmy sunshine by the Lake of Geneva; crossed the barely roadworthy Simplon pass, teeming with flocks of goats and their brave little kids, and dined and slept in Italy. Next afternoon we'd cross the Ligurian Sea from Piombino to the isle of Elba; then we'd drive west along the coast and up through the scented groves of a marvellously unspoilt island, where an isolated house overlooking an idyllic bay could be bought for £500 in 1951, to Marciana Alta and the Hotel Palazzo Fonte Napoleone.

The enthusiastic *direttore*, Signor Umberto Chioffi, greeted us with a welcome bottle of chilled champagne and a telegram. Behind us the evening sun turned Monte Capanne to gold. A Lewis de Freis travel article in the *Sunday Express* would have introduced a Gigli lookalike on a neighbouring balcony. Even without this embellishment the climate seemed propitious for good tidings. The cable read: 'Horse ran bad. Sorry. Charlie.' Started 5/2 favourite, too.

Fred Winter, who had won on the old horse when he was in previous ownership, was back in action for his next race. The site was Towcester on 21 September. 'I think I'll hold him up,' said Fred. Well, somebody had to. He ran sixth, little more than thirty lengths behind the winner, and he did beat four. So you couldn't say the tactic had been a failure. But Fred thought the ploy had disappointed him. As I'd had a 'pony' each-way, that made two of us. Next time he would let him stride on.

Meanwhile we had him entered all over the place on Boxing Day, so as to take advantage of the most favourable handicap at a time when fields might be depleted. Wolverhampton looked the least competitive. 'I can't see more than six dangers there,' said Charlie, adding, 'and they're not all bound to run.' As Fred was required at Kempton (me too, for TV), we decided to 'claim' and give a lad in the yard a chance. 'He's a right good boy this,' opined The Solid Man's trainer. 'You'd best have a bit each-way, he'll be any price.' I backed him SP. My money didn't get back (he drifted from 8/1 to 10/1), but nor did the horse. The evaluation of the 'dangers' proved remarkably accurate. After one had run out in the nine-horse field and another had unseated his rider, it took exactly six to beat the representative of Upavon who finished (tailed off, reported *Chaseform*) seventh. It transpired that he had spread a plate (twisted a shoe), so the form, like the money, was best forgotten.

After a morale-restoring interval, Lingfield was selected for the recovery mission early in the new year. 'If it's heavy, that'll suit him well,' said Fred.

Extremes of surface had long been 'lovely Lingfield's' principal problem. On 11 January 1952 it was on the soft side of unraceable. Fred was sanguine that The Solid Man would handle it OK, and anyway they would look after each other. Those connected with some of his competitors in the seller viewed conditions a lot less optimistically, inviting the inevitable conclusion that 10/1 could be value. I helped to back him down to 13/2, and relished the sight of the old fellow galloping through going like partially set cement as if it were the lightest soufflé and treating the fences with the respect he had shown for coiled barbed wire. Running down the hill into the left-hand bend and level home straight, with three plain fences to jump, he was five lengths clear and showing no signs of weakening – not to us riders in the stands, anyway. When Ted Binns called, 'I'll take five to four The Solid Man don't win,' he was almost trampled in the rush.

As the leader jumped the third last he really looked as though he'd be very hard to beat, unless you were the man on top and could feel the weariness draining into the fourteen-year-old legs beneath you. By the second last younger legs, bearing a lighter burden, had joined issue, only to be overtaken themselves after jumping the final fence. Sympathetic horseman that he was, Fred gave his partner the office to spare further effort and, on the run-in, as others trudged by, they appeared secured by an invisible anchor. Whatever flickering flame of unwarranted optimism encouraged the duo to make a further appearance together later in the month at Hurst Park, where they were tailed off, I cannot remember.

With honourable retirement The Solid Man's imminent due, Charlie Bell heard that I might be able to acquire another personal favourite, Fidonia, without extravagant outlay. His owner, D'Arcy Halford, and trainer, Snowy Parker, had fallen out, and since winning the 1949 Midland Cesarewitch at Birmingham, the Manchester November Handicap and other races, Fidonia had undergone a long period of inactivity. He was seven when sent to Ivor Anthony to be schooled in the autumn of 1951. Fidonia had always taken good care of himself – he would only entertain serious effort in yielding ground – and it took him a while to get the hang of the hurdling business. After several runs on an unsuitable surface he was reasonably, but not strongly, fancied to win his Novices' at Newbury, where the ground was soft, on 24 January 1952. Starting 7/2 second favourite to Fon Portago's much-expected Farad (2/1), he didn't jump all that fluently but had the class to win very comfortably indeed.

He returned to Newbury a month later and, now rated a good thing despite the officially good ground, he started 6/4 in a twenty-runner field, was never going well, and had no chance when falling at the last. D'Arcy, an enthusiastic owner on the Flat, was infinitely less keen on the jumping game. Ivor Anthony told him he didn't think Fidonia was totally sold on it either, though he'd like to give him another run in a smaller field at Hurst Park.

While the owner concurred, the horse had become an embarrassment to him and, with the Snowy Parker dispute unresolved, he really wanted 'out'. We had a mutual firm friend in George Todd, who was an outstanding all-round trainer but had a particularly marvellous way with old horses. 'If you will send him to George I will gladly give him to you,' proposed D'Arcy, 'otherwise I'll sell him to you for £150.' He repeated the offer in writing, making it unconditional on how he performed in the Tudor Rose Hurdle at Hurst Park on 27 March. Talk about temptation! I would love to have had a horse with George and, the trainer apart, Manton would have been ideal for Fidonia. But Charlie Bell would have been understandably hurt, and it just wasn't on.

I discussed the proposition with my friend Pat Butler who trained with Tom Yates, for whom we both placed commissions (Tim Forster has his old betting book now), hoping that he might come in halves with me. £150 may not sound a fortune but in relation to late eighties' values it represented over £1500. Pat favoured coming in at the 'nothing' rate and sending him to George but, understanding man that he was, he signalled readiness to sign for £75. When making his last appearance for D'Arcy Halford on 27 March 1952, Fidonia was clearly rehearsing for carrying my colours. He finished sixth of seven behind 1950 Derby fourth and recent hurdles hat-trick scorer Telegram II. The ink was barely dry on the cheque before Fidonia developed the first of a series of impediments which were to interrupt activity and render him a bountiful source of veterinary income. Understandably he needed the race when Harry Carr, who had shared his more memorable moments, renewed their partnership at Wolverhampton on 20 October.

Although he finished well down the field, Harry was quite pleased with him and promptly agreed to ride him in the Manchester November. Meanwhile there was an ideal race, the Duchy Stakes at Liverpool on Friday, 7 November, in which he would receive generous weight allowance in consideration of his long absence from the winner's circle. Hopefully the ground would be favourable. Well, it bucketted down on the Thursday before the race, and Harry Carr, carrying a sopping saddle into the weighing room after the last, predicted: 'The old fellow'll swim in on his own tomorrow.'

Harry was claimed to go to Windsor, where he rode a double, so Bill Rickaby took over. I guess my copy reflected a degree of optimism and, fortified by BBC earnings including a mammoth 35 guineas fee for scripting and narrating a programme – *The St Leger* – broadcast from the Mansion House, Doncaster on the eve of Tulyar's 1952 victory, I helped to back him down to 11/4 second favourite in a five-horse field.

The two-word greetings telegram I received from the Editor shortly after the race read 'ALAS – CHRIS'. He beat one, and we abandoned thoughts of the November. There are more excuses for beaten horses than there are verses in the Bible, which George Moore (the writer) described as containing 'very good prose but a hellish complicated plot', and by the time Bill Rickaby had pulled up Fidonia, which didn't take a lot of doing, I was receiving the knowingly whispered knowledge that he had definitely been 'done'. In the pre-virus era interference was widely held accountable for poor form. More often than not horses run below expectation for natural reasons, but malevolent dopers were unquestionably active at this time.

While Fidonia appeared an unlikely candidate for their attention (subsequent running suggested that if he did receive stopping mixture, he became addicted to it), there were strong grounds for suspecting villainy in the 1952 Triumph Hurdle at Hurst Park, where the fifteen-horse line-up included Mercury IV and Magnibois, owned by the twenty-three-year-old Spanish Marquis de Portago. They were part of a ten-horse team he had sent over to be stabled at Cuckfield, Sussex, under the supervision of Willie Adèle.

The going at Hurst Park was very soft and Fon Portago, who rode mud-loving Magnibois, reported afterwards: 'He was well beaten before he reached the first hurdle.' Mercury IV went to post in a lather with René Emery, who said: 'He was like a dead horse under me from the start.' Magnibois was last and Mercury IV thirteenth. Six days later, at Sandown, Mercury IV met the Triumph Hurdle fourth Hilarion (who had beaten him all of thirty lengths at Hurst Park) on 8 lb worse terms and, in winning the Select Open Hurdle very comfortably, beat him five lengths.

Fon called in a private detective agency and we debated whether it would be best to publish the story and maybe scare off any predators, or keep quiet and hope the agency would come up with a lead. We figured the latter contingency good odds against, so I phoned the story of events which appeared under a banner heading – RACE DOPING SENSATION – leading the front page of the *Express* on 15 March 1952 with a photo of Mercury IV jumping the last at Sandown captioned: 'This horse was got at, says owner.'

The account, which reported that the Marquis, champion amateur of France, was convinced that both his horses had been got at in 'a further sensational case of suspected doping', accelerated the predictable mail from cranks and opportunists ('For £5 I will send you the name of the man that done it') but inspired one interesting development.

A caller rang me at home saying it was about my article on Saturday. He was, he said, a bookmaker I knew by sight, and he'd give me his name if I'd go to a specific public call box which he indicated and where he'd call me whenever I could get there. Like now. He was sure I'd be interested in what he had to say. I agreed to be there at 10 a.m., and in case it was engaged he said he would keep ringing every few minutes. He had checked that the phone would actually ring – some of them don't.

It was a cold March morning and there were two kids in the box, keeping warm. They welcomed an inducement to change location to the sweet shop. I was holding the handset to my ear and keeping the ringing tone depressed, so as to appear to be talking when, on the dot, I got the buzz.

'I'll tell you my name, Peter,' said my caller, 'although I don't have to, as long as you'll give me your word that it is never, ever, mentioned in connection with what I have to say. I don't want to get my throat cut,' he continued, 'but I want to do what's right.'

He had my word.

'I don't know about those two horses,' he said, 'but I was offered to have one "done up" last week for a monkey [£500] and I'd be the only one to know. And it wasn't a con, I guarantee.'

He told me the name. I thanked him and made an appointment with a friend in Racecourse Security who didn't inquire the source. But he did observe, drily, a while later, 'Any more "winners" like that, I'll be pleased to hear about.'

I have seen both horses and greyhounds that have suffered interference from human flotsam, and I do not take kindly to the perpetrators. Clearly a bookmaker is advantaged by the knowledge that a short-priced one has been stopped, but so is a punter. The bland assumption that banning bookmaking is an automatic recipe for the suppression of roguery is unsupported by some notorious happenings in *Pari-Mutuel*-monopolized France. That said, it has to be conceded that, excepting the existence of ante-post betting, the Derbys of 1958 and 1961 would probably have been won by the nefariously nobbled Alcide and Pinturischio respectively. As bookmakers in general bet to a profit margin, they have a vested interest in the sport being vigilantly monitored, as well as in employing mutual safeguards against what might be construed as excessive punter opportunism.

Among the unsuccessful post-war coups containing an element of deception, including the over-planned Francasal plot at Bath in 1954, the under-planned Gay Future affair twenty years later came nearest to fulfilment. It was loosely based on a ploy which, amazingly, was said to have succeeded before the introduction of overnight declarations. A stable would cover two of its runners in a double to win, say, a monkey during the afternoon. The first was a presumed good thing; the second a long odds shot. If the good thing won, the second leg didn't run and the bet became a winning single. If the good thing was beaten, the second leg ran and the long odds ensured that the outlay was minimal. I doubt whether it worked very often.

In fact the Gay Future coup was far less devious. The horse was prepped in Ireland for an August Bank Holiday engagement in Cumbria before being sent over to his new owner-trainer, Antony Collins, to run in the Ulverston Novices' Hurdle at Cartmel on a day when the stable had two other presumed runners elsewhere. Bookmakers favour multiple bets, so doubles and trebles would be more readily accepted.

Gay Future won at 10/1 while the other duo not only didn't run, they didn't leave home base.

There were other circumstances surrounding the operation which alerted the president of the Betting Office Licensees Association, Lord Wigg, to the possibility that bookmakers' rule number one, 'Thou shalt not win', had somehow been transgressed. George Wigg advised members of BOLA to withhold payment. I am simplifying this story a bit but, in essence, from this point it started to look a little messy. George made a solid contribution to racing during his chairmanship of the Levy Board, but he tended to vault on to a moral high horse quicker than most of us could jump off a live one, and he was breathing fire, brimstone and the law when Tony Collins, whom I had never met, wrote me from Stock Exchange House, Glasgow, asking if I would mediate with the bookmakers.

It occurred to me, and many more, that if Gay Future (who wasn't a ringer and wasn't doped) had lost, no grounds would have been discovered for returning the stake; that the 'crime' scarcely warranted jeopardizing the career of the prominent Irish trainer who prepped the horse. And that the processes of law would inevitably contrive to reflect discredit on racing. I said I'd do what I could and, two days later, I put the case to Cyril Stein over a 'working breakfast' at Claridge's. He was very agreeable, and said he'd discuss the matter with George.

In the interim Tony Collins ('We made two unfortunate errors', he put it when writing me about the affair) offered compromise suggestions. But it was soon clear at the second breakfast with Cyril that none would be entertained. He took the view that it was conspiracy and, as such, they (the bookmakers) could not reach any accommodation with the instigators.

It was a long while before the Director of Public Prosecutions decided that there was a case to answer. When he did it was not heard at Preston Crown Court until 3 February 1976, eighteen months after the race in which Tony Collins realized an unwelcome treble. He was not paid out over Gay Future (which he personally had only backed in single bets); he forfeited the cash he had placed on the stable's other runner, Racionzer, to improve the odds of Gay Future; and, although the judge appeared to sum up for acquittal, he and the originator of the scheme, Tony Murphy, were each fined £1000. The Irish trainer, Edward O'Grady, had no case to answer.

And what of Gay Future himself? Amateur-ridden on 16 August at Cartmel, he was partnered next time out by one of jumping's legends, Jonjo O'Neill, at Hexham where, even-money favourite, he won by fifteen lengths. Subsequently offered for sale and bought, largely for the

Left: Mr Truelove, Fairy and reluctant Indian, 1925

Under orders in Iceland, 1938, *(bottom)*, where there was a Tote monopoly *(below)*, and ...

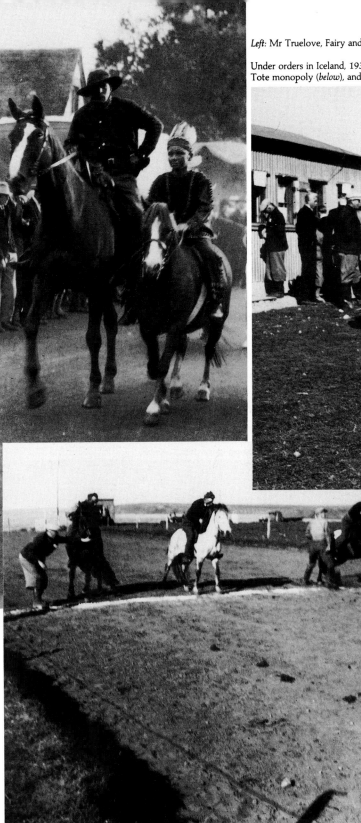

... the ground was a little uneven in the collecting ring

Slim, alias Rosebud, in Carlyle Square

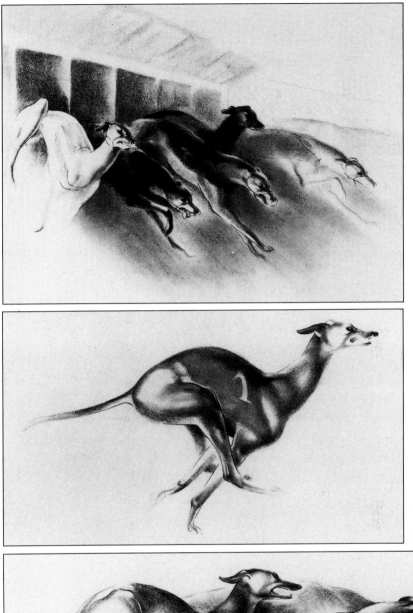

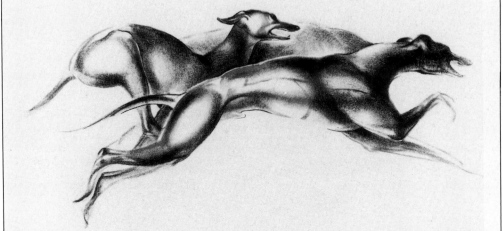

Three of 'those bloody drawings', as John Skeaping referred to the £15 set of five – drawn in 1938 and signed in '45

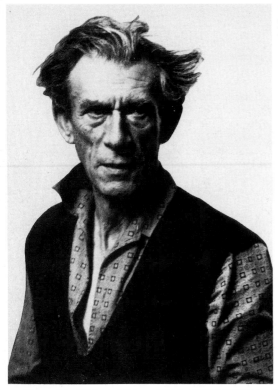

'No one of his generation was born with greater natural facility,' said Henry Moore of Professor John Skeaping RA

Opposite:
Early morning mist at Chantilly with Percy Carter (*above*) and Freddy Palmer (*below*)

Below: Dante (*nearest camera*) winning the 1945 Derby on Saturday 9 June, Newmarket

Left: 'A beautiful girl, the most striking in the ballroom,' said bandleader Joe Orlando – Pat

Below: Racereading with subsequent O.B. chief Peter Dimmock

Bottom: Sir Alfred Munnings at the start, Newmarket

Sir Alfred and Sir Gordon

Below: Commentary point – 1950s style – Newmarket; and (*bottom*) improved vantage site for TV, Doncaster

Scene-set for BBC *Grandstand* at Kempton

Amenities progress twenty years on at Ascot – with Clive Graham and Jean Rook

publicity value, by flamboyant Scottish bookmaker John Banks, who didn't endear himself to all his colleagues by referring to betting shops as 'a licence to print money', Gay Future was sent to John Sutcliffe senior at Epsom. Reappearing as a five-year-old, more than five months later, he showed enough sparkle to inspire a gamble in Liverpool's Coronation Hurdle. But he failed here, and twice subsequently before changing ownership again at the end of 1975. Then, first time out for his new connections in January the following year, he fell at Wetherby and, sadly, was killed.

There was an unhappy sequel, too, following the nobbling of Fon Portago's pair, Mercury IV and Magnibois, in the 1952 Triumph Hurdle. Although the former zipped back to form within the week at Sandown, his once useful young stable companion, Magnibois, never showed a glimmer of ability again.

Mercury IV was a tough horse, and I had reason to be grateful for his resolution on 21 December 1951. His owner, champion amateur on the Flat as well as over obstacles in France, champion over the Cresta Run, star racing driver and Davis Cup tennis player was constantly travelling the world. He would ring his trainer from Mexico City or wherever and then call me to have a bet for him – in this instance £500 each-way Mercury if he was 4/1 or better (it was a quarter the odds a place at that time), otherwise £1000 to win.

That race in December 1957 was a juvenile hurdle in which he was one of two previous winners. Getting on each-way in non-handicaps wasn't easy, especially when there was a short-priced favourite (Florus) and they bet 100/8 bar three. It was the last race, so there was plenty of time to make inquiries about the confidence behind the opposition. There were six newcomers among the sixteen probables, none of them remotely expected, as far as I could discover. In fact there wasn't any discernible fancy in the race, apart from the widely touted recent French import, Florus, partnered by that very stylish hurdles rider, Johnnie Gilbert; the three-race winner Owen O'Cork, trained by Peter Cazalet; and Mercury himself.

I've always found punting for others more fraught with anxiety than betting with my own money. At the outset they went 5/2 Florus, 3/1 Owen and 7/2 Mercury. If there wasn't to be any money for anything outside the front three, the percentage indicated that one of them would have to shorten. If I went in and took £3500–£1000 and they came for one of the other two, strongly, afterwards, Mercury could ease to 4/1 or bigger. If I waited, I might miss the 7/2.

I was standing on the members' lawn near the rails, having a dither, wondering which way to move, when a friend came up and inquired the 'strength' of Mercury. He wasn't the only one who knew I'd be aware of the stable estimate. Sometimes insignificant acts can affect the market. I produced five large white £5 notes and asked my friend to go into the ring and put me a pony on Florus – not necessarily following suit himself – and asking him to meet me at the top of the stands for the race. I went to the paddock to have another look at them, and when I returned they were going 5/4 Florus, 9/4 Owen, 6/1 Mercury and 8/1 bar three. Whether or not my gesture had affected the trend or, more likely, merely coincided with serious support for Florus, is irrelevant.

There was certainly nothing very bright about my next move. Walking in the general direction of the rails, and trying to resist the temptation to break into a run, I caught the eye of Willie Preston, one of the shrewdest rails operators at the time, who signified with a magnanimous wave his willingness to place the house of Preston at a disadvantage on my behalf. Leaning down from his stool, he placed a hand on my shoulder and muttered, 'What can I do for you?'

I asked him how he bet on the front three.

'Never mind about that,' says Willie. 'You shall have the best.'

I knew that the bet to ask for was £3000–£480 each-way, but I thought I'd got more chance if I forgot the fraction. So I said, 'It's 6/1 everywhere, I'd like six monkeys each-way Mercury IV.'

Willie had an 'outside man', Joey Cox, who, when it came to getting about the ring, could make any fly-half you care to name look web-footed. His governor turned towards him, whispered a word or two and unleashed a flurry of activity in the ring. The 6/1 had gone, the 5/1 was going and I hadn't struck a bet when Willie, once again, favoured me with his undivided attention. He expressed deep regret that the place contingency was impossible, but that, at what he implied amounted to great personal sacrifice, he could do me four and a half monkeys (£2250–£500).

I said 'No bet' and sprinted across the enclosure, followed by the admonitory bark of Lady Munnings's dog, Black Knight, reaching the paddock just as Willie Adèle was legging up Roger Obry. 'I'm going to back him to win for the Marquis,' I told Willie breathlessly. 'Not for a place at all – to win only.'

'*Vous avez parfaitement raison, monsieur,*' reacted the trainer, '*il va gagner.*'

Yes, I continued in French, I hope so, but what I want you to remember is that I have told you I am going to back him to win only, not each-way.

Maurice Adèle's nephew eyed me nervously and repeated that I was right to back the horse to win.

This conversation could have continued indefinitely without resolving my anxiety to 'declare' the bet beforehand. It was going to be pretty embarrassing, if Mercury started 4/1 or better and finished second or third, to have to explain the loss of £1000. I met my friend at the top of the stand. 5/1 was a common offer now. I asked him to put me £250 on and had £200 with each of four rails layers myself.

At the 'off' they bet 13/8 Florus, 100/30 Owen O'Cork, 9/2 Mercury IV, 10/1 Nepaul, 100/8 Jokkmokk and 20/1 others. It was one of the least enjoyable races I have watched – most of it. Owen O'Cork, a front runner, looked as though he was going to jump them cold until the third last, where he made his first mistake and Mercury took over. But Florus, receiving 12 lb, was sitting on his heels and when Johnnie Gilbert 'kicked' two out, that was it. My only hope was for Mercury to fall at the last; otherwise he was guaranteed to be second or third.

Despite making a mistake at the final flight he was still assured of second spot until, all of a sudden, Florus began to falter. English-trained horses were usually popped over three flights of hurdles when schooled; their French-tutored counterparts would jump a succession of obstacles, so that they learned how to handle themselves when tired. If anything, Mercury's error gave him impetus. Halfway up the run-in, victory became a possibility. At the line it became fact. Violet Munnings's dog, Black Knight ('Pussy' to his intimates), barked his approval. 'He was on it,' exclaimed Violet as Mercury IV entered the unsaddling enclosure. She carried around her voluble peke in a shallow bag from which he reviewed the parading horses through the eyes of a hyperthyroid, yapping hysterically when he spotted a likely winner, or when, as I always suspected (though she strenuously denied it) his owner gave him a little tweak. I'd written a column on Black Knight after he'd 'barked' a series of winners at Hurst Park in July that year. The Sports Editor showed it to Chris and it was commandeered for the front page, a staff photographer having been dispatched to Chelsea Park Gardens to 'shoot' Pussy for the next day's paper. I'm not sure that President of the Royal Academy Sir Alfred was all that chuffed by the realignment of attention, but Lady M. loved it. She wrote:

c/o Black Knight
from LADY MUNNINGS,

31. 7. 51

FLAXMAN
9236
Castle House
Dedham Essex

BELDON HOUSE,
96, CHELSEA PARK GARDENS,
LONDON, S.W.3.

Dear Mr O'Sullevan!
    We have had to leave London!
The=phone never stops!! At Alexandra
Park Mon- even Americans snapped
Pussy!   There isn't a shop in Chelsea
that doesn't take the Expens! & there seem
masses of people who ring up that want
to see the dog, & so we came back to find
letters, letters, letters — newspapers
=phoned for interviews, "Our dogs"
"Illustrated". —   any way its
done one good thing taken peoples
minds off those awful child murders.

AT Goodwood Today under the notice "No Dogs"
Pussy was admitted & welcomed !!!
being on private property & not on the racecourse —

I do wish your hir Joyce who came
with the photographer had kept my
name out ! So ordinary (lady M
says, so commonplace !!)
everyone knows who Black Knight
is without me   I've a lovely
photo of him unpublished sitting in
the Gold Casket presented to my husband
when he received the Freedom of the City
of Norwich. 11 ins by 9 ins. If you
would like to print in — write to
Douglas Hunt. Tower Street —
      Brightlingsea. Essex, & he
will send you a print. Do it soon
OR Illustrated will get it.
He got 4 winners at alexandra Park Bunkered
                                          voted m___

After Black Knight died he was taken to a taxidermist and his owner
continued to carry him round wherever she went. When I told John
Skeaping that I found this rather macabre, he reacted, 'The time to

worry is when the old boy goes and she continues to take *him* to the races.' Violet gave me a very good gouache of Black Knight by her distinguished husband, saying, 'It's only a print, dear, but it's signed and no one will know the difference!'

Alfred Munnings, who had a great feel for the countryside and horses, was renowned not only for his talent with brush and pen but for making probably the most controversial presidential address in the history of the Royal Academy when, in 1949, for the first time since the war, he revived the annual dinner which had begun in the era of Joshua Reynolds. He abhorred modern art, and art critics more so. He didn't care for dressing up in boiled shirt, white tie and tails, but, as he expressed it on one of the occasions when I was lucky enough to be shown the work in his Chelsea studio, 'If a thing is worth doing, it's worth over-doing.'

For the first time the services of a top-flight toastmaster were employed. By the time the President was due to address his guests, including Sir Winston Churchill, whose splendid grey Colonist II he painted the following year, he had already proposed and drunk five toasts and had not exercised obvious restraint in the interim. He was in no mood to pull punches. And he didn't. Contemporary sculptors, curators, critics, churchmen, fellow committee men, art teachers, the Surveyor of the King's Pictures, Anthony Blunt (later the centre of espionage controversy, and who had roused Alfred's wrath by pronouncing Picasso a finer artist than Reynolds), were lambasted with vigour and impartiality to a worldwide audience through the presence of BBC radio, which he had not anticipated but by which he was totally uninhibited.

Preoccupation with the genus equus naturally condemned Sir Alfred Munnings in the eyes of 'serious' critics but he did, unquestionably, paint some splendid pictures through which less perceptive eyes learned to appreciate more acutely the colour and magic of the racing scene. One of the last pictures he ever showed me was a portrait of Hyperion, which he considered one of his best works. The great little horse was a source of inspiration to many besides, including Edward Seago, the Norfolk artist, who painted a fine series of Lord Derby's best horses. During the early days of the war I often visited his Chelsea studio, in Justice Walk, and he generously gave me several of the original pen and ink sketches he did for the entrancing *I Walked by Night* – the life of a Norfolk poacher edited by Lilias Rider Haggard. When signing the book Edward also did some marvellous drawings on the fly-leaf. Some years later, on 3 January 1962, I recorded in the *Express* the process involved in John Skeaping's creation of the permanent memorial to Hyperion at Newmarket:

Hyperion II has his all-night guard

A FIVE-WEEK night vigil over the horse of the century has ended for Chagford, Devon, builder Leslie Jarvis and his wife Norma.

For during the doping scares of the post-war years no "live" classic prospect has been as meticulously cared for as the equine model of the era, Hyperion, created by John Skeaping, R.A.

When Professor Skeaping began to create the life-size model of the little wonder horse who was painlessly put down in his 31st year (in December 1960), one and a half tons of clay were imported to his Chagford studio from the Bovey basin near Newton Abbot racecourse.

He remembered!

Before John started to re-create the 1933 Derby and Leger winner, progenitor of champions throughout the world as well as winners of 744 races worth £584,854 in England alone, he made a small scale model from memory (the memory of seeing Hyperion beat his own Derby bet, King Salmon, by four lengths!) and photographs.

For his full-scale operation, involving slide-rule measurement of every bone, cottonwool-wrapped from Newmarket's Equine Research Station, a steel frame was erected with suspended wooden platforms and lead piping (which could be bent) for the legs, head and tail.

During the first two weeks of modelling in clay he used atomisers by day and damp rags and cellophane overnight to maintain essential dampness.

But throughout the final month of modelling the weight of rags would have suppressed delicate forms. Which is where Mr and Mrs Jarvis, who live in the house, Ford Park, of the artist's studio, came in.

Every three hours of every night they "watered" Hyperion to prevent him "cracking".

Next step was to take a plaster mould in 14 sections of the clay model. These sections were then rebuilt and liquid plaster poured in through steel rods so that the exact replica of the clay model was reproduced in plaster.

Bronze next

The next move – if you're still with me – was to cut the plaster in 14 sections. These go to a Cheltenham foundry on Monday to be filled with liquid bronze.

The bronze sections are then welded together, and Lord Derby's commission, after polishing by the 60-year-old sculptor, is complete.

Taking into account all ingredients – including a specially built turntable which had to support one and a half tons and be finger-turned, and a five-ton granite plinth – the materials and operational costs alone amount to £5,000.

It's a safe bet that this latest work of the man whose animal studies are renowned throughout the world will be a fitting memory to the great little horse – who'll be viewable for ever from the Snailwell Road, Newmarket, as he stands framed by cypress trees in Lord Derby's Stanley House Stud.

A horse in the stable meant a lot more to Fon Portago than money in the bank. Barely had I broken the news to him that, due to bookmakers' unwillingness to bet each-way in Hurst Park's Mitre Juvenile Hurdle, he had won £5000 instead of £2182 10s, than he converted the surplus into a Grand National ride by buying Icy Calm out of Willie O'Grady's stable. Two years earlier, aged twenty-one, he'd brought over his useful chaser Garde Toi, on which he'd finished third to Cottage Rake in the Gold Cup before getting as far as the seventh (the fence after Becher's) in the National. Since my involvement in broadcasting, the 1952 Aintree renewal, in which Icy Calm was one of forty-seven runners, was the only Grand National that I have anticipated without a feeling of acute apprehension.

One-time Gaiety girl Mirabel Topham, a formidable and strong-willed administrator who inherited the onerous task of staging the world's most famous steeplechase over the family land, took a long-sighted view that, were she able to establish copyright in the broadcast of her product, she could both develop income and attract sponsorship. She employed a communications enterprise, Mercury Sound, to represent her in negotiations with the BBC, and what began as a narrow breach between the parties widened into a chasm. The upshot was that 'Ma Topham', as she was widely known, with a blend of awe and affection, defiantly told the BBC to go to hell – or Yorkshire as they spell it in Lancashire – and appointed her own commentary team. So for an unrepeated occasion, instead of dining solo in an anonymous restaurant while trying to memorize the big race colours for the morrow, I joined Fon and his striking brunette American wife at the time, Carol, in a National eve Adelphi party which included his Anglo-Irish mother, Olga, and Spanish stepfather, Isidro Martin-Montis, who had flown over from Biarritz; uncle and aunt, Charlton and Jean Leighton, and his equally horse-orientated sister, Sol (the Marquesa) de Moratalla.

Although Icy Calm was a winner (under 9 stone 9 lb) at Leopardstown, his unexalted position in the National handicap did not instantly recommend him as an ideal purchase. However, despite carrying 11 lb overweight, he gave a noble account of himself. There were ten fallers at the first and a further twenty-six had departed come the Canal Turn, second time round, at which point Fon decided his game partner had done enough and pulled up. Headed by Teal, who had been turned down by two prospective buyers at £5 as a two-year-old, there were ten finishers. Typically, Fon took Icy Calm back to France to ensure that he always had a good home.

The race was even more difficult to broadcast in that era than later, due to inadequate vantage points and technical problems which invariably prevented one commentator from hearing another. Added to these hazards, the visibility was very poor this year, and Mrs T's commentators, who had done a fair job under the circumstances, were harshly criticized.

Mercury Sound had sought to book the BBC's commentary team which included Michael O'Hehir, Bob Haynes and myself. Although none of us were Corporation staff we felt a certain allegiance to the pylon-tall, languid Head of Outside Broadcasts, Seymour Joly de Lotbinière, who was in his last year of office, and this, coupled with Topham's intention to transmit the race 'live' overseas but recorded and delayed for UK listeners, decided us to decline. 'Lobby', who had managed to survive Eton without emerging totally convinced of his superiority to less favoured mortals, wrote to each expressing his appreciation; the following year his successor, Charles Max-Muller, increased individual Grand National fees from fifteen to twenty guineas.

As the wrangle continued I gathered the Topham side had gained limited ground, since my 1953 National contract read 'Copyright shall vest in Tophams Ltd who have agreed to pay you a fee of 5 gns for the right to sell records of the commentary to overseas broadcasting organizations.' Whether they recovered this extravagant outlay I did not learn. I do know that Fidonia's countrywide excursions to such locations as Birmingham, Lewes, Sandown, Warwick, Wincanton, Wolverhampton and Worcester, over hurdles and on the level, were conspicuously unfruitful, notwithstanding assistance from a variety of talented practitioners including Harry Carr, René Emery, John Hislop and Tim Molony, as well as encouragement in the form of open letters – illustrated, on occasion, by Osbert Lancaster or Roy Ullyett – which I addressed to him in the paper.

After John Hislop, champion amateur on the Flat from 1946 to 1956, had ridden Fidonia at Lewes on 9 June 1953, he expressed the charitable view that his partner 'went well for the first hundred yards', leaving his opinion of Fidonia's performance over the remaining 2540 yards unspoken. As they finished tailed off last of nine it was, perhaps, unsurprising that John politely regretted a previous engagement when invited to renew the association at Warwick on 1 August – the first occasion on which I struck a winning bet on a horse carrying my colours. Another friend, Vic Wark, took over and conscientiously walked the course beforehand. Vic, who rode out regularly for Johnnie Dines, was a film production manager and was associated with 'Tibby' Clarke in that rare phenomenon, a passable racing film – *The Rainbow Jacket*.

As the six runners were leaving the paddock to contest the two-mile Willoughby Amateurs' Handicap, Geoff Kennedy, the trainer of Sampa, said, 'Peter, I'll bet you £1 mine's last.' I hoped Geoff had struck a winning bet. But in the race, won by the subsequently successful trainer and apprentice tutor, Reg Hollinshead, Geoff never looked in danger of collecting. After Sampa had finished fifteen lengths behind the fourth horse, with Fidonia the same distance away, last, Vic reckoned he'd covered the ground in faster time on foot in the morning than he had in the afternoon.

My broadcasting progress around this period seems to have been marginally less sluggish. Appreciating their scarcity value, I retained and cherished approving messages, especially from professional colleagues. It was Jimmy Snow, Northern correspondent of *The Times*, who generously exceeded all permissible levels of journalistic licence when writing: 'The large crowd at Thirsk on Saturday gasped in admiration at the drama and excitement you conveyed in a magnificent broadcast of the big race at Ascot.' However, Arthur Christiansen, whose approval I needed most, remained unconverted. In the two years since I had joined the *Express*, correspondence had progressed from 'Dear O'Sullevan' to 'My dear O'Sullevan' to 'Dear Peter' to 'My dear Peter' and 'As always, Chris'. (Magpie-like, I have every letter and memo ever written me from the *Express* – and the BBC, come to that.) We lunched together from time to time, often with his Australian restaurateur and on occasion talked into the early hours in my Chelsea flat over Dom Pérignon – Moët champagne's pride was then £24 a case. But in a racing context, broadcasting was not discussed.

Early in 1952 Ralph Hubbard, clerk of the course at Goodwood since 1938 – a charming, far-sighted administrator whose selection was a tribute to the judgement of the Duke of Richmond – talked to me about his ambition to provide racegoers with a broadcast commentary of each race over the public address system. There were, he felt, only a very small minority who had a coherent picture of a race as it was run. The Jockey Club had given qualified approval for the innovation. Would I like to tackle it? For a commentator there is no substitute for 'live' practice. If ever one was going to improve, develop confidence, reduce nervous tension and, hopefully, fulfil a useful role in the process, this was a great opportunity.

I couldn't envisage there being any objection, but thought it prudent to tack on the request at the end of one of the usual notes seeking permission to broadcast on specific dates. It evoked the reply, dated 7 July 1952,

While I herewith give permission for your BBC commentaries from Ascot and Goodwood on the dates mentioned in your letter of July 6th, I am getting a little bothered by these constant applications, for I feel that they must affect the amount of time at your disposal for *Daily Express* work.

I do not understand the application you make in relation to broadcasting to the Goodwood race crowd. This seems to me to leave pretty well nothing for the *Daily Express* the following day so far as the people at Goodwood are concerned, and I must reluctantly say no.

Obviously I had expressed myself badly. I wrote back forthwith, pointing out that all I would be doing was reading a race aloud, anonymously, instead of reading it to myself. There was no way this could place me at a disadvantage vis-à-vis my work. Within six weeks Chris was writing in affectionate terms and announcing a bonus 'in gratitude for helping so significantly to keep the prestige, influence and importance of the *Express* at such a high level', but before that, dated 11 July, back came the reply,

I take a very strong view that your value to the *Daily Express* would be completely lost so far as thousands of people were concerned if you were to broadcast race commentaries to the crowds at race meetings. It is not merely a question of reading the race aloud instead of reading it to yourself – it is a question of whether any racegoer will buy the *Daily Express* if he can have your views over the loudspeaker system!

Ralph Hubbard wrote on 14 July to say he was very disappointed by the unwelcome decision, as he thought we 'would have put racecourse broadcasting on the map from the outset'. That is precisely what he did do. Bob Haynes, especially, set a particularly high standard in this sphere, his calm, accurate delivery bravely masking the anxiety of one of the most calamitously addicted gamblers on the course at that time.

Ralph had also hoped to arrange for Clive Graham to broadcast comments on the horses in the paddock – which he was later to do so incomparably for the BBC. He wrote to me nearly twenty-two years after Chris's refusal asking what I thought of his idea to name a race after Clive 'who has done so much for racing', adding, 'It seems such a pity to wait until someone dies before their contribution is recognized.' I thought it a marvellous idea. But, sadly, it had to be posthumous after all. In the second week of June 1974 I had to ring Max Aitken, chairman of Beaverbrook Newspapers, and make an appointment.

'Problems with you-know-who?' asked Max.

This was a reference to the new Sports Editor, three and a half weeks after whose appointment, on 1 July 1973, I was to resign.

'Unhappily, nothing so trivial,' I told him.

When we met I had to report that Clive was terminally ill and would never work again. Max was genuinely distressed. We discussed the future and, particularly, the question of replacing 'The Scout', traditionally the principal racing writer on the *Express* until 1973, when Clive and I contractually became Joint Chief Racing Correspondents. Such following as I had attracted had been acquired while writing under my own name, and the chairman agreed emphatically that this should not be forfeited for a pseudonym. 'I suppose', he reflected, thinking aloud, 'we shall have to get somebody in.'

Charles Benson had been contributing the Bendex column for several years without leaving an impression that his health was ever likely to be impaired by overwork. I suggested that, given greater responsibility, he might respond to the challenge. Max looked sceptical, very, but he did ask, 'What would be the chance of him taking over from Clive with the BBC?' adding, 'Your broadcasting partnership has been such a bonus for us.'

Well, that was rich. On the one hand I was receiving unprecedented hassle over appearances on BBC programmes and attendance at minor meetings due to the Corporation's forfeiture of many major events, and here was the boss requiring sustained involvement! I said it was very possible. Though, secretly, I doubted whether 'your man' would be willing to surrender so much of his life to toil – and who could blame him for that? – while it was a long way from a certainty that he could fulfil the role which Clive made appear so easy but which certainly wasn't.

More immediately, Max's concern was Clive. He was currently in a ward in the ageing St George's Hospital at Hyde Park Corner and, although uncomplaining, was not over-happy there. Mercifully the Fleet Street invasion by property developers, asset strippers and accountants had not yet gathered full momentum. There still existed, exceptionally, power with responsibility. Within twenty-four hours Max had arranged his transfer to a large private room in the London Clinic and funded his stay there for the duration.

As so often happened when treatment was less advanced, Clive rallied fleetingly from the scourge which affects one in four of us. He made it to Diamond day and the paddock commentary box for the last time at Ascot, where I warned Julian Wilson privately that he was a very sick man. Neither the Graham wit nor wisdom deserted him on his final broadcast, but the voice was sometimes agonizingly slurred.

Back in the London Clinic, his personality transformed by the steroids with which he was being treated, Clive became uncharacteristically aggressive, bombarding the Sports Department with a fusillade of articles which were either spiked or rewritten; summoning the Deputy Sports Editor, Norman Dixon, to his bedside to appoint him head of the department in place of the incumbent who had become the target for his fury; and requesting (successfully) the presence of MPs to receive his protest over the discriminatory application of VAT to bloodstock.

Poor Marie, Clive's third wife, who suffered so much longer before she too died of cancer, asked me to fulfil Clive's wish and scatter his ashes by the winning post on the Rowley Mile course at Newmarket. When I arrived, early, on a race day, torrential rain was washing the windswept heath and I caught myself thinking, 'Poor lad, he'll catch his death of cold in this,' And I always hope Clive forgave me for keeping him in the boot overnight. The next day the sun shone and there was a gentle breeze on which, with the larks, he soared into the blue summer sky.

CHAPTER 11

The Boy

I left Saint-Cloud in a hurry on the crisp spring afternoon of 9 March 1953, convinced that I'd seen the winner of the Lincoln in sixteen days' time. In a hurry because I had eighteen minutes in which to collect my thoughts, drive back to Paris, find a parking spot in the place Vendôme or rue Cambon, and be on the phone to London. Convinced because the Aly Khan's Nahar had just featured in the most dramatic public big race trial I'd ever seen. Much earlier in the day, during a stables tour of Chantilly, twenty-eight-year-old Alec Head, who had topped the list in France the previous year with sixty-seven winners, had shown me Nahar, among others, expressing the hope that a 'nice race' that afternoon would put him just right for Lincoln.

Well, the 'nice race' was going well until a quarter of a mile from the finish in the six and a half furlongs Prix Auguste du Bos. At this point Roger Poincelet's partner, who had been running well off the pace, suddenly grabbed hold of his bit and flew. Now both Aly and his American partner Laudie Lawrence had already bet on Nahar for the first leg of the traditional spring double, and they intended to go in still more seriously, provided their son of Stardust showed the expected sparkle today.

It was not until 10 October, five years later, that French technicians first inspected Ireland's film patrol apparatus with a view to its introduction to France. So there is no record of the acrobatic manoeuvre which prevented the short neck runner-up collecting a 10 lb penalty for 25 March – a circumstance which would have meant the cancellation of his journey.

At the *moment critique* Roger's foot slipped out of his nearside iron, unbalancing Nahar while in mid-thrust to the line. Looking suitably crestfallen after his consequent narrow defeat Roger declared, with a broad wink, that but for the misfortune he'd have won by two or three lengths.

Alec said he'd be giving Gordon Richards waiting instructions at Lincoln and, respecting a racewriter's obligation simultaneously to observe the laws of libel, exercise discretion and properly inform his readers, I reported that the trial had sent local *turfistes* scurrying to get on for the 25 March handicap, with a well-known trainer eagerly accepting 10/1 from a clandestine bookmaker. Leaving a sequence of successful naps unsupported, I preserved all ammunition for 'Nigger' – so called in the stable because he was black as settling day. Backed down from 8/1 to 6/1, Gordon's burnished ebony partner shared the market lead with Kara Tepe in the forty-one-horse field. 'Nigger' not only tended to be moody, he would do no more than necessary to take the lead. Having struck the front he reckoned, not unreasonably, that he had achieved his objective and declined to proceed further.

With two furlongs to run up the Carholme straight mile Gordon found himself with what he termed afterwards 'two or three double handfuls'. It occurred to me that even a 10 lb penalty would have been no hindrance. To Gordon it was just a matter of picking the right horse to take him closer to the line. There was a choice between following both Bill Rickaby (Fastnet Rock) and Arthur Roberts (Sailing Light), who were towards his inside, or tracking Johnnie Greenaway, on his outer, on Dignitary. Noting that Bill and Arthur were already pushing and scrubbing, he tucked in behind Dignitary. Barely had he done so when the Scottish-trained five-year-old packed in and Nahar, left in front, abruptly signed on with the same union. And that was that. Sailing Light went on to beat Fastnet Rock half a length.

Two hours later I was phoning the alibi from a hotel in Chesterfield while *en route* to Liverpool and the Grand National meeting, which featured eleven Flat races in the mixed three-day programme. My seventeen-year-old travelling companion would drink a cup of sugarless tea during the halt and eat sparingly when we stopped for dinner at the George Hotel, Knutsford, while bound for Liverpool's Adelphi. It was a trip we undertook for several years, ever since his father had asked, 'Can you look after the boy and give him a lift to Aintree?' Before I put over the next day's selections 'the boy', who never talked a lot, said he'd been told that the one he rode in tomorrow's seller, Terrorist, would go well. It did, winning by a short head and becoming the 190th winner in the meteoric career of the boy, Lester Piggott. Twelve months later, during the corresponding journey, we would be discussing a more significant Liverpool ride on whom he was to experience the extremes of racing fortune.

Alec Head decided that Nahar, having shown himself well able to win a Lincoln granted the necessary luck in running, should be set along the path to redemption in 1954. Which was why on 9 March that year Alec and I were driving at first light from Chantilly to Compiègne racecourse to see the seven-year-old 'Nigger' take part in a serious trial over seven furlongs with the useful import from England, Masai King, and a leader. The breakfast *en route* was delicious country pâté, a hot baguette, coffee and a carafe of Calvados. I remember, after a glass or two of calva, reminding myself not to get too carried away by the work-out. But it sure looked good. Nahar, who was due to meet the previous winner, Sailing Light, on 22 lb better terms, did not have Gordon's weight. So twenty-two-year-old Jean Massard, who had never been to Lincoln, was to take over. Alec said, 'For goodness sake make it your business to find the right one for him to follow.' Since the ante-post favourite, Dumbarnie, was a confirmed front runner, carrying the readily identifiable maroon and white colours of Major Lionel Holliday, it wasn't a very difficult choice.

Once again I had led my French stables series with Nahar. He was 20/1 in the overnight betting and, although I'd napped him in 1953, it seemed prudent, knowing him better now, to advise an each-way interest. At that time I was contracted to broadcast the first six furlongs from a mobile truck, which was intended to keep pace with the thirty-two-horse field as it sped along the adjacent roadway. A quarter of a mile from the finish, there was a sharp bend in the road which diverted round the stands. At this point the field was lost to my view and I would hand over to Raymond Glendenning in the grandstand.

There's a nice relaxed atmosphere down at the start, a mile away from the hubbub in the enclosures – nice and relaxed providing you're not broadcasting, that is – and Massard, who had arrived too late to walk the course as intended but had hopefully received my message apropos Dumbarnie, gave a friendly wave over to my truck and with a broad wink indicated another horse altogether! So when Raymond handed over to me as the five-strand tapes were lowered in front of the field, I caused a momentary break in transmission and yelled to Nahar's rider: '*Non, celui-là!*'

In fact he was just having a little joke, and as they jumped off he was soon tucked in behind Frankie Barlow and Dumbarnie, who set a terrific gallop. Well, the van started a bit abruptly and my engineer companion landed flat on his back. I was anxious to see what I could of the finish, and had arranged with the BBC driver that when I banged on the side he would apply every aid to come to a standstill instead of swinging round behind the stands. Apparently, every time I went through the field I made a flattering reference to Nahar, because, honestly, he really looked to be cantering.

Just before I was due to hand over, I was saying something like: 'Well past the halfway mark, and it's Dumbarnie still from Nahar. Amabassador's Court, Postman's Path next, followed by Monsieur Isy, and then Sailing Light making ground, Langton Brig is fading, so with Dumbarnie still in command but Nahar cruising on his heels, it's over to Raymond Glendenning in the grandstand.' I banged on the side of the van, the driver slammed on the brakes, we slewed across the road, the upright I was holding was split, so was my nose, but there was no serious damage to anyone and I retrieved the headphones in time to hear Raymond repeating the result – 'First, Nahar. Second, Sailing Light. Third, Ambassador's Court.'

Nahar, who started at 100/7, had already been led away when I reached the weighing room area where Alec was surrounded by my colleagues. A little detached from the group was his father-in-law, Lulu Van de Poele, who'd been persuaded to accompany him on the trip (which started with a puncture on the way to Le Bourget). I asked him how easily the old horse had won, and he replied that unfortunately he'd no idea. Two furlongs out, Alec had clapped him over the head in his excitement and jammed his pork pie hat down over his face. Then he looked at my bleeding nose and black eye and asked, 'Were you standing the other side of him?'

I was giving a lift to Lester Piggott. My nap, Red Mill, trained by Towser Gosden and ridden by Jimmy Lindley, was running in the last, but Lester had no more rides and I'd got quite enough to write about, so we left early to avoid the traffic. As we sped out of the car park Lester was already deep into tomorrow's probables: 'I suppose,' he grinned, 'you'll be able to retire now.' In fact, I'd had a very modest interest, discouraged by Charlie Smirke, who had known Nahar's gallop companion, Masai King, from the time he was trained by Marcus Marsh at Newmarket and who, when I told him about the work-out, reacted with: 'I wouldn't rely on that bastard as a guide – he wouldn't tell you the time if he had ten watches.' Still, I'd had a £4000–£10 double with Tudor Line in the National.

When we reached our usual stop in Chesterfield and I phoned the office, the copy-taker expressed generous approval.

'A pity I didn't nap him like last year,' I said.

'Well,' he countered, 'with your nap winning at 4/1 you still had a 74/1 double and I was on it.' Maybe I should have stayed for the last. At Knutsford we drank a little Cheval Blanc in honour of the *cheval noir*, and on arrival at the Adelphi there was a greetings telegram from the Editor which read:

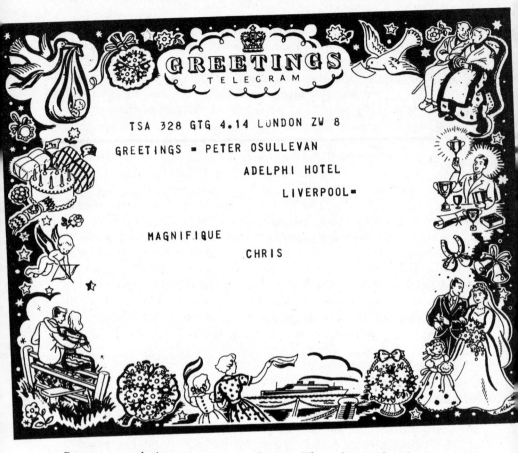

TSA 328 GTG 4.14 LONDON ZW 8

GREETINGS ▪ PETER OSULLEVAN

ADELPHI HOTEL

LIVERPOOL▪

MAGNIFIQUE

CHRIS

But commendation was not unanimous. The solitary 'fan' letter among the following week's mail was penned by an immoderately aggrieved reader who complained vehemently that my 'each-way' proviso was a deliberate put-away, since 'anyone could tell by the tone of your voice on radio that you *knew* from the start Nahar would win'.

During dinner that evening Lester, who was expected to win tomorrow's seller on Richmond Street, which he did, talked about his Union Jack Stakes ride, Never Say Die. 'They think a lot of him, you know,' he said, referring to trainer Joe Lawson, and Gerald McElligott, racing manager to the colt's charming American owner, Robert Stirling Clark. We agreed that, although the son of Nasrullah had probably not been hard trained as a two-year-old, he would need to have improved considerably to reach top flight. In the Free Handicap he'd been assessed 18 lb below the top-weighted Gimcrack winner The Pie King; and 3 lb behind Jack Jarvis-trained Tudor Honey, who had to give him 5 lb tomorrow. The race should have been renamed the Union Jack Jarvis

Stakes, for year after year the Newmarket trainer who was knighted for his services to racing in the 1967 Birthday Honours produced one – hatrack-lean and supremely fit – to win this first of the classic trials.

Tudor Honey was no exception. Looking as if he could do with a good meal, he beat the relatively portly Never Say Die by a length, with Gordon Richards' well-fancied but disappointing partner Chalybes six lengths away third.

Joe Lawson figured the race would have put the Nasrullah colt just right for the Free Handicap, for which he started a well-backed 9/2 favourite. He looked fitter, but found the seven furlongs trip too sharp. Lester was not impressed, and although he did not dispute Joe Lawson's contention that the current 100/1 Derby outsider would be better suited by a mile and a quarter plus, he said he'd rather go to Bath, where he could have five rides, than renew their association in the Newmarket Stakes. There was no contract between them, so Joe got Manny Mercer to ride on 12 May.

A brilliant, instinctive jockey, Manny probably didn't ride a handful of bad races in his too short life, but this appeared to be one of them. Making up his ground very quickly on the 20/1 chance in the ten furlongs trial, he hit the front in the Dip and was run out of it close to home.

Because the thick-set chestnut had a tendency to hang to the right, Gerald McElligott was not keen to run him at Epsom. Joe Lawson was contrastingly in favour, pointing out that the horse was improving hourly, needed the distance and was owned by a seventy-seven-year-old who might not have many more opportunities of realizing a long-cherished ambition. (Joe was seventy-three himself.) They couldn't advise Mr Clark to make the trip, but run they would; and it was by only half an hour that Joe Lawson failed to secure Charlie Smirke. The bold 'Smirkie' told him, 'I'm sorry, governor. I would have been pleased to accept, but I've just taken the ride on Elopement.'

At the corresponding period two years earlier, when Etienne Pollet of Sea Bird II fame handled the first and second ante-post favourites, Silnet and Thunderhead II, for the Derby, Smirkie asked me to try and get him the ride on the 2000 Guineas winner Thunderhead II. I'd been in Paris, reporting daily, for a week before Etienne agreed and I cabled the news. Back came a wire from the Aga Khan's jockey: 'Tulyar won Lingfield today stop will have to ride him now.'

That 1952 race didn't go too well for Lester, when he rode the runner-up Gay Time behind Tulyar, with no fewer than eight French-trained horses in the thirty-three-runner line-up. But 1954 was better.

After Lawson and McElligott had decided to ask 'the boy', Lester rang to say, 'I'm going to ride that horse.' He couldn't see that he had a big chance, and when reporting on 24 May 'Never Say Die will no longer be 100/1 after this evening's call-over. Lester Piggott rides the American owned and foaled colt', I did not appreciate how limited would be future opportunity to obtain three-figure odds about L. Piggott riding the winner of the world's premier classic.

The Derby was a very different race before the introduction of the film patrol camera and before turf husbandry became a priority under Peter Beckwith-Smith. The top of Tattenham Hill could be more like Harrods during the January sales than a horse race. After the experienced thirty-three-year-old Freddy Palmer had earned the gratitude of both O'Sullevan followers by winning on Phil Drake in 1955, he confessed: 'The first time I rode in the Derby I was totally lost, the second time I was all at sea, and by the third I was just about getting the hang of it.'

Freddy, the Chantilly-born son of an English father and a French mother, nearly got the hang of it for the last time in 1958 when his mount, Wallaby, did the splits at the treacherous mud-and-tan intersection five and a half furlongs from the finish. Max Garcia and the American Johnny Longden were other near victims of the hazard, to which I had drawn repeated attention and which was finally closed as a crossing and properly turfed later in the year. This welcome development prompted a letter from Clerk of the Course Major John Watts, who had taken exception to my criticism in previous years, stating: 'Lest you should think otherwise, this action has nothing to do with your comments.'

Lester's swiftly developed ability to reach the Derby flashpoint with minimal interruption – as a skilled footballer creates his own room to manoeuvre – meant that Never Say Die enjoyed a seemingly effortless route to victory. But two weeks later the Ascot flight path proved contrastingly encumbered. With a little more than a quarter of a mile to run in the King Edward VII Stakes, anyone watching on an imperfect TV set could have been excused for thinking they'd tuned in to stock car racing. I was commentating on the race, and for that reason did not retain a reliable impression of the sequence of events, but it was a certainty that, unless the stewards were fulfilling their popular image by nodding over the port, there would be an immediate inquiry. Which there was.

Arabian Night, two lengths runner-up in the Derby, now received 8 lb from his Epsom conqueror and started marginal favourite (13/8) in the eight-horse race with Never Say Die 7/4, Rashleigh 5/1 and 100/8 bar three. Rashleigh, ridden by Sir Gordon Richards, passed the post a length ahead of Tarjoman (Roger Poincelet), who beat Derby sixth Blue Prince II (Harry Carr) by a half, followed by Never Say Die, Arabian

Night (Tommy Gosling) and Garter, ridden by Lester's cousin Bill Rickaby. In the days before the film patrol the stewards tended to rely as much on jockeys' evidence as their own observation, and on this occasion the eminently fair-minded Sir Gordon was uncharacteristically harsh in condemning his young rival. *Raceform* recorded that there had been impact between Blue Prince II, Never Say Die and Garter, while Arabian Night had swerved and struck the rails. It may be that in his testimony Gordon, who described Lester as having 'a touch of genius – a touch of the devil', was being a little self-protective – ensuring that, whatever action was taken, his finishing position would not be compromised.

Later, when I met the favourite's rider, Tommy Gosling, while we were both holidaying in Mauritius, he recalled: 'My horse was wandering all over the place. We were all getting in each other's way . . . it was very much six of one and half a dozen of the other.' This was not a view shared by officialdom. Less than three weeks after riding the first of his nine Derby winners, the *Racing Calendar* carried this communiqué: 'The Stewards of the Jockey Club informed Lester Piggott that they had taken note of his dangerous and erratic riding both this season and in previous seasons and that in spite of repeated warnings he continued to show complete disregard for the rules of racing and the safety of other jockeys.' He was banned for six months and ordered to leave his father's Lambourn yard and join a trainer in another area.

The punishment appeared excessive in relation to the crime, but racing's rough justice is probably administered with greater fairness and understanding than in the civil courts, and extreme measures to curb the 'wonder boy's' reckless zeal seemed both inevitable and even desirable. By the time he had won his first apprentice title at the age of fifteen, Keith and Iris Piggott's only son had collected more 'yellow cards' than most of his contemporaries would gather in a lifetime. I remember Keith complaining: 'They [the stewards] seem to think that I'm to blame.' Frankly I believe that, to a great extent, he was. Brought up in a tough school himself, Keith would just as soon arrange for a rival to go through the wings as go home to tea. While Iris was caringly concerned to encourage thrift in her young son, having seen other successful jockeys dissipate their earnings, Keith's priority was to sustain the fire which fuelled 'the boy's' ardent endeavour and which, he feared, discipline might dampen.

It is a fact of Lester Piggott's traumatically climaxed racing life that, if he had not commenced his sustained battle with the scales in his very early teens, there would have been no hope of him conditioning a 5 feet 7½ inch frame to operate for thirty years at 21 lb below the bodily norm. The austere regimen further isolated him from his fellow men, promoted irritability and fostered the gunfighter's delusion of being above the law.

The degree of his single-mindedness was illustrated midway through that post-Ascot ban when the stewards unexpectedly commuted his sentence. The scales revealed that, wearing jodphurs and a polo neck, he weighed 9 stone 7 lb. Ryan Jarvis, for whose uncle, Jack Jarvis, Lester had worked for the past three months, offered him the ride on Cardington King six days thence, provided he could do 8 stone. I tipped him both to make the weight and to win, and when he brought off the double at Newmarket on 29 September 1954, beating thirty-five opponents in the process, and returning to sustained rapturous applause from the eight thousand crowd, the pale young rider did go so far as to admit that the reception had been 'a pleasant surprise'.

Less successful was my 400/1 spring double bid, initiated by Nahar. For the second leg, Tudor Line failed by a shrinking neck in the closest finish for sixteen years, to catch Royal Tan, one of the components of Vincent O'Brien's unprecedented Grand National hat-trick. In this year Vincent had an equal stake on his stable companion, Churchtown, who changed ownership on National eve. Favourite was Aintree regular Irish Lizard, whose trainer, 'Frenchie' Nicholson, had won just about every big NH race as a jockey bar the National. 'He seemed to be under the impression that the race ended at Becher's second time round,' observed his wife, Di. The Sefton winner, Coneyburrow, partnered by Pat Taaffe, was very strongly fancied, and Tudor Line, unbeaten in his three lead-up races, had been backed from 50/1 to 10/1, largely by Alex Bird – a keen supporter of the nine-year-old's trainer, Bobbie Renton.

As my broadcasting point was at the twelfth (and twenty-eighth) fence, I had an imperfect view of the climax, but a close-up of many incidents only dimly visible from the stands. For twenty years Clive and I combined the following day (Sunday) to tell our story of the race, contributing individual impressions until, hopefully, we had built up a comprehensive thousand-word picture of the sequence of events and background of the winner for Monday's paper.

Among the thirty-nine who set out in that National, three fell at the first and Tudor Line, my *Express* selection (each-way), all but made it four. After Becher's on the final circuit we reported that,

The struggle centred between Sanperion, Churchtown and Tudor Line who appeared to be going quite the easiest of the survivors. Royal Tan was tracking the group with Coneyburrow and Irish Lizard on his heels. At the last ditch (28th) Coneyburrow crashed heavily. Pat Taaffe waited sadly beside him until the horse was given a pain-killing injection.

He had to wait too long in my view. And we went on to ask:

Are there sufficient veterinary surgeons in attendance to ensure that this is done with the minimum delay?

Approaching the second last, Tudor Line led from Churchtown with Royal Tan third, followed by Sanperion and Irish Lizard. As they jumped the fence Churchtown broke a small blood vessel and gave way to Royal Tan, whom Bryan Marshall, having noted his rival's tendency to jump to the right, drove up on George Slack's 'inner' as they raced for the last. Once again Tudor Line, who was running without the corrective brush 'pricker' which he wore on park courses, forfeited valuable ground by jumping to his offside. When Royal Tan landed on the flat he was two lengths clear and set for an easy victory. But the roar died in his supporters' throats as, inch by inch, Tudor Line closed the gap.

As we wrote: 'Both jockeys had Flat race experience and were mounted on super-game horses who ran unflinchingly straight. Even ten yards from the post, the issue was still in the balance. It seemed a shame that either had to lose.' It so often does.

CHAPTER 12

Off the Record

I had just completed my annual frenetic pre-Flat season stables tour in 1953 and was boring Arthur Christiansen and Ken Hall with tales of the turf. Transported, no doubt, by the Château Haut Brion – that marvellous sequel to the peaceful invasion of the region of Bordeaux by the O'Brien clan in the nineteenth century – which accompanied our lunch at Le Coq d'Or (later Langan's Brasserie), Ken proclaimed with the conviction that is generated by very superior claret, 'Peter *must* write a regular special feature of these off-beat stories and news items.' The patron, Henri Sartori, one of my very favourite restaurateurs, had produced his best Armagnac by now and Chris, who was rarely inclined to oppose Ken's racing judgement, raised a balloon of the golden liquid and said, 'What about it?'

Frankly, I wasn't over-keen to increase my workload. Would he consider it fair to allow a day off a week to gather material? Chris, who had taken over editorship of the *Express* from Beverley Baxter in 1933, had added 2,338,000 to the daily circulation by 1950. It was now running at well over the four million mark. He had not done this by being in the business of making too many concessions. He looked flushed and benign, and I thought I was in with a chance.

'No,' he said.

When we parted I crossed Piccadilly for a chat with George Criticos, the head porter at the Ritz, who always had some news and, importantly, held funds for Aly Khan who would ask me to collect from George when I had a losing bet for him. By the time I got back to the office, Sports Editor Harold Hardman had received a memo. We had to determine the day of the week this *magnum opus* was to appear. I opted for Friday, because it would give me a chance both to gather material during the week and to look ahead to weekend racing. It was to be called 'Racing off the Record'.

Billed as 'An entirely new feature for racing followers never before attempted in daily racing journalism' (I thought that was a bit strong!), it was launched on a hopefully indulgent readership on 17 April 1953 and ran for a decade. Ironically, in view of Chris's refusal to sanction my participation in racecourse commentary, one of the twenty paragraphs in the inaugural feature related: 'Running commentaries to the enclosures at Epsom will be tried for the first time next week. If successful the Derby will be relayed round the track.'

Among the 'Off the Record' paragraphs after that coronation year Derby, an emotional renewal reputedly attended by a crowd of 750,000 and featuring the triumph at his twenty-seventh attempt of lately knighted and immensely popular Gordon Richards, was a conversation piece between two hard-bitten professionals at the unsaddling ringside.

'You look as though you've been crying,' said one.

'You *are*,' said the other.

I liked, too, the spontaneous reaction of the winner, Pinza's trainer, Norman Bertie. A modest, unassuming former stableman (who had been slipped half a crown − 12½p − after showing an *Evening News* correspondent round his stables that year), Norman was escorted to the Royal Box where the radiant young Queen, whose Aureole had finished second, shook his hand and said, 'Congratulations, Mr Bertie, on winning the Derby.'

To which the little man, who was no taller than Gordon, reacted: 'Congratulations to you, Your Majesty, on winning the world.'

One of the disadvantages of this weekly 'spread' was a tendency to withhold items from my daily column to use on Thursday for Friday, only for another paper to get in first. On the other hand, once the feature was established, friends and contacts would ring with valued contributions − like my pal Steve Ahern, who inspired a September 1953 comment apropos the Cesarewitch: 'One you can expect the money to be shovelled on, provided he remains sound, is a horse who cost 35 guineas as a yearling named Chantry.' Shovelling began at 25/1 and his bold trainer, Staff Ingham, went in again on the day, Wednesday, 14 October, after walking the course and satisfying himself that conditions were right. 'Never in the slightest danger of defeat,' was pilot Ken Gethin's verdict on the ultimate 4/1 favourite who landed one of the biggest gambles in the history of the Newmarket marathon by a comfortable 1½ lengths, having been allowed to go to the front when, as Ken put it, 'I couldn't hold him any longer.'

There were few complaints about that one, but not every reader who wrote in agreed with the conclusion to this item: ' "Steeplechasing at Ascot", one of the racing scenes depicted on a set of Swiss-made napkins on sale in England, causes much amusement among the cognoscenti. But let's hope it is prophetic. What a course could be built on the inside!' Twelve years later, when reporting the success of the first chase at Ascot, which the Queen Mother supported so enthusiastically, I liked the quote from Jack Duggan, ebullient boss of County Kilkenny's premier jumping circuit, who observed with a twinkle, 'This place looks like rivalling Gowran Park!'

Among the more bizarre Friday feature reports in 1955 was the brief account of: 'An unusually cautious expedient adopted by a trainer who had a "touch" at Newmarket. "I took out an insurance policy on your life," he explained to his commissioner, "in case of accidents before the cheque arrived." As a matter of interest the policy covering a period of fourteen days for £2500 cost him 18s [90p] out of his winnings.'

This one didn't involve a lot of research, because I was alerted by the surprise arrival of a Lloyds insurance policy – the (slightly reluctant) commissioner having been myself. Shortly after the 2.30 at Newmarket on 29 June, while I was innocently watching the Apprentice Handicap winner being unsaddled, 'Ginger' Dennistoun, who trained at Childrey and who moved in a more or less permanent cloud of pipe smoke, approached me with purposeful gait, snatched an incinerating branch of briar from his mouth, pointed the sharp end at my chest and hissed, 'You can get a bet on, can't you?'

Now for all his virtues Major John Dennistoun MBE, late of the 14th/15th Kings Hussars, did not have a reputation for lightning-prompt settlement of accounts. I knew what my response ought to be, but were medals awarded for moral cowardice I would have been profusely decorated. I had got as far as saying, 'Well . . .' when the Major interrupted sharply with, 'Be a good chap and put me two hundred quid on this filly in the next and get the best price you can. She'll win all right.'

The contest was a six furlongs two-year-old 'seller', in which 'this filly', Sapphire Queen, bought in Ireland on behalf of John and Nancy Dennistoun by former jump jockey Johnny Gale for 100 guineas, was making her second appearance. She had shown promise in a Worcester maiden, but there were no unwarranted restrictions on running in selling races at this time, and good 'platers', like the Brighton winner and automatic favourite Clyde Emblem, usually won them.

When I went into the ring the first thing I heard was that 'one of Dennistoun's people' had been round with 'readies' taking the long prices about Sapphire Queen. So the £200 on tick was to be the icing – granted there being any cake. She was 10/1 generally, 100/8 in places. I took £1000–£80 two and a half times for 'Ginger' and, as an afterthought, although I couldn't really fancy her, had a 'pony' each-way at 10/1 with Hill's representative Peter Blackwell. What I didn't know, nor did he, was that there was a letter in the post closing my account.

Sapphire Queen jumped off smartly under Joe Mercer and made every yard of the running to win by one and a half lengths. The next morning at breakfast I opened a registered envelope, forwarded from Chelsea to Newmarket, which contained notification of the closure of my account – sequel to my criticism in the *Express*, following the telegraphed complaints from readers, of Hills' advertising ante-post odds which were either unavailable or remarkably short-lived.

That long-time outstanding stipendiary steward Brigadier Roscoe Harvey was a breakfast-time witness to the day I had received the missive from Hill House – as I pointed out to 'WH' in a less than entirely friendly telephone discussion. The wager was very properly settled, but we did not speak for many months. Not until an afternoon at Maisons-Laffitte, where, after a good lunch at ex-jockey Marcel Lollierou's café-restaurant (*poulet basquaise* was the unsophisticated speciality), I overlooked the late start and, primed with a generous ration of marc de Bourgogne from the patron, arrived all of two hours early. The only other racegoer to make this miscalculation was 'the world's biggest bookmaker', according to the adverts at the time. We circled each other warily for a while until articulating the thought, more or less in unison, 'We'd best have a drink, hadn't we?' Bill, probably the greatest exponent of betting on the rails in the history of the game, had by now given up this activity in favour of concentrating on his bloodstock interests (in which he was so well advised by Phil Bull) and SP business. After an hour we resumed betting, tossed a coin and I lost. It was my dinner that night.

In November 1955, when 'Off the Record' asked 'Does National Hunt racing need a camera?', initial reaction among around five hundred responses was against: 'It would spoil the splendid atmosphere and character of winter sport . . . surely if a judge cannot decide, a dead-heat is fair for both . . . etc.' Final conclusion was 15 per cent in favour. Two years later the photo-finish camera was operated officially for the first time at the end of an NH race in the London area, at Hurst Park on 21 October 1957. Use of the camera for jumping finishes was then at the option of executives. On the same day that long-defunct Hurst Park used the mechanical aid, Kempton said: 'Considerable reconstruction would be required and none is contemplated in the immediate future.' Also 'doubtful' were Lingfield and Sandown.

Following outraged reaction to the Friday column 'lead' on 2 December 1955, I often wonder how protesters responded to the ultimate fulfilment of their nightmare. Under a caption 'Advertising could assist to boost stake money', a leading advertising executive was quoted saying: 'Almost unlimited funds would be made available by big firms were they permitted to endow race prizes.' He asked, 'How much dignity would be forfeited were Liverpool's Christmas Cracker Chase (for example) to be styled Bloggs's Christmas Cracker Chase – with a £5000 endowment from Messrs Bloggs?' Few propositions evoked comparable indignation. Typical of letters on file . . . 'a preposterous suggestion which would totally undermine the character of the sport'. Yet the Whitbread and the Hennessy were only two years away. When they arrived, 'Off the Record' was saying (3 May 1957): 'I should like to see a prize included for the lad who "does" the winner the next time special awards are made for the successful trainer and jockey of a big sponsored race victor.'

Course bookmakers who bet at the 'away' meetings were neither generally accepted nor, according to some, acceptable in 1956. Personally I felt that, provided punters were given the alternative of taking SP or the odds displayed, they were providing a service. Typical was the resourcefulness illustrated in a paragraph on 6 April 1956:

Such a commotion around the 'joint' of a southern racecourse bookmaker betting on an 'away' meeting when it was discovered that an incorrect result had been signalled and the client had been paid £50 to £6 over a horse who hadn't won.

'We've done it now,' he lamented to his clerk.

'Never see that punter again.'

'Not to worry,' said the clerk, pointing out that the backer had invested £4 of his winnings on the following race (3.0) at the 'away' meeting.

At 3 o'clock sharp the bookmaker bellowed: 'X (the punter's horse) has won.'

Up came the jubilant backer – to be greeted with the news that he had to refund £56 as his first choice hadn't won after all. Added to which, when the proper 3 o'clock result came up, his second bet turned out to be a loser too!

A contrasting paragraph on the same day, telephoned in a mood of wrath which I controlled with difficulty, was the sequel to a grim visit to the loading quays of Dublin and was to become a recurring theme. . . 'Note to my Irish friends and others – do you take every conceivable precaution to ensure that the horses that have served you ill or well do not become part of a grim and horribly discreditable consignment to the Belgian abattoirs?' More cheerfully. . . 'Anyone doubting that twenty-two-year-old ex-pageboy Geoff Lewis from Breconshire is a champion of the future should have been at "Ally Pally".'

Broadcasting generated considerable correspondence, which frequently yielded items like:

'What a wonderful horse that must be,' observed a lady televiewer soon after she and a party of friends had watched Pidgin win Kempton's '1000' Trial. Mrs

Blank's husband was surprised that his wife, normally uninterested in screened racing, should have been so impressed by the event. 'Didn't you hear what the commentator said?' she quizzed the assembly. 'He said they got Pidgin out of a *cellar* in France.'

I received several indignant letters at this time protesting over the cruelty of keeping horses in cellars, and resolved to speak of selling races in future. Apropos of which I liked Robert Morley's quote (27 June 1956) after winning a Folkestone 'seller' with his £100 horse, Anything, 'I didn't realize I had such a good horse until I heard the auctioneer describe him.' There was still no bid. Towser Gosden (father of John) kept his admiration for jockeys well under control, and responded in character when quoted (but not identified) on 13 June 1956 after the announcement that skullcaps would be obligatory equipment for Flat race riders from 10 September 1956: 'They've got nothing to protect, so what's the use of covering their —— heads?'

An 'Off the Record' item on 31 May 1957 which heralded a welcome innovation was subtitled 'The film patrol':

Interesting development at The Curragh was the erection of a tall tower beyond the winning post. Not, as someone suggested, a jumping-off platform for punters in despair, but a film unit installed by the Irish racing authorities. If the experiment is successful the film patrol will become standard equipment for the first time in Europe. The idea is to film activity in the straight for reference in the case of objections; as a guide to the handicappers; and means of instruction to young jockeys.

More than a year later, on 11 July 1958, 'Off the Record' was reporting: 'A French Jockey Club member studied the recently installed film patrol unit in Ireland this week. Probable sequel is that the system will shortly be introduced in France.' Fifteen months on (13 October 1959), and:

I have just seen the most dramatic racing film ever recorded (PO'S clearly seeking to justify staying over in France after the week-end) on celluloid – thanks to the courage of the French stewards. This is the film of the £37,000 bumps in France's Arc de Triomphe which resulted in the highest-priced objection ever adjudicated in Europe and the relegation to second place of dead-heater Midnight Sun. There is little doubt that without the third eye of officialdom – the film patrol camera – the mammoth prize would have been shared last Sunday week by Aly Khan and François Dupré. For it is known that the general astonishment evoked by George's Moore's complaint on behalf of Saint Crespin was shared by the stewards. This factor encouraged a large sector of the French racing press to campaign for a view of the photographic evidence. Just as different experts can come up with opposing opinions on X-ray pictures, so is the evidence of the film patrol camera capable of conflicting interpretation.

The stewards who reached their verdict after twenty-one minutes' deliberation originally felt that what had been decided 'in camera' should remain secret.

Their change of attitude which means that their view will stand public trial from the French racing press in a showing this afternoon is a courageous precedent for European racing.

The Secretary-General of the society that controls Longchamp kindly gave me a private showing yesterday – running the film in quick time and slow motion. So that I saw the horses running head-on up the straight and even – in the manner of too many O'Sullevan selections – in reverse.

The ultimate startling revelation of the film left me in no doubt that there had been a decided infringement of the rules and that Saint Crespin had been severely bumped twice.

But it was a generally desperate finish in which it is asking a lot for horses to maintain an absolute direct line. Will the official interpretation be endorsed by local race writers? The future status of the film patrol camera will depend somewhat on their conclusion. The fact that it is established as essential racecourse equipment must, however, remain incontestable.

My Gallic colleagues supported the verdict.

I had been banging on for some while about the film patrol camera, not because I considered it an infallible purveyor of truth – of course it is capable of conveying false impressions – but because I was, and remain, convinced of its value as an aid to safety. One day in 1960 on the Rowley Mile course at Newmarket, during his senior stewardship, 'Bobo' Roxburghe, the Duke of, walked across the weighing-room enclosure to tell me with mock huffiness (at least, I hope it was mock), 'Well, you've got your bloody camera, now we'll see what good it does.' After its employ later in the year I reported on 1 August:

The Epsom stewards invited Lester Piggott to a very private film show on Saturday. For the patrol camera was operated on the course for the first time. And the private eye of officialdom recorded in detail the action-packed drama of the 2 o'clock duel between Scobie Breasley on neck winner Fobdown and Lester Piggott on Spanish Polka. What Lester saw at the pictures is understood to have evoked a becoming blush and left the season's leading rider in no doubt that had he won the Tattenham Selling Plate his partner would have been summarily relegated to last place. As Spanish Polka, who appeared to allow Fobdown the minimum space in which to exercise his limbs, did not succeed, no action was taken. Because of the unique camber at Epsom the problem of maintaining a straight course is probably more acute than anywhere else. But the camera's presence will surely encourage riders to exercise maximum endeavour.

For sure, few of the incidents which occurred in the roughest Derby I ever saw (1952) were ever likely to be repeated under camera surveillance. In that year Marcel Lollierou, rider of Ralph Strassburger's French-trained Worden II, was almost blinded in one eye (I quoted him relating diplomatically 'A stone or something hit me' when he had been slashed by a whip). Poor Marsyad broke a fetlock and had to be destroyed while Ted Fordyce (Thunderhead II) and Willie Nevett (Torcross) reported having been put out of the race altogether in the top-of-the-hill mêlée. Still, it is a personal view that the electronic monitor has rendered obsolete that section under the rule relating to Riding Offences which binds the stewards to disqualification of a horse if a jockey has been considered reckless. In Ireland, correctly, the stewards *may* disqualify: in England they *shall*. This situation leads to such manifest injustices as the relegation to last place of 'winners' like Nureyev (1980 2000 Guineas), Forest Flower (1986 Tattersalls Cheveley Park Stakes) and Royal Gait (1988 Ascot Gold Cup).

My 1956 Derby hope Lavandin, whom I'd started to plug (thanks to Alec Head) in stables tour copy on 14 March when he was '50/1 others', was well beaten on 6 May at Longchamp. As a result there was a stewards' inquiry into the riding of thirty-five-year-old Roger Poincelet, nine times French champion. I quoted Alec: 'I was not satisfied with the way my horse was ridden and it is unlikely that Poincelet will ride him at Epsom.' But I left out his postscript: 'I'd rather put you up. And I'm not kidding!' A fortuitous meeting with the colt's owner, Pierre Wertheimer, in the Paris Ritz that evening led to speculation: 'Lavandin may now become a third Derby winner for Rae Johnstone.' And in 'Off the Record' on 11 May I wrote: 'Sequel to Rae Johnstone winning the Irish 1000 Guineas on Pederoba for Messrs Wertheimer and Head is that he'll ride Lavandin at Epsom. And win.'

I should have known better than to add those last two words of glib comment. They were prompted by the knowledge that Rae was going through a difficult period in his life. He was subject at the best of times to bouts of melancholy, and now his riding confidence had weakened through shrinking patronage. 'Copy' invariably has to be cut due to pressure on space, and in my 7 May report on Lavandin's Longchamp defeat in the previous day's Prix Hocquart, a paragraph reflecting my view that his Epsom prospects were enhanced, rather than diminished, was missing from some editions. When Rae rang me and mentioned, in the course of conversation, 'I notice you wrote that the faith of Alec and the others was unshaken, but you didn't mention your own'. I didn't explain the reason – first, because it always sounds like an excuse for incomplete coverage to be eternally laying the blame on 'subbing'; and second, because it had little relevance, since the hope of Rae getting the ride was then only a tenuous one.

As every horse handler is keenly aware, the route to the winners' circle is permanently mined with more hazards than there are cones on the

M1 motorway. I remember Michael Beary's lament when the fit and fancied horse he was preparing for an important race trod on a flint and lamed himself just before a final gallop. 'And to think,' he reflected, resignedly, in that soft Tipperary brogue, 'there are ten thousand eggs laid in Berkshire every day and my horse has to tread on the only stone!'

Lavandin may have avoided treading on 'the only stone' in Chantilly, but Alec Head's worries were little diminished for that. He was facing the same problem which his friend Sir Noel Murless surmounted so brilliantly with Crepello a year later: how to give a heavy-topped horse sufficient work to attain vital fitness without prejudicing a suspect undercarriage. It was a measure of the confidence in his trainer's ability that a horse who remained a maiden after his only run as a two-year-old – and who had won a modest nine furlongs event on his reappearance at three, followed by defeat over the Derby distance – was now, three days away from the world's premier classic, favourite to beat twenty-six opponents.

As I wrote when ghosting *The Rae Johnstone Story*, which was first published in 1958, 'A race-writer wants to select the right horse in his paper; a jockey wants to ride the winner; but for the trainer, "the day" represents the culminating point in many months of carefully practised skill, keen observation and persistent worry. And in this instance peculiar circumstances heightened the tension for Alec one hundred-fold.' Even granted favourable portents, the confidence of those most closely associated with an ambitiously targeted horse tends to weaken as the hour approaches. As it was, six weeks had elapsed since I had dissuaded Rae from fulfilling his expressed intention to retire forthwith, and he was on a losing sequence of sixty-one in France; while my own nap selections had not been promoting obvious distress among members of the BPA. Always good company, 'Quinnie' Gilbey, who had joined us for dinner, may have found the assembly rather heavy going as well as sensing more bravado than conviction behind my aside to the maître d'hôtel at the Mirabelle that we would need a larger table on Wednesday night. Within eight hours three of us were painfully convinced that grounds for celebration on 6 June were virtually a non-runner. Lavandin was Rae's only ride at the Epsom meeting. Roger Poincelet had been switched to the stable's Buisson Ardent, winner of the French 2000 Guineas, and Alec had borrowed a horse from his cousin, Vic Smyth, to give them a 'lead' in work over the course on Tuesday morning.

Horses travelled in advance of major events to a far greater extent in this era and, although Rae wasn't required at Epsom until just before 8 a.m., he liked to take every opportunity to study the opposition. We left London at 6 o'clock, driving through rain-darkened, deserted streets which, at the corresponding hour on the exit from Paris to Chantilly, would already be humming with traffic.

Many of the home-trained horses were as unfamiliar with Epsom's gradients as the visitors, and Pirate King, from Newmarket, was one of the first to take a spin round Tattenham Corner, led by a senior stable companion. 'If our fellow handles the course as well as that, I'll be satisfied,' reflected Rae. Unlike six other runners, which included the Lingfield Trial winner Induna, with whom he started joint second favourite, Pirate King had not won over the distance. But it was widely, and reasonably, assumed that this would present no problem.

Most horse race writers develop allegiance to certain trainers. Clive Graham was a firm Humphrey Cottrill man. 'Humph' trained Pirate King, a handsome son of Prince Chevalier out of an Oaks runner-up, Netherton Maid, who was unbeaten as a three-year-old – having won the Craven and Newmarket Stakes. Clive, blue-suited and otherwise unprotected against the chilling rain, had come straight on from the Stork, accompanied by two of the night club's waiters and its entertaining boss, Al Burnett, who liked to go racing occasionally 'to see what my customers look like in the daylight'.

Although Clive and I would debate, without overbearing solemnity, both current form and the merit of succeeding generations, we never collaborated over final selections. These were determined in a spirit more of rivalry than of collusion. When Chris inquired during the fifties, 'How much "needle" is there between you two boys?' I suggested, 'Enough to benefit you, but not enough to damage us.'

Throughout nearly twenty-five years' working together, during which time we lived within a furlong of each other in the 'Royal Borough' of Kensington and Chelsea, we agreed on few Derby winners. Exceptions, providing relief for the caption writer of the time, included a quartet between 1964 and 1968: fifty-year-old Scobie Breasley's thirteenth ride, Santa Claus ('We believe in Santa'); the great 1965 winner, Sea Bird II ('Sea Bird to fly in, say the Big Two'); Jim (HJ) Joel's Royal Palace, who followed the Crepello pattern when winning the first stalls-started Derby under forty-three-year-old George Moore in 1967; and another irresistible joint nap, brilliant Sir Ivor, one of Lester's very favourite horses, the next year.

I must say the volatile and immensely successful Australian trainer Tommy Smith had me worried about the selection of Royal Palace. While on a fleeting visit to the UK he'd seen the colt work, and thereafter given it as his opinion that the prospects for George Moore's partner staying a mile and a half were, at most, zero. The view was doubtless coloured by the detail that while Tommy and George had been associated, as trainer and jockey, in more than a thousand winners during a quarter of a century back home, they had rarely been known to agree on anything beyond the day of the week. After the race – in which George, a very fine rider, beat the nearest of his twenty-one rivals by 2½ lengths – I reported:

During the closing stages of the 188th Derby, none shouted 'Come on, Jim' louder than the owner's box neighbour, Bill Hill, whose ante-post book alone showed a £25,000 loss on the favourite, and who has £80,000 double liabilities with stable companion Fleet. How come he, of all people, could shout the favourite home? 'Because I am sentimental about horses,' he explained, 'and this is a good one with the right owner who will not sell him abroad but will stand him in England and make him available to all breeders.'

The Sydney champion had won the first two classics that year, and in the same report I related, 'A tall, blonde and beautiful racegoer named Iris Moore will have a job to maintain her customary cool composure at 3.35 tomorrow afternoon, when her husband George goes to post on the now 3/1 favourite for the Oaks – Fleet. She has a bet, £5000–£1, G. Moore to ride the first four classic winners in 1967.'

Needless to say Fleet, who didn't stay and later won the Coronation Stakes, was sunk without trace behind Bill Elsey-trained, Edward Hide-ridden Pia, owned by Countess Margit Batthyany, proprietor of the Erlenhof stable in her native Germany. The Countess, whose filly had failed to reach a 1500 guineas reserve when submitted at Newmarket as a yearling, had sixty horses in training in England, France, Germany and Ireland, and was a constant, unwitting source of embarrassment to this commentator – televiewers protested over my discourtesy in referring to an owner, and a countess at that, as 'batty Annie'!

Scobie's victory on Santa Claus, bred by a Warwickshire GP from a £300 mare, evoked the most astonishing and little-known professional reaction to a Derby winner in my experience. According to the transcript of my TV commentary, reproduced in *Timeform*'s *Racing Weekly*, Indiana and Jimmy Lindley were well clear inside the final furlong before Santa Claus, who had been tenth rounding Tattenham Corner, loomed on his wide outside in the closing stages and, with Scobie barely moving a muscle, took an unhurried length advantage at the line.

The Queen sent for the quiet-mannered son of an Australian sheep-drover and trotting-trainer from Wagga Wagga to congratulate him on achieving a lifetime ambition. Lester Piggott, who had been born in 1935, the same year that Scobie had married his wife, May, said, 'We are all pleased he's done it. He deserved it, and I tell you I am really glad for him.' Paddy Prendergast, trainer of the third, fourth and sixth, characteristically shrugged off his own disappointment and exclaimed:

'That was one of the finest races I've ever seen ridden at Epsom – if he hadn't nursed him like that he'd never have won.'

Darby Rogers, however, father of both the winning trainer, Mick, and one of Irish bloodstock breeding's greatest allies, Tim, had walked down from the stands seething with indignation. A respected figure, who combined experience with reticence, he was convinced that the winning rider had done everything to get beaten; that quite simply he was 'not off'. Scobie was never invited to ride Santa Claus again or any other horse in the stable. Unaware of the reason until some years later, he recalled, 'I remember how well I was going at the foot of the hill and saying to myself, "Hang on now, don't lose your head, take your time." I thought I rode him all right. He did it nicely. Now you come to mention it, I thought the old captain seemed a bit funny afterwards.'

As a compulsive ante-post player I tended to signpost intention ahead of the top races. Clive preferred to play his cards close to the chest and took impish delight in dealing a joker in the pack. Even so, by 8 o'clock on the morning before the 1956 running, Clive's preference for Pirate King seemed as secure as my allegiance to Lavandin. In fact The Scout was to select joint second favourite Induna – winner of the Lingfield Derby Trial and believed by Marcus Marsh to have come to himself, Tulyar-like, right on cue – and by 8.30 I was agonizing whether or not to abandon the cause of Lavandin.

Twelve months ago to the day, Rae's intended Derby partner, Hugh Lupus, had slipped at a tan crossing after completing his morning spin, pulled a back muscle, and, to the chagrin of his owners, Stephen and Lady Ursula Vernon, been put out of action on the eve of the race. I had then been lucky enough, encouraged by François Mathet, to switch to the 100/8 winner Phil Drake. Now here was Alec Head, trainer of French 2000 Guineas winner Buisson Ardent (Roger Poincelet) and Lavandin, looking as white as a freshly laundered number cloth . . .

The nearer a race approaches, the more vulnerable appears a horse's fragile frame. While others explored the local contours at a good half-speed, at least, Alec had dispatched his Derby duo along the outer perimeter of the last seven furlongs of the course, under firm instruction to proceed at a leisurely jog before quickening the tempo, marginally, over the last quarter mile. When they pulled up and Rae slid from Lavandin's back, Reg Perkins, the travelling head lad who had been with the Head family all his working life and who is now with Alec's daughter, Criquette, stepped forward, slipped the reins over the Derby favourite's head and let him bend for a pick of the rain-freshened grass. It was then, as he redistributed his weight, that the colt appeared to 'prop' – as if feeling a stab of pain in a tendon. Perkins looked up sharply and caught Alec's eye. Rae and I exchanged anxious glances.

Lavandin continued to crop unconcernedly. 'Walk him round, Perkins,' said Alec. There wasn't a trace of heat. Maybe we'd misinterpreted the movement. Maybe. The prospect of him becoming a first Epsom Derby winner for his trainer, a first in forty-six years' ownership for Pierre Wertheimer, who had never been represented previously, and a thirtieth classics triumph for Rae Johnstone, had not improved.

Alec, who planned to equip his chief hope (he doubted Buisson Ardent's stamina) with supportive bandages, decided to stay on at Epsom for a while and see the horse back in the yard. Rae and I returned to London, stopping off for a coffee in a joyless Epsom café which our presence did nothing to enliven. For those of us engaged in tipping for a living it is always important to select winners – doubly so on Derby and Grand National days, when the racing pages will be studied by many more of a paper's regular readers and by new ones too. Supposing the worst happened and Lavandin's suspect off-fore gave way and he broke down during the race? Alec would be quoted, saying it was a fear he had had to live with. What was I doing, not only tipping a 'suspect' horse, but failing to forewarn potential backers of the favourite that there was an additional hazard involved?

I could hark back to my 14 March stables tour article in which, while advising 50/1 Derby speculation, I'd stressed that 'this heavy-topped horse, who ran only once, without success, as a two-year-old, has a lot of weight to support on legs which it will be hard to keep trouble free'. And, having done so, I could now reveal that the favourite's bandages would not be worn simply for protective purposes, but to support a significant weakness. Hence my rejection of the horse whose cause I had championed for so long. And then suppose he won? It is far easier to forgive a man for tipping a loser than it is to absolve him for stopping you backing a winner.

The Epsom summer meeting ran from Tuesday to Friday at this time, with morning dress obligatory in the Members' Enclosure on each of the four days (later amended to Derby Day only, with the programme running Wednesday to Saturday), and while changing to return to the course on D-Day minus one I was still dithering. Alec, who had a runner in the Woodcote, reported that so far 'Johnny' (Lavandin's stable name) was fine. I went to a public phone – and reaffirmed my faith, admitting that, 'If "Johnny" does not come marching home (in front) this afternoon, I haven't the faintest idea what will.' I had a premonition, justified as it turned out, that this was all going to end in tears.

The windscreen wipers on the cars which transport the jockeys from weighing-room to paddock at Epsom were working overtime when the twenty-seven riders entered them shortly after three o'clock on Wednesday, 6 June. Rae, who hated the cold and wet, looked less than happy and more than his fifty-one years as he waited his turn for transport. During the race the driving rain reduced visibility but there was no mistaking the fact that, as the strung out field descended the hill into Tattenham Corner, Lavandin was a long way off the lead. Monterey led into the straight, followed by Pirate King. Several lengths behind him came King David II, Tenareze and Jimmy Eddery on Roistar. Then Pearl Orama, Induna and Lavandin. The favourite (10/1 to 7/1 on the day) sure had it to do.

The rain, which temporarily obscured the weakening Monterey from Rae's vision, had at least taken the sting out of the ground. Once 'picked up', therefore, Lavandin really used himself, surging towards the lead with power and determination. Inside the final furlong Alec Head released months of tension in a devastating roar of acclaim which left his immediate neighbour, Aly Khan, maintaining: 'I doubt if my eardrums will ever be the same again.' Having struck the front, Rae was already thinking of Johnny's future and nursing him home, when Freddy Palmer came at him with a late flourish on Montaval. The judge called for a photo but there was no doubt that number 27 had won. The verdict – a neck, with two lengths back to the third, Roistar.

Disregarding the damp, the crowd round the unsaddling enclosure gave the winner an ovation when Rae rode in, misty-eyed. At least I think he was misty-eyed. Maybe it was my own blurred vision. Some events in a racing life are capable of instant recall. I remember the highly excited racegoer who ran up to me with a fistful of white £5 notes, insisting I distribute them as I wish, but agreeing to pass them on to Tim Molony's wife, Stella, who was fund-raising for an injured National Hunt jockey. I remember when I ran into Alec's wife, Ghislaine, and mine in the mêlée outside the weighing-room, Pat exclaimed in a tone which reflected both surprise and incomprehension, 'Good Heavens, you're crying!' To an infrequent racegoer the emotion aroused by a horse race is a strange phenomenon.

'Of course I'm bloody well crying!' I reacted, adding, 'Try and get through to the Mirabelle and confirm my reservation.'

I remember my contemporary, John Rickman, of the rival *Daily Mail*, generously offering 'Congratulations on a great journalistic coup'. I wondered then (and still do) whether he knew that, nine months earlier, I'd been offered his job? Pat Reekie, Sports Editor of the *Mail*, had approached me the previous October. I was certain I wouldn't want to move, but he said there was no harm in talking. He lived at Bletchingly, on the route to Lingfield, and after I'd called in to see him on the way there he made an appointment for me with the Editor, Arthur Wareham. The attraction was that the *Mail* would give me complete broadcasting freedom and, whatever my current salary (£2500), an additional £500 and increased expenses. I told Mr Wareham that I was very flattered (amazed would have been more accurate), but that since Arthur Christiansen had given me my first chance on a national daily I could not give an answer without talking to him.

'That's not the usual way in Fleet Street,' he reacted, adding, 'I hope you'll think about it.'

Chris said he'd have my contract revised favourably as soon as possible (which he did), and gave permission for me to sign a three-year 'exclusivity' agreement which the BBC were requesting – as long as he had sight of it. Then, suddenly, he leant forward in the Editor's black leather chair, fixed me with a steely look, adopted the air of a villain in a Victorian melodrama, and almost hissed, 'If you ever quit journalism for broadcasting, I will personally destroy you.' I was too surprised to react, before, equally swiftly, like a horse who has flattened his ears unaccountably, he was back on the bridle and inquiring amicably: 'When are you going to tear yourself away from the racecourse and have lunch?'

Chris was delighted about Lavandin – he even had £1 on himself – and attached to a personal letter ('straight from the heart!') posted me a copy of the in-house *Bulletin* for 7 June which read:

We regained the initiative on the ETU story today. The last editions of the paper were fine and vigorous on this subject.

But, of course, it was Peter O'Sullevan's Derby tip which made the day for most of our readers. The path of the racing writer who has to tip is well-nigh intolerable. No other people in our profession have such a difficult task. But everywhere I go I hear eloquent praise for the gifted men of our racing service – Clive Graham and Peter O'Sullevan.

I'd made only one concession to my benefactor's potential infirmity. Obsessed by a desire to show a seasonal profit on the nap selections a two-year-old Nearco filly, Kahira, whom Alec rated pretty useful, seemed a safer vehicle for the star. Running less than three-quarters of an hour after her stable companion, backed from evens to 6/5 on, she won the Lonsdale Produce Stakes handily under Roger Poincelet and boosted the lifetime prize-winnings of Aly's father, the Aga Khan, beyond the £1 million mark. This circumstance inspired a remarkably unprophetic paragraph in which I wrote of it as: 'A record in European racing which is unlikely to be surpassed.'

Lavandin's success – which, sadly, was never repeated (he was struck into during the Grand Prix de Paris and did not run again before export as a stallion to Japan) – had a lasting effect upon my attitude to writing about selections. On the occasions between March and 6 June when I had expressed such flippant comments as 'the Derby winner, Lavandin's, odds have been shortened from 20/1 to 100/8 . . . after Lavandin's Derby victory has been officially recognized . . .' etc., I assumed these would be accepted in the spirit of extravagant optimism which they represented. Judging by the content of the post-Derby mail, this was a dangerous miscalculation. It was chilling (though rewarding in this instance) to learn that there were OAPs who had invested meagre life savings; a hospital matron who could now anticipate her first holiday abroad, but who would have forfeited any sort of break in the event of failure; and punters as far afield as Ceylon who had interpreted reckless anticipation as supernatural knowledge. From then on, I took a firmer grip on over-exuberance.

As for Rae, whose career in the saddle had appeared virtually at an end before that wet afternoon on the first Wednesday in June, the tide of fortune turned abruptly. After winners at Chantilly and Saint-Cloud, he returned for six booked rides at Ascot, winning on four of them to become the top jockey at the Royal Meeting. Usually on TV I particularly enjoy calling home a winner for the Queen, but loyalty was divided when sentiment (and cash) went along with luckless Lady Ursula Vernon's Rae Johnstone-partnered Jaspe in the Hunt Cup. Drawn 18 in the twenty-seven-runner field, Jaspe raced into the final furlong well clear of those on the far side. Meanwhile the royal colt, Alexander, who started from 3, had shaken off all pursuers up the stands rails. The judge called for a photo, but although Alexander's rider, Harry Carr, was uncertain – he saved a 'pony' with Rae as they pulled up – there was little doubt that in the ninth race of the 1956 Royal Meeting Alexander had not only become the first winning favourite, but the first clear favourite to win the handicap (then worth £3500) in forty-six years.

Hugh Lupus later achieved handsome consolation for the Jaspe connections in the Hardwicke before being beaten under a big weight in Goodwood's Chesterfield Cup. Then, as a prelude to winning the Champion, Noel Murless, who now had charge of the horse who had been so unluckily prevented from running in the previous year's Derby, reverted to a mile with him in the Scarborough Stakes at Doncaster. Clearly the trip might be too sharp – but not necessarily.

Rae had, a while back, taken a firm vow against betting while he held a jockey's licence. Since then his racing-wise Australian friend Fred Angles, who had justifiably high regard for Rae's judgement when he wasn't betting, asked him to have up to a 'monkey' (£500) for him on anything he fancied. The 'Angles bets' were seldom far away.

Shortly before the Scarborough, due off at 4.40 on 13 September, I had phoned over the nine hundred words of the following day's 'Racing off the Record' and was, unusually, in conversation with the senior steward of the meeting and a rather staid member of the Jockey Club outside the weighing-room when the jockeys exited *en route* to the paddock. As Rae walked by in the black and yellow Westminster family colours, he gave me a playful tap with his whip and said, 'Put Fred a hundred on this, will you, Peter?' It is, of course, a breach of the rules of racing in Great Britain for jockeys to bet on horse racing or for a person to bet on their behalf. This was tantamount to overtaking a police patrol at 100 m.p.h. in a 30 m.p.h. built-up area. Admittedly the request was delivered quietly, as an aside, which I acknowledged with the merest flicker, but despite the popular perception of stewards being deficient in the auditory and visual department it seemed unlikely that I was alone in receiving the message.

By the time conversation had been disengaged the tapes were lowered and I was hastening to the rails, trying to appear unhurried. I couldn't see Hugh giving 7 lb more than weight-for-age to the Paddy Prendergast-trained filly Carezza, who was fractional odds-on, and didn't add to Fred's £100 other than a cautious 'pony' a place. Carezza looked like trotting up until, burdened by my nap, she faltered in the last fifty yards and Hugh Lupus (after drifting from 9/2 to 15/2) got up to win cleverly.

Back at the hotel – the Mount Pleasant at Rossington – Rae found it hard to believe that he could have got us both warned off. 'You know I've given betting away and you know the money is Fred's, so I can't see there can be anything wrong,' he reasoned. A clear conscience is no guarantee against the gallows, I pointed out, figuring that, if required, it might be no easy matter to locate a third party who would accept the simple truth. Agreeing to be more circumspect in future, he said I should put the winnings on Borghetto in next day's Cup, provided he seemed OK after his trip over. A sound, unspectacular stayer who had won the two miles Sunninghill Park Stakes as well as the longest race in the Flat calendar, the twenty-two furlongs Queen Alexandra, he was allergic to air travel and Dalton Watson had sent him across from Chantilly by road and sea. Rae was to ride him a canter in the morning.

Among fellow seniors, Jack Gerber's By Thunder, who had a marked preference for heavy going, seemed the only possible threat, though the good ground would be against him and two miles two furlongs was probably further than he cared to run. Walter Swinburn's father Wally, claiming 3 lb – reducing his weight to 6 stone 12 lb – had won the Ebor on him as a three-year-old on a very holding surface in 1954. And ridden by another talented young Sam Armstrong apprentice, Josh Gifford (the same Josh Gifford as pictured in 'Off the Record', aged five, jumping a fair-sized fence on his pony, and showing the style which made him a record-breaking NH champion), he had been runner-up this year.

No three-year-old had won the Doncaster Cup since 1934, and this year's duo didn't look anything special. Phil Bull's headstrong Souvrillus had won a Redcar maiden and modest events at Bogside (on a disqualification) and Beverley, but his resolution had been suspect in other less successful efforts. The Queen's muscular little son of Djebel, Atlas, had won the Dee Stakes and run a respectable fifth, behind Lavandin, in the Derby. However his subsequent performance in the King Edward VII Stakes had been so moderate that, whereas it often paid to overlook Epsom runners who reappeared at Ascot, it was difficult to entertain any excuse. And, in any event, he had to get the trip. George Todd, who knew as much about handling stayers as anybody, reckoned that 'For every twenty-five horses that get two miles, only five stay two miles and a quarter.'

Rae and I were on the course when Borghetto pulled out of the racecourse stables shortly after 7 a.m. I was glad I'd put the nap on him. He looked great and felt likewise, reported his pilot. I was broadcasting the race, so would have to get someone to put on Fred's £750 to which I was only adding a 'pony', as it would be enough to see a losing nap run interrupted. When George Cooper, a Cheltenham bookmaker, whom I particularly liked, called into the hotel for a coffee before racing, I gave him the small commission and he said he'd send one of his men up to the commentary point to let me know the price I was 'on' at. George (real name Johnnie Whitnall), who bet at Cheltenham and Gloucester greyhounds, built up a big racecourse credit business and professional connection through ability and personality. His weakness was too high a tolerance of the 'knockers' and slow payers who are the bane of the betting ring and who left him acknowledging, 'If I could recover a tenth of what I am owed, I'd be a rich man.'

Shortly before post time at Doncaster one of Johnnie Whitnall's men nipped up to the commentary box and slipped me a piece of paper on which was written the odds returned over Borghetto. 'Carpet, it read, which is the same as 'half a stretch' – a stretch being a six months' sentence, half that is three, therefore 3/1. Had it been in France, the message would have read: *'avec l'amant'*. Just as there is a 'secret' method of conveying numbers between bookmaker and employer, so is there a language of the Hippodrome, dating from the pre-electronic era when the chief *Pari-Mutuel* odds relayer would call the 'shows' to his employees, who would then distribute them to subscribers on flimsy tissues. The 'language' was developed to inhibit the activity of enthusiastic freelances who would listen in and offer a cut-price service.

Why *avec l'amant* for three? Evens (*égalité*) is *tout seul*; two is *toi et moi*; three is 'with the lover'. The French method of misrouting 'ear-wiggers' is based on a more intimate formula than the English. There is only one common denominator: five is 'hand' (*poing*) both sides of the Channel. Easily confused are 'cockle' (ten in English) and *à la coq* (nine in French). Cock and hen is rhyming slang for ten (hence cockle), though many refer to the number as *net*. *A la coq* is a boiled egg. An egg, of course, is *un oeuf*, which, when you say it, is like *neuf* (nine).

As far as Borghetto, the ultimate 9/4 favourite for the Doncaster Cup, was concerned, he might just as well have been returned 'double carpet' (33/1) – *les deux bossus*. Although he ran an honourable race, when Harry Carr 'kicked' on Atlas just outside the quarter-mile pole he initiated a royal procession.

Tales of larceny are the oxygen of the ring; acts of villainy probably occur in the ratio of one in a hundred compared with the City. It isn't saintliness that keeps racing as straight as it is, it's the fact that, in a small community, there are no secrets, or precious few. Here's one which didn't result in villainy; had it done so, it would be common knowledge.

It was 1954, the year Sir Ken went for his Champion Hurdle hat-trick, and Johnnie Whitnall and I were having a drink at the end of a local dog programme which followed Cheltenham racing. He always appeared to me more like an innocent farmer's lad than a pretty sharp bookmaker, and I remember thinking what a funny question when he asked, 'What do you think of that Tim Molony?' Five times champion before he retired, Tim was a hell of a brave jockey.

'A real good man,' I replied.

'I *know* he is,' said Johnnie, bright-eyed with admiration. He leant forward: 'I offered him £10,000 to get beat on Sir Ken, and do you know what he answered?'

£10,000 represented close to £100,000 in the late eighties and, at the 1954 level of Champion Hurdle prize money, a jockey would have had to win it twenty-five times to earn that amount.

'I'll assume you're joking,' Tim had reacted, adding, 'but for my own protection I must report the conversation to Willie [Stephenson] and Mr Kingsley.'

Discussing the matter thirty-four years later at Cheltenham, Tim recalled, 'Willie just shrugged and said, "You did right to tell me." But Max Kingsley was hopping mad about it.'

As it happened odds-on favourite Sir Ken was struggling from three out and looked sure to be beaten by locally trained Impney, who led over the last, until he got up close home and won by a hard-fought length.

The following year, Johnnie, who was known to have laid heavily against one of the market leaders in the Gold Cup, was himself approached with an offer to have the horse 'seen to'. Nobbling people may have been entertainable to the principal of the George Cooper firm, but interfering with horses was altogether different. He made sure security was alerted and, shortly afterwards, the originator of the proposal took up residence elsewhere . . .

*   *   *

My tipping fortune turned shortly after that 1956 Doncaster meeting with a 64/1 treble. I wasn't 'on', but relieved. I was beginning to worry about the Earl of Normanton's pictures – the marvellous examples of the works of Reynolds, Gainsborough, Rubens, Canaletto and so on – at Somerley in Hampshire. Chris liked to remind his journalists: 'Always remember you are writing for the man in the back streets of Derby.' Why Derby I never learnt. What I did know was that those who were foolhardy enough to take note of selections covered a wider social spectrum. One of them was 'Boy' Normanton. As everyone associated with racing knows, the only way to end up with a small fortune by backing horses is to start with a big one. The then owner of the fine estate at Ringwood may well have been in a position to achieve this situation. I was concerned, nevertheless, to learn from him by enthusiastic letter that he had developed a positively infallible staking method in connection with my naps. The system did necessitate heavy outlay at times, he explained, but it yielded 'regular and excellent' profit. He was eager to demonstrate, and Pat and I must come and stay for a Salisbury meeting. Unsociable, I demurred at first, preferring the independence of hotels when working, but ultimately we did.

Boy and Fiona were marvellous hosts and we became firm friends. His system was horrendous, depending, as it did, on virtually unlimited resources and incorporating the ingredients of self-destruction. The fifth Earl of Normanton, whose boyish charm made him so well suited to the nickname which replaced the generous quota of seven with which he had been christened, did much of his betting with a Bournemouth bookmaker. While the O'Sullevan naps were scoring regularly – a circumstance which arose with less frequency than intended – the betting pattern was fairly normal. After a losing sequence of five, the stake on the sixth had to be sufficient to recover the loss; likewise if the sixth failed, and the seventh, and so on. This situation accounted on one occasion for such a substantial sum being 'blown' down to Bath by the bookmaker, who naturally got the best of the odds, that a horse which would normally have been sent off at 6/4 won at long odds-on. Sometimes at dinner parties, after the ladies had left the dining room and the port had been round two or three times, I thought I had convinced him that there was no reason why a losing nap sequence should not be sustained for three weeks. Happily it never happened. And he did, wisely, modify the system. But, aware of the grounds for bare walls in other stately homes, I still worried about the pictures. They were still *in situ* when, sadly, Boy, wartime captain in the Royal Horse Guards, died, a young fifty-six.

CHAPTER 13

Unprofessional Conduct

Variety was not a conspicuous feature of the BBC's Sunday television programmes in 1954. After the morning service, which usually opened the day's viewing, there were rarely any further pictures until the children's programmes at 5 p.m. So it was a surprise, to say the least, to be invited to commentate from Milan on an international trotting race, which was to be transmitted direct to England, France, Germany, Holland and throughout the host country on Sunday, 28 November. It was to be the first trotting race screened in England, and the first time that local horses had competed against foreign specialists in Italy on equal terms. The Grand Prix des Nations would feature eleven of the top international trotters and drivers, racing over an extended 1¼ miles for a first prize of more than £6000.

What I knew about trotting could have been written on a horsemeat trader's heart and still left room for the horse's prayer. Also, I had barely recovered from the trauma of covering the first Arc de Triomphe televised to England the previous month. This couldn't be worse. 'Yes,' I said, and then wondered how the *Express* would react to a column about the European trotting championship on Monday the 29th. Probably not too enthusiastically.

The weather had been playing havoc with fixtures, and Clive and I had lately been asked to produce our 'twelve to follow' for the current jumping season. He readily agreed to write about his on the Friday for Saturday the 27th, so that I could phone mine in on the Sunday. The timing was lucky, because Lingfield, Wetherby and Worcester were all waterlogged that weekend.

The Gordon Richards and doyen of trotting drivers at this time was the veteran, Irish-born Charley Mills, who had lived most of his life in France. In 1953, the previous year, trotting races in France (4345) had outnumbered those on the Flat by 1549. I learnt as much as I could about the game from reading before Charley Mills kindly gave me a crash course on the morning of the race, in which the driver of more than four thousand winners was to partner the young four-year-old queen of French trotting, Gélinotte.

If the Arc de Triomphe programme was any guide, it was essential to have plenty of 'waffle' in reserve to survive the long periods of picture failure during, what appeared to me, a dauntingly lengthy transmission from 2.30 to 3.10 p.m. The schedule for the day was 11 to 11.45, morning service from Winchester Cathedral; closedown until the Grand Prix des Nations; followed by a further interval until 5 p.m. and children's hour – *Quick on the Draw*. At least the day's output gave one a chance of reaching the first three in the ratings.

In contrast to my sensibly relaxed fellow Eurovision commentators, one of whom didn't even bring any binoculars because looking through them gave him a headache, I had lugged over on an early morning Saturday flight a giant naval submarine pair with heavy tripod support. These were viewed with deep suspicion by Italian customs, who held me up almost as long as their British counterparts had – though with less good humour – on a recent return trip from Paris to Heathrow. Then, asked the routine question, I was obliged to declare the acquisition of two pairs of rubber bootees for our poodle, which I had bought from Le Chien Elégant in the rue François Premier, and twelve glass phials of toad's venom, a gift from the Chantilly trainer, Jack Cunnington, to an English colleague. It was reputed to be an efficacious remedy for horses who break blood vessels.

The Grand Prix promoters gave the visiting commentators an excellent dinner, after which my French counterpart, Georges Decaunes, joined me when I said I was going to a shop where I had previously bought very good silk ties. I thought it was odd when, after I'd selected a couple, he asked, pointing to the first one, 'What colour is that?' Then, indicating the other, he repeated the question, 'I am quite colour blind,' he laughed, and, forestalling my question, continued, 'Tomorrow? I shall stand next to you. What they hear in England, they will hear also in France.' Nice, I thought. The possibility of misleading the citizens of one country would already have me pounding the San Siro circuit (I can still recite the dimensions!) before the roosting birds had whistled a note. Was it worth going to bed?

As usual, it was marvellous to see the horses exercising in the early morning. Trotting – a two-time diagonal gait in which the off fore and near hind strike the ground simultaneously – has infinite aesthetic appeal when the horse is pulling a light (20–25 lb) sulky, but, to me, contrastingly little when the horse is mounted and his natural grace is diluted by the relative ungainliness of man. A trotting race introduced a new dimension to commentary for me, in that one had to be alert to possible disqualification through a runner breaking into a gallop or pacing (a two-beat lateral action, like a camel).

The organizers had thoughtfully provided us commentators with photographs of the horses. The six representing Italy were all US-bred imports, including a five-year-old, Hit Song, who had been one of the best three-year-olds in America, and was the top local hope. The Dutch runner, McKinley, also of US origin, had proved a star at home and was the first from Holland to race in Italy. Germany's crack home-bred, Ejadon, had been preparing on the Milan training circuit well in advance of the event. As well as Gélinotte, the French fielded the prestigious Prix d'Amérique winner Feu Follet X and Gutemburg A, who had already beaten Gélinotte but been disqualified for passing the post at a gallop – an infringement which most O'Sullevan horses carefully avoided.

Although the day had dawned bright, the sky was ominously dark by midday when the commentators were shown their work site. We were aligned along an open section of the main grandstand beneath an improvised awning which did little to exclude daylight from the small monochrome monitors. These, theoretically, would enable us to see the images being transmitted. I hoped it wouldn't rain. The big event was number five on the card. By race three it was tipping down. At 3.30 local time (2.30 in England) we were lined up, poised – like earnest performers confronting a non-existent audience at the end of a storm-lashed pier – and ready to commence our polyglot rendition of Sunday at San Siro.

From left to right, rain pulping their notes, there were Italy's long-serving interpreter of the racing scene, Alberto Giubilo; Holland's Hans Eysvogel; Germany's Hans Stein; Georges Decaunes for France; and his neighbour from the UK who was welcoming viewers to 'the first telecast of the most popular sport on the Continent with which the horse is associated' – when the technician in charge of my circuit indicated that I should stop. The sound wasn't getting through. The second effort also foundered somewhere on the airwaves, but, third time round, we were away. The excellent producer, Giovanni Coccorese, had scripted every shot in the build-up to the 'off', so despite hazy images it was possible to follow the action. It was quite a race and, after missing the break and trailing, Gélinotte took off on the home stretch, caught Hit Song and won at the wire.

I thought it might have gone all right and, soaking wet but relieved, drank more grappa that night than I was entitled to survive. But there were clearly no grounds for developing a big head to go with the sore one I woke up with. Georges Decaunes took a sabbatical shortly afterwards to forestall a nervous breakdown, and the Gran Premio delle

Nazioni, to give it its local title, was the last trotting race to be televised in England.

At least I didn't manage to kill off coverage of the Arc de Triomphe in the same year, and it wasn't until 1986, thirty-two years later, that BBC TV forfeited transmission of one of the highlights of the European racing season. By that time, although the interview area remained a chaotic shambles, the commentary point in the 'new' 250 metres long, six-tiered grandstand, created in 1966, was impeccable – a contrast to 1954, when I was somewhat perilously located on an open roof which had not been constructed to accommodate such intrusion.

French television racing coverage was not at a very advanced stage of development at this time, and the producer did not appear to be fully *au fait* with his responsibilities. It was, I gathered, his first horse-racing assignment and, while I was seeking to learn what camera angles he intended to employ during the race, and particularly what procedure would be followed when, after 400 metres or so, the field was obscured from the grandstand by *le petit bois*, I understood him to say that if the horses were going to run around behind trees, he wouldn't bother about them at all. Encountering my gifted and versatile colleague, Léon Zitrone, a Gallic Richard Dimbleby with a passion for horses, outside the weighing-room, I expressed doubt whether the producer was fully informed regarding the direction the horses in the Arc would follow, adding that this impression was doubtless due to my incomplete comprehension of the language.

'*Mon cher ami,*' reacted Léon, 'sadly, you have understood only too well.'

Generally, once they're off I commentate from the 'live' action, with only an occasional quick glance at the screen. This time a peek at the monitor, when the field was hidden behind the little wood, revealed that we were looking at the feathered headdress of tipster Ras Prince Monolulu. At the halfway mark, when England's only hope, By Thunder, who had been accompanied over by Susan Armstrong's (later Susan Piggott) pony, Smokey, was showing prominently, the screen was decorated by a mannequin. But, although I was focusing on the straight at the time, and did not re-refer to the monitor, I gather there was a shot of the closing stages.

Rae Johnstone, riding for the youngest trainer with a runner, Pierre Pelat, for whose father he had won on Nikellora in 1945, had arranged for his car to be washed over the weekend to ensure rain on behalf of his partner, Sica Boy. There had been a meteorological over-reaction, and conditions were very arduous. They proved no handicap to the beautifully ridden 4/1 favourite, who took up running inside the last

furlong and readily fulfilled the prediction of his owner's, Mme Jean
Cochery's, parrot, who had been repeating his lines for the past week –
'Sica Boy has won it.'

When I looked at the monitor it was blank. There was no way of
knowing whether pictures were still being received in England, so I kept
burbling on until a French technician signalled that their transmission
was ending in two minutes. A bonus in that era was the absence of any
requirement to maintain precise timing schedules. The Arc de Triomphe
programme had opened television on that Sunday, 3 October. It could
end when it cared to; the next offering was not until children's hour at
5 o'clock.

A further bonus of working abroad was that viewers were less
exasperated by the absence of news of betting, to which, as I mentioned
earlier, any reference whatever was comprehensively banned on BBC
TV and radio until the embargo, in respect of starting prices only, was
lifted in 1958. By 1955 60 per cent of my mail included requests to
'please refrain from talking while the starting prices are being given over
the loudspeakers', or, more directly, 'why can't you bloody well shut
up?' The answer was because the studio would scream at the producer,
'what's happened to Peter's mike?' Dennis Monger, who covered racing
for a long stretch and was very good at it, was accustomed to me trying
to arrive at a 'natural break' when the SP's came up and would interrupt
my silences by interjecting, 'OK they've heard the price of the winner.
Now for God's sake carry on talking.' Barrie Edgar, who handled many
of the Midlands meetings, like Birmingham, Nottingham, Stratford,
Uttoxeter, Leicester, Warwick, Worcester and, most importantly, the
Cheltenham National Hunt meeting, was, for all his virtues, less of a
racing man. He would invariably react to a momentary hush with a
startled cry to the chief engineer, 'Peter's mike has gone,' or, with a
double take, and anxious appeal to his assistant, if I mentioned before
a race that a horse was (say) 'bison arf' (bice and a half, or two and a
half, or 5/2). I suspect, however, that he cottoned on before a big event
at Cheltenham in which there had been much speculation as to which
would head the pre-race betting. 'There goes everybody's favourite',
observed Clive Graham drily, as the horses left the paddock. And as the
camera panned on to his chief market rival, I added, 'And there's
everyone's second favourite.'

Barrie was in the production chair on 14 November 1959 when I
committed a 'crime' which inspired a two-page reprimand ('unacceptable, unprofessional conduct' etc.) from the Head of Outside Broadcasts, Peter Dimmock who, as luck would have it, happened to be in
the racecourse 'Scanner' (mobile control room) at the time. The
Hennessy Gold Cup, in which I'd gone for that excellent Verley

Bewicke-trained mare Kerstin, was then run at Cheltenham. The incomparable Cotswold course looked its best, but, despite a personal leaning towards the jumping game, my thoughts on this occasion were at Manchester and the last day of the Flat.

The previous Saturday's programme at Windsor had been abandoned owing to fog, resulting in the prospect of bigger than ever fields for the final cards at Manchester and Lingfield. Also there was an acute jockey shortage. I'd already backed a personal favourite, Operatic Society, at 25/1, for the Manchester November Handicap when Vincent O'Brien rang to say he would like to run Ross Sea, and have a bit on him, if he could get a decent jockey. The three-year-old had won three times at The Curragh under Garnie Bougoure that season, but Garnie was needed at Naas on 14 November. I thought there might be a chance of getting Geoff Lewis. Fine if you can, was Vincent's reaction. So I booked him, put the money on, and reported, 'Twenty-three-year-old Geoff Lewis, one of the star riders of the season, will partner Ireland's "November" hope, Ross Sea, on Saturday week. Penalised 6 lb for a recent smooth Curragh success the Vincent O'Brien-trained colt will be Geoff's first ride on a horse trained in Ireland as well as a first ride in the big handicap in which Vincent seeks consolation for the narrow defeat of Knock Hard in 1952.'

Operatic Society was a Goliath of a horse. Sent to Ascot sales as a two-year-old, he was knocked down for 310 guineas to that good judge, Peter Thrale, who freely confessed he thought he was three. To win the 'November' he would have to establish a weight-carrying record for a three-year-old in a record field (forty-nine) for the one and a half mile handicap. He'd won a string of races over a variety of courses including Lewes, twice, and was set to concede lumps of weight to all but one of his thirty-five senior rivals. If ever a horse was constructed to do it, it was he. And, significantly, the regular man aboard, Ken Gethin, was convinced he was still on the upgrade. He'd travelled well, I learnt on Friday morning, and the going, exceptionally, was perfect. I needed a winning nap at 4/1, or better, to show a profit for the tenth time, Flat and National Hunt, in the last twelve successive seasons, and wrote, hopefully, 'While respecting, and fearing, Ross Sea, I am going along with Operatic Society (1.55 nap) to establish a record.'

The Hennessy was due off at 2.15, twenty minutes after the Manchester contest, so there should be no problem about hearing Raymond Glendenning's radio commentary. I'd got a small radio with an ear jack which fitted under my TV headphones. The racecourse number board, rather than a studio caption, was used for screening the runners and riders in this era. By the time I was called upon to read through the Hennessy field, it was getting near the off up north. I went through them as if they were entering the last furlong and, without waiting for a cue, handed over to the paddock. 'My God, that was quick,' exclaimed Barrie Edgar, adding, 'go ahead, Brommers.'

Peter Bromley was standing in for Clive Graham, who was in America for the Washington International. Along with coils of cables, two monitors, the intercom system and a floor manager, we were both operating from the same box, in which there was insufficient surplus space to introduce an anorexic hamster. Peter was crouched on the floor trying to screen the monitor, from which he had just started to commentate, when I turned up the radio volume and heard the glorious, unforgettable words, 'Operatic Society is racing away all on his own now.' I just had time to thump Peter on the back and acknowledge his thumbs up sign before Raymond completed his sentence, 'and Ken Gethin is running after him!'

Bursting with *joie de vivre*, the gelding had unshipped Ken and indulged a little sensibly unexacting solo tour before allowing himself to be recaptured. They were not yet off at Manchester when the Hennessy horses began to leave the paddock and Barrie was saying, 'OK, hand over to Peter O'Sullevan now.'

I shook my head vigorously at Peter and whispered, 'Carry on, for Heaven's sake!'

He'd already said just about everything he knew about the big 'chase runners. So he said it again.

Barrie repeated his instruction, in a slightly sharper tone.

Peter Bromley kept going strongly and, at last, Raymond announced, 'They're away.'

Reception my end was not as coherent as it might have been because, by now, the senior Midlands sports producer was expressing extreme agitation over complete loss of contact with his commentators. Raymond Glendenning was saying, 'I am waiting for them to come out of the fog now. I won't see a horse until about a furlong from the finish. Here they come and something is well clear.' Let it be him, I muttered to myself.

The light on the intercom flashed, the floor manager picked up the phone and I heard Barrie's anguished appeal: 'What the hell is going on up there?'

I turned up the volume of my transistor. 'Yes,' shouted Raymond, 'it's Operatic Society, the horse that got loose before the race. Operatic Society has won the Manchester November Handicap easily from Ross Sea second, Sunrise third.' The SP 18/1, 18/1, 25/1. And Kerstin (4/1) won too, at Cheltenham.

Without the introduction of ITV, the announcement of starting prices might have remained unacceptable to the BBC Board of Governors indefinitely. As it was, resistance to any indication of pre-race betting moves was sustained for a further two and a half years – placing BBC TV racing coverage under a handicap, vis-à-vis the opposition, which was virtually doubled on Saturday, 29 October 1960 when, as one paper put it, 'The farce came to a head with the commercial boys gleefully dealing a knockout blow for the BBC by giving the betting at both the Corporation's televised meeting and their own.'

By this time the war between the rival bodies had been running for several years, with Commercial scoring the first significant hit in 1955 by annexing one of the BBC's prime sites, Sandown Park, for a five-year period. This coup Peter Dimmock swiftly countered by heading for the Jockey Club and making a good catch (which he later dropped) by securing Newmarket for the 'old firm'. Harry Middleton, racing's most staunch and knowledgeable ally within the Corporation administration for nearly twenty-five years, promptly released me from radio commitments on the Rowley Mile and July courses and, four years later, greatly strengthened BBC TV's racing lobby when transferring from Assistant Head of Outside Broadcasts (Sound) to the corresponding position with Peter Dimmock.

Paul Fox, the brilliant inspiration behind *Sportsview* and the long-running *Grandstand*, the first frenetic screening of which, on 11 October 1958, I remember so well, saw racing as a prime ingredient of both programmes, though there were occasions when our correspondence reflected disagreement over priorities. Among early *Grandstand* producers, racing was to such an extent a linchpin that one of the dynamic (or do I mean manic?) orchestrators, Bryan Cowgill, would change location overnight when winter racing was threatened by bad weather. On one occasion when there were to be early Saturday morning inspections at Windsor and Sedgefield, he had me drive to Nottingham (which I was happy to do) so as to be within striking distance of whichever meeting got the go-ahead.

It was obvious in the 1950s that BBC TV racing's freedom of choice would be reduced by the advent of Commercial, and that screen time would be limited by the demands of an increasing variety of other sports. But, in view of the enthusiasm of the time, it was difficult to foresee that, by the late eighties, the BBC would have been outmanoeuvred to the point of conceding all five English classics, sixteen of the twenty-three Group I races in the racing calendar, and virtually the whole spectrum of international horse races outside the British Isles.

CHAPTER 14

Allez Johnstone!

It was just coming up to 10 p.m. on Saturday, 29 June 1957. As the prospective commentator on the twenty-seventh Greyhound Derby I was standing, dinner-jacketed, facing the camera, and offering a silent prayer that the electronic eye was not about to perform its familiar trick of extinguishing all coherent thought.

At that time annual greyhound racing attendance figures for the sixty-five GRA-licensed stadia exceeded 16 million. Nor did the 120 flapping tracks lack enthusiastic support. The audience potential for the sport's big night of the year, brilliantly orchestrated by the White City's racing manager, Major Percy Brown – responsible for seeding the 140 entries, so that 48 remained to compete in the qualifying rounds for the six-dog final – seemed dauntingly unlimited.

Throughout the drive from Newcastle to London, after covering that afternoon's Northumberland Plate, I had been continually repeating to myself the opening words with which I hoped to greet the unseen audience in a simulated relaxed manner – rather than, as one producer gently put it, 'as if you were facing a bloody firing squad'. Over and over again, I repeated, 'Good evening and welcome to this great stadium, White City, where you are joining a crowd of fifty thousand [Percy Brown's figure] who are currently being entertained by the immaculate floodlit Band of the Royal Marines as a prelude to the introduction of six of the fastest greyhounds in the world who will shortly be competing over 525 yards for a first prize of £1500 and a £250 trophy.'

Take-off, as it were, accomplished, I reassured myself that the rest would be no problem. After all, the 'City' was familiar territory, from the old shilling ring to the winner's circle where, on occasions of comprehensive celebrity absence, I had even been required to present prizes. And, more importantly, to receive same, following successes by my brindle benefactor, Cloughgriffin Cottage, acquired under the stimulus of a favoured refreshment (black Russian, a nourishing blend of draught Guinness and vodka) from the racing sage of the *Cork Examiner*, Tommy Lundon.

During a twenty-five-minute transmission scheduled between the other two evening programmes – *Light Music from the Royal Festival Hall* and *Today at Wimbledon* – there might be time to relate that, because the roar of the crowd reaches such a crescendo as the electric hare nears the traps, on this one night of the year, greyhounds are obliged to rely more on sight than sound at the off – a circumstance which may adversely affect normally fast breakers. There could be opportunity also to correct a widespread misconception that, because greyhounds hunt by sight, they have no sense of smell. My irreplaceable wartime greyhound, Slim, frequently confounded this assumption – notably on a well-remembered occasion when his twitching nose foretold the contents of a parcel which a generous countryman had left with the porter at my Chelsea flat. Chickens, a rare luxury then, had not yet been introduced to factory production and were flavoured by free-range life. Unpacked, the fine roasted bird was placed well beyond greyhound sight and reach while I went out to purchase an appropriate bottle. On return, I found a polished wooden skewer, as used to pin the body of a plump fowl, and no further trace of chicken. Not even a wishbone.

I had dubbed commentary on to the semi-finals in the studio several days earlier, and afterwards visited the track with the producer to see the three camera positions and the commentary point, which was in the open area in front of the glassed-in Directors' Box. It looked ideal. What we had not taken into sufficient consideration was that there would be others, apart from the greyhounds and ourselves, present on the night. A rehearsal on the event prior to the Derby revealed the startling detail that, like the finish-line TV camera, I had a very good view of the backs of a forest of heads, but of virtually none of the actual circuit. Frenzied readjustment – two wine crates providing a makeshift commentary platform – were completed just in time for me to hear through the earpiece, 'Opening titles going out.'

The Royal Marines were marching proudly in a pool of dazzling light, encircled by the billiard-table green track. There was an atmosphere of eager expectation among the immense crowd who had made the Dennis Hannafin-trained Wimbledon dog Ford Spartan, drawn in trap one, a warm favourite. I licked my lips and waited for the cue to launch into the indelibly digested opening phrases.

Ronnie Pantlin, the studio manager, was posted by the camera (into which I was staring with all the rapt attention of a rabbit caught in the beam of headlights) ready to give the signal if the ear attachment failed. There are more sophisticated appliances nowadays to enable commentators or presenters to receive directions from production. At that time the fallible earpiece sprouted a cord as subtle as a domestic clothesline, inspiring a 'fan' to write, following a commentary which he regarded with particular disfavour, to inquire whether I was blind as well as deaf. Sound was entering my ear with crystal clarity.

'Good luck, Peter,' said producer Douglas Fleming, 'and for God's sake don't mention the band.' He had just received a solemn reminder that acknowledgement of the gallant musicians could, through their union, involve the BBC in extravagant disbursement; a situation which, excepting the acquisition of a remarkably ancient film or, later, to score a point over ITV, the Corporation properly sought to avoid. For an instant I thought it might be easier to do the commentary without reference to the dogs.

But I guess it worked out all right. Brian Johnston was his usual professional self in the paddock. It was a fine race, with the evens favourite, Ford Spartan, getting home by a neck from an 11/2 chance, Highway Tim, in trap two. And I was even asked to cover it again: for the next three years, in fact.

For more than a decade, the Greyhound Derby was the second leg of what my *Paris Turf* colleague, Jacques Orliaguet, referred to as '*le tiercé Peter O'Sullevan*'. The weekend treble started with the Northumberland Plate – until my duties switched from Newcastle to The Curragh for TV coverage of the first sponsored Irish Derby in 1962 – and was completed by Sunday's Grand Prix de Paris, at that time run over one mile seven furlongs, and the richest three-year-old prize in Europe.

Bob Wigney, the cheerful, runcible clerk of the course at Brighton, was in the habit of offering a prayer on the eve of a local meeting in favour of a sufficiently cool breeze to deter holidaymakers from languishing on the beach; yet not cool enough to discourage them from ascending to the grandstands atop Whitehawk Hill. If the Longchamp promoters sought divine intervention on behalf of the 30 June 1957 renewal of the Grand Prix, it was not acknowledged. After an oppressively hot night, the early-rising sun beat down on the roofs of Paris with such intensity that, by 9 a.m., a steady flow of traffic was imprinting a Michelin tattoo on the melting exits from the capital. The cool forests of Fontainebleau to the south and Ermenonville to the north were diverting erstwhile Sunday racegoers from the Bois de Boulogne.

Throughout my race-reporting life I never overcame the fear that, come 'copy' time, I would have gathered no news worth relating, no story worth repeating. British interest in the outcome of the Grand Prix would be reduced by the defection of two intending Newmarket challengers. Lester Piggott had been approached to ride the favourite, Aly Khan's Magic North, but was already committed the same day to

Orsini in the West German Derby – which he won. It was a good programme: the Prix d'Ispahan included several possibles for the King George VI and Queen Elizabeth Stakes the following month, while an earlier feature was the reappearance of the useful grey filly Midget, runner-up in the 1956 English 1000 Guineas. But news could be sparse as ice in a racecourse bar.

Personally I love the sun. However, Paris this day was a little overheated. Shielded by tall buildings on either side, the bleak rue Lauriston, haunted by wartime memories of Gestapo occupation, would be cooler than most. Here, at number 72, Signor Conti served the lightest pasta, the freshest, most succulent scampi to be found in the 16th – or any other – *arrondissement*, to a clientele drawn largely from the world of racing. To this community he gave both nutritional and pecuniary support by regularly passing on income from the small, distinguished restaurant Chez Conti to the unsmiling servants of the *Pari-Mutuel*. When I rang and booked the corner single at which I could, discreetly, continue to study the day's prospects, the *patron* reported that he had reservations from five owners of Grand Prix runners. So there should be no shortage of misleading guidance. There wasn't. Though Pierre Wertheimer helpfully gave me news that he was importing Australia's leading rider, George Moore, who would be leaving for France on 27 July.

At the track the torrid temperature inspired some female racegoers to degrees of exposure which even the most devout students of equiform found distracting. I was seeking to focus attention appropriately when Rae Johnstone caught my eye. He signalled for me to come into the jockeys' dressing room, which was permissible for pressmen at that time, and walked on ahead to his bench. Wearing the blue and white silks in which in the last race he'd be riding Midget, his only ride of the day, he reached up for the white cap on the peg above his place. Then, when I had sat down beside him, he said, 'This is my last ride, Peter.'

I reacted with, 'You can't be serious!' and was going on when he gently cut me short.

'No,' he said, 'you've talked me out of it before, and you were right. But this time it's final. I told Mary when I left the apartment, and I'm telling you, Peter – but no one else.'

Historically the Grand Prix programme is one of the great events in the French racing year, and I felt that Rae should let the Société make an announcement over the public address. But he had never forgiven the few for booing and stoning him when he'd been beaten, irrespective of how he had ridden, and cheering success on occasions when he had shown less skill than in defeat. He wouldn't hear of it.

Although Alec wasn't certain that he had Midget positively 100 per cent, I had a lot more on her than I intended. They set off at a blistering pace over the seven-furlong circuit (in this era they tended to gallop from the outset in France and dawdle early in England; later the fashion was reversed), with Rae settling Midget towards the rear of the nine-runner quality field. I get the impression that Longchamp needs knowing as much as any course in the world – it took Lester a couple of years to get the hang of it – and the grey filly's partner knew every nuance and how to exploit it. The very speedy Polic was beaten, and well-fancied Wayne was fading, when the duo cruised towards the lead. Rae had timed his run with, seemingly, devastating precision. He'd picked off all but one of his rivals without seeking serious effort. The only remaining threat was the progressive second-season colt, Balbo – to whom Midget was conceding several pounds more than weight-for-age.

Knowing him for a dour, competitive opponent, Rae challenged a little wide and took a neck on him well inside the final furlong. I'd run up to the top of the old public stand, to watch the race on my own, and, as the fairytale ending looked a *fait accompli*, I yelled: '*Allez Johnstone!*' Then, all of a sudden, I was darting anxious glances towards the winning post and back to the action. Balbo had taken a few strides to respond to the challenge, as Rae had hoped, but now, roused by the presumption of his grey-coated adversary, he stretched his neck like a swan in flight. In the same instant Midget appeared to falter, as if her heart, like mine, had missed a beat. Maybe she caught a powerful whiff of the garlic with which Balbo's trainer, Percy Carter, liberally dosed his horses. Whatever, it was Balbo's number that went up in the frame.

As I turned to descend the stairway a fellow racegoer tore up his tickets, spat with the accuracy of one accustomed to a life of expectoration, and announced to no one in particular: '*Johnstone a mal monté.*' Among several personally favoured Sunday lunch sites was the family-operated stall in the tree-shaded area opposite the Longchamp stables – then almost exclusively patronized by lads and their 'clientele': clandestine bookmakers, card sharps, touts and the occasional family. (It probably would be still had I not blabbered so incontinently about the marvellous value of the rare roast beef, pâté, farmhouse Brie, oven-warm baguettes and chilled Brouilly, resulting in an English invasion.) As well as providing good food and refreshment, it had always been a rich source of vocabulary expansion for me. As a result, when I rounded on Rae's critic – who was, after all, merely exercising the normal punter process of disclaiming personal miscalculation – and loosed a torrent of invective with the malevolence of a llama spewing grass, I must say he did appear rather surprised. To me he represented every unwarranted critic who had ever hurled abuse and, in my over-excitement, I almost added that Johnstone, who had ridden more than 1400 winners in

France alone, was appearing for the last time in colours. Nice way to handle an 'exclusive'!

It was Midget's fourth run of the season and her fourth successive second before she came good under George Moore in both the Maurice de Gheest and Prix de Meautry at Deauville. Then Scobie Breasley rode her to win the Queen Elizabeth II Stakes at Ascot. But no wonder the talented daughter of Djebe found Georges Wildenstein's Balbo a tough opponent at Longchamp. He next won the valuable Prix Eugène Adam over ten furlongs; beat all the specialist milers in the prestigious Jacques le Marois at Deauville; and finished fastest of all when third in the Arc de Triomphe.

After Rae had carried his saddle into the weighing-room for the last time, he showered, changed into an immaculate dark suit, lit a cigarette and left the track. Back in the 'fried haddock' (slang for paddock) the thirteen runners for the Grand Prix included one, Sertorius, with a kitchen cloth soaked in cold water wrapped round his chestnut head – thanks to his solicitous lad. As the crowd melted in the torrid heat the third favourite, Le Haar, delayed the start by indulging in a voluntary pre-race gallop which effectively put paid to his chances. When they got under way on the sun-baked ground there was certainly no hanging about. My report in Monday's paper began: 'Paris, Sunday. A subnormal crowd, grilled by an abnormal temperature, saw Altipan lower the Grand Prix time record at Longchamp this afternoon.'

I hurried from the course to a public call box between races – so as not to be overheard – told Bob Findlay, the Sports Editor, about the Rae Johnstone story and suggested that, to do it justice, I should hold it over until Monday for Tuesday. He fully agreed, as long as it would 'keep' (remain exclusive), and arranged to send a photographer to Rae's Auteuil apartment in the avenue Maréchal Lyautey.

Although Roger Poincelet had failed only twice to win the French Jockeys' Championship during the eleven seasons from 1944 to 1954, Etienne Pollet-trained Altipan was his first winner of the Grand Prix de Paris, after which he kindly invited me to a small celebration party that evening at Maisons-Laffitte's Vieille Fontaine, where the salmon soufflé was light as my pocket after the defeat of Midget.

On Tuesday, 2 July 1957 the *Express* carried a front page piece across three columns – 'RAE JOHNSTONE RIDES HIS LAST RACE' – in which I outlined his record, with a cross-reference to Peter O'Sullevan's column on page nine, which appeared like this:

If you go racing most days of your life, you spend a lot of time hoping fervently that this horse or that will win.

I have done, and shall continue, my share of hoping.

But seldom with the fervour evoked by the spectacle of Rae Johnstone (see page one) and Midget entering the final two furlongs of Sunday's Prix de la Porte Maillot at Longchamp.

It wasn't a very important race as races go.

It was simply that, six or seven minutes before, sitting in the torrid heat of the weighing-room, making the final adjustment to his cap, Rae Johnstone had declared quietly: 'This is my last ride, Peter.'

The announcement, delivered in the familiar laconic, emotion-concealing manner, evoked a flood of reminiscence – and not a little remonstrance.

How would the Parisian crowd have reacted had they known that their idol for a quarter of a century was appearing in colours for the last time?

Even in the overwhelming heat of Grand Prix day the reaction would have been deafening – as it had been before here, at Epsom, The Curragh, and any other track in any one of nine countries you care to think of.

But it wouldn't have affected the outcome as Rae challenged with his renowned timing, moving from nearly last place to first – only to find Midget faltering at the all-important point.

But Rae preferred to exit quietly – and firmly. Remonstrance was of no avail.

'Thirty-six years is a long time to have been riding,' said Rae, 'and I have decided to call it a day.'

It's a highly competitive business, the race game. A lot of things are said in the heat of the moment that would have been better left unsaid.

The impressive statistical record of the Johnstone saga, you can read elsewhere. I would like to record that, over a long period, I have never heard Rae 'knock' (to use an Australian euphemism) a fellow rider, and that as the French would say is *déjà quelquechose*. If excess of self-criticism is a fault in a jockey, Rae had it to a degree.

For as Roger Poincelet (echoing the view of so many as he described his colleague as '*un vrai gentleman*') observed philosophically at a post-Grand Prix dinner – 'better not criticise yourself too much; your "friends" will do that for you!'

One more quote from Rae Johnstone himself – 'I've made some good friends in the game. I'd like to express my gratitude to those who have supported me and that, needless to say, includes the racing public.'

Those win tote tickets associated with No.5 (Midget), loser by a neck of the Prix de la Porte Maillot at Longchamp on Sunday June 30, I shall keep.

Bob Findlay was immensely supportive. He emblazoned the back page with 'scoop! Peter O'Sullevan gave first news yesterday that Rae Johnstone had decided to retire. scoop! Peter O'Sullevan landed a 9/2 nap when Penultimate won the last race at Brighton. scoop! Peter O'Sullevan is £26 up on his naps this season. scoop! Peter O'Sullevan is showing a substantial naps profit for the seventh season in eight.'

Less impressed was the reader who wrote from one of Her Majesty's detention centres to inquire whether I had ever been bitten by a kangaroo, and if there was any chance of hearing about a jockey 'other than one of those Aussie bastards'. *Sport Complet* followed up the next day, under the heading 'W. JOHNSTONE ABANDONNERAIT LA CRAVACHE', with a report that:

According to the *Daily Express* the crack Australian jockey W. Johnstone revealed on Sunday before the Prix de la Porte Maillot that, win or lose, he would retire forthwith. It has proved impossible to verify this astonishing news as W. Johnstone is absent from Paris for several days. However the article, which appears under the signature of Peter O'Sullevan, details so fully the sudden, dramatic, decision of the champion jockey that it must be regarded as official.

Within a week I was reporting the retirement of another star in his own riding sphere, the perennial amateur champion, John Hislop, who figured that, at forty-six, 'One hasn't the energy and timing that seemed to be there at thirty.' Few have reached the top in so many spheres of racing as the wartime paratrooper who competed with such outstanding success during a golden era for amateurs – jumping and Flat; became a distinguished author on Turf matters, often in collaboration with the artistic skills of John Skeaping; and, as an owner–breeder, was responsible for one of the outstanding horses of his era, Brigadier Gerard. It was during the latter stages of the creation of John Skeaping's marvellous lifesize bronze of the Brigadier that the two Johns, between whom there had been such close rapport for so long, fell out irreparably. It was a regrettable failure on my part that, as a friend of each, I was unable, despite persistent endeavour, to make any progress towards healing the breach between them.

The immediate sequel to Rae's decision was that, individually, we received letters from a literary agent and publishers inquiring whether either, or both, would be interested in a book on the life of Johnstone. As Rae said he would only entertain the project if I wrote it, and as I was working a full seven-day week for a combination of the *Express*, TV and radio (the consistent drain on O'Sullevan resources at this time was a quite remarkably unathletic filly named Big Sister), the answer was a polite no. As Rae remained adamant that he would not collaborate with anyone else, I began to feel guilty about shirking the job. Provided he told all – and Rae would have it no other way – there were the ingredients of a good story. Our prospective agent proved as resolute as Big Sister was lethargic. He telephoned daily and even 'got at' a fellow guest attending the farewell dinner party given by Pierre Wertheimer, '*Pour les adieux de Mr W. R. Johnstone*', at the Pré Catelan in the Bois de Boulogne on 22 July 1957.

Pierre invited just about every trainer in France for whom his guest of honour had ever ridden, many of the owners whose colours he had worn and the majority of the jockeys he had ridden against. Rae's weighing-room colleagues in England entrusted me with a presentation on their behalf at the end of dinner which, I am reminded by the menu in front of me, was appropriate to a warm, candlelit evening in the Bois: Billi By en tasse (mussel soup), Charentais glacé (iced melon), Suprême de barbue Bercy (brill, cooked in white wine, fish stock and shallots), Chaud froid de volaille à l'ancienne (glazed cold chicken), Coeurs de romaine (cos lettuce) and Bombe Johnstone – accompanied by Pouilly Fuissé, Château Beychevelle 1953, Pol Roger 1949, coffee and a rather exceptional Calvados without which I might have felt better the following day.

Menu

Diner

Offert par Mr Pierre Wertheimer

Pour les Adieux

de Mr W. R. Johnstone

Pouilly Fuissé

Château Beychevelle 1953

Pol Roger 1949

Café

Billi. By en tasse

Charentais Glacé

Suprême de Barbue Bercy

Chaud. froid de volaille à l'Ancienne

Coeurs de Romaine

Bombe Johnstone

Friandises

Pré Catelan 22 Juillet 1957

Seventy-three-year-old Dick Carver, the grand old man of French training, for whom Rae rode Derby winner My Love, paid a glowing tribute to the guest of honour; likewise one of the top jockeys of the time, Freddy Palmer, who was to have his first ride for Paddy Prendergast in the Irish Oaks on the morrow. The principal guest himself served a notable apprenticeship as a speechmaker, addressing one of his favourite themes when underlining that a jockey is acutely aware that in a minute or so he can destroy an owner's hopes and undo weeks of hard work by a trainer and a horse's lad. 'He needs,' said Rae, 'all the confidence he can be given to help him ride to the best of his ability. To all those who have placed their trust in me and given me confidence I say a special thank you.'

Maybe if a few of us, including Roland de Chambure, whose sudden death at the age of fifty-four in September 1988 was such a loss to French bloodstock breeding and to all his friends, had not moved on to a night club, 'the book' would have been forgotten. As it was, it seemed that everyone who hadn't got to write it thought it ought to be written. 'It would make a film for sure [that was the agent, Stanley Barnett's, pitch too] and George Raft is the man for the part,' insisted Frank Vogel. American-born Frank had stayed over in Paris after the war and, whether in the role of owner, trainer, manager or punter, and sometimes all four, was part of the Gallic racing set-up. At sixty-five he was still an ardent collector of remarkably young female company; otherwise – a retired advertising agency executive – he was unemployed. He lived within a kilometre or so of the subject, whom he knew, and understood, as well as anybody in the world. 'You're the perfect ghost writer for the job,' I told him.

'Frank,' interjected Rae, 'can't keep his hands off a girl long enough to write a cheque.'

The upshot was that I started writing at 6 a.m. – until it was time to leave for the track – for three months. Often stopped off, *en route* to Midlands meetings, at the British Museum Newspaper library at Colindale to check dates. And occasionally, in desperation, I made expensive telephone calls to Tokyo (where my subject had gone, at the invitation of the Japanese Racing Association, to coach the local riding talent) to establish facts. It was written in the first person, as an autobiography, and when I expressed the first two chapters east, Rae reacted with such limited enthusiasm that, excepting the publisher's vehement encouragement to stay on course, I'd have ducked out immediately.

When he returned to Paris and flew over for dinner one evening, I set a bottle of Dom Pérignon in front of him, put on a tape of his favourite Nat King Cole, and insisted he read to the end before the soufflé went in the oven. My reward was the unashamed tear or two at the end – and he'd only drunk one glass. Rae inscribed his book to 'My staunchest supporter, father confessor, author and best friend'. It had been hard work, much of it 'taped' in racecourse car parks and written up when I got home. However I found adopting the skin of another less forbidding than writing, naked as it were, in my own.

Although my name was not associated with the production of *The Rae Johnstone Story*, I'd sought permission to write it, so as to avoid being in breach of contract. This had been granted on the understanding that the *Express* had first refusal in the event of serialization. The option was exercised and on 17 March 1958 Arthur Christiansen wrote:

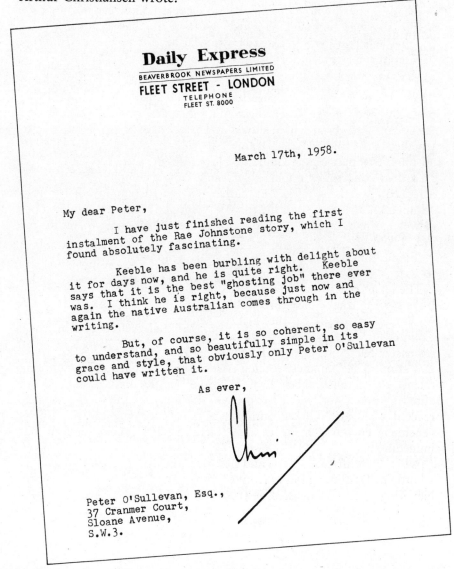

Daily Express

BEAVERBROOK NEWSPAPERS LIMITED

FLEET STREET - LONDON

TELEPHONE
FLEET ST. 8000

March 17th, 1958.

My dear Peter,

I have just finished reading the first instalment of the Rae Johnstone story, which I found absolutely fascinating.

Keeble has been burbling with delight about it for days now, and he is quite right. Keeble says that it is the best "ghosting job" there ever was. I think he is right, because just now and again the native Australian comes through in the writing.

But, of course, it is so coherent, so easy to understand, and so beautifully simple in its grace and style, that obviously only Peter O'Sullevan could have written it.

As ever,

Peter O'Sullevan, Esq.,
37 Cranmer Court,
Sloane Avenue,
S.W.3.

If Chris and Features Editor Harold Keeble meant half what they generously said, I had, at least, not screwed up a good story. The reviews were similarly flattering, and after the first impression had sold out the second and last did likewise. Thirty years after its publication at 18 shillings (90p), London bookseller Joe Allen, who founded what is, probably, the most comprehensive equine library in the world, had a copy for sale in his secondhand list for £15 – better than being 'remaindered'.

Before long Rae was to lease a Chantilly yard, order smart paddock sheets embroidered with a crocodile emblem instead of the traditional trainer's initials, and launch into a new career. And I, too, was making what was for me a new departure. During a dinner party in London, Stephen Raphael, who had trained with George Lambton and Billy Laye before the war but who had been without a horse in recent years, inquired whether I would care to buy a yearling and go into partnership. Several of the eighteen horses (yielding one winner of a Windsor selling hurdle) to carry my colours so far had been in joint ownership, only one of them having cost three figures! And every one had been 'secondhand' – if they'll forgive the term. To buy a yearling would be a new experience.

I went to Dublin to see my friend Bert Kerr, a very professional bloodstock agent who was permanently visiting studs and observing the development of young stock. We looked at several and he agreed to bid on two, with the first choice a clean-limbed, sharp-looking, early foaled chestnut daughter of Ballyogan. The dam hadn't produced anything worthwhile, but Bert insisted that none of this one's predecessors had her conformation. She cost 600 guineas.

At the same time Greville Baylis, a shrewd interpreter of the 'book', gave his wife Katie Boyle an advance Christmas present in the form of a 1000 guineas colt by Denturius, who would be the first to carry her blue and gold colours. I reported in 'Off the Record' that Catherine, our friend and neighbour, had enthused, apropos her gift horse, 'I would prefer him to be friendly than fast'; an original preference which was not fully shared by her trainer-elect, Staff Ingham. I suggested that honour and expectation might be satisfied by christening him Fast and Friendly, while I would name the Ballyogan filly Just Friendly. The first to win to pay for dinner.

Just Friendly's target was the Stonebow Selling Plate on 24 March, the opening day of the 1958 season at Lincoln. She had a perfect temperament and worked nicely. After Cyril Mitchell had sent her along one morning with a few of Ron Smyth's, Ron said, 'If yours doesn't win I'll shoot mine.' He definitely wanted to be 'on'. She'd clearly shown enough to take some beating, unless there was a useful plater in the

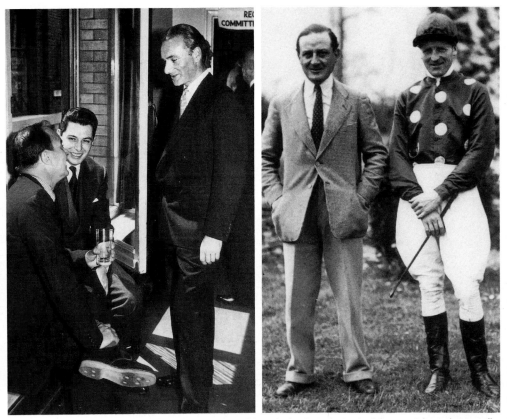

Above left: Aly Khan and Roland de Chambure at the Press Club Derby lunch. *Right:* A splendid team – Johnnie de Moraville and Dicky Black

With Rae Johnstone on a damp day

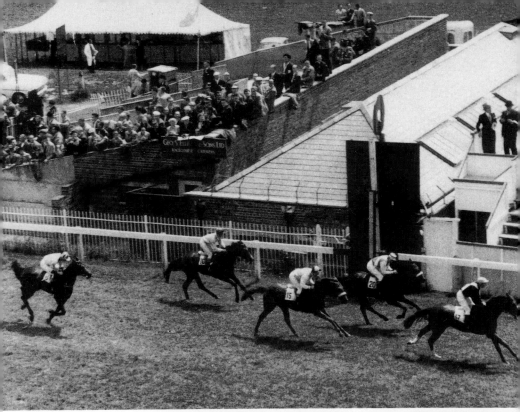

Just Friendly wins
'sellers' at Lincoln (*top
left*), Hurst Park (*left*),
and Epsom (*above*),
where (*right*) Mrs Lorne
(third from the rostrum)
appraises her before the
auction on 3 June 1958

Lavandin brightens another wet afternoon and (*bottom*) Pierre Westheimer and
Alec Head with the 1956 Derby winner — watched on the right by Lord Rosebery

To Peter all my thanks and love Rae.

Above: Midget II – Rae
Johnstone's last ride

With Russian jockeys
Nikolai Nasimov and Viktor
Kovalev, from Soviet horse
factory no. 33, before the
dramatic 1958 Washington
DC International

Fred Winter and Friendly Again on their way to post for Cheltenham's Clive Graham Handicap Hurdle on 11 April 1964

Below: Paddy ('Darkie') Prendergast on Town Moor with the next day's 1963 Leger winner, Ragusa (Garnie Bougoure)

And (*right*) thirteen years later, flanked by Richard Baerlein and P.O'S, receiving a 'Trainer of the Month' award

Fred Winter and Friendly Again lead on the first circuit and (*below*) finish second – the last time the great four times champion jockey was placed under National Hunt rules

The young grey mare later gets a photo verdict at Lingfield under 16-year-old Andy Turnell – his first ride outside his father, Bob's, stable, 19 December 1964

Lester Piggott and P.O'S at Laurel on the day before America's equine idol, Kelso, won the 1964 Washington DC International

Later at the Stable Lad's Boxing ...

... and later still

eighteen-runner field.

Two-year-old sellers, as they were then constituted, provided the best market guide in racing, as well as, in the case of higher-prized ones, post-race entertainment. After the traditional Findon seller at Good-wood's summer meeting the previous year I had reported:

Idler became the centre of the liveliest racecourse auction for many years after achieving a first-ever Goodwood success for the distinguished Norfolk colours. How much in keeping with the luck of the game too that the first winner for the Duke and Duchess at their local course should be a bargain purchase whose future as a racehorse was once despaired of. The horse for whom the Queen watched the keenest competition ever evoked by a Findon Selling Stakes winner cost the Duchess of Norfolk 360 guineas. He was such a little handful in his early days that Bill Smyth, twelve years trainer at Arundel, reported: "The sooner we get rid of him the better." Hardly were the words spoken than Idler began to show signs of being more amenable. He progressed so rapidly that he was rated a good thing for an Alexandra Park seller – which he duly won. Then he picked up two non-sellers prior to yesterday's triumph over seventeen opponents.

At the outset of the bidding, starting at 200 guineas, Idler appeared bound for a long journey on a boat – to China. But at 1500 guineas the Chinese who coveted the active little colt reluctantly dropped out. The bidding progressed to 1900 at which point Graeme Whitelaw, whose light blue and scarlet colours have for long been familiar to racegoers, staked a brief claim. At 2000 guineas Bill Smyth, bidding to retain the youngster for the Duchess, nodded no further. Enter Epsom trainer 'Snowy' Parker, playing up his winnings at the meeting, but in vain. At 2600 guineas 'Snowy' bowed his grey head and called it a day, leaving Jack Gerber (evidently undaunted by the subsequent failure of Guinevere's Slipper whom he had bought for 1400 guineas after the 1955 Findon seller) to secure the prize at 2700 guineas.

Altogether a nice afternoon's work for auctioneer Bob Wigney (five per cent is the usual commission) and a handsome £1250 'surplus' for Lord Ranfurly, Ben Hilliard, Ralph Moller and Nicky Morris, partner-owners in Idler's nearest pursuer – Touché.

For the record, Idler went on to win the Bentinck Nursery under 8.13 at Newmarket, followed by victory over the Noel Murless-trained filly, Court One, to whom he conceded 13 lb, in the Prendergast Stakes. As if to say, 'That's your lot,' the senior assessor rated him a mere 9 lb below the top-weighted Major Portion in the Free Handicap, so that, secured by an invisible anchor, he failed to revisit the winner's circle in eight attempts the following season. It was hard to foresee then that unrestricted two-year-old sellers would be eliminated from race prog-rammes within two years.

This heedless prohibition, regarded with concern by both trainers and the less affluent owners and breeders, was the consequence of an

opinion expressed by a committee of inquiry established to determine
the effect of the current race pattern on the production of horses capable
of winning from one mile to one and three-quarter miles at the age of
three. Responding, within its terms of reference, the committee, under
the chairmanship of Lord Rosebery, pronounced, *en passant*, that two-
year-old sellers did not serve this end.

It did not require a high-powered committee to reach such a
conclusion, nor was the 'production of horses capable of winning from
one mile to one and three-quarter miles at three' the sole purpose of
conducting Britain's greatest sport. Because of the artificially low selling
price associated with the winner, a gentleman's agreement had
developed against bidding up an owner who wished to retain his horse.

While banging on about the 'ban', I suggested that the introduction
of overnight declarations presented a new element; that the minimum
selling price must be raised and the surplus above the selling price of
the winner be distributed on a different basis. Formerly the owner of
the second had received the entire residue. I proposed 'fifty per cent of
the surplus from the sale of the winner to the second; thirty per cent to
the third and twenty per cent for the establishment of a school for
apprentices'.

At this time, 1961, trainers were not represented by an association.
Several asked me if I would get up a petition on their behalf. Among
them was Susan Piggott's father, Sam Armstrong, whom I quoted:
'Selling-race auctions are one of the attractions of racing, apart from
the fact that two-year-old sellers bring new owners into racing and are
essential for other equally obvious reasons.' I canvassed opinion during
the December sales, and everyone I approached, bar two, signed. The
exceptions were Bernard van Cutsem, because he never ran a horse in
a seller, and Derrick Candy, who felt that compliance might upset the
Jockey Club member for whom he trained. I forwarded the signatures
to the senior steward, Major-General Sir Randle Feilden, who
responded on 11 December: 'Thank you for your note together with the
petition on behalf of the trainers which you enclosed. As you know I
hand over this morning as Senior Steward, therefore I have passed the
petition on to my successor.'

On 14 December, under the caption: 'SELLERS AGAIN' PLEA BY 100,
I wrote,

A petition signed by one hundred licensed and incensed Flat trainers has been
presented to the new Senior Steward of the Jockey Club, Lord Crathorne,
expressing regret at the discontinuation of selling races for two-year-olds and
requesting that 'their re-introduction be considered.' There is no intimation that
the 'one-hundred' – who represent a great many more members of their

profession – plan a sit-down strike in Cavendish Square at the moment, but I can confirm that this year's precipitous ban has evoked very high feeling.

The plea was only partially successful. The 'ban' was lifted in 1963, but the events were only reintroduced in an emasculated form which severely limited spectator appeal and, unacceptably, merely benefitted the racecourse.

Lincoln's 1958 Stonebow Selling Plate, in which we were to run Just Friendly, carried a first prize of £196; the winner to be sold for 100 guineas upwards. So if the successful owner wanted to buy in his winner, he had around £300 to play with, as it were. Hence the need to bet. Just Friendly was generally forecast between 8/1 and 10/1 – not that Fleet Street assessment necessarily reflected available odds – and I tipped her each-way. She'd always been small, but looked to me to have shrunk on the journey from Epsom. Jack Leader warned that his filly, Lily Drake, was pretty sharp and Harry Blackshaw, who specialized in these events, vowed that no youngster trained in the north was fitter than Five Trumps.

I'd intended to have £200 on her, but after each confidence-weakening encounter with one of the opposition I knocked a 'pony' off, and the wager was soon halved. My absent partner, uncontaminated by well-intentioned late advice, had asked me to bet £200 for him. Cyril Mitchell wanted £50; Ron Smyth likewise. There were a few 'ponies', including one for Greville Baylis, who probably asked to be included in the 'commission' more out of courtesy than expectation, and Nico Collin, who had travelled up to the fen country with Ron Smyth and been brainwashed by him *en route*.

In the days before rat-catchers became known as rodent officers and horse hustlers as bloodstock agents, Major Collin's transparent integrity did as much to confer respectability on a profession which had long been regarded as the last resort of the black sheep of the family as his keen eye for the finer points of the thoroughbred. It was during his early years as an agent shortly after the war, while travelling horses to America, that the notable US trainer, Benjamin Allyn Jones, advised him, 'Young man, one day you will have a lot of other people's money to spend. When that happens always remember this: the three most important elements in a horse are brain, heart and lungs – in that order – and you can't see any of them.'

'Why do you put the brain first?' queried Ben Jones's disciple.

'Because,' pronounced the handler of such Olympian gallopers as Whirlaway and Citation, 'you can't train a stupid horse.'

Ballyogan's daughter out of Drizzle by Brumeux, christened Just Friendly, wasn't stupid. She surveyed the unfamiliar activity in the paddock with total detachment, hacked to the start under Ken Gethin with unhurried calm and, drawn seventeen of eighteen, lined up behind the five-strand barrier as if waiting to be called to choir practice. Her serene demeanour was in marked contrast to the feeling of apprehension being experienced by the punter who was standing in my shoes on the top level of the grandstand.

A seller is a drama in two parts. First there's the race; then the trauma of the aftermath, involving not only concern over the extent of the bidding in the event of success, but anxiety over the possibility of a 'claim' after failure. Every runner, excepting the winner, could be claimed for the selling price plus the advertised value of the race, and many were hijacked to Belgium and elsewhere by this means. So why compete for a seller, some would ask, if you're afraid of losing your horse? The answer was, and remains, that an owner's principal objective is to win a race. In theory, selling races represent the most modest company, so for players whose involvement is in the lower end of the market they afford the biggest chance of success.

When the tapes whipped skywards Just Friendly's outside neighbour spun round, losing lengths, and a white terrier slipped its lead and sped after the field. My recollection thereafter was a little hazy, though I remember thinking that, although prominent, the white-faced chestnut on the stands side was not exactly putting life and soul into her effort. After dealing with possibly more significant matters in the following day's *Express*, I reported, 'Anyone who requires an accurate description of the last two furlongs of the Stonebow Selling Plate will have to apply elsewhere. The hands holding my race glasses might well have belonged to an advanced case of DTs. Ken Gethin confirmed (once he had recovered sufficient breath to express an opinion): 'Two furlongs out I was saying to myself, "The poor so-and-so's done his money again".'

She had, in fact, crossed the line with a heart-stopping head advantage over the runner-up, who was a head in front of the third. When I reached the unsaddling enclosure, rather more breathless than its four-legged occupant, Cyril said, 'She's a lot better than that, I promise you. Hang on to her if you can.' I had given 'the business' to the rails bookmaker Maxie Parker. There had been a little 10/1 on the boards; 7/1 on the rails; and she'd been backed down to 5/2 favourite. I figured we'd be returned around 6/1; fives at the worst.

Before the auctioneer mounted his rostrum I hastened to our commissioner to learn the precise extent to which my heroine had modified her supporters' financial status. Although Maxie Parker, the second of four brothers whose father was a World War I immigrant, bought Ladbroke's in 1957 he continued to operate Max Parker Ltd of 653 Commercial Road. Without the flair of his bookmaker brother,

'Snouty', or the charm of his immediate junior, Jack, who was the father of Cyril Stein, Maxie was not given greatly to social badinage. Without waiting for the question, he leant down from the wooden crate which conferred stature on his short, stocky frame and pronounced with singular gracelessness, 'You had 3/1.' It would have required far more unfavourable news to dilute my euphoria, but the thought of declaring such a paltry return to the others was embarrassing to say the least. Maxie waited for me to conclude a summary of my opinion, which cast doubt on both his competence and reliability, before delivering the – to me – unforgettable line, 'If I returned you any bigger I'd lose on the race.'

My discontent was fuelled by the founder of the Laurie Wallis firm, who occupied the adjacent pitch, confiding, 'There was plenty of 7/1 and I laid Maxie £1000–£140 twice.' And Cyril Stein, who served an exhaustive apprenticeship at Ladbroke's Old Burlington headquarters before taking over and becoming one of the leading entrepreneurs of his generation, was correct when he observed, with a wry smile, a little later, 'I hear you are not very pleased with my uncle Max.'

Happily the selling ring-siders were more indulgent. Just Friendly was led out, to the accompaniment of generous applause, without raising a bid. Among telegrams which flowed in to the press room at Lincoln and the Saracen's Head Hotel from all over – Ireland, USA, France – Alec Head's message read: 'TOUTES MES FELICITATIONS POUR TES VINGT ANS D'EFFORT EN ESPERANT QUE TU N'AURAS PAS VINGT ANS A ATTENDRE POUR LE SECOND AMITIES = ALEC.' Cyril Mitchell was convinced that there would be no waiting for nearly twenty years for another success on the Flat. 'We'll fit a pair of blinkers next time,' said he. 'She'll improve three or four lengths on that.'

There was a £500 seller at Hurst Park nearly three weeks away. Three or four days before the race Monty Smyth offered the discouraging advice, 'You'll be wasting your time if you take on my filly, Go Lass, at Hurst Park.' He said she'd needed the race when second, beaten a neck, at Leicester and had 'come on a stone' since. I consoled myself that Monty, an ex-Flat jockey, told a good story – like the occasion when he had a brief flirtation with riding over hurdles. He'd always fancied himself at the game, as he told it, and was full of confidence when he got this good ride on a novice which had 'schooled' like an old hand and over which connections were going for a nice little 'touch'.

It was in late spring at Folkestone, when there was a fine covering of lush, naturally irrigated grass. Related Monty, 'The further we went, the more I was enjoying myself and the further I got up his neck. By the time I got over the far side I was making George Duller look like a policeman. I'll show 'em what style is, I was saying to myself – when, all of a sudden, he's flicked the top of one and I'm flying out the front door. I hit the upright of the rails a horrible smack and lay in the infield for dead. I seemed to have been lying there for hours, groaning, when, finally, I hear someone approaching and there's this fellow looking down on me. I'm almost in too much pain to speak. "Get me some help," I ask him. "I think I've broken my leg."

"Broken your leg?" he says, turning on his heel and spitting into the grass. "You ought to have broken your —— neck!" '

Apart from Go Lass at Hurst Park, there was a colt, Ushant, trained by Jack Jarvis, which had already run in a maiden – in which it had been said to be rehearsing, so to speak. But Just Friendly had worked like a bomb in blinkers. So it was reasonable to be hopeful, and I put the nap on her, as well as modifying the punting arrangements. Five of the ten runners were quite seriously backed, with Go Lass opening 5/2 favourite, and Just Friendly 9/2. Market positions were reversed before the off, where our filly jumped so smartly that she won, easing up, by five lengths.

The subsequent auction was, understandably, a little less friendly than at Lincoln – southern attitudes have long been more commercial than those of the north – and we had to go to 680 guineas to buy her in. However, that's a chance you take.

Planning a horse's races, irrespective of the level of competition, is one of the most important aspects of the game. We had a peach of a race for her within the fortnight at Alexandra Park – the Enfield Plate, for maidens at starting, selling races excepted. In a big field over five furlongs she drew Ally Pally's most favoured number, nineteen of nineteen. She had the advantage of experience over 60 per cent newcomers, and was backed from 6/4 to 11/10 on. The start was out of sight of the stands, but when they raced round the allotments into the hairpin bend for home the 'good thing' was virtually out of touch. Apparently, overlooked in her position directly beneath the starter, she had been taking a turn when the tapes were released. Under the circumstances it was no mean performance to run on into sixth place, as she did.

Unsettled, maybe, by this reverse, I then made the disastrous recommendation that we have one more run in a seller in the opening race of the Epsom summer meeting. Here she would meet, among others, Staff Ingham-trained Lady Cobbler, who had won a Windsor maiden by three lengths, and another sharp Epsomite in Boggy Whelan-handled Rhythmic Queen, who had shown promise in a similar event at Newbury. She could be claimed for peanuts in the event of failure, and could be bid out of reach if she won. Lady Cobbler opened 6/4 favourite, Just Friendly 9/4, Rhythmic Queen 4/1.

Knowing that Staff wasn't at all confident of beating us, I took the 9/4 and we went off the 6/4 favourite. No sooner had the tapes risen than Willie Preston was calling, 'Three to one Just Friendly.' She'd jinked sideways at the off and lost two or three lengths. But, still able to join issue a furlong out, she ran on to win by a length.

Nominating her for the race wasn't my only error in connection with the Mynne Selling Stakes. On the previous day my three personal guests at the traditional Press Club Derby luncheon were Comte Roland de Chambure, Prince Aly Khan and Frank More O'Ferrall. While discussing the four-day meeting, at which Aly and Roland had classic prospects, I suggested that Just Friendly was possibly the best bet in twenty-four races, confiding to Frankie, head of the Anglo-Irish Bloodstock Agency, that my main concern was whether I'd be able to retain her afterwards. The chances of doing so were not improved when Ken Gethin returned to the unsaddling circle and exclaimed, in ringing tones, 'Sorry, mate. I lost my irons at the start or she'd have won a minute.' It may have been coincidence that one of Frankie's co-directors, Ben Hilliard, was leaning over the rail within earshot, accompanied by a lady who appeared to be taking an analytical interest in the winner of the 2 o'clock. I hoped she didn't like what she saw.

At 650 guineas it was my bid and the auctioneer was saying, 'Is there no advance on six fifty for this very attractive filly?' Isn't that enough, for heaven's sake? I was thinking, when Ben's neighbour inclined her racecard towards the rostrum. Stephen and I had agreed beforehand that, if we had to go to 1000 (almost five figures in terms of the late eighties), we would. I'd seen it done before and trusted it would work now. In what was intended as a polite gesture, designed to silence all opposition, I raised one finger.

'At one thousand I'm bid,' intoned the auctioneer, stirring a little buzz of anticipation. (Among the ringsiders after a seller are those who suspect some thieving owner of having a 'touch', and they come to see him pay for it.)

One of my pressroom colleagues gestured towards the lady bidder and whispered the unwelcome news, 'She's loaded.'

The loaded one nodded discreetly. 'Eleven hundred I'm bid,' said the auctioneer, calculating his 5 per cent. He swept his gavel round the gathering crowd and inquired, 'Is there no advance on eleven hundred guineas?'

Geoffrey Gilbey materialized by my side, festooned with cameras, saying, 'I've taken some great shots of your filly.' He added, 'That's Margot Lorne bidding – she's a Frightfully Nice Woman.'

The auctioneer announced that he was selling.

'Eleven fifty,' I said. The FNW nodded, sharply.

'Twelve I'm bid,' intoned the man on the rostrum.

'She's got a lovely place in Rhodesia,' offered Geoffrey. I wished she was there.

'Has nobody got thirteen hundred guineas for this comfortable winner?' inquired the tireless salesman.

'Twelve fifty,' I said.

The loaded lady with the lovely place in the future Zimbabwe nodded again. While Just Friendly continued patiently circling the ring in which Charlie Smirke's fourth Derby winner, Hard Ridden, would be unsaddled on the next day, the bidding advanced, in slow motion, to 1500 guineas.

'For the last time at fifteen hundred guineas,' announced the auctioneer, 'and it's against you, sir.'

As if I didn't know. I could see her slipping away now; she looked more beautiful by the minute. 'Fifteen fifty,' I said.

At this point the unmistakable, trenchant voice of Tighie Nickalls, wife of the *Sporting Life*'s chief correspondent, floated over the crowd, inquiring of nobody in particular, 'Has he *got* fifteen hundred and fifty guineas?'

The question became purely academic after Mrs Lorne had nodded again and I had raised my top hat, bowed, and given Just Friendly a final, grateful pat.

In the following day's paper, after expressing the opinion: 'Quite the livest outsider this afternoon I consider to be Hard Ridden with veteran Charlie Smirke aboard,' I regretted that Mrs Lorne had proved a better stayer than JF's owner, adding: 'But the possibility of losing one's horse in a seller is a perfectly fair hazard. It is consoling to know that, after a short period in Jack Gosden's stable, she'll be going to her new proprietor's attractive stud, near Salisbury, in Southern Rhodesia.'

She reappeared twice before shipment; winning the 8.55 at one of Ally Pally's evening meetings, which I used to cover for BBC TV, and then trotting up, under nine stone top weight, in a nursery at Lewes. On both occasions she was ridden by a young man whom I had earlier described as 'One of the brightest young apprentices I've ever seen' – Jimmy Lindley.

CHAPTER 15

Big Race Sensation

Shortly after 6.30 p.m. New York time on Thursday, 13 November 1958 I took leave of my boss, Lord Beaverbrook, in his Waldorf apartment and sprinted to the elevator, leaving the legendary newspaper proprietor resigned to the realization that he had an obvious nutcase on the payroll.

I had been drinking his vodka with fresh lime and admiring his pictures when he generously proposed that I take a short vacation, fly up to New Brunswick to see his art collection, thence to California and Florida to cover the US racing scene for a while, and return on the *Queen Elizabeth* in comfort. 'I've been reading your stories. I like them,' he said. 'I like them a lot.' I glanced at my watch. Flight check-in was in forty-five minutes. How do you tell someone who has invited you to dinner at Le Gavroche that you'd prefer a Wimpy? I couldn't tell the truth – that I'd signed a contract to cover Cheltenham for BBC TV at the Hennessy Gold Cup meeting tomorrow. And that if I missed the flight I'd be in dead trouble. 'It's a marvellous suggestion, Lord Beaverbrook, and I am extremely grateful,' I said, 'but I hope I am building up a following in the paper [well, I was getting sixty to seventy letters a week, even if they weren't unanimously loving] and I feel that, generally, they may be more interested in what one expects to win tomorrow.' Max Beaverbrook wasn't given to looking nervous, otherwise he might have done so now. He simply said, 'Well, if you change your mind let me know.' And we were on our feet in unison.

The excursion had started unpropitiously a week earlier when the original plan that I should leave London on Saturday night, 6 November, to cover the Washington DC International at Laurel on the following Tuesday was suddenly revised by the Editor, Arthur Christiansen. Chris took the not unreasonable view that the *Express* would get better value for the travel expenditure if they received 'build-up' pieces for several days. My concern was that BBC TV expected me at Liverpool on the Friday and Saturday at the mixed meeting which featured the Grand Sefton Chase. Bob Findlay, *Express* Sports Editor, was sympathetic to my remonstrance but stressed that the Editor's wishes were paramount. Technically I was in the clear because the BBC Aintree contract had not yet reached me, and Peter Dimmock was very indulgent under the circumstances, but the change of plan evoked some aggrieved correspondence. My highly accomplished colleague, Peter Bromley, filled the breach in the very year in which Peter Dimmock unavailingly sought to persuade him to stick with TV – instead of going over to 'sound' – on the grounds that he would be directly in line to take over from Peter O'Sullevan. 'That,' laughs Peter now, 'would have made me just about the longest living understudy in the world.'

Once committed to a Tuesday departure I rang Vincent O'Brien to synchronize flights to the USA, where Ballymoss was assured favourite for the seven-country International.

I'd bet for Vincent from his Cheltenham days, and we'd already been through two dramas with John McShain's champion. The first occasion was at Doncaster on the eve of the 1957 St Leger, when the vouchers I still hold read:

£4000–£640 each-way Max Parker Ltd
£2000–£300 each-way Laurie Wallis Ltd
£1000–£160 each-way Jack Woolf Ltd
£800–£128 each-way D. Upex Ltd
£100–£16 each-way Stafford & Co. Ltd

Meticulous as ever, before proposing the speculation Vincent had walked the Yorkshire circuit and verified ideal conditions for a horse whom he rated unsuited to soft ground. I napped the son of Mossborough, writing: 'The greatest danger to Ballymoss is rain.' Within half an hour of phoning copy from the Earl of Doncaster Arms the danger had materialized.

I didn't see Vincent the next day until shortly before saddling time for the big race, which I was due to broadcast, in part, from a point down the course.

'I've just walked out there,' he said anxiously. 'We'll have to get out of the bets, he's got no chance in this.'

I daren't delay, I said, because I had to drive down to the radio point and wouldn't have time. 'Here's a list of the bets with each bookmaker on the rails. He's down to 5/1, so there should be no problem.'

Vincent is basically shy. He didn't want to go into the ring and, anyway, the horse was uppermost in his mind. 'Let's leave it,' he said. So we did.

I hurried off to the secondary commentary point, which is a good one on the inside of the course about five furlongs distant from the stands and the Leger start. There is public access to Town Moor, and crowds gather here on a natural mound where the BBC van was stationed. The engineer in charge had thoughtfully, and exceptionally, provided a long enough headphone and mike 'lead' for me to climb on to the roof of the vehicle. It was a fine vantage point. A 'live' broadcast is worrying at any time – the day you give the wrong result from the number one position is the one commentary you'll be remembered for. It's less of a worry for a supporting contributor. After all, if you get it wrong out in the country, how many will know? So because I was working that day from a site that gave me a perfect view, and because the pressure had been reduced by having tipped and backed a runner whose failure was already both accepted and accounted for, I was fairly relaxed for once. And, maybe, better for that.

After describing the action in my area I rattled through the order of the sixteen-horse field as they entered the straight, with Arctic Explorer (Lester Piggott) taking over from Barred Rock (Geoff Lewis); Tenterhooks (Edgar Britt) and Brave Buck (Stan Clayton) were next, followed by Tommy Burns on Ballymoss who was still moving very easily. Last was Malacca III (Serge Boullenger). I recapped the leaders and, with Ballymoss going to the front, called, 'Over to Raymond Glendenning in the grandstand.' Then I blushed scarlet with shock as there was a sudden outburst of spontaneous applause from the crowd round the van. My next day's *Express* copy, reporting Ballymoss's success, was headed: 'Just a canter, claims rider.'

Although Vincent always thought a lot of Ballymoss he hadn't wanted to be 'on' for the Derby because, owing to a stone bruise, the colt's preparation had been interrupted. But Michael O'Hehir thought we should both have an interest and on the very morning he rang, 24 May, a fortnight before Epsom, I received another call from a rider who had taken part in a mixed gallop at The Curragh in which Ballymoss had created a very favourable impression. Although he was among the '100/1 others', this isn't a rate which bookmakers generally favour laying in great volume. As Bill Hill used to say, 'If you can sell a horse at 6/4, you're a fool to lay 13/8.' I took 100/1, 50/1 and 40/1. Among the more attractive looking vouchers were:

£2500–£25 each-way David Cope
£2500–£25 each-way Ladbroke
£2000–£40 each-way Ladbroke
£1000–£10 each-way Jack Woolf
£1000–£10 each-way D. Upex
£1000–£10 each-way Albert Williams

Ballymoss wasn't a horse who attracted much attention. At the paddock side on the day of the race I heard the high-pitched voice of the *Sporting Life*'s Colonel Tom Nickalls noting, 'That's a damned nice-looking horse, Ballymoss. I've never heard of him.' The unheard of 33/1 chance looked all set to achieve extravagant reward for his sparse band of followers when striking the front two furlongs out. Then Lester changed gear on Crepello and we settled gratefully for the 25/1 a place.

Tommy Burns, who had ridden a fine race in what was a pretty rough event to be second on Vincent's first Epsom Derby runner, had no problem whatever in landing the odds (9/4 on) in The Curragh equivalent on 26 June. After his further exemplary partnership of John McShain's colt in the Leger, Tommy was beaten on him in the Champion Stakes after Ballymoss had lashed out and struck the parade ring rails beforehand. Although I got Scobie Breasley his first ride for Vincent (Lester too, come to that), I thought it tough of the owner to replace the quiet Irishman with Scobie soon afterwards – especially since Vincent wrote on 23 October 1957, when enclosing a four-figure cheque in settlement for Newmarket, 'Thinking over Ballymoss's running, I do not think there can be any doubt that his poor showing was due to the shock he must have got as a result of kicking the rails.'

The second betting drama I had with Vincent over Ballymoss occurred before the following year's Arc de Triomphe, and followed the Doncaster pattern. The Bois de Boulogne circuit was no drier than the adjacent Seine. 'Any hope of laying off my bet?' inquired Vincent despairingly. There wasn't. Rae paddled into the weighing-room to advise Scobie to swim round the inside. He did so, and halfway up the Longchamp straight the winner of that season's Eclipse, Coronation Cup and King George VI and Queen Elizabeth Stakes accelerated like a power boat to give his barely recognizable mud-spattered partner his first victory in France.

As the torrential rain continued to soak victor and vanquished impartially, Vincent agreed that the Laurel International – five weeks away – would be the next and final appearance of the product of a flat-sided chestnut mare, Indian Call, whom breeder Richard Ball had bought in the bloodstock bargain basement for fifteen guineas at Lord Glanely's dispersal. So on Tuesday evening, 4 November, we were sitting in the plane, enjoying a glass of wine and discussing the obstacles that might lie ahead for Ballymoss and his year-junior stable companion, Tharp, before retiring to our respective sleeping compartments. Yes, they had couchettes in those days, like the Orient Express. When we reached New York the following day I had to forgo the connection down to Baltimore or I'd have missed the deadline for copy, which had to be telegraphed from the airport. The piece concerned Ballymoss's antipathy to ponies, and ended with a footnote: 'Quick Approach is expected to run well at Liverpool'.

The tip for Quick Approach – who won by eight lengths at 100/30 – was inspired by Vincent, who sent the horse to the Newmarket Sales, where he was bought by Fred Rimell on behalf of a Kinnersley patron for 6000 guineas. The horse had won four for Ballydoyle and was to win another twenty for Fred; his last success was achieved on 13 May 1967 as a sixteen-year-old at Devon and Exeter, where he won cleverly, ridden by Terry Biddlecombe, giving over a stone to his nearest rival.

Typically, Fred and Mercy kept him in comfort until, aged twenty-nine, it was kinder to put him down on the premises. As Mercy Rimell says so rightly, 'When they have lived their lives in a five star hotel it is wrong for them to be relegated to inferior conditions.' Further it is shamefully wrong for a sensitive thoroughbred to be subjected to the final ordeal of an alien abattoir, where his cash value is so much greater than the carcase of a horse who has been despatched among familiar sights and scents, in order to appease the greed/ignorance of trainer/owner. While the majority of trainers are both caring and responsible, I would like proper safeguards to be a condition of receiving a licence. And I would not be overcome with grief were the watery-eyed predators who infest the minor bloodstock sales, waiting to gather up the cheap ones and transport them to misery in appalling conditions, to be inhibited in their unlovely trade.

After sending my offering from the airport I'd grabbed a cab in time to make New York's Jamaica Track (since closed), and later cabled a requested piece to Features, to which they gave the full treatment. To my dismay the piece evoked the response from Ted Pickering (later Sir Edward), who was in charge at the time:

NOV 7 PM 2 03

AW810 WRD197 EXP5 LONDON 16 7 649PM

PRESS PETER OSULLEVAN MAYFLOWER HOTEL WASHINGTONDC

07183 NOTHING BETTER SINCE RUNYON WROTE ABOUT THE

DERBY

    PICKERING

07183

Laurel was a sharp track all right – it reminded me a bit of Staines – but its pioneering president, John D. Schapiro, who made such a significant contribution to international racing, had sure assembled the ingredients of an entertaining event. Covering it was no sinecure. I'd had a severe reaction from the obligatory inoculation and little opportunity to catch up with the five hours' time differential between GMT and Eastern Standard Time. TV cameras were to relay the race for the first time, and I was to record a commentary which would be flown back to London with the film. A US camera crew filmed interviews which were recorded daily at morning work and during afternoon racing. I had to get up at 5 o'clock every morning in Washington to drive to the Maryland circuit, where track work was the most enjoyable and informative feature of the day; then back to Washington after breakfast to write and transmit copy and do a piece at the BBC radio studio where the Corporation's very nice man in charge was Gerald Priestland.

In contrast to the US horses, who were out of their barn for little over ten minutes in the morning, the Russian trainer Eugeni Gottleib, an unmistakable horse enthusiast, kept his duo out in the crisp, invigorating, autumnal air for at least three-quarters of an hour, evoking the caustic local reaction: 'Those horses will be just dead meat come post time.' It would not be very diplomatic to include this quote, I decided, when sending a first Laurel communiqué to the sports desk:

Russians worry over Ballymoss
Laurel (Maryland), Thursday

WITH a gay wave to early morning bystanders, the respective riders of Russian hopes Garnyr and Zaryad, Messrs Nikolai Nasimov and Viktor Kovalev, stepped out on to the Laurel sand track to breeze the products of Soviet horse-factory No. 33.

In the past few days the locals have not been vastly impressed by the visitors from behind the Iron Curtain. But largely I suspect because of their unfamiliar work tactics.

This morning for the first time, the Russian pair were equipped with aluminium plates, in which they walked a mile and then completed a quick zip around the seven furlong track.

Russian trainer, Eugeni Gottleib, is satisfied that the 5,500-mile journey has taken little out of his charges. He says frankly that the change of food can be no disadvantage to the horses since it is so similar to the home menu.

He adds that he personally is very happy with the steaks he's getting on his visit.

The big query

Of course, I had to get around to the 64,000-dollar question: 'What do you think of your chances of coming out on top in next Tuesday's International?'

To which he replied, as you would expect: 'There is no way of comparing the form in one part of the world and another. Only the race will show.'

Then he went on with the query which is on everybody's lips: 'This Ballymoss. Is he a truly great horse?' . . .

In deference to the European horses, who were not then familiar with starting stalls, Vancouver-born Eddie Blind (who retired aged seventy-three after starting twenty-eight Laurel Internationals) had the unenviable task of despatching the ten-horse field by flag. My responsibilities were somewhat more mundane, but dependent for fulfilment on Mr Blind effecting despatch at official post time, 15.45 Eastern Standard or 20.45 GMT. John Schapiro had kindly assigned to me a phone in his bureau; the *Express* would call me on it at 9.10 their time, twenty minutes after the off, so that I'd have plenty of time, theoretically, to put over the story of the race with quotes, odds, and all relevant details. As soon as possible after the commentary I was to do a filmed interview with Scobie, win or lose, for the BBC.

The razzmatazz which preceded the star attraction, seventh race on the card, made the fairground hubbub of Epsom on Derby Day positively sombre by comparison. The appreciation of the 40,276 paying customers may not have been fully shared by the contestants, several of whom were near boiling point by the time the polyglot assembly had come under the jurisdiction of Eddie Blind. They were supposed to walk up in a perfect line abreast and, at the drop of the flag, surge forward in unison. As one false start succeeded another the crowd became as restive as the horses. Determined to do credit to Soviet horse factory No. 33, Zaryad and Viktor Kovalev repeatedly broke the ragged ranks, hotly pursued, on one occasion, by Venezuela's Escribano. As the minutes ticked by my anxiety increased, but personal concern was nothing compared with the situation of the NBC producer, who had to be off air at 16.02. Germany's Orsini II, patience exhausted, staged an impromptu rodeo show to the apparent total unconcern of Lester, who was instructed to move him from the favoured number two starting position to the far outside before one of his twin barrel kicks connected. When the track caller, Ray Haight, informed the multitude, a little superfluously, that 'Eddie Blind with his black homburg and red flag is having trouble with these horses', the producer yelled at the operator of camera number one, 'Go in on the man in the red hat with the black flag.'

My watch showed just after five minutes to four (barely fifteen minutes to copy time) when Mr B. finally released them beyond recall, with the over-eager Zaryad now hopelessly left. Tudor Era broke smartly, followed by Sailor's Guide, and the duo were to be front rankers throughout. The autumn sun was low in the Maryland sky and shining directly into the riders' faces as they raced down the home straight on the first circuit. The inside was defined by a hedge rather than the customary rail, and as Orsini made the clubhouse turn he struck the shrubbery, raising a cloud of dust and twigs, and bounced off it into Ballymoss who, in turn, did no favours to Clem.

It continued to be that sort of race, and when calling Tudor Era the winner from Sailor's Guide and Ballymoss I warned that there might be an objection. Unless my binoculars or eyesight were seriously defective, Tudor Era's rider, Willie Harmatz, had slammed his closest pursuer into the hedge in the vital stages. Eddie Arcaro had had as good a view as anybody of action in the front line, and when he pulled up fourth on Tharp he called over to young Howard Grant, 'Claim a foul, boy, claim a foul.' Already seething with indignation, Sailor's Guide's partner needed little encouragement. Without consulting the runner-up's Australian connections he steamed into the weighing-room and lodged his protest. Tudor Era was already supporting a kaleidoscope of floral tributes and Mrs Herbert Herff, from Memphis, Tennessee, had her arms outstretched to receive the trophy from the Governor of Maryland when the buzz of the crowd was suddenly silenced by the public address announcement of jockey Grant's action.

The stewards retired to the 'motion picture room', and I bolted for the phone. Midway through relaying a story which wrote itself but would require adjustment once the outcome of the protest was known, Bob Findlay interrupted and I learnt, with misgiving, that 'news' were very excited and wished to lead the front page with it. I say I had misgivings because the strident, nuance-free page one treatment invariably made me squirm. I broke off to find out the result of the inquiry, but the stewards were still deliberating. Then, just as I was heading back to the phone, it came. Twenty-five minutes after being hailed the winner, Tudor Era was demoted in favour of Sailor's Guide. And all hell broke loose. The Herffs' hero, who had been bred and raced in England before export, had an excellent record at Laurel and a consequent strong local following. The punters, who staked a record $2,645,834 during the afternoon, had sent him off a warm third favourite.

American horseplayers tend to disgruntle more readily than their British counterparts, and while Tudor Era's supporters were clearly displeased, many Sailor's Guide backers were frantic. In the interest of domestic harmony track attenders prefer to avoid crowding their pockets with valueless Mutual tickets, and there ensued a hectic scramble for recovery of those associated with the new winner. Punters who weren't searching were booing. This is how the front page of the *Express* looked on 12 November 1958:

DAILY EXPRESS

WEDNESDAY NOVEMBER 12 1958   Price 2½d.

Peter O'Sullevan, only British daily newspaper racing expert on the spot, tells of the most dramatic finish ever

BIG RACE SENSATION

OBJECTION TO U.S. WINNER TUDOR ERA	*SO, SAILOR'S GUIDE IS FIRST*	*BALLYMOSS COMES IN THIRD*

Uproar greets the result

I WATCHED today the most dramatic end to an international horse race I have ever seen.

The crowd of 40,000, warmed by the Maryland sun, is still booing the result.

1. SAILOR'S GUIDE   (8—1),
2. TUDOR ERA   (13—2),
3. BALLYMOSS   (11—10).

John McShain quit the scene without a word to the favourite's jockey, who never wore his white, red and black colours again. Scobie, who had exclaimed before our filmed interview, 'It was bloody rough out there', was diplomatically reserved once recording began. It was an invitation race and all horses, owners, trainers, lads and jockeys were guests of the executive. He could not say for sure that the clubhouse turn crash as well as further interference in the backstretch had made the difference between success and failure. John Hislop, then writing for the *Observer* and the only other British racing reporter present, expressed the view that Ballymoss might have trained off, and he said it before the race. John was champion amateur rider thirteen times, riding 102 winners on the level and 48 under NH rules. He rode 150 more winners than I did, is a distinguished author and surely a better judge of a horse than I. But his was a very lone voice. Every US turf writer thought the O'Brien-trained champion looked great and moved likewise. Scobie thought he was better than ever before the contest, and such a connoisseur as George D. Widener pronounced him in magnificent condition.

'Sadly,' wrote the *Morning Telegraph*'s Charles Hatton, 'it was just a messed up race. Maybe Peter O'Sullevan has a point with his suggestion of a tape start.' (It was adopted in 1959.) Meanwhile Tudor Era's rider, Willie Harmatz, received twenty days' suspension for shutting off Sailor's Guide entering the stretch.

At 5.30 on Wednesday morning I received a call from London asking me to send a follow-up to Tuesday's big race story. I'd dined with Lester and Noel and Gwen Murless the previous evening, and my copy went like this:

I saw jockeys fight – Piggott

Laurel (Maryland), Wednesday

BY SIX o'clock local time on the evening of November 11 the horseplayers had departed from the Laurel Racecourse, scene of the seventh anticlimactic running of the seventh International.

They departed leaving a sea of uncashable Mutual tickets and the melancholy atmosphere of a party which promised to be so successful but which did not quite work out. Only 48 hours before had we not heard the representatives of the seven competing countries each expressing the pious hope that such an event would play a permanent part in furthering international relations?

The Russian Ambassador, whom I met at the Irish Embassy, stressed the point, particularly the point that the Russian horsemen themselves were received with almost overwhelming hospitality by the warm-hearted American people.

For the parade before the big race, which was preceded by national anthems by massed bands, scarlet-tunicked girls, and, in fact, almost everything bar a strip-tease display, it was the Russian horses that attracted the greatest volume of applause.

The introductions were fine but the cordiality was soon replaced by frustration as the starter, unaided by the European-style starting barrier, attempted the unaccustomed feat of despatching the competitors from a walk-up flag start.

Too eager

Twenty-four-year-old ex-farm hand Viktor Kovalev, who became a jockey 'because I like horses', was determined that 'his' Zaryad, with whom he obviously formed an affectionate partnership, would not be left.

It was over-eager Viktor who repeatedly broke the tattered line.

And then, chaos having been reduced to disorder, it was the Russian cavalier who was hopelessly left.

His mount had been unintentionally held over-long by an over-zealous official accustomed, no doubt, to American-type starting stalls which are dispensed with out of courtesy to visitors who are unacquainted with the contrivance.

Who was to convince the accordion-playing jockey from the Kuban area that this was not a dark capitalist plot? Viktor, to his credit, having sounded off in incomprehensible but understandable terms, later declared that he believed it was an accident.

Of course it was an accident. But if Laurel is to have a European-style start a European-style gate must be installed.

The race was rough. Lester Piggott, dining later with Noel Murless, who flew 2000 miles from Arizona to view the contest, declared: 'Two jocks in front of me were having a fight going to the first bend.'

Hedge rail

Exaggerated hairpin bends obviously tend to promote over-intensive rivalry. The inside running rail is a hedge in which Scobie Breasley once nearly left his near-side boot.

The outcome was finally determined by an objection which 'amazed' the Australian Dibb family, who 'would not have dreamed of objecting in an International'.

Which is not to deny that young Howard Grant was doubtless fully entitled to do so.

But the Laurel executive who conceived this bold and felicitous idea is not unaware of the simple fact that the party must be held in a larger room.

Imaginative track extensions are way beyond the blueprint stage and will, in fact, be fully completed by 1960.

So if your horse gets an invitation from Laurel Park one day don't be deterred by the fact that 'even Ballymoss got cramp.'

Granted those larger premises, this party should not be missed.

I had a flight out of Washington the following morning which would get me back in time to learn colours for Cheltenham. Then, when I phoned copy, they told me, 'Lord Beaverbrook wishes to see you and will await your visit in New York at his apartment at 5.45 tomorrow [Thursday].'

Trying to serve two masters had raised problems before and would do so again, though seldom more critically. 'I hope this isn't too inconvenient,' said my host with a warm handshake. I remembered Jacob Epstein having said that when the Canadian tycoon visited his studio for a sitting, he brought a secretary who read to him every word in his papers. Racing might not have been Lord Beaverbrook's favourite topic since Lord Rosebery persuaded him to take up ownership – with short-lived and unrewarding results. If he's read my stuff, I reflected, he'll have been bored beyond endurance. But, remarkably, it was a couple of drinks later that he made me an offer which, under normal circumstances, only a lunatic would refuse. He must have forgiven me for doing so because eighteen months later, after TV commentating the 1960 Derby, I received the following charming message:

FROM LORD BEAVERBROOK

95, ARLINGTON HOUSE,
LONDON, S.W.1.

June 2nd, 1960

Dear Peter,

I heard your television story of the

Derby.

It was a wonderful effort and I do

congratulate you most warmly.

I could hear every word of your narrative.

And that is a compliment for old men don't hear as

clearly as youngsters.

Don't bother to reply to t is letter.

It is what you call a fan letter.

Yours sincerely,

Peter O'Su..levan, Esq.,
Daily Express,
121 Fleet Street,
London, E.C.4.

For the record, the Laurel executive announced on 1 December 1958 that the eighth running of the International, on 11 November 1959, would be held over 'a new turf course'. The circumference of the track to be increased by a furlong; the front and back stretches widened to eighty feet; the turns to be a hundred feet wide and well banked; a new finish line to be introduced for the big race, lengthening the run in considerably, and the hedge which formerly represented the inside running rail to be replaced by an aluminium rail. The inside turf to be preserved specifically for the International runners, which will be started by European-type tapes instead of the walk-up. Repatriated after failing to reproduce his positively brilliant Newmarket homework in public, Nasrullah's son Bald Eagle won the next two runnings of the Laurel Prize with impressive ease.

CHAPTER 16

In Memoriam

'Oh, my God!' exclaimed the racegoer beside me in the Epsom stand. 'He's dead.' George Moore, the Sydney champion, was lying prone in my colours, two hundred yards from the winning post. A St John's Ambulance man was running towards him. Seconds earlier the Australian whom Sir Noel Murless reckoned 'one of the greatest jockeys in the world', was making what looked like a winning challenge on my grey filly Chinchilla when the saddle suddenly spun round her slender frame and he was catapulted into unresilient turf.

George was first jockey to Alec Head this season, 1959, and they'd made a great start with the fluid-actioned Taboun in the 2000 Guineas – doing any O'Sullevan readers a good turn in the process. During an annual winter break in Switzerland I always spent a little après-ski time preparing imminent stables tour material and learning colours of the entrants for Cheltenham's more nightmarish events, like the Foxhunters and NH Chase. Alec had advised that Taboun should not be lightly opposed despite defeat by Hieroglyph in the Coventry.

When I saw the colt in March, he looked terrific, and a 33/1 interest ('Sure to show good hedging – granted survival') was firmly recommended. Taboun, who had been brought up on the bottle following the premature death of his mother, was not well disposed towards humans in general but would do anything for his devoted Arab lad, Ababsa. While other Chantilly residents were still wearing winter coats, Ababsa's pride shone like polished mahogany. He won his prep race, the Prix Djebel, by three lengths and, starting 5/2 favourite, had the Guineas won at the Bushes.

Now George was to ride the Derby favourite, Princillon, for the stable. Alec also had Telemaque in the Craven Stakes on the first day of the meeting, and George, who had never ridden Epsom, wanted to get the feel of the course before partnering him. Ken Gethin couldn't do the weight in the Mynne Selling Stakes without drastic wasting, so Chinchilla seemed the ideal opportunity. Not much bigger than a rabbit – I'd upset my friend Bertie Kerr who'd bought her, by writing that on arrival at Cyril Mitchell's she got out of an empty horsebox – she'd run very respectably in a similar event at Lingfield, and looked to have a good chance. Cyril had remarked, when collecting the tack, that he didn't like elastic girths, but George reassured him that he'd never had any bother with them.

While Alec and I were running anxiously down the course, George, to our intense relief, was already getting up and dusting himself off. 'Sorry,' he said, fingering a dented skullcap, 'I didn't mean to feel the course with my head.' He added, in case it was any consolation – which I wasn't too sure about – that he thought she was sure to have won. As it was, the poor girl, frightened by the flapping equipment, careered on into the paddock and collided with a clearly shocked Telemaque, who was being led into a saddling stall. 5/4 favourite, he was beaten by the outsider of three. 'Not satisfied with nearly killing my jockey,' complained Alec not too seriously, 'you try to finish off my horse as well!'

In what appeared to be a less than trouble-free Derby, Princillon, whom I tipped each way, confessing to little confidence, finished seventh behind Parthia. During the following day's report I commented:

Since post-race interviews followed the pattern of Grand National post mortems (with riders claiming, 'I was on the floor at the end of half a mile' . . . 'Mine was clouted right out of the race,' etc.) it was appropriate that the rider of a National winner, Bruce Hobbs, should have played no small part in securing Parthia's presence. For had not Captain Boyd-Rochfort's assistant caught Parthia, when the horse got loose in the vast paddock beforehand, the winner might have been in Epsom Town instead of on Epsom Downs at Derby time.

Undoubtedly the unlucky horse of the race was Shantung. Freddy Palmer explained: 'Mine and Princillon were nearly down when horses converged on us after half a mile. Shantung was struck into and I thought he'd broken a leg, so almost pulled him up.' Yet Baron Guy de Rothschild's good-looker ran on to deprive Saint Crespin of third place on the line. So that, once again, a first jockey picked the wrong one.

This was a reference not only to George having switched from Saint Crespin a week earlier, but also to Lester Piggot having chosen Collyria (unplaced) in preference to successful stable companion Petite Etoile, in the 1000 Guineas, and then having opted for Dame Melba instead of Park Hill winner Collyria at Doncaster. After this I recall him saying, 'I dunno, I might as well go and have a fourpenny ice cream. Want one?'

Reverting to the Derby report, during which Roger Poincelet (on Dan Cupid), was quoted ('I was just knocked to hell'), as was Doug Smith ('A very rough ride on Above Suspicion'), I related that 'Aly Khan, one

of the first to congratulate Sir Humphrey de Trafford, would like to
have kept Saint Crespin for the French Derby. The reason he didn't was
"Because he had been ante-post favourite for so long and I thought it
would be unfair to the public".'

That was typical Aly. And it was a shock to all who relished both his
racing involvement and his infectious *joie de vivre* when the elder son
of Sultan Sir Mahomed Shah, Aga Khan III, and an Italian ballet dancer
was killed in a Paris car crash on the night of Thursday, 12 May 1960.
The following morning I was summoned to the office to write a feature,
with the brief, 'Let it run. You can have all the space you want.' (I tend
to panic first, fearing insufficient material, and then to overwrite.)

Aly would often ring to discuss horses, bets and, before he died in
1957, the father he greatly admired and whose pragmatic approach to
life included the employment of a wise Persian to give his offspring
sophisticated sexual instruction at an appropriate age. Once the media
has typecast an individual, the role is immutable. Aly was represented
exclusively as a playboy – which, of course, he was. But not exclusively.
I hoped to illustrate the point in a tribute to a man who had the natural
gift of making everyone with whom he came in contact feel better for
the encounter.

This did not automatically apply in my case, since I was at pains to
avoid striking bets on his behalf unless they could be recorded in his
name, with one of the firms with which he was currently in credit, or
in my own – provided George Criticos held requisite funds to cover the
wager. Crete-born George, *concièrge* of the London Ritz and universal
confidant, was the repository of more secrets than MI5, and a lot less
leak-prone. 'Mr Peter,' George would say. 'The Prince has no got more
than a thousand pound here. You tell him that is enough to bet or we
all go skint.' Like so many people, George was shattered by the tragic
news.

I wrote my piece, conscious of inadequacy, but feeling that, if it was
printed as submitted, I needn't feel ashamed. Pressure on space means
that there are very few journalists whose copy appears without a degree
of trimming. It certainly wasn't a status I ever attained, and I was well
into my racing piece for the day, and intending to ask Features kindly
to leave in certain paragraphs in my Aly story, when there was a call
from the Editor's office. That's nice, I thought – if a rewrite's required
I'll go mad. Ted Pickering, dark-suited, owlish behind tortoiseshell
specs, more senior Foreign Office than the popular image of a shirt-
sleeved Editor, stood up courteously and waved me into a black leather
armchair. 'I've been reading your Aly story,' he beamed, 'and I just
wanted to tell you it's great stuff, great.' The relief. It was like hearing
'Objection overruled' when you've just backed a 10/1 winner. I

explained that I was going to ask Features to retain certain paras which reflected the subject in an unfamiliar light; but Pick could not envisage any pruning whatsoever. Well, he's the Editor, I figured, so I went home happy, without bothering.

I should have appreciated that an editor generally leaves each department to get on with its own production, which is, inevitably, subject to swift-changing pressures. The next day the following article appeared – one-third of my submission had been cut out, and every favoured paragraph eliminated:

My luck may be running out
Aly Khan told me under the chestnut trees at Longchamp last Sunday

WHEN Aly Khan crashed finally and fatally in a Paris suburb on Thursday night there ended one of the most consuming love affairs of the century – between Aly Khan and life.

The "Golden Prince" of the headlines loved and was loved by many women of course. But it was his passionate, restless, zest for living that was his outstanding characteristic. That made him the compelling personality he was.

"I'll be with you at 11 o'clock at the Travellers' if I can make it," he told a friend during that Thursday afternoon of what was to be his last day's racing.

Not that Aly was a member of the staid Travellers' Club in Paris. He did not care much for men's clubs. Though he always said he wouldn't turn down an offer to join a women's club.

His "date" was to play bridge, which he liked to play for as high stakes as possible at the time, until three or four a.m., without a cigarette or a drink.

At 17 . . .

"If I can make it," he had said. But nobody worried when he didn't. For he would change his course in a second. Like the time nine years ago when, having persuaded his second wife Rita Hayworth to overcome her fear of air travel and fly to Nairobi immediately, she arrived to find a note saying he had left for a week's hunting in the jungle.

What was the source of this compelling restlessness and need for speed? Maybe the lack of home life from the time at the age of 15 when his mother, Theresa Magliano, an Italian ballet dancer, died. Aly never went to school.

"Stables were my school," he said. And it was as a 17-year-old that, with his father's jockey Michael Beary, he started to visit Dick Dawson's stables at Marlborough and began to accumulate the knowledge which was to serve him so well both as a rider (he rode more than 100 winners) and in the direction of what became the world's greatest racing empire. An empire founded on 14 stud farms in five countries which produced stakes winners of a record quarter of a million pounds in 1959.

Records

There was no need for Aly to gamble – no need for speed. But from the day of his 21st birthday, when he immediately bought an Alfa-Romeo, he set about establishing personal records.

From the Ritz to Newmarket (over 60 miles) in an hour. From Paris to Deauville (130 miles) – in 89 minutes.

I knew Aly well on the racecourse, attended his glittering parties in Paris when he always had time for everybody. But let's face it, only his women and his horses really knew him.

I remember many of the fantastic gambles in which he took such impish delight. And which caused him no slight embarrassment at times.

Like the year 1955 when he left Epsom (where one of his bets was £9,000–£4,000 on his winning two-year-old Palariva) with a credit of £26,000. Only to be showing a loss of £32,000 by the end of Ascot.

"Please don't report the figures, Peter, not till I'm dead, anyway," said Aly laughingly in the Newmarket paddock in 1957 as he flourished a voucher from his bookmaker, Jack Wilson Ltd., of Dover Street, London, showing a bet of £12,000–£2,000 each way Rose Royale and £20,000–£1000 each way Sensualita after the horses had finished first and second in the 1000 Guineas.

His father's horse won, his own was second. And he was genuinely happy that they finished in that order.

Ironic

In the middle of a bad run – a run which necessitated stripping the walls of all his pictures in his Paris house not long ago – he would ask Mr. "Beau" Goldsmith, managing director of Jack Wilson Ltd.: "Please hang on until Christmas, I'll have money then."

And, contrary to rumour, "he always paid every penny," said Mr. Goldsmith last night.

"I've always been lucky," Aly observed to me beneath the chestnut trees at Longchamp last Sunday as he fidgeted restlessly with the clothes he wore as though they were a tiresome restriction on activity, "but my luck may be running out this season."

He liked to bet a long way ahead to prove to himself his judgment. He was referring to Charlottesville, a horse in whom he had invested £2,000 for the Derby. And which had met with a setback which looked like preventing him running.

Death cancels ante-post bets. And only Aly Khan would have gaily appreciated the irony of the so sad fact that he had to die to get out of his last bet.

When so much that one has wanted to say is suppressed, it is difficult to evaluate what remains. Personally, I felt that I had betrayed a friend, so it was particularly comforting to hear from Vi Aitken (wife of the chairman of Beaverbrook Newspapers), who wrote:

FROM:
MRS. MAX AITKEN, THE GARDEN HOUSE, CHERKLEY, LEATHERHEAD, SURREY
LEATHERHEAD 3162

16ᵗʰ May 1960

Dear Peter -

How very well you wrote about Aly in the Daily Express - I thought that it was exactly right - warm, friendly and extremely perceptive. I hope that you don't mind me writing to you and saying so - but I was so horrified by the Evening Standard the night before - and was longing for someone to write about him who really knew him.

I think that a lot of people are going to miss him very much - he had many, many friends here - mainly because he himself was such a good friend.

I know that I, for one, will never have a better one -

Yours,
Vi

CHAPTER 17

An Irish Volcano

To connoisseurs of unquenchable, unbridled enthusiasm among train-ers, Paddy ('Darkie') Prendergast was top of the handicap with 7 lb in hand of his great English counterpart, Ryan Price. And that, believe me, was going some. As one of The Curragh maestro's owners, Bing Crosby, once observed to me in his dry, off-beat, manner, 'After listening to Paddy talk about your horse for two minutes, you just had to feel real sorry for the opposition.' Or as another transatlantic proprietor, Max Bell, put it, 'As soon as I've called Paddy and discussed prospects I spend the purse!' Every year from 1950 onwards, before visiting the Prendergast team during my March stables tour, I'd remind myself not to get too carried away and launch into an ante-post speculating spree. Every year 'Darkie' would present his new collection with the panache of a ringmaster, the pride of a perfectionist. In every box there was a burnished crock of gold, and I'd fall – like a novice at Becher's.

Atty Persse, who both bought (1300 guineas) and handled the 'spotted wonder', The Tetrarch, reckoned that 'good trainers are born, not made'. Paddy was born thirty-two years before he requested and was granted a trainer's licence by the Irish Turf authorities in 1941. A failed jump jockey, as he would readily acknowledge, he had unsuccess-fully tried his luck in Australia, and later obtained work with the Epsom trainer Harry Hedges, for whom Fet, ridden by Midge Richardson, landed a Cesarewitch gamble in 1936. Paddy was still working for Harry on and off, and odd-jobbing in Epsom, at the outbreak of World War II, when he returned to Kildare. 'He'd no money,' recalls his pal Mick Connolly, who had begun training at The Curragh in 1939, 'and was as near to the floor as a man can get. Yet when Cecil Boyd-Rochfort wrote, offering him a job as head lad, he tore up the letter, saying, "Maybe Boyd-Rochfort will be applying for a job with me one day."'

While Paddy was cycling through Newbridge to his rented boxes, a bale of hay on the handlebars, a yearling who was to be his meal ticket for nearly a decade was attracting minimal attention in Goff's sale ring at Ballsbridge. By Sea Serpent out of Dinah's Daughter, he was knocked down to Kerr & Co. for 30 guineas on Tuesday, 30 September 1941. Paddy bought the chestnut gelding, named Pelorus, from Bertie Kerr for £200 on behalf of one of his first patrons. From then on whatever the season, whatever the going, whenever required, Pelorus was there, ready to assume responsibility for redressing the shortcomings of others and to sustain the Prendergast *équipe*. Towards the end of an honourable career, on 26 November 1949 in the Troytown Chase at Navan, he was one of five winning rides for Martin Molony in the five races open to professional jockeys. The other event went to Mr Pat Taaffe. Twelve months later the versatile ten-year-old was back on the level winning the Naas November Handicap.

Top jockeys are best placed to evaluate a trainer's skills. Lester Piggott says of Paddy Prendergast, 'There's no doubt he was a great trainer. His horses knew what to do, like Staff's [Ingham], they ran straight because they'd been properly taught.' During my visit in 1954, when Paddy was banned from running horses in England for most of the season, I remember being surprised to see one of his classic hopes, Moonlight Express (six lengths winner of the previous year's Convivial at York), working in a wide circle on The Curragh, and quoting him saying, 'They learn a lot more that way than galloping in a straight line.'

By the time the war ended 'your man' was flying at home and set to fire a salvo or so across the Irish Sea. First of a steady stream of raiders was a 350 guineas Denturius filly, Port Blanc, who, ridden by Michael Beary, won Goodwood's Harvest Stakes by four lengths, head in chest, on Friday, 30 August 1946. By 1951 I was reporting from 'The biggest stable in England and Ireland – the 85 horse-power team of Paddy Prendergast' (Walter Nightingall's 73-horse Epsom stable was the largest in England), and drawing attention to a 700 guineas youngster who would make a gale-force wind appear sluggish by comparison. Named Windy City, he was owned by the most colourful and entertaining American in the horse-hustling business, Ray Bell, whose leathery countenance cracked into a Grand Canyon-wide smile when Paddy told him, 'There isn't a two-year-old foaled who could blow wind up this fella's tail.' He'd heard it all before.

But Paddy was right. Following his sensationally easy five lengths success in Chester's Oulton Stakes, there were those who doubted whether, in view of his exceptional speed, the son of Wyndham would handle the extra furlong of the Gimcrack. Ridden by Gordon Richards, he won that by five as well and, not surprisingly, headed the Free Handicap. Ray flew him to the States at the season's close and sold the 700 guineas yearling for $165,000. Injured while running second in the Santa Anita Derby, he was retired to stud.

When Rae Johnstone started training he and I bought a half-sister, Just Windy, who also went like the wind. But only a puff, unfortunately. When we ran her over 4½ furlongs at Compiègne she got four furlongs; when we ran her half a mile in Saint-Cloud's 800 metres Prix Yong Lo on 24 July 1961 she lasted three furlongs. Despite her shortcomings, underlined by continued failure when we sent her to a provincial trainer for a spell, JW's family connection secured comfortable retirement to the eminent stud of Mme Jean Stern.

By 1953 the feature which the *Express* styled 'Peter O'Sullevan's Who's Who in the stables' was recording, 'It's not in accord with tradition for classic winners to be trained in Tipperary, but I'm developing the opinion that with Vincent [O'Brien], one of Ireland's youngest trainers (he's already won four Gold Cups and three Champion Hurdles), almost anything is possible.' And in County Kildare, 'The powerful offensive by 'Darkie' Prendergast's 90-horse team will get under way at Liverpool via The Lotti and Fast Lady. Gordon Richards rides both.' The Lotti got beat; Fast Lady won (4/1).

This was the year in which another Ray Bell juvenile star, The Pie King, who cost 1850 guineas, outshone his contemporaries on his three visits to England, during which he won the Richmond, Coventry and Gimcrack by an aggregate of ten lengths. Sharp stable companion Sixpence also won the Cheveley. But Blue Sail, a 'punt' in the Cornwallis (then run over the Old Mile, at Ascot), despite Tommy Gosling putting up 3 lb overweight, went under by half a length.

Bred for stamina, by Tehran out of a Blue Peter mare, Blue Sail had run twice, unplaced, over six furlongs in Ireland. The Ascot stewards held an inquiry into his form and, unsatisfied by the explanation, referred the matter to the stewards of the Jockey Club. There followed a notice in the *Racing Calendar* to the effect that no further entries would be accepted from P. J. Prendergast. The affair aroused considerable feeling. 'Off the Record' reported, 'It is being said in Ireland that the English are determined to win the Gimcrack themselves for a change.' Both the stewards of the Irish Turf Club and the Irish National Hunt Committee held an exhaustive inquiry, interviewing officials, jockeys and owners from three countries, before satisfying themselves that there was no evidence of any unexplained discrepancy in the running of Blue Sail at Ascot.

The ban had been in force for nearly a year when it was lifted in time for Ireland's leading trainer to mount a five-horse challenge for York's principal fixture. When Prendergast-trained Panalley won the opening race of the meeting, the Prince of Wales's Stakes, Sir Humphrey de Trafford, who had been Senior Steward at the time of the Ascot affair, strode across the unsaddling enclosure and grabbed the trainer's hand, saying, 'Welcome back! Well done, Paddy.' The stable proceeded to win the next, the Nunthorpe, with the Tommy Carter-ridden two-year-old My Beau, and on the following day they took the two-year-old seller through Gipsy Rover (Rae Johnstone) and the Voltigeur with none other than Blue Sail (Bill Rickaby), who stormed clear at the quarter pole and won by a long-looking official ten lengths.

Come 1965 Patrick J. Prendergast had not only trained winners of the English 2000 Guineas, 1000 Guineas, Oaks and St Leger, he had twice been leading trainer under Jockey Club rules and was about to complete the hat-trick. But his obsessive target, the Epsom Derby, continued to elude him. Year after year, transported by his own enthusiasm, by which I was unfailingly contaminated, he would pledge his ante-post support to the most favoured member(s) of the team.

Like in 1952, when I'd arrived late in Dublin from Paris and my phone call interrupted Paddy's poker school. 'Wait now while I go into another room,' he instructed. Then, in a half whisper, 'Be at Baldoyle [racecourse] at eleven o'clock tomorrow morning and I'll show you the Derby winner. Don't tell a soul now, God bless.'

There was time to call in early in the morning at the up-to-date Glencairn stables, seven miles out of the fair city, where Seamus McGrath was the first to introduce electrically operated starting stalls to his complex. He had trained his first winner aged twenty and achieved a personal highlight when turning out Levmoss to win both the Gold Cup and the Arc de Triomphe in 1969. And there would be time after leaving Baldoyle to visit Mick Rogers (Derby winners Hard Ridden in 1958 and Santa Claus in 1964) and still make evening stables at Vincent O'Brien's Ballydoyle, where a feature to this regular tourist was the extent to which the uncrowned King of Cashel had affected the living standard in his area. Within a short while the shed which once housed the bicycles of the stable personnel had become a car port; the fields a private racecourse; the infield a helipad.

'Darkie' had obtained special authority to work Europe's darkest Derby hope – un unraced son of Caracalla II – on Baldoyle's otherwise deserted seaside racecourse. They went a mile and, work completed, the trainer eyed the only other spectators – a flock of uninterested seagulls – suspiciously in case there was a carrier pigeon amongst them. Then he said, 'Right, let's get to the Gresham [the best hotel when Toddy O'Sullivan was the manager] and have a coffee.' The likelihood of an Irish-trained horse winning the Derby at this time was insufficient to inspire terror among the most timid bookmakers. 'Having a coffee' involved my ringing round the firms and taking 200/1 and upwards, and downwards, about Kara-Burnu for the first Wednesday in June. I wrote,

I did not see Orby win the Baldoyle Derby 45 years ago as a prelude to Epsom success, but I doubt if a better horse than Kara-Burnu has printed this seaside turf since. Ridden by 'Corky' Mullane, he fairly sprinted past his four-year-old pacemaker, as well as 'Paddy' Powell-partnered Mardol (an Irish Derby hope) in his first serious spin. His trainer made no secret of his satisfaction afterwards. 'Never,' said his rider, 'have I ridden a horse with such an action.'

Later in the piece I hazarded, cautiously, 'It may be that when Kara-Burnu meets serious public opposition his limitations will be exposed,' adding, 'I'll believe it when I see it.'

Well, I didn't see it, but I had to believe it. Kara-Burnu didn't make it to England at all. There were several in between, but come 1956 dear Paddy had, and I quoted him, 'the best horse I have ever trained'. Which, as I mentioned at the time, were 'powerful words for a man of prodigious achievement'. He was a great big eyeful of horse who had been too backward to do much with as a two-year-old. This was the year in which I was already sold on Lavandin, so I resisted, for once, going overboard with Paddy while backing Al-Mojannah for him to win everything bar the Boat Race. He made his first appearance before the racing public in England, ridden by Lester Piggott, in the Ormonde Stakes at Chester where he finished last. If anything, he ran worse in the Derby, abysmally in Germany afterwards, and ended the season stigmatized by *Timeform* with the uncompromising symbol employed to represent 'an arrant rogue; a thief; a horse so temperamentally unsatisfactory as to be practically worthless for racing purposes'.

While Paddy's Derby luck remained consistently out, he had the last laugh in another sphere in 1960. The *Express* had prefaced that season's stables tour with a series of exuberant 'blurbs'. On my return from holiday to cover the Cheltenham NH Festival, as usual, for the paper and BBC TV, the Champion Hurdle nap, Another Flash, obliged in style. Entirely thanks to my friend and colleague Michael O'Hehir, I had been plugging him since mid-December when he was a 100/6 chance. His achievement inspired a telegram from Sports Editor John Morgan: 'FANTASTIC STOP WHAT A MARVELLOUS RETURN FOR YOUR FANS STOP I KNEW YOU WOULD SAVE MY LIFE STOP ALL MY CONGRATULATIONS AND GRATITUDE MORGAN.'

The form was maintained at Cheltenham, and as I'd been lucky enough to show a nap profit of £71 5s 5d the previous Flat season and for nine of the last ten seasons on the level, there were bullish references to 'king of the naps' and 'now for his unique, inspired stables guide' etc. So when I phoned a fairly positive proposal on behalf of Venture VII in the 2000 Guineas, it received unequivocal display under the heading, 'VENTURE? I RATE IT A CERTAINTY.' I'd written:

If City column colleague Frederick Ellis knows a better investment than 4/1 Venture VII for the 2000 Guineas – we're in the wrong business. Admittedly there are around 250 other hopefuls still holding the engagement – including a pack of unraced star potential – which make the current odds *appear* somewhat cramped. But in this Venture-struck horsefancier's view, Aly Khan's colt has only to remain alive during the ensuing 44 days to the running of the first 1960 classic to collect. And in Venture's present state of exuberant health 4/1 about survival seems fair value.

I'd gone on in this vein for several acres, reinforcing expectation with quotes from Aly Khan, who loved the horse, and from Alec Head who had confessed, 'If one could construct a horse for the Guineas, it would be difficult to create a better model.'

So when I arrived at Keadeen, where Paddy was at the time, he said, with a twinkle in the eye, 'I suppose it's no good showing *you* a 2000 Guineas horse!' He did all the same, telling his man, 'Give him another lick out of the pot' (Paddy was a great man for giving them at least one wooden ladle of Australian honey at evening feed). We stood back to admire the son of Kentucky Derby winner Hill Gail and winner of the 1959 Coventry. He was a really massive individual, and I was pleased to see he looked to have done himself extremely well during the winter. As if reading my thoughts, Paddy said, 'You needn't worry. I'll never get this fella right for Newmarket. But you'd better not be backing Alec's horse to beat him in the St James's.' While Venture won his prep race, the Prix Djebel, by three lengths, Martial was beaten by the same margin in the Thirsk Classic Trial. When they went to post for the big one, Venture VII was 6/4 favourite, Martial 18/1.

The race wasn't one of my favourite TV broadcasts. By this time Peter Bromley had moved over to 'Sound' and was covering the first half of the race for radio before handing over to Raymond Glendenning, who was sited in an absurdly positioned rabbit hutch on the first-floor roof of the Tattersalls Grandstand. I'd worked from there pre-TV and knew it to be impossible since the flat roof totally obscured horses finishing on the stands rails. When Peter Dimmock secured the contract for TV I insisted that I must be allowed to operate from the sometimes gale-swept main roof, from which there was a magnificent view of the course. This was strenuously resisted by the Newmarket authorities on the grounds of safety, but ultimately acceded to upon the assurance that the body, if swept from the site, would fall on the second roof, some forty feet below, rather than on the public. The riggers lashed down a tarpaulin night watchman's shelter as a commentary box and tied a rope between it and the distant trap-door access, for clutching in unfavourable weather.

Typically, a fine, permanent, wooden commentary box, for which I had been nagging and submitting blueprints since 1956, had only lately been completed when BBC TV lost the contract in 1968. And how did they lose it? Clerk of the course Pat Firth and Jockey Club agent Robert Fellowes were invited to London by Peter Dimmock to discuss the future at a time when the agreement was due for renewal. 'I remember the occasion well,' recalls Pat Firth. 'Before we sat down to the biggest steaks I had ever seen – in fact before we had sat down at all – Peter Dimmock said, "Well, you boys, I might as well tell you from the outset you're not getting any more money. And that's final." There didn't seem to be a lot to say after that. We reported back to the Board, who had been very happy with BBC coverage and expected it to continue, but who naturally hoped for a favourable revision of fees. Within next to no time ITV had offered more money (£500) and that was that, we signed up.'

Pat, who later took over responsibility for Doncaster, continued, 'When I informed Dimmock, he said, "A pity you didn't come back to me."' Had they done so, Peter related some thirty years later, 'I'd have gone to my bosses and asked for more money.' As it was, his job was to secure contracts on the most favourable terms to the Corporation, and he acted in the belief that there existed a tacit agreement between 'Auntie' and the newcomers to avoid potentially costly competition. To the extent to which this understanding existed it was negated when Commercial went regional, and ultimately BBC cameras were left without an English classic to aim at.

Right now, on 27 April 1960, the producer was concentrating on the Guineas runners on the far side of the course. Filipepi, ridden by Geoff Lewis and drawn fourteen of the seventeen runners, was leading from Red Gauntlet and Tudorich, with Venture tucked in nicely behind them. As the camera switched to a wide angle over the great breadth of the Rowley Mile, Great Faith, Oak Ridge and Martial were prominent on the inner. With a quarter of a mile to run, George Moore gave Venture a little extra rein and, as Geoff Lewis expressed it afterwards, 'I nearly caught pneumonia in the draught as he went by.'

While calling the favourite in front I had a sudden recollection of his lad, Charlie Eva, warning me at Chantilly, 'As soon as he hits the front he goes to sleep.' George's fellow Aussie, Ron Hutchinson, was having his first ride at Newmarket. Peter Bromley had walked the course with him earlier, pointing out the advantage of gaining impetus running into the Dip, and now Ron was scooting along the stands rail on Martial. As Venture applied the brakes, Martial, racing wide apart, lunged for the line and, as the photo confirmed, got up for a head verdict. 'If only he hadn't been left on his own,' was George Moore's despairing post-race comment. But it was some training performance by Paddy to have 'Hutchie's' so well-handled partner in such shape on the day.

The next time the Guineas principals met, in the Sussex Stakes, Venture, admittedly receiving 6 lb, ran all over his Newmarket conqueror. But the bookmakers had long since pocketed the Guineas money. And, at last, BBC radio appreciated the absurdity of their commentary point. Poor Raymond didn't call Martial in the first three.

It was the year in which Paddy's Epsom fortune finally took a more favourable turn that, in a melodramatic Derby — the first televised by the BBC since Thomas Woodruffe and Richard North commentated on it in 1938 — the Prendergast duo, Alcaeus and Kythnos, finished second and third respectively to, of all horses, St Paddy.

As the last race on the previous day was run over the Derby distance, a camera rehearsal was scheduled. I was asked to be *in situ* and to give a commentary without bothering about the content, since the principal object of the exercise was to check camera angles.

The race was the Durdans Handicap, in which I'd napped and supported Apostle, a Staff Ingham-trained runner, ridden by Scobie Breasley. Already haunted for days by dread of some commentary disaster on Wednesday, I welcomed the opportunity for a little light relief. Unaware that, on the eve of the big event, the run-through was being solemnly monitored by a watchful in-house audience in London, I mentioned one horse throughout the one and a half miles. And from the foot of Tattenham Corner, where Scobie's partner, who had been backed from 9/4 to 11/8 favourite, was moving sweetly in third place, I launched into a vociferous repertoire of traditional punter encouragement, yelling, 'Apostle for evens,' as he took up running, and 'Go on, my son . . . not too far . . . what a little beauty . . . good on you, Scobe . . . etc.', rising to a peak of enthusiasm which, I was given to understand, was not fully shared. The producer, Dennis Monger, relayed a message from base to the effect that a marginally less partisan commentary would be appreciated tomorrow.

The classic had been marred by fatal injury to France's hot favourite, Angers, who suffered a multiple fracture on Tattenham Hill and was immediately put down on humane grounds. I had the unenviable task of breaking the sad news to his frail, eighty-year-old American owner, Mrs Ralph Strassburger, in her private box on the West Tier. Her husband 'Strass', a long-time stalwart of French racing, had died a year previously after trying, unsuccessfully, to win the Derby for thirty years. For his widow, Angers's bid was the occasion of her first public appearance since his death.

She left the course heartbroken but, gamely, returned the following year with another favourite in the betting, Moutiers, a half-brother to the family's 1956 runner-up, Montaval. A horse who preferred a right-hand circuit, he gave a fair impression of an uncoordinated crab on the descent to Tattenham Corner, but did at least return unharmed behind the 66/1 winner, Psidium. This result prompted the elder statesman of the turf, Lord Rosebery, to observe, 'It is seventy years since I saw my first Derby, won by Common, and that is the second most surprising result I've witnessed in the period. The biggest shock was the 100/1 winner Signorinetta in 1908.' Lèster, who could have ridden the horse on whom Roger Poincelet improved from twenty-eighth place to first, had declared after riding him behind Moutiers over one and a quarter miles in France, 'He wouldn't get a mile and a half in a horsebox.' I had admitted in my Derby guide that if Psidium won I'd be 'psurprised'. So in response to the happy owner, Etty Plesch's, query 'What are you going to say now?' I wrote contritely, 'Consider me in psackcloth.'

Paddy Prendergast kept going, winning everything except the Derby, in which Cipriani was a creditable fifth in 1961; Pavot, who later won the Queen's Vase, was outpaced in 1962; strongly fancied Ragusa (third) proved best of the stable trio in 1963; and 100/1 chance Dilettante II was also third, behind Santa Claus, in 1964.

Come 1965 the Rossmore Lodge stable, already responsible for the Anglo-Irish stakes-winning record in a season, held a hand of unlimited potential. The ingredients included Jim and Meg Mullion's unbeaten pair, Prominer (National Stakes and Royal Lodge) and Hardicanute, bred by the actor Richard Greene in Ireland, bought for 4700 guineas, successful in the Champagne Stakes and Timeform Gold Cup; Larry Gelb's runaway Duke of Edinburgh Stakes winner, Carlemont; and Meadow Court, a partnership horse between Max Bell, Bing Crosby and Frank McMahon, a handsome son of prematurely exported Court Harwell and winner of the Sandwich Stakes at Ascot. It is four years from conception to Derby day, and the notable quartet shared a common misfortune – they were foaled in the same year as Sea Bird II.

To know Paddy Prendergast was to have relations with a volcano. There can have been no man or woman with whom he was ever associated whom he did not fall out with at some time or another. Our rift occurred in 1965.

CHAPTER 18

Guinness, Garlic and Gremlins

To me one of the most intriguing aspects of touring the stables was the trainers' varied approach to the conditioning and nourishment of the horses in their care. 'Training', said Noel Murless, who believed in Australian oats and Canadian hay, 'is four-fifths experience, one-fifth intuition. And it's the last fifth that counts.' Noel would visit and feed a carrot to every one of his horses at evening stables. François Mathet who, like Noel, started with very modest jumpers, never entered a box unless a horse was ill. 'They look much better inside,' insisted the first hundred-horse trainer in Europe. 'I prefer to see them out.' He regarded '*le coup de la carotte*,' as he termed it, with contempt, and cited a trainer's task as requiring 'the assessment of a horse's aptitude; the need to create a harmony of peak physical and mental fitness; not to over-tax him at home; and not to exhaust him by setting tasks beyond his ability'.

Having started in 1945 with two horses whose aggregate cost was £375, he achieved a record 111 winners in 1958; was leading trainer on the Flat for the sixth successive time in 1962; and the first 200-horse trainer in the world by 1965. He had a horror of owners who wished to visit their horses, never received the local press, and was generally as gregarious as a Trappist monk. Further, although he patronized a London tailor and shoemaker, he was said to dislike the English.

The portents for a prospective interviewer were not wholly favourable when, during my 1952 tour, after leaving Geoff Watson who presided over the Rothschild collection, I spotted the hermit, as some referred to him, in a clearing alongside the main Chantilly workgrounds. I pulled off the road and, with the apprehension of a sacrificial offering hoping to find the lion in benign humour, introduced myself. Monsieur Mathet shook hands courteously enough. He had little to show me (I soon learnt that he seldom admitted to having any horse worth more than a passing interest in his care: when he confessed otherwise, it was worth heeding), but if I wanted to see his second lot they would be along in three minutes. They were, with military precision. In response to my request for a list of his horses – very few of the French stables featured in *Horses in Training* then, and Mathet's never – he invited me to his *bureau* for coffee and arranged for his secretary to send me details. We had an animated exchange (his, 'I thought they only bred cattle in Ireland', kept the conversation going when I was extolling Irish bloodstock) and it became an annual date. By the late fifties the local specialist weekly was printing a translation (an excruciating one effected by a non-racing professor) of our March interviews which appeared in the *Express*. It was through François that readers were on Derby winners Phil Drake (1955) and Relko (1963), and on Bella Paola in the 1958 1000 Guineas and Oaks.

As unorthodox as he was brilliantly successful, François Mathet ridiculed the concept of horses being trained to stay or to sprint. 'They run,' he affirmed, 'according to their inherent capacity, which cannot be changed. Sometimes, of course, superior class enables them to win outside their distance. That has nothing whatever to do with a particular training method.' Although his patience with horses was in direct contrast to his intolerance of people, he was nevertheless responsible for the development of France's greatest jockey, Yves Saint-Martin. Reserved by nature, Mathet surprised me in September 1963 by sending an enthusiastic message following the success of Grey Lag, trained by Rae Johnstone, ridden by Roy Higgins and carrying the O'Sullevan colours in a Chantilly seller on a day I had to be working at Doncaster. Except during a short-lived rupture in June 1976, which is another story, we maintained regular friendly contact for thirty years.

Etienne Pollet's recipe was to restrict his stable complement to fifty; to pamper them with sweet-smelling hay from the deep south and get them up in the dark, if need be, to ensure working on fresh ground. Although he had a fine classics record, his touch with the youngsters was uncanny – in a nine-year sequence he had six winners and four seconds in the Grand Critérium, France's richest two-year-old prize. Right Royal was a fair horse – winning the French Derby and King George VI and Queen Elizabeth Stakes in 1961 – but after visiting the stable for fourteen years, 1965, the year of Sea Bird, was the first in which I'd known him confident of there being a proper three-year-old in the yard. Those of us who experienced the exhilaration of seeing Sea Bird gliding to glory on the four spectacular public appearances of his second season – Prix Lupin, Derby, Grand Prix de Saint-Cloud and Arc de Triomphe – will be lucky indeed to see his equal.

Etienne Pollet did not enthuse readily over horses or jockeys. I always remember his reaction when he rang towards the end of April the following year saying, *'J'ai besoin d'un jockey pour dimanche,'* explaining that this was for a light-mouthed filly in the '1000', and I proposed Scobie Breasley. 'Good heavens,' he exclaimed. 'He's older than you and I added together, isn't he?' Scobie was, in fact, a week off his fifty-second birthday when he rode Right Royal's daughter, Right Away, in the Poule d'Essai des Pouliches. But after winning his first French classic on his first ride for the stable, Scobie earned the comment from the trainer, 'What a fabulous jockey that is!'

Etienne was always good for 'copy', but he reluctantly embargoed a good story in 1968. Vaguely Noble, object of intense competition at the Newmarket sales where he was part of his late owner Major Lionel Holliday's dispersal draft, had recently arrived at the exclusive Chantilly yard, having been bought by agent Albert Yank for a world auction record of 136,000 guineas on behalf of Hollywood plastic surgeon Robert Alan Franklyn. The immensely impressive seven lengths winner of the Observer Gold Cup had no classic engagements and was to be trained for the Arc de Triomphe. The spectacular bloodstock gamble made the son of Vienna the hottest horse news of the moment. After we'd looked him over, a powerful, commanding individual with a charming disposition, Etienne said that he would first carry the all gold Franklyn colours in the Prix de Guiche (one and a quarter miles) on 7 April, 'Provided I still have him.'

Immediately after purchase Vaguely Noble had been sent to Paddy Prendergast. It was after Nelson Bunker Hunt had bought into him that, since the horse was to be campaigned in France, Nelson strongly counselled his transfer there. Now here was the three-year-old's new host saying, 'Provided I still have him.' In response to my look of surprise, he went to his desk and handed me a letter which had arrived from Dr Franklyn the previous day. The writer indicated that Vaguely Noble would be running in the name of his wife and, when he did so, he wished the animal's feet to be painted gold. He added that if this posed any difficulty he could arrange to have it done. Etienne Pollet stood back and awaited my reaction. Aware that the proposition would not hold great appeal for the perfectionist, who was already looking dangerously close to a stroke, but reluctant to kill a good story, I offered, lamely, *'C'est un peu bizarre.'*

'Bizarre!' he almost screamed, hurling his arms in all directions (he was a little like Jacques Tati). 'It is utterly monstrous, totally *inadmissible.'* But what a story! I was already envisaging the caption, 'VAGUELY NOBLE TO BE GILDED'. 'I am sure,' I suggested diffidently, 'there is nothing in the rules of racing which stipulates that a horse's feet shall not be painted in a preferred colour or, for that matter, that his/her eyebrows might not be touched up.' (Would Mrs Franklyn think of that?). Etienne Pollet assumed his Queen Victoria mask. 'Irrespective of whether Vaguely Noble represents a gold mine,' he pronounced

solemnly, 'the owner will be asked to remove him if he persists in his wish,' adding, '*Ici ce n'est pas un cirque!*' Surely I could still write the story so far?

'*Mon cher* Peter,' regretted the trainer, 'I would love to *te rendre service*, but I don't *want* to lose the horse and my protest may be accepted, so I'd rather you said nothing.' He promised to ring me immediately if the Franklyns insisted. Wisely they didn't, and while the medium of the biggest gamble in bloodstock history to date turned himself into gold, another good story was mentally spiked.

Wherever Lester Piggott went in the world, earning the money with which he fortified the Exchequer below the level of requirement, he took note of local horse husbandry, retiring with the conviction that 'Noel Murless was the best feeder in my experience'. He goes for English oats, local hay (Michael Dickinson, at the peak of his jump training brilliance, was another English hay man, on the basis that 'compression in transit can create break-up and create dust; while mineral content can be boosted by soya meal'); and molasses and salt in the feed. Lester believes, 'It is a great thing for a horse to drink well.'

To South American Angel Penna, who has been at the head of his profession in four countries, this is the paramount requirement. Angel, who favours powdered glucose and salt tablets, says, 'The more they drink the more I like it. I want them to sweat – that's how they eliminate toxins.' Carrots he abhors ('No donkey food for me – it's too heavy'); garlic ('It makes them stink!') likewise. There is no breakfast *chez* Penna. First feed is at eleven o'clock; evening meal between 6 and 7 p.m., with fast feeders receiving some at the first 'sitting' and the rest at 9 p.m.

Barry Hills, who kicked off with seventeen winners in 1969, then built up by steady progression to eighty-one by 1975 and three figures in 1987, is another twice-a-day feeder on similar lines. He uses chaff to slow down the guzzlers, and a bran, oats and linseed mash twice a week. 'Most people eat too much, and horses too,' says Barry, who cultivates comfrey for the Manton horses and grows good hay on the estate, supplemented from the source, near Huntingdon, where Henry Cecil, Dick Hern and Michael Stoute get theirs. Barry was delighted with Finnish oats for six successive years until a poor harvest interrupted supplies. After he switched to equally appreciated Scottish oats, his agent found difficulty in maintaining an adequate supply for a 160-horse team and he is currently on Canadian, which Maurice Zilber says lack calcium.

Maurice, born in India, the son of a French father and a Turkish mother, was regarded as a bit of a joke when he first started training at Chantilly. He had been twelve years as leading trainer in Egypt until 'all my property was confiscated, everything, in 1962'. He arrived in Paris the following year with £6 and an Egypt–US transit visa, and within six years had created a record by enabling his employer, Daniel Wildenstein, to top the prize money, both Flat and obstacles, in a season. As Zilber's horses appeared to enjoy the £50,000, sixty-five feet long, heated equine pool which his patron provided, I asked François Mathet what he thought about swimming his horses. 'When horse races are run in water, I'll do it,' he said.

In contrast to Angel Penna, Maurice Zilber was a firm believer in the efficacy of garlic. 'Every day they get powdered garlic in their feed, and quick eaters are fed four times – French oats, bicarbonate of soda in their linseed and barley mash.' When I asked in 1973 if he was concerned about the unsocial aspects of garlic, the ebullient handler of a hundred Bunker Hunt and Boussac horses at the time exclaimed, 'Other horses, they do not get near enough to smell mine!'

An enigma to both fellow trainers and most jockeys, he achieved remarkable global results with a variety of horses, including Vaguely Noble's daughter Dahlia (who followed up her second successive King George VI and Queen Elizabeth Diamond victory by winning Canada's Woodbine), Nobiliary, Exceller, Empery, Youth etc. . . . He had a great partnership, and friendship, for years with the excellent Australian jockey Bill Pyers (who created a major Arc de Triomphe shock on Suzy Volterra's Topyo in 1967). But, in truth, for the big occasion there existed only one jockey for him. 'Can you get me Pee-gott?' he would ring and inquire. Even Lester found him difficult to 'read', saying, 'You can ride one of Maurice's in the morning and it wouldn't win an argument. Then the next day it wins a classic.'

Nine times Australian champion and brilliantly successful in Europe, George Moore brought a wealth of experience to his new profession when in December 1971 he started training, close by Chantilly, a team which were largely Bunker Hunt-owned. He figured at the outset 'I probably haven't got the patience of Noel Murless or Alec Head, though I'll be more cautious than Tommy Smith,' for each of whom he'd ridden a series of classic winners. He gave himself little time in France to exercise patience or caution.

George was outspokenly critical of the gastronomic amenities available to his horses. Preferring peanut oil to linseed and unable to buy it in bulk, he became an astonished Italian delicatessen proprietor's best customer. The high-concentrate glucose he sought was unobtainable, and the hay of a quality he would not accept as cattle fodder on his 6500 acre New South Wales farm. Worse, he was far from happy that American vets, employed by Nelson Bunker Hunt for his horses, were turning up to administer treatment without proper consultation. While I went round the stable with him in March 1972, just after he'd won with his first runner, Proud Prince, ridden by his nineteen-year-old son Gary, he asked what I thought the chances were of his securing the trainer's job advertised by the Royal Hong Kong Jockey Club. I rang Gerry Feilden, who was Senior Steward then, and explained the situation. He in turn contacted General Penfold in the colony. In a letter dated 29 May 1972 George wrote gratefully from the Hong Kong Hilton to say that he had been granted a licence for the following year, noting, significantly in the light of subsequent events, 'The only trouble here is that the jockeys seem to control most of the horses and all you are is a glorified head lad. But I am hoping this can be overcome.' He didn't do too badly. Third in the trainers' list in 1973, he was champion trainer eleven times in thirteen years.

As it was put by ace Australian commentator Jim (JA) McGrath, who was employed there to call the horses between 1973 and 1986 before moving to Europe, 'George Moore mastered the system from the "off" through sheer ability and strength of personality.' George and I met up again in 1979, when I was lucky enough to be invited to Sha Tin racecourse. It was opened in October 1978 after 16 million tons of mountain had been removed in reclaiming 250 acres from the sea. Amenities for the horses, in one of the most advanced racing complexes of the era, included two-storey air-conditioned boxes with piped music, sand rolls, hosing rooms and heated indoor pool. To give some idea of the scope of the 700-feet-long, eight-storey grandstand, the biggest building in Hong Kong, the management would reckon to employ 1250 catering staff and serve 35,000 race day customers. Catering equipment included 60 tons of stainless steel hardware.

On the outward flight a racing-orientated British Airways steward not only prescribed Château Mouton Rothschild as a cure for the feverish cold with which I had left Heathrow on a frosty January morning, but thoughtfully placed an emergency bottle of the medicine in my overnight bag as a stumbling-off present. When I checked into my room at the Mandarin around breakfast-time, there was a note from George and Iris Moore, propped against a bottle of Dom Pérignon, counselling sleep to offset jetlag before they collected me for dinner. With the irresolution of a Piscean I had got as far as deciding to have a bath and think about it when the unmistakable voice of Lester Piggott came on the phone and asked, simply, 'What are you going to do?'

Lester, a regular winter migrant, had been there for ten days. It was more than twenty-five years since he had deftly slipped a neatly folded, large white five pound note into my hand as I was walking down the iron stairway from the press room at Newbury. Reacting to my surprise, he explained, 'That ride you put me in for for Vincent O'Brien.' Conscious of both appearing basely ungrateful and sounding self-righteously pompous, I returned the offering to his jacket pocket, explaining that being first with the news was reward enough. He shrugged. His expression reflected faint annoyance, as if a presumed ally had suddenly turned out to be dangerously unbalanced. He mentioned a long since retired colleague on another newspaper. '*He* doesn't object to a few quid when he gets me a winning ride,' he said. It was my turn to shrug.

I always felt that, from there on, he regarded me as being mildly quixotic. Not that our friendship was affected, and when I replied, in answer to his immediate query, 'What are you going to do?', that I was going to bed so as to feel fresh in the evening, he told me, 'That's the worst thing you can do. You'll feel like death. The only way to adjust is to keep going. I'll meet you down in the hall in half an hour.'

Lester had arrived from the Hilton and was signing autographs in the Mandarin lobby when we met. He introduced me to his tailor; we explored the markets; took the Star Ferry to Kowloon; visited his shirtmaker; and had a cheery lunch in a restaurant in which he was treated with reverence appropriate to the Emperor of China. He advised against a too-late night as he would pick me up at 4.30 a.m. to watch work at Happy Valley, the course, deep in the city. The horses were led down there from their multi-storey stables in the early hours – rubber-booted so as not to disturb the citizens in the high-rise blocks along the Shan Kwong road. On Wednesday evenings, 42,000 would pack into the floodlit arena before a red flag was hoisted, signifying house full. It was relatively deserted at morning worktime when Lester was riding for the outstandingly successful and colourful White Russian trainer, George Sofronoff, who had dominated his profession in the pre-Moore decade as emphatically as his successor.

All horses are purchased by the Royal Hong Kong Jockey Club for allocation to owners by ballot; all are stabled in identical surroundings (on the completion of Sha Tin, horses were transferred there from Happy Valley); all are exercised in the same area; all are pre-race tested; and all have access to the same no-expense-spared nutrition, which is imported by the Club, whose officials monitor its preparation. So there seemed little scope for the emergence of a dominant trainer. Yet, just as Arkle's superiority over his 'chasing contemporaries in the sixties led to modification in the rules of handicapping, so there was a limit imposed on Sofronoff's intake; and, later, on George Moore's too.

Scrupulous attention to detail was a characteristic common to both. When Sofronoff, who had earned a considerable reputation as a horsemaster in Shanghai, took me round his horses after morning work, he'd already checked each one at 4 a.m. and varied their activity according to appetite. George Moore would meanwhile have been doing the rounds of his feed bins at Sha Tin. While top-quality lucerne hay from Canada and Australia, oats from the same source, and Australian honey and supplements were basics on the Jockey Club's *en pension* menu, approved 'extras' had to be ordered through the stable manager, and paid for. These included the Australian-manufactured vitamins favoured by George, and injections, carried out by the on-site veterinary department, of B.12 or folic acid, the latter to compensate for the lack of green grass. Such injections were prohibited in the week before running. The Moore stratagem included a comprehensive record of the daily work, gallops and nutrition variation of every horse in his care, as well as far from disinterested observation of the homework of his competitors. George fed twice a day, sometimes three.

Whether his owners were personally able to sustain this rhythm was doubtful, judging by results during the week of my visit. A jockey, my good friend Johnnie Roe, nine times champion of Ireland, was the sole purveyor of fruitful counsel during my stay, though Lester nearly landed a touch for Irish-born Yorkshire immigrant Frank Carr on a horse named American Eagle. Before the photo verdict went the wrong way by an inch or so, Lester's whip and that of his challenger, French ex-champion Philippe Paquet, had appeared to become temporarily interwoven and, unless the incident was an optical illusion, American Eagle's rider had leant over and pushed the head of his rival's horse. The evidence of the patrol cameras, which monitor every stride, left no scope for doubt. 'I thought he was going to run into me, and I did it on the spur of the moment,' explained the guilty party disarmingly. But he failed to disarm the stewards, who charged him 5000 Hong Kong dollars (£500) for the offence. 'It didn't look too good on the film,' he admitted afterwards, adding, 'I thought they were a bit hard, but I've no complaints.'

As well as the incident I recall the thoughtfulness of my press room colleague George Ennor. Although we worked for rival newspapers, George, who knew I was hurrying from the course to view conditions in a riding school, took the trouble to leave a message at my hotel in case I had missed official details of Lester's penalty.

Prosperity and compassion are not automatic allies. Although the zealous punters among the four and a half million population had enabled the non-profit-making Royal Hong Kong Jockey Club to contribute £38 million to charity and social services between 1972 and 1978, there was no guarantee that racing's rejects would share the benefits of one of the world's richest racing plants. In fact, the club exercises a high standard of responsibility towards the horse. When a thoroughbred has to be put down for any reason, the deed is performed on site, as it should be. Horses that are passed on to a local riding school

are supervised weekly by a Jockey Club inspectorate. Those that are
retired to a similar life in Thailand or Taiwan are sent under agreement
that they never race again and are visited at intervals by a member of
the Sha Tin-based veterinary corps.

Religious custom and ignorance remain the twin adversaries of the
horse; otherwise an equine historian might accept that the quality of life
in general has improved for the breed in the last half century.

Clive Brittain, who trained that outstanding filly of 1985, Pebbles, with
such a sure and delicate touch, was with Noel Murless for twenty-three
years until he started out on his own in 1972. During my stable rounds
in March that year, when I called on Willie Carson in the Snailwell Road
he suggested I look up his friend and neighbour Clive, who had some
nice horses which he'd be pleased to show me. They looked big and well
in the manner of those of his old governor, who liked to turn fat into
muscle through steady homework. Clive recalled that, as a youngster,
he used to cycle six miles to Beckhampton during the Fred Darling era,
when Norman Bertie was head lad, to look at the horses. At evening
stables they'd be tied up with three-rack chains, one fastened from the
hayrack to the head collar and one to each side while they were wisped
and strapped. 'They could be tied without being able to move or scratch
an itch for up to three hours to prevent them grabbing a lump out of
you,' he related. 'There wasn't a yard in the country that didn't have
two or three savages.'

Within two years of Noel Murless's moving there in 1947 there was
not a chain to be seen. Whenever Noel's horses travelled, their own
water supply went with them. It is a formula that Clive has followed
scrupulously – to the point of including five-gallon containers in the
luggage of a runner in America or Japan, where he won the Cup with
the game and durable Jupiter Island. Like his old governor, he includes
Guinness and eggs on the menu, and calcium for the youngsters. The
vital, skilful feedman's day begins, checking on appetites, before 5 a.m.;
but the stable, which transferred from Pegasus House to Carlburg in
1975, is essentially a team – if any resident needs feeding as much as
five times a day there is 'room service' from 5 a.m. to 9 p.m. Canadian
hay is on offer in the morning ('too rich in protein to be overdone') and
English fare from Devon in the evening. Horses are required to crush
their own oats, which are only lightly bruised to avoid losing the
essential goodness. Garlic honey is served and comfrey, used internally
and externally (as a poultice), has been a feature at Carlburg ever since
it was proposed by the longest-serving Brittain supporter, Marcos
Lemos, for whom Clive trained the 1978 Leger winner, Julio Mariner.

Among the several problems associated with stables touring was the difficulty of contriving fresh approaches to the annual assignment. In 1965, while on holiday in Switzerland, I rang Paddy Prendergast to hear news of his big four classic hopes who had swept the board as youngsters, winning six of their eight races. Remarkably, the three-year-old he was bubbling about was a colt who had not yet run. After calling in at Rossmore Lodge on 15 March, I wrote in the following day's paper:

The chef is *maître* Prendergast. The recipe is as follows: Take 7 cwt of prime yearling horseflesh – preferably grown on Irish limestone soil. Break gently. Apply 16 lb of oats at regular intervals. Season with chopped hay, molasses, carrots, etc. Add one large (s)table-spoonful of honey daily. Allow to mature. Serve in the spring. And, DANDINI, you have a 2000 Guineas favourite! That's him, the masculine-looking grey (cost £6 per lb), half-brother to Clear Sound, working half-speed on The Curragh with another three-year-old maiden, Newsrullah, and the 1964 Derby third, Dilettante, at a difference of 5 lb. Dandini, unraced in public, untried at home and yet favourite for the first colts' classic at Newmarket on 28 April. How come? You may well ask. Let's recap the career of this slightly wilful, talking, rocking, or racehorse. Once expected to be the Rossmore Lodge 'Timeform' colt, Dandini rapped a joint, was lightly blistered for the injury and sent to the seaside for a recuperative holiday. He found that the site fell somewhat short of the holiday brochure promise, went off his feed and returned unrefreshed. He was 'fired' and given time. What a build-up for a horse about whom one 'leviathan' bookmaking firm offers no more than 4/1 against winning the 2000 Guineas. So I came to The Curragh expecting to write down the grey talking horse. Instead, I found myself reaching for the phone and making him the first leg of some playful classic doubles! Wait till you see that stride. Better still, maybe, wait till the moment of truth for Dandini which will be at Phoenix Park on Saturday when Vincent O'Brien fields the highly regarded Tomahawk IV against him in the Athboy Stakes.

Paddy had withdrawn the established stable stars – Carlemont, Prominer, Hardicanute and Meadow Court – from the Guineas to remove the temptation to get on with them too early. They were all Epsom-targeted but the trainer's choice was Carlemont, a late foal with scarred knees, the result of falling on the road with shock when a bullock poked his head over a hedge. I had a double for him to win five figures, Dandini (2000 Guineas) and Carlemont (Derby). And ignoring my own counsel, to await Dandini's debut, had a similar interest.

When phoning 'copy' I asked if the art department could put a chef's hat on a good picture of Paddy to go alongside the opening paragraph. It was very successful (I thought), which was more than could be said for Dandini, who started even money four days later and, as well as Vincent O'Brien-trained Tomahawk, was well beaten. When I rang Paddy a week afterwards, he was hopping mad. 'You've made me look an idiot,' he fumed, 'a right blithering idiot.' I couldn't think what the hell he was raving about, and said so. It was the hat. I said the piece I had written was intended as acknowledgement of his wizardry. And surely he hadn't lost his sense of humour? 'You don't put a chef's hat on your Mathets and Pollets, do you?' he shouted. 'You don't try and take the mickey out of them!'

We went on for a while, to no purpose, and must have just about run a dead-heat in putting the phone down. And starting a long period of non-speaks. Until Saturday, 26 June. Before that, the season which promised so much for Rossmore Lodge had fallen far short of expectation. After failing at the 'Park', Dandini was an odds-on flop in the Craven, unplaced in the Guineas and likewise in the St James's Palace. Neither Prominer nor Hardicanute got beyond their first race; Carlemont (later to win the Sussex) didn't make Epsom, leaving Meadow Court the stable standard-bearer. Having made a heroic effort when runner-up to the redoutable Sea Bird in the Derby, here he was winning the Irish Sweeps-sponsored equivalent, a first in The Curragh classic for Lester Piggott. As I wrote the next day, 'Meadow Court's appearance was sheer delight to all whose pleasure it is to look upon a perfectly conditioned thoroughbred.'

Television outside broadcasts from Ireland were invariably bedevilled by more gremlins than there are excuses for beaten favourites. Relieved to have survived this BBC *Grandstand* transmission without any apparent breakdown in communication, I had hurried from the commentary point and was running across the course to congratulate Bing Crosby and his partners when I ran straight into Paddy. Totally forgetting our rupture, I grabbed his hand and was about to congratulate him when he seized my left arm in a firm grip and threatened, 'If you don't come to the party tonight, I'll never speak to you again!' I said I thought we weren't speaking now. 'That,' he said, 'was a green-eyed, jealous, so-called colleague of yours, putting in the poison and saying you'd made me a laughing stock. I shouldn't have listened to the git. He'll not be entering my yard again.' Paddy added for good measure, 'You'll get your money back over Dandini in the last.' At 5/4, and with Lester putting up 5 lb overweight, I decided to sit that one out. And missed a winner. But I didn't miss the party, at which, when it came to singing Irish songs – as it inevitably did – Paddy was generally rated no more than 2 lb behind Bing.

Meadow Court went on to win the King George and Queen Elizabeth Stakes on 17 July, when Bing couldn't get over. 'These producers', he wrote, 'have little understanding of the important things in life,' so I sent him a recording of the race. 'It's a fine job', he wrote generously of the BBC TV production. 'You get the whole studio real excited every time I run it, and that's plenty.' Ironically, Bing made it to Doncaster for the Leger, having written that he'd have to work nights to fulfil a film schedule on time, only for Meadow Court, who started 11/4 on, to get bogged down in a sea of mud through which 28/1 chance Provoke (allotted 7 stone 13 lb in the Cesarewitch) powered to a ten-length victory.

The Irish Derby and Ascot winner also found the going more resilient than he cared for in the Arc de Triomphe. Not that there was a horse in the world on Sunday, 3 October 1965 capable of matching the momentum of the amazing Sea Bird II. I cannot remember commentating on a Flat race in which the quality of performance exceeded the breathtaking achievement of this glorious galloper, who had six lengths to spare over the hitherto unbeaten French Derby winner Reliance, with winners of three more Derbys and the subsequent Washington International winner, Diatome, toiling further behind. The exhilarating flight of the bright chestnut bird was seen by 75,000 racegoers and an estimated TV audience of 75 million in six countries. The BBC's ambivalent attitude to France's great international horse race, which resulted in forfeiture of access to it in 1986, had already led to uncertainty regarding coverage. Ultimately, commentary was recorded and transmitted on BBC1 after the event.

While Meadow Court went to stud, Paddy Prendergast sustained his pursuit of Epsom glory with undiminished fervour. He had a pair of aces to deal in 1966: a new stable jockey, twenty-four-year-old Desmond Kenneth Lake, whom he described unequivocally as 'the best Australian to ride in Europe since Brownie Carslake himself'; and Khalekan, whom he rated 'the best son of Alycidon to have set foot on a racecourse'.

It was Des Lake who was indirectly responsible for one of my less creditable contributions to the *Express*. Encouraged by his Sports Editor, Jim Manning, the *Daily Mail*'s racing columnist, Tim Fitzgeorge-Parker, who had given up training horses for the less demanding task of writing about them, was turning out good knockabout stuff – as long as you weren't the one being knocked about. He deplored the multiplicity of non-triers (losing tips?), demanded that once a horse had worn blinkers in public he should be forbidden from running without them, named two lesser-known jockeys who had come to blows in the weighing-room, and generally projected minor squabbles within the closely woven family of racing as traumatic confrontations.

On 18 May the first race at Brighton was not until 6.25 p.m., so I went into the office to reduce a backlog of correspondence. Sports Editor John Morgan who, like his predecessor Bob Findlay, was ideal to work for – since he left Clive and me to get on with our jobs – was

thumbing through rival sports coverage before the 11 a.m. editorial
conference. He said, 'I see the *Mail* quotes Lester Piggott saying he
hasn't decided what he'll ride in the Oaks, and we say he rides the
favourite, Valoris, for Vincent O'Brien.' 'He does,' I told him.

'They imply that in that case there would be a fall-out between Lester
and Noel Murless.'

'There is,' I said.

John knew I didn't greatly favour making 'copy' out of racing's
wrangles. 'Do you think,' he asked diplomatically, 'that we [meaning
you] give enough coverage to behind-the-scenes rows within racing?'

Quite enough, I thought. And I said, rashly, 'Mixing it isn't clever. I
could write a mud-slinging story any day that would cause a bit of a
stir, but so what?' I was shuffling through the mail piled on to the coffee-
stained table-top, littered with half-empty cups, which passed for a desk,
when John wandered past on his way out to conference and said, 'I bet
you couldn't write one today.'

I had rung Paddy Prendergast that morning, before leaving the flat,
to ask about the progress of his Derby horse, and he'd launched into a
fluent tirade against a 'dirty, rotten, stinking little bastard' who would,
he assured me bitterly, 'never put a leg across one of mine again as long
as I live'. The 'little bastard', Lester Piggott, was inclined to greet visiting
Australian jockeys with a welcome which, at times, fell a little short of
ardent cordiality. And it had occurred to me at Chester that he wasn't
going out of his way, during action round the Roodee, to do Des Lake
any obvious favours. To Paddy, apparently, it appeared that he had
acted with open hostility.

After our one-sided morning conversation, I'd intended to give Paddy
time to simmer down; to have a word with Lester; and, hopefully, to
bring about a *rapprochement*. Unworthily, rising to John Morgan's
legitimate bait, I rang Paddy again and asked him whether he meant
what he had said for the record, or just between us. If anything, the
wrath of Ireland's leading trainer had intensified since our earlier
conversation. 'Print it, Peter, every goddam word of it,' Paddy growled,
adding, 'The little swine hardly gave the lads a present after winning the
Derby here and the King George [very much out of character, according
to Vincent O'Brien's travelling head lad, Gerry Gallagher, who says,
"Nobody can criticize Lester to me"] and they won't miss him, I tell
you.'

If I'd behaved half decently I would have rung Lester for his side of
the story, but I knew he'd ask me not to print it, so I didn't. A 'good
story' can go stale during the day if transmitted too early; it can also
get 'leaked'. I left a message on John's desk: 'To my discredit lively piece
to follow. Will need front page cross reference, Peter.' I shovelled the

mail into a bag, to cope with at home, and drove to see Ryan Price at Findon on the way to Brighton. *En route* I phoned:

Ireland's top trainer Paddy Prendergast yesterday announced a bombshell for Britain's champion jockey Lester Piggott. 'He will never ride a horse trained by me again – never.'

The Curragh maestro, angered by Piggott's attitude to his jockey Des Lake, revealed that he had lately informed a Rossmore Lodge patron: 'I wouldn't engage Piggott under any terms – not for the Crown Jewels of England.'

Paddy Prendergast recalled that he had stood by Britain's mercurial cavalier – who rode both his first Irish Sweeps Derby winner and King George VI and Queen Elizabeth Stakes winner for the stable – when others were 'gunning' for him.

The declaration [which I had cleaned up considerably!] by the trainer, whose Khalekan is moving into the forefront of the Derby market, follows extreme tension in the Murless–Piggott partnership.

In fact it was soon after this column's query (18 September 1965): 'How much longer will the association which has yielded seven local classics triumphs in eight years be maintained?' that the partnership was severed contractually.

Lester has had a verbal agreement only with Noel this season.

The champion's acceptance, announced yesterday, of Vincent O'Brien's offer of the Oaks mount on Valoris, left Noel Murless adamant that he would henceforth look elsewhere for a partner for the Warren Place stars. 'I took on Lester following his suspension,' said Britain's record-breaking trainer, who attained an all time high with £145,727 stakes winnings in 1959, 'and he is not going to play ducks and drakes with me.'

Stan Clayton has been engaged to ride Varinia, with whom Noel had expected Lester to be associated in the Oaks. 'Scobie Breasley will help out when available, and I shall be contacting Freddy Head for Ascot,' added the Newmarket trainer. Even so, a personal view, unsupported by the current climate surrounding the brilliantly talented thirty-year-old champion, is that an ultimate renewal with the Aunt Ediths of Newmarket Heath will be effected before very long.

The article appeared in the southern editions of the *Express* under the headline 'TRAINER BARS PIGGOTT', subtitled 'Never again says Paddy Prendergast', and with front page details. Manchester's front page referred to 'PIGGOTT SENSATION' and the racing lead to 'STORM OVER PIGGOTT'. I didn't see Lester for a couple of days, until he caught my eye outside the weighing-room at Newmarket, sauntered over and asked, 'What did you want to write that for the other day?' I told him, adding that I wasn't very proud of myself. Most of us, in Lester's place, would have been angry or resentful – or both. He just shrugged and said, 'I shouldn't worry. It'll all be forgotten in a day or so, won't it?'

Within two months Lester had ridden Noel Murless-trained Aunt Edith to win the King George VI and Queen Elizabeth Stakes, and three more Warren Place winners at that Ascot meeting. On 11 September he decided to be contract-free and go freelance for 1967, at the outset of which Paddy Prendergast declared their breach to be healed. I quoted him, 'Things happen in the heat of the moment that are best forgotten.' What I could have added was that, while they were staying in the same hotel, Lester borrowed the key to Paddy's room from the chambermaid one morning and walked in to inquire what all the fuss was about. 'He dived under the bedclothes,' the intruder related gleefully. 'Thought I was going to hit him!'

Paddy and Des Lake parted at the end of the 1967 season, during which the stable's heavily backed Dominion Day never raised any hope of ending an eighty years' sequence of failure for maidens in the Derby. Paddy and I were 'on' the ultimate 8/1 third favourite to Royal Palace at long odds. Typically, when promptly forwarding his cheque for £1600, he wrote, 'I am sorry I dragged you into the "gulf" with me, as I am more upset about this than anything. I am at a complete loss for an explanation as to why he ran so badly. Hope to see you at Ascot, and once again I cannot say how very sorry I am.'

There was no evidence that Paddy's Epsom expectations were ever modified by disappointment. When he rang during May 1971 to ask me to put him 'a towsand' on Lombardo for the Derby, I had to remind him that he'd already requested £1000 on Credit Man ('and have a word with Saint-Martin about riding him') a week earlier. There was a moment's hesitation. 'I can't separate them,' says he, 'they'll be first and second.' They were last and fourth, respectively, in the only classic to elude him on either side of the Irish Sea. It was a sad day when I had to stand in front of the BBC TV camera on the press balcony, before the first race on the last day of the 1980 Royal Ascot meeting, and bid a final adieu to Patrick J. Prendergast, who had fought a brave fight against terminal illness for the past six months.

Paddy was survived by two fine trainer sons – Kevin, who was a star amateur before becoming a leading member of his profession, and 'Young Paddy', whose sharp wit always enlivens morning work-watching for me when he visits Cheltenham or Ascot. As it was, within half an hour of paying tribute to his father I was calling home Cooliney Prince, trained by Paddy Junior, as winner of the Windsor Castle Stakes.

CHAPTER 19

Divided Loyalties

By 1962 ITV was really up and running and BBC employees were channel-hopping with the speed, if not the grace, of Arkle jumping fences. Even sports commentators were being propositioned and Peter Dimmock (General Manager BBC TV Outside Broadcasts) wrote me that year, 'I am sure that Independent Television would be willing to offer a substantial bait in order to lure you from us, but at the same time I feel sure that on a long-term basis you will never regret staying with the "old firm"!'

It wasn't changing horses that was my concern, it was sustaining the momentum required to fulfil a dual role. When Peter's admirable aide, Harry Middleton, wrote on 22 March 1962, 'You will be delighted to hear that this year at Lincoln we are providing you with a commentary box on the roof of the grandstand, so that, for the first time, you may possibly go on to Liverpool without suffering from influenza,' his welcome news followed apologies from producers at Birmingham, Chepstow and Sedgefield for the absence for various reasons (structural weakness, high winds) of any rooftop cover. For six months of the year I ran a temperature with greater consistency than any horse ran to form. Apart from the detail that the scaffolding struts made my tripod-mounted binoculars inoperable, it was a very nice little box at Lincoln. But not for race commentary.

Competition from ITV increased emphasis on the importance of 'scene-sets', whereby each outside broadcast location was visited briefly at the start of the weekend programme, *Grandstand*, for the commentator to stress the significance of the action to follow. The more the BBC forfeited its major racecourse contracts, the higher the premium on imagination. I recall facing the camera at Uttoxeter on 1 May 1971 and experiencing some difficulty in summoning the necessary conviction to persuade viewers that, notwithstanding ITV's simultaneous screening of the clash betwen Brigadier Gerard, Mill Reef and My Swallow in the 2000 Guineas at Newmarket, this was the place to be at 2.45 p.m.

211

But Saturday, 27 January 1962, about which Peter Dimmock complained, was different. We were not opposed by a significantly superior programme to the one we were covering at Warwick. Here the twenty-six-runner Studley Novices' Hurdle (on which I'd spent around two and a half hours learning the colours) featured the jumping debut of that splendid Astor-bred stayer, Trelawny, who had already won the Chester Cup and Brown Jack Stakes for Mrs Leonard Carver since being bought as a three-year-old for 2500 guineas, and who was twice to achieve an Ascot Stakes–Queen Alexandra Stakes double, as well as winning a Goodwood Cup. 'In the one o'clock "teaser" for *Grandstand*,' wrote Peter, 'you mentioned that, among the afternoon's runners, viewers would see Trelawny. But you did not suggest this was a highlight. Nor did the producer, whom you usually make aware of the news value of such a horse, feature him prominently. Even in the race you made little reference to Trelawny until stating that he was coming with a strong late run to finish third.' He added, 'We must remember the marginal viewer of *Grandstand* who only watches racing because he is waiting for the next event in the programme.'

In replying I confessed that the viewer who was waiting for the next programme had not occupied a high priority in my approach. 'I arrive at the course early,' I explained, 'in the hope of gathering immediate news for the "scene-set". In this instance one item of information I received was that Trelawny was having an "easy race". Under the circumstances, it seemed inappropriate to feature him too extravagantly. For the record, he drifted in the betting from 4/1 to 100/8.'

Heavily backed in his three subsequent races that season, he was second on each occasion. But after George Todd had performed legendary feats with him on the level, the old horse returned, aged ten, to Kinnersley where Fred Rimell produced him in great heart to win his Warwick Novices' by ten lengths, and the Spa and Coronation Hurdles, at the Cheltenham and Aintree festivals, in a common canter.

Mrs Carver seemed to me a fairly formidable lady. When I decided to retire my first jumping winner, Pretty Fair, in 1954, Mrs C. offered £100 for him as a hunter. But he was only a little fellow and, with respect, I thought she might be a pound or two too heavy for him. So I gave him instead to lighter-framed Diana Hellyer who, as Diana Byrom, had caused a stir at Epsom as one of racing's first and most decorative stable girls back in 1945. Pretty Fair carried her happily with the Cottesmore before retirement, which Trelawny also enjoyed for several years.

Fred Rimell was not too happy when Trelawny's owner asked him to school the ten-year-old over fences – he feared injury to the immensely popular son of Black Tarquin. Terry Biddlecombe, who had partnered him to each of his three sparkling hurdles victories, was equally apprehensive. When they took him to the schooling ground, where three generations of Rimells practised their art before one of the twentieth-century scourges – the property developers – stepped in, they were the only two present. Trelawny 'popped' a fence neatly. 'Want to do it again?' asked Fred. Terry, three times champion during his cheerful career, indicated negative. When they returned to breakfast Fred rang Mrs Carver. 'He doesn't like fences,' he told her, with a wink at Terry. 'You'd best retire the old fellow.' And she did.

By 1962 the ratings war, which was to become such a significant aspect of TV life, was at full gallop. A decision was delayed until the deadline for *Radio Times* billings before coverage of Ireland's first Hospitals Sweeps-sponsored Derby was agreed. At over £50,000 to the winner, the twenty-four-runner race was the richest classic ever staged in Europe. When Alec Weeks, *Sportsview*'s producer, wrote the following month thanking Clive and me 'for a marvellous job' (and apologizing for working conditions!) he revealed, significantly, 'Our one fear on *Grandstand* was the loss of Wimbledon viewers to Commercial when we went over from tennis to The Curragh at 2.30. Our fears were needless as figures have proved that 5¼ million viewers tuned in at 2 o'clock and stayed with us until 4.15.' The short-head Irish Derby winner, Tambourine II, first runner in Ireland for Etienne Pollet, completed a notable double for the Chantilly trainer who had won the 2000 Guineas with his first English runner, Thunderhead II.

By 1962 the attitude of the *Daily Express* towards their employees becoming involved in TV seemed to have undergone a considerable change, for the time being anyway. On the final day of the Flat at Manchester on 10 November, Clive was in Washington covering the Laurel International. Under the circumstances I figured I'd better forgo TV at Wetherby, which featured the Whitbread-sponsored Mackeson Novices' Chase, and report the last round-up on the level. When I went into the *Express* on Sunday, all anyone seemed to want to know was why I wasn't on *Grandstand* on Saturday!

Peter Dimmock, on the other hand, was not happy about my absence from commentary. He sent a letter by hand on Monday morning in which he stressed that there would be star-quality jumping every weekend for the next five months, through Kempton's King George VI Chase to the Grand National itself. After extolling the 'great contribution of Wetherby's spectacular big race to Saturday's *Grandstand*', he added, a little testily, 'there was only one element missing – Peter O'Sullevan.' He acknowledged the 'problem of divided loyalties', and continued, 'That is why I am so keen to have details of what might be involved should you change your mind about coming to us full-time.'

This proposition had cropped up several times during my annual contract renewal and, with it, the faint undertone that there might be difficulty in continuing to allocate prime commentary dates to one who was not exclusively available.

Peter had written already that year, on 23 October, 'What is the minimum for which you would be prepared to leave Fleet Street and turn your attention full-time as a racing commentator, expert, and correspondent for the BBC?'

The truth was that, much as I hoped to continue and, hopefully, improve commentary, I found that reporting offered greater scope for reflecting the racing scene and for exercising the effrontery of seeking to influence opinion on contemporary topics. I had, however, told Peter that I'd set out conditions under which I would quit journalism full-time (but not wholly) and I asked my accountant, Frank Stacey, who was fully appraised of both contracts, to come up with the answer.

While Frank was doing his sums, I was preoccupied with such matters as dope (testing methods were questionable, and 'positive' reaction led to automatic warning-off for the trainer – a situation which led to manifest injustices); the (to me) unsatisfactory new Ascot stand which was to be the forerunner of others, Sandown excepted, in which the general racegoer received a far lower priority than the box holder; the news that stalls starts (to which I'd become a convert) had 'split French trainers'; the first endeavour of international racing officials, who met in Marcel Boussac's house, to seek to agree a 'pattern' for major horse races; the vexed question of the pending ban on two-year-old 'sellers'; and a variant on the perennial question 'What will Lester Piggott ride in the Derby', which, following a report by the Lincoln stewards to the Jockey Club on Wednesday, 30 May, was amended to 'Will Lester be available to ride in the Derby?' In my search for the answer I have to admit to exercising a one-off experience of what my disgruntled colleague Norman Pegg of the *Daily Sketch* referred to at the time as 'dirty cheque-book journalism'.

I'd reported on 1 June that, after a prolonged inquiry into the Riseholme Selling Plate, the stewards had suspended Lester Piggott, who would be interviewed at Cavendish Square (the Jockey Club headquarters) on the Monday of Derby week. In the race which inspired official action, Polly Macaw (backed from 3/1 to evens), ridden by Peter Robinson, had won by two lengths from stable companion Ione (who drifted in the market from 4/6 to 11/8), ridden by Lester whom I quoted as saying, 'I don't know what it's all about, but I've been told not to say anything. So I'd better leave it at that.'

In that era, on the advice of their legal counsel, the Jockey Club made no statements after inquiries before their findings were published in the privileged official Thursday publication, the *Racing Calendar*. So a reporter's only source of publishable information was the interviewee. No quote – no story. I was in the office, two-thirds through my piece for the day, when, a bit late, I woke up to the fact that if the Press Association reporters who would be waiting outside 15 Cavendish Square, along with a pack of newsmen from the dailies, failed to extract a quote, there would be no means of knowing whether Lester was free to ride in the Derby – not until he had been tracked down anyway. I rang the dentist who practised his painful skills on me across the Square from the Jockey Club and asked Fiona, his tall, blue-eyed nurse, if there was a crowd outside the building on the corner of Harley Street. There was, and had been for hours. If I parked my grey Jaguar below her window in fifteen minutes, would she be able to give a sign when two figures emerged from number fifteen? Her boss had finished torturing for the day, and she would. Sports Editor Bob Findlay agreed in a flash that if Lester revealed the outcome, exclusively, £100 would be fair reward.

Talk about luck! I had barely driven into the Square when there was a flurry of ninon curtains from the second floor of number nineteen. I waved thanks and spun round the corner. Lester and Peter Robinson were trying to make their way through a posse of photographers and reporters. I leaned over and released the catch of the passenger door, shouting, 'Lester!'

I remember once, before a big race, asking Paddy Prendergast Junior, 'How's your horse?' His reply was, 'Sharp as a cowboy's gun!' That was Lester. He was in the front seat and Peter had piled into the back faster than the stalls open after the starter has pressed the electronic button. If I interpreted the expressions of some of those left on the pavement correctly, Lester's comment, 'That wasn't bad!' was not universally shared. In reply to my question, he said, 'They done me, not only for Epsom but Ascot too. And I didn't do anything wrong. That Bob Ward put me on the one he fancied least to get the odds.' Peter chimed in with, 'Bob told me mine would win when he legged me up.'

The panel, headed by the Duke of Norfolk, had not been convinced. Lester had left his car nearby in Wimpole Street. As we drove round there I said that if he took the phone off when he got back to Newmarket, and the *Express* had it exclusively that he was off Young Lochinvar in the Derby and 'out' until 28 July, I could give him £100. The only trouble was I hadn't made any provision for Peter. 'That's all right,' says Lester. 'I'll look after Peter out of mine.' But Peter Robinson was adamant. 'You don't have to. I won't talk to anybody, and I owe

Peter one anyway.' Apparently, a while earlier, I'd written an 'Off the Record' paragraph about a young apprentice who would be well advised to place a lot less reliance on the whip. 'You were right,' related Peter, 'but you didn't name me, and I was grateful for that.' So next day the front-page lead of the *Daily Express* (price 3d) was: PIGGOTT SHOCKED: OUT OF THE DERBY AND SUSPENDED UNTIL 28 JULY.

It was a horrendous Derby – the worst classic to commentate in my experience. The point at which the runners begin the descent from the top of Tattenham Hill is the least visible from the stands. Here the twenty-six-horse race was suddenly transformed into a battleground. Romulus and Crossen fell, bringing down the favourite, Hethersett, and four more, including trainer Tom Masson's first two Derby runners and the Ryan Price-trained King Canute II, which shattered a leg so badly that he had to be destroyed.

Nine days beforehand the ultimate winner, Larkspur, who had been rejected in favour of Sebring by Vincent O'Brien's stable jockey Pat Glennon, was receiving veterinary attention for a swelling below the hock. For two days he was box-bound, undergoing fomentation. Under the circumstances, Vincent thought it fair to issue a warning that participation was uncertain. When the renowned Ballydoyle vet, Bob Griffin, gave the all-clear, Raymond Guest, the colt's owner, who loved a bet and was about the only member of the entourage who fancied the son of Never Say Die, had a playful 'punt'. But it made no great stir in the market, and on the day Larkspur eased from 20/1 to 22/1. If Vincent, for whom Larkspur was the first of six Epsom Derby winners between 1962 and 1982, inclined to reticence in making public pronouncements thereafter, it was hardly surprising in view of the stewards' immediate post-race demand for an explanation from him as to how he accounted for support for a winner who had been declared a doubtful runner.

Personal criticism of the £1 million Tattersalls grandstand which was opened at Ascot in 1961 – criticism on the grounds that it was set at an absurdly inadequate angle for viewing the straight, and incorporated no top-level area for the general public – was inspired, as I wrote at the time, by the fear that it would be accepted as a blueprint for future developments when Levy Board grants became available. Generally it was, despite an avalanche of supportive readers' letters, including a lovely one from actor, author and racing aficionado Robert Morley, who wrote:

Fairman's Cottage,

Wargrave,

Berks.

Dear Peter,

You are right about the new stand at Ascot nót
being what its cracked up to be.   As a distinguished
foreign correspondent perhaps it has never occurred
to you that Ascot, unlike the surrounding countyside,
is a Police State.

Have you ever noticed all those unsmiling gentlemen
wearing bowler hats and expressions ofextreme
suspicion forever tapping the public on the arm
peering into their faces, examing the various passes
and throwing rope barricades across the paths to
close thoroughfares whenever distinguished party
members or their horses are preparing to leave the
paddock ?

If you have ever spoken to any of these watchful
zealots you will know that their attitude to the
members of the proleteriat is one of extreme disdain
coupled with a reluctance to give information equalled
only by the staff of British Railways.

It came as no suprise to me that having ridden up
the shining new escalator which stops so abruptly

Fairman's Cottage,
Wargrave,
Berks.

at the first floor that none of the security agents stationed
at the top were prepared to tell me where the office of TOTE
Investors had been moved to.   Nor later when having sat down
for tea in what appeared to be a worker's restaurant that the
waitress who took our order dissapeared for ten minutes to return
not with a tray but with form signed possibly by the Duke of
Norfolk himself authorising the serving of tea at a table
which although, so she informed me , had been unoccupied all day
was offically designated as reserved and therefore not normally
available for casual visitors.   As the next race was now due
to start I asked her to get the tea and strawberries and promised
we would return and consume them in ten minutes, only to find
when I did so that a uniformed official had thrown a barrier
across the entrance and refused at first to allow us to pass.
"But those are my strawberries" I told him and "I've paid for them"
N̶o̶t̶x̶n̶n̶i̶i̶x̶y̶n̶u̶
Finally he relented on the ground that both of us were at one
time connected with the theatrical business.   He had I learned
later actually buried Fred Barnes.   I dread to think what would
have happened to him had he been caught but he undid the barrier
and loosed us on the strawberries and cream.

Fairman's Cottage,
Wargrave,
Berks.

Ascot is like that presumably it always will be.   The public
puts up with the apartheid and red tape and when like me
on Saturday they climbed the endless stairs of the new stand
expecting not unaturally that they would be able to see the
the racing and discovered that all they were permitted was
a view of the backdoors of the private boxes they were dissapointe
but never out of temper.   It was no one s job to tell them
that if they wanted a view of the racecourse they must climb
down again and stand where they always used to stand on the
grass.   At a cost of a million pounds all that the public
is provided with are a few concrete steps rather narrower
than before.   Profits from Ascot are used not to improve
facilities which are ^now worse for the silver ring and the Iron
Stand but to make bigger profits in the years to come.
Gone are the days when ~~thextheak~~ at the Heath meetings the boxes
were free.   Ours-not to reason why and certainly not to be
told that on these occasions there is no room at the top.
But the horses are still there, Lester Piggot is still there,
and I hope very much that you and I will be still there
if we don't get ourselves deported to Ally Pally as counter
revolutionaries.   YOURS EVER *Robert Morley,*

Some years later Ascot's urbane, widely travelled clerk of the course, 'Nicky' Beaumont, who makes it his business to sound out public opinion, figured he'd solved one of the problems – the provision of viewing for three thousand racegoers above box level. But the contractors regretted that, the way the stand was constructed, it would not support the weight. 'They'll have to do it at the next rebuilding, when we're no longer here,' says Nicky. Let's hope they do.

In the interim I was to undergo a wholly unexpected experience of racecourse management from the administrative side of the rails. Soon after the Beckwith-Smith family put their 350-acre Lingfield Park on the market in 1974 it seemed that the eighty-four-year-old circuit was doomed as a racecourse, since neither the Levy Board, nor United Racecourses (Epsom, Sandown and Kempton) nor the Jockey Club subsidiary, Racecourse Holdings Trust, was interested in purchase. John Sutcliffe, who sent out the 1971 National winner, Specify, from his immaculate Headley yard, had a horse of Cyril Stein's at the time. He persuaded Ladbroke's chairman that acquisition of Lingfield would benefit the Group as well as ensuring the continuity of racing on one of the most attractive racecourses in the south of England. It was probably the latter consideration which largely motivated Cyril when he gave the OK – provided John could assemble an 'appropriate' board from within racing. Sutcliffe senior's quixotic insistence that he needed my support in this area was politely undiluted by the doubts I expressed regarding competence to interpret a balance sheet.

Both I and my fellow board member John (Lord) Oaksey had at the outset less than nil expertise in the financial world, and neither of us would readily forget the stern address of chairman Sutcliffe at the initial board meeting following Ladbrokes' £½ million purchase. Glaring round the table, he proclaimed: 'Gentlemen, let me first welcome you by saying that I wish you to keep in mind at all times that a board of directors has one absolute clear priority, namely to remember that the principal purpose of their presence is to promote and safeguard the interests of shareholders. That said, let's get down to business.'

It was the forerunner of many brilliantly chaired, relaxed and constructive meetings, before which I showed a fair profit betting on the late arrival of Lord Oaksey. John only let me down once when, obviously due to an oversight, he arrived three minutes before the 'off'.

As a team, which included the notable expertise of Chris Collins and John Hughes, we were also involved in Ladbrokes' Grand National rescue. This spanned seven years, starting in 1976 (Rag Trade's year), when for the first time the TV coverage was properly marketed worldwide. As a result the income from sales exceeded the aggregate of TV's previous fifteen years at Aintree, when negotiations were handled by a less than universally admired outfit inappropriately styled BBC Enterprises.

Before Lingfield's resale to Ron Muddle in 1981, extensive and, hopefully, beneficial changes had been made. Sequel to our first board meeting was the establishment of a two-enclosure course with the Silver Ring and Tatt's amalgamated for a £1 entrance fee, while a personal whim was satisfied with the introduction of the first realistically priced wine bar on a British racecourse. I never succeeded, however, in another aim – the employ of distinctively dressed rubbish collectors who might shame racegoers into keeping Lingfield lovely. It should not be impossible to discourage backers and bookmakers alike from littering the enclosures with spent tickets and other refuse.

Few issues polarized Anglo-French racing opinion in the early sixties to the extent of starting stalls. No sooner had an experimental set been introduced to the Chantilly training grounds on 1 December 1961 than feeling ran as high as the Eiffel Tower. The following year I reported Alec Head, supported by Miguel Clément and Rae Johnstone, to be a passionate advocate; François Mathet, backed by George Bridgland and others, vehemently opposed. I quoted Alec, 'First, present starts in France are terrible.' This was the one point over which protagonists were solidly agreed. 'If you have a photo-finish at one end, it seems absurd to be completely haphazard about the other,' he continued, adding,

'I have schooled my sixty two-year-olds in the stalls without a single accident. With the tapes start I had three kicked and two loose the other morning. Rubber suction pads make the opening and shutting of the stalls noiseless, and instead of ribbons flicking up in a horse's face the doors just part naturally. So there is nothing to distract him. They quickly get used to walking into the stalls, and the lad can just sit quiet and pat them – instead of hauling them about and trying to keep them straight.'

One of Alec's senior lads, fifty-nine-year-old Charlie Eva, chipped in, 'Stalls-starts for me. What's the good of "my" horse having perfect manners if another ignorant one crashes into him at the start, or an ignorant starter lets 'em go just anyhow?'

Trainer, like Alec, of more than a thousand winners by 1962, François Mathet insisted, 'What we need is a competent starter, not traps. Their introduction would mean the reconstruction of French courses which, as in England, traditionally call for a variety of talents in a horse. On American tracks they have one object – to get out as quickly as they can, and get home as soon as possible.' To which George Bridgland added, 'We train our horses to settle down, not to bolt from starting-boxes like greyhounds.'

Personal experience in the United States left me firmly opposed to their noisy stalls, in which many horses appeared terrified. But this new, light, highly mobile Australian type was very different. After pressing the button to release a group of Alec Head youngsters, I felt the same way as hundred-horse trainer Max Bonaventure, who told me during racing at Saint-Cloud, 'I was strongly opposed until I saw Alec in action. Now I've had a positive rethink.' Alec's father, Willie, one of whose happiest achievements during an outstanding career was training an Arc de Triomphe winner (Bon Mot III, 1966) ridden by his grandson, Freddy, recalled 'the outcry when the present system replaced flag starts. The diehards all thought the horses and riders would get hanged in the tapes.'

Newmarket's top trainers, Noel Murless and Cecil Boyd-Rochfort, both 'hated the sight of American stalls', with Noel going so far as to say, 'I'd rather not train if the American gate was introduced here.' But he did add, 'I have no experience of the Australian type that I know Alec Head favours, so I have an open mind about them.' After watching Harry Wragg 'clock' his two-year-olds across the ice-cold Heath, I sought his opinion. 'I gave a talk in America some years ago about their method,' he recalled, 'and I told them our gentler system of both educating and starting horses was much more likely to produce good stallions. I suppose,' he added wrily, 'if I'd been right, they wouldn't have bred any good horses by now!'

On 26 July 1962 I was reporting:

The French starting stalls experiment was widely accepted as a triumph at Chantilly yesterday. The first event to be stall-started in France, the Prix de Chaumont, was won appropriately by Britannia. Appropriately because Alec Head, who trains the winner for his wife, Ghislaine, is a principal advocate of this form of start. The seven two-year-olds walked into the stalls very quietly and quickly, and were off in a few seconds. The stalls experience of Neville Sellwood, who won this and two other races, served him well. So delighted with the experiment were the French authorities that two more two-year-old races will be started by this method at Chantilly tomorrow. There will remain for several years a powerful body of diehard opinion opposed to the introduction of stalls-start in England. There is no doubt that operational difficulties will be a bigger factor here than elsewhere. But many will share the view expressed to me by Lester Piggott yesterday when he said, 'stall-starts are the fairest method of all . . . they've got to come sometime, there's no doubt about that.'

They were a long time coming alright. Two years later, in February, when the *Sporting Life* arrived at my holiday address in Switzerland, it contained a letter from John Oxley, who had trained that season's Oaks winner, Homeward Bound, regretting that 'Those great advocates of starting stalls, Messrs Graham and O'Sullevan, were noticeable by their absence from the farcical demonstration of starting-stalls laid on by the Jockey Club at Newmarket.' Following condemnation of the system, which was obligatory for all two-year-old races run in 1963 on France's six top courses, John gave thanks on behalf of all those who, like himself, 'hope we shall never see starting stalls on an English racecourse', for the intervention of the Minister of Transport, Mr Ernest Marples, who had objected to the transportation of stalls units which exceeded an approved width. The respected and successful Newmarket trainer felt that stalls would inhibit training initiative and prevent jockeys 'riding a race as we know it'.

I gave up a morning's skiing to regale readers of the *Sporting Life* with a lengthy defence of the stalls, concluding with the detail that *all* Flat races on the principal French courses would be started from stalls that year, 'which may be considered a reason why English-trained horses should be stall-conscious'.

It wasn't until 8 July 1965 that starting stalls were used for the first time in England. The next day I was able to report:

Following minimum delay and maximum efficiency at the despatch end, Newmarket's first stalls-started race ended as a lot more events should – with the jolly favourite streaking home a clear three lengths winner. It may have been no more than coincidence that four of the five jockeys with previous stalls experience taking part in the contest filled the first four places. But familiarity with the medium must be an advantage – as in any other sphere of activity. Snap interviews among riders of the 'also rans', behind Lester Piggott-partnered Track Spare, produced such observations as 'Super; mine flew out.' 'Very good indeed.' 'Absolutely perfect.' And from five-times champion Doug Smith: 'It was a first time for me and I thought they were very good indeed.' Many among the crowd, which was 16 per cent up on the corresponding day last year, walked down the course for this historic start. In the stands bookmaker Ted Binns only just had time to shout, 'They're going into the traps' before they were under orders and off. It is doubtful whether many previously prejudiced observers remained unconverted to the view that this is the fairest method for horse, rider, and punter.

CHAPTER 20

A Commercial Proposition

At a personal level, Frank Stacey had long since (6 November 1962) come up with a figure which would enable me to join the BBC full time, and continue to maintain a racehorse – of not necessarily outstanding ability – and like essentials. I would need a car to the value of £2500 and a salary of £7500 (he pitched it high, knowing my reluctance to quit the *Express*), and Peter Dimmock wrote back:

Very many thanks for your letter. Exactly what I wanted to learn. I am afraid that the terms suggested are so far in advance of anything that anyone is paid here that I doubt whether we could even suggest a compromise that might be acceptable to you. At the same time, it is most useful to have this information should the situation change at any time. I have asked Harry [Middleton] and the boys to give Peter Montague-Evans some more commentating experience during the winter. If the weather remains fair we should have an excellent double bill from Newcastle and Chepstow.

Peter Montague-Evans, a highly accomplished race reader, became the Corporation's official racing correspondent, winning a narrow verdict over Raleigh Gilbert who had lately returned from Kenya, after considerable commentary experience there, and who was to become regularly associated with both the RTS (Racecourse Technical Services) and ITV teams. Peter Montague-Evans enjoyed working for the BBC as a freelance but felt less happy 'being owned by them', as he put it, and in 1965 he decided to live abroad and left.

So the Corporation advertised for the position and Scobie Breasley reminded me to put in a good word for the young Barbadian, Michael Stoute, about whom we'd talked previously. John Goddard, the West Indian Test cricketer and a lifelong friend of the Stoute family, had earlier contacted Scobie about getting the horse-mad son of the Barbados chief of police a job in England, and the twenty-year-old was currently working in Pat Rohan's Malton stable. He was, in fact,

Left; Tony Boyle about to lead in Be Friendly and Geoff Lewis after their Prix de l'Abbaye victory stroll in 1968

Below: Be Friendly and Maureen – Elms Stud

Isidro Martin-Montis, Pat, Sol Moratalla and self at Chalet Isga, Gstaad

At one of our dear friend Dick Wilkins's (background) splendid parties Queen Elizabeth, The Queen Mother, receives Pat and me

Attivo leads the 1974 Daily Express Triumph Hurdle field

Attivo is clear in the 1974 Daily Express Triumph Hurdle before making a heart-stopping hash of the last, and is led into the winner's circle by Derek Wilmot – owner following

Vi Aitken presents the Triumph trophy; (*above right*) Attivo cuts it a bit fine in the Ladbroke Chester Cup

Lester going to post on Attivo at Lingfield

Pat Eddery partners 'Percy' in his last race on the level, 9 May 1980

strapping a horse when called to the telephone and asked to present himself at Newbury on Friday, 26 November 1965 for a test.

BBC cameras were set up that day – although there was no transmission – in preparation for the next afternoon's Hennessy Gold Cup, in which the amazing Arkle (6/1 on) gave 32 lb and a fifteen lengths' beating to the closest of his seven pursuers, the splendid Berwickshire horse Freddie, himself runner-up when handicapped with top weight in the National. Although Michael had commentated in Barbados and Trinidad, he'd never been to a jumping meeting, so his boss advised him to travel down early and walk the course beforehand. The BBC, having narrowed the field of applicants to six, would require each to perform a scene-set to camera, followed by paddock and race commentary.

Four of the 'runners' assembled on platform thirteen at Paddington Station. They were: Gavin Pritchard-Gordon, twenty, who was working for a ship-broking firm in Paris; Tim Richards, twenty-two, who was with the *Sporting Chronicle*; Julian Wilson, twenty-five, and David Phillips, thirty-five, who were both with the *Daily Mirror*. 'We all went second class,' recalls Tim Richards, 'except Julian, who travelled as he clearly intended to continue – first.' Jack Millan, twenty-nine, columnist in *The Racehorse* and the sixth contestant, made his way to the trial ground independently, like Michael Stoute.

Jack, from Dundee, drew round one, the first division of the fourteen-runner Freshman's Hurdle. He'd familiarized himself with half the field and had expected to be free to study the others in the paddock. But he was required to take up his position in the commentary box, equipped with headphones, to listen to the paddock commentary of David Phillips. 'So I only knew half of them,' he remembers. 'By the time they turned into the straight I knew I'd blown it. I was humiliated. So I just said, "There's an unidentified object in front"!' Jack consoled himself with the thought that his broad Scottish accent might not have been understood anyway, and went on to achieve distinction as Robin Goodfellow of the *Daily Mail*, which he joined in 1974.

Tim Richards felt that things could only improve after he had 'frozen' before the cold eye of the scene-set camera, so that his only recorded words were, 'Hell, I've cocked this up!' The following year he was appointed to his first 'outside' job, succeeding the charming northern correspondent, Claude Harrison, as syndicated columnist for the Thomson Group morning papers. In his first season he won the *Sporting Chronicle* and *Sporting Life* naps tables, modestly attributing the feat to 'beginner's luck', and adding 'I was near enough bottom the next year.' Respected for industry and integrity, Tim was sixteen years with the *Mirror* before being appointed Chief Racing Reporter and later News Editor to the *Racing Post* in 1985.

Gavin Pritchard-Gordon drew the short straw when lumbered with a thirteen-horse novices' chase, involving two colour changes, run in suddenly descended thick fog. He reminds me that I entered the box and advised him, 'You'll have to read this from the monitor.' To which he reacted, 'What's the monitor?' Reading off the screen in fog isn't too easy because it's hard to tell where the hell they are. Gavin did a good job under the circumstances, but even better in training well over one hundred winners in the three years after taking out his first trainer's licence in 1972.

David Phillips had no problem calling home Dicky May (4/6) in the Oxfordshire Chase when the Tom Dreaper-trained six-year-old became my fifteenth winning nap in the last sixteen (had to get that in somewhere!) during a run, generously termed 'phenomenal' by the *Life*, extended to twenty-two out of twenty-four when Gobion Goblin (6/4) won at Sandown on 11 December. But David did have a problem the following year when becoming Pay TV's paddock commentator throughout the duration of the service. The subsequent Racing Editor and Newsboy of the *Daily Mirror* made the mistake of taking a couple of mild drinks before climbing a series of ladders to his Kempton platform, where he was obliged to remain uncomfortably seated throughout the six-race programme. Very uncomfortably!

Considering that Michael Stoute had been in the country for less than three months and had never seen National Hunt racing, it wasn't surprising that he was a little tense. Even so, he called the second division of the Freshman's Hurdle flawlessly and, twenty-four years later, could remember that Bobby Beasley, who was having a great run for the Arthur Thomas–Paddy Sleator team, won by three lengths on Harwell. In fact, had it not been for the pale young applicant, whose lips moved as silently as a novice monk while he rehearsed his scene-set in the corner seat of a first-class carriage, Michael Ronald Stoute, assessed runner-up in the BBC rating of talent to Julian David Bonhote Wilson, would not have trained more than one hundred winners in the first three years since receiving his licence in 1972 – the same year as his Newbury rival Gavin Pritchard-Gordon. Neither would he have achieved a century in 1980 and become champion trainer for the first time, with ninety-five winners of £723,786, in 1981.

Peter Dimmock appointed Julian Wilson TV Racing Correspondent on 1 January 1966. Patience was not a natural front runner among the virtues of the General Manager of BBC TV Outside Broadcasts, and he had barely nominated the new man than he was telling me, 'This one's no bloody good!' But it was not long before he realized that he'd backed a winner.

The following year London Weekend Television's Head of Sport, Jimmy Hill, wrote me to make 'a very important offer on behalf of independent television'. We got on particularly well and enjoyed a series of excellent lunches, making serious impact on dear Henri Sartori's stock of most notable Bordeaux at Le Coq d'Or. Foolhardily I was reluctant to quit the BBC for cash and must have been very tiresome to negotiate with. Jimmy changed tactics towards the end of the year and, as a result of my half-serious response to his question, 'What can we do to tempt you to sign up as senior ITV commentator for a period of your own choosing?' he wrote on 16 January 1968:

I have already made arrangements for a yacht for you in the Mediterranean. I enclose a list of the most important meetings we cover. If you would prefer to work for nine months in the year, as you intimated, the gaps for consideration appear to be between 2 November and 1 January and 4 April to 3 May. I do hope we are on our way to finding the right formula for you and for an immensely enjoyable and successful association.

The list included all the top fixtures at Sandown, Redcar, York, Lingfield, Doncaster and Epsom. So they had three of the five classics already, though, as a designated 'national event', the BBC had access to the Derby.

I'd been plagued with bronchitis that year and pined for a little warm sun before Pat and I had our fortnight in Switzerland. Wanting to avoid the long flight to Mauritius or the Seychelles (which tended to be prolonged by breakdowns in those days) or even my favourite, Antigua, I flew to Malta (which must stretch the brochure writer's imagination) to think about 'Commercial's' proposition. Tracked down, through the head porter of the Sheraton, to the apartment I had rented, I received a cable from David Montagu on 20 February with an 'urgent request' to call him that evening in London. Speaking as both a director of London Weekend Television and a friend, he assured me that I would never regret the move. It had to be good advice. In the same year the BBC was to lose Newmarket by default and ITV had every classic. Yet somehow I think Jimmy knew and I knew, throughout our negotiation, that I would stick with the Beeb, as I did; with not a few disputes to follow throughout the duration.

In fact the 'old firm' showed no little enterprise in 1967 during a six weeks' racing ban owing to an epidemic of foot and mouth disease. With domestic racing 'off' throughout December, Clive Graham, Julian Wilson and I went to Saint-Cloud to cover three races for *Grandstand* on the second Saturday of the month. It occurred to me that there were better ways of spending a Friday night in Paris than staying in my hotel room learning the colours of sixty-one runners, but, hopefully, I would know them by morning. The following Saturday *Grandstand* featured the World's First Electronic Horse Race, which I commentated from the Atlas computer at London University.

The next assignment, Boxing Day transmission of jumping from Cagnes-sur-Mer, might have been more enjoyable without the accompaniment of 'flu. But only just. The engagement meant spending Christmas in the vicinity of the South of France circuit – which should have been no hardship, except that I left the hotel booking to the BBC for the first time in my life. And the last. I didn't expect to be booked into La Réserve at nearby Beaulieu or that delicious little hideaway, just above the Côte d'Azur racecourse, Le Cagnard, at Haut-de-Cagnes, or even that monument to Victoriana along the coast, the Negresco. But neither was it my ambition to spend Christmas in the red light district of Nice in an establishment which featured linoleum flooring throughout, a jug of cold water and a chamber pot in the bedroom, a single cigarette-scarred blanket on an iron bedstead and, presumably to inhibit the suicidally inclined, no hanging space. There was no service, though an arrangement could be made for the delivery of *petit déjeuner* from a 'local' café. Well cooled in transit, the coffee was served at room temperature, which was arctic. The only communication with the outside world was via a pay phone in a dark lobby which featured the sole concession to luxurious living – a dead plant.

When Pat learnt that I had left the reservation of my room to the BBC, she reacted with the divine instinct of her sex by inserting a hot water bottle in my suitcase. When I took it to the deserted local café for filling, in the interest of reducing the dampness of the sullen grey sheets, and ordered a *vin chaud* to wash down the antibiotics, I have to admit that the generous offer of the well-upholstered young waitress to provide more substantial warmth was, like the proposition of ITV, declined with just an element of regret.

The object of the visit might have been a greater success without the intervention of a near-cyclonic Boxing Day storm which burst over the Alpes Maritimes at midday, snatching racegoers' headgear and creating an undulating background of spray as mountainous waves crashed against the promenade on the far side of the course. The duckboard which was my commentary platform on the flat, open grandstand roof was two inches below the waterline. The tangle of cables made it an ideal site for the electrocution of those in the area. Twice *Grandstand* lost pictures. As I wrote at the end of 'copy', phoned from Nice Airport shortly after coming off air and while changing my socks and shoes,

No sooner had an engineer pronounced the situation 'excessively dangerous' than smoke from an exploding monitor enveloped cameramen and commentator. It wasn't easy to distinguish the producer's 'talk-back' above the rooftop gale, but I was grateful for his comforting observation: 'If that bronchial cough doesn't get you first, you should have the consolation of dying in microphone harness.' Hope you enjoyed your Christmas too.

At £50 for the assignment I did not feel I had been extravagantly overpaid.

The next time I got out of bed was to take myself to the English Electric Computer Centre in Bayswater on Saturday, 30 December when, in the absence of the real thing, I was to 'call' the *Evening Standard*-sponsored, computer-programmed King George VI Chase. As with the earlier electronic race, the *Grandstand* feature received widespread coverage, in France and Ireland as well as England. Betting shops reported plenty of business and very little money for the 100/1 winner Master Mascus, owned by Essex estate agent John Bairstow, trained by David Thom and ridden by the amateur John Lawrence. After the twenty-one-runner race, in which the 1963 Gold Cup winner, Mill House, was fourth, and the Queen Mother's Makaldar a faller, the *Standard* gave me a cheque for £1000 to present to John on behalf of the Injured Jockeys' Fund.

And what a happy day it was for the world of racing, when legally qualified John Lawrence, the future Lord Oaksey – whose more actively achieved triumph aboard Taxidermist in the Hennessy Gold Cup I enjoyed commentating at Cheltenham in 1958 – opted for appraising innocent horses in preference to defending guilty men. For thirty-one years obligatory reading in the *Daily Telegraph* and twenty-nine in *Horse and Hound* before joining the *Racing Post* in 1988, John teamed up with ITV in 1970. It was a significant year in the history of televised racing. Ex-BBC man John McMillan, then Director of ITV Sport, had reinforced Commercial's negotiating team. And the Corporation's racing horizon was shrinking fast. On 16 September 1970 I wrote,

ITV, which already has exclusive rights to the screening of four of England's five classics, could achieve a nap hand in 1971. 'Commercial' has just renewed a high-priced three year contract with the Epsom–Sandown combine. As the Derby is a national event BBC cameras have access to it – providing they can pay the asking price. 'We have made a financial proposal and we are awaiting the Corporation's reply,' said the Director of ITV Sport, John McMillan, yesterday. 'Of course they may not reply at all,' he added, 'in which case we'll assume they don't want it'. By the end of the current year ITV will have arranged to screen 157 programmes compared with the BBC's 83. Two years ago ITV covered 110 days. 'We are relentlessly pursuing our expansionist policy,' declared Mr McMillan, confirming that the exclusive Newcastle contract looked like becoming 'Commercial's' latest acquisition.

ITV's aggressive strategy coincided with demands for greatly increased fees from racecourses – a short-sighted policy in view of the benefits conferred by TV in the area of sponsorship – and Peter Dimmock reacted like a wounded and cornered bear. In October 1970 I reported that *Timeform*'s £40,000 charity race day at Doncaster the following July, which had been offered to BBC and ITV, would be covered exclusively by 'Commercial'; that Peter Dimmock would relinquish the option to extend the Corporation's contract with Cheltenham following unacceptable proposals; and that extension of agreement with Good-wood was in jeopardy. I quoted him saying, 'There are a substantial number of viewers who do not like so much horseracing on the screen. Our job is to maintain a balanced output in sport.'

I reacted with, 'It would be interesting to know how many top "live" race-casts could have been transmitted for the price of last night's brief recorded film of a boxing walk-over.' Paul Fox, then Controller of BBC 1, courteously responded by letter, 'The price for last night's recording of the Clay fight would have brought us *either* the 1971 Derby *or* half the 1971 Grand National *or* two-thirds of the 1971 Royal Ascot meeting.' When I reacted with a fusillade of protest, Paul, who left to become Director of Programmes at Yorkshire TV in 1973, returning fifteen years later, patiently asked:

to be allowed one come-back so that our dialogue on the Derby v. Clay may be based on fact.
1. Derby 1970; Live, mid-week afternoon – Audience: 3 million.
2. Clay ('non-event' in your phrase); Recorded and shown 17 hours after it happened: Audience: 15 million.
In this harsh, harsh world, which is better value for money?

As Professor Joad used to say, 'It depends what you mean by "value for money".' My guess is that a higher percentage of the total audience were more entertained, enthralled and uplifted by the privilege of viewing the vibrantly 'live' action at Epsom, where the majestic Nijinksy outran Gyr – a horse who would himself have won nine Derbys out of ten – by a remarkable two and a half lengths, to become home-grown champion Lester Piggott's fifth winner of the most renowned horse race in the world, than they were by the unappetizing bloody demolition of J. Quarry by C. Clay in a non-championship, one-sided encounter in Atlanta, Georgia, which was stopped in the third furlong.

The embattled bear, Peter Dimmock, hoping to draw the attention of the Racecourse Association to the benefits of television coverage, announced the withdrawal of BBC cameras on three Saturdays (23 and 30 January, and 6 February) as 'an experiment'. Clerks of the respective courses were not overjoyed by the decision, and on 7 January 1971 I quoted Kempton's Henry Hyde: 'We have the Ladbroke Handicap Hurdle on 30 January and when arranging this with the sponsors, I stated, in all good faith, that the event would be televised. Happily they have generously agreed to abide by their commitment.' By way of a postscript to the report I added, 'As an alternative to live colour race coverage, it is understood that the BBC is now facing up to the task of finding films of sufficient antiquity and banality to qualify for TV screening.' Henry Hyde's prediction that 'The BBC will "miss out" by tossing the ball into ITV's court' was later fulfilled at Kempton, and on 8 April 1971 I was further reporting, sadly:

Scottish racing will be shunned by BBC TV on all but one day in 1971. 'It's disgraceful', declared Ayr's secretary Bill McHarg when revealing the Corporation's intention yesterday. Although less than fully serious when suggesting, 'the Scottish Nationalists should rise up against the English dictators', the boss of Scotland's premier racecourse, which has been a mainstay of BBC coverage since telecasts began, is clearly upset by the regrettable development.

I asked Lord Rosebery to intercede with the upper echelons of the Corporation. And he did, willingly. But all he received was a bland acknowledgement, marginally less exasperating than the response I elicited on another occasion from a dweller in the Corporation's ivory tower when protesting over the BBC's failure to exercise its option to televise the Derby. 'After all,' he wrote, 'it is an event of relatively short duration'. In retrospect, for all the good I did and all the hostility I engendered by bombarding heads of this and heads of that with a plethora of protest, I might just as well have saved the stamps for returning the occasional commentary contract and kept my mouth shut, except when calling the horses.

There were only two occasions when, indirectly, I may have exercised a little influence. After fifteen years' consecutive Derby coverage, 'Auntie' absented herself in 1975 (year of the gallant chestnut Grundy) on the grounds of acute financial constriction. It was supposed to be a 'one-off'. But like taxes – once imposed, seldom rescinded – it became a 'two-off' in 1976 when I reported on 15 April:

BBC TV is 'out' of the classics. Following a 'top level' decision within the corporation, the Epsom Derby will be shunned by BBC cameras for the second successive year. In consequence ITV has exclusive rights to all five English classics. Epsom's impresario, Air Commodore 'Brookie' Brooks, understated his feelings yesterday when reacting to the BBC news by saying: 'It is a tremendous shame. As a national event, the Derby is, of course, available to both channels, irrespective of contract.' 'Brookie' shares a widespread view that the BBC function is to provide a service. To opt out of association with the most renowned horserace in the world, is not only to fail in the context of service. It means that BBC viewers are deprived of access to a vital recording in the build-up to subsequent events, such as the Irish Derby, King George VI and Queen Elizabeth Diamond Stakes and (until they lost it) Prix de l'Arc de Triomphe.

International rugby star Cliff Morgan had lately been appointed Head of Outside Broadcasts, with equally likeable former *Express* colleague Sam Leitch his sports chief. When it came to renegotiating my annual contract – on my part seeking to improve commentary fees while agreeing to broadcast only for the BBC – I proposed 'exclusivity' on the understanding that we went back to Epsom on D-Day. It could not be agreed contractually, but there was a tacit understanding. And we did indeed cover The Minstrel–Hot Grove epic, which of course the Beeb might have done anyway. But they defected, once again, the following year.

As I've said before, I expect, if you are going to drop names, you might as well drop good ones. Bob McCreery and I had taken over a Chelsea restaurant to give a little racing party of sixteen to Queen Elizabeth the Queen Mother. Apart from an unexpected diversion when the jazz pianist booked for the occasion froze everybody in their tracks by striking up a lengthy rendition of the national anthem as the guest of honour entered from Walton Street, conferring that uniquely heart-warming smile on the gathered assembly, it was a great evening.

Before coffee, when Bob and I surrendered our dinner-table places to Willie Carson and John Francome, who gave the royal guest animated instruction in the art of playing spoof while Peter Easterby worked on selling a horse to Jim Joel and Dick Wilkins, I had played the well-worn O'Sullevan LP on the BBC and the Derby to my captive neighbour – not for the first time. It would, the Queen Mother concurred, be very disappointing if the Corporation were to spurn the imminent (1979) celebration of the bicentenary classic. In her irresistible, almost impishly conspiratorial manner, blue eyes sparkling, the Queen Mother saw no reason why I shouldn't associate her thoughts with my annual plea. In addressing it to Sam Leitch, and stressing the historical significance of the event, I did add the reminder that the Queen herself was patron of the Jockey Club.

The BBC did it. And it was one of my worst broadcasts – which is saying something. Willie Carson made a bold decision, widely criticized at the time, when he elected to ride Troy for Sir Michael Sobell and his son-in-law, General Electric chairman Sir Arnold (later Lord) Weinstock, in preference to stable companion Milford, owned by the Queen. Willie had won that classic 'bogey' race, the White Rose Stakes, by eight lengths on Milford. Subsequently he broke his right collarbone at Chester and Lester took over on the home-bred royal colt, first produce of the Queen's 1000 Guineas and French Oaks winner Highclere, in the Lingfield Derby Trial. They won a fairly modest contest by seven lengths. Willie was back in action in time to partner Troy, who started 11/4 on in an uncompetitive Predominate Stakes at Goodwood, where he also won by seven. Although Dick Hern rated the decision, 'difficult, and one I would not like to have to make myself', and Willie said he'd sleep on it, I did suggest in the following day's *Express* that 'with over a furlong to run, the clear indications were that Mr William Hunter Carson would defer hopes of a knighthood in favour of a seat on the Board of GEC'. Even so, at the Derby Club dinner my neighbour, Senior Jockey Club Handicapper David Swannell, and I nodded our heads sagely and agreed that, notwithstanding Troy's success over one and a half miles on soft ground against moderate opposition, we could not stand for a son of Petingo getting the trip in a fast-run race.

Maybe that's why I was still saying, 'Troy is coming there strongly,' when he had already streaked clear to become the widest margin winner (seven lengths) of the world's premier classic for fifty-four years. The viewing figures (for what they are worth) showed that, although ITV covered the races which preceded the Derby, a very significant majority tuned in to BBC coverage for the big one. 'Brookie' Brooks, the United Racecourses supremo, noted, 'Your people must have been pleased with the figures, I wonder if that'll mean you're back?' It didn't. Roger Mortimer, one of the most entertaining chroniclers of the racing scene of his era, was already writing in *The Racehorse* on 14 March 1980:

It is typical of the BBC to decide not to show England's greatest race, the Derby, on TV this year. That the loftier echelons of the BBC have little love for racing is well known, but it really is a bit thick putting up financial reasons for the decision while apparently money is available for dreary American sludge like *Wonder Woman*, the only excuse for which is that it is presumably designed to cater for viewers who find *Blankety Blank* too intellectual.

Roger was surely right about the 'upper echelons', but the Head of Sport at the time, Alan Hart, would have firmly favoured sending cameras to Epsom, his departmental budget permitting. From 1968 to 1977 he was a skilful editor of *Grandstand* and, as far as I was concerned, a particularly supportive one. But we had a regrettable falling-out after his promotion, when I strongly criticized jettisoning a late-starting Hennessy Gold Cup (1979) to avoid missing the preliminaries at a Twickenham Rugby International. Under the *Sporting Life* headline on 26 November 1979 'O'SULLEVAN SLAMS BBC OVER "LOST" RACE', their reporter John McCririck accurately quoted me: 'It confirms a long held conviction that the BBC hierarchy simply regard racing as a filler', and a lot more besides.

It was a view with which BBC's longest-serving, outstanding racing producer, Dennis Monger, fully concurred. But at a small dinner party a few of us gave for him in Chelsea the following month to mark his retirement, Dennis questioned my wisdom in speaking and writing as I had. And Julian Wilson told Pat, 'They'll get him for this.' Of course it may have been sheer coincidence, but after belting from racecourse to studio every Friday evening for eighteen months, to contribute a brief racing insert to a TV sport slot, my presence was never again required.

If the grounds for the BBC's Derby defection were financial, a significant reason was the high participation fee demanded by the contract holders, ITV. Their long-time key man, Colonel Peter Moor, wartime DSO and MC, who became a founder associate of 'Commercial' in 1954 and bought the rights to their first classic when paying Doncaster £5000 for the 1957 St Leger, saw to that. Although the Epsom agreement incorporated eight other racing days (Oaks, Coronation Cup and so on), he virtually assessed the total contract value to be represented by the one event. 'It obviously suited my purpose and I was amazed to get away with it,' he reflected after retirement in 1981.

It was this valuation that I repeatedly, and unavailingly, sought to have queried. The nearest I got to doing so was on Friday, 1 July 1977. During racing at Sandown that day 'Brookie' Brooks, who had masterminded the first Hong Kong day programme, discussed the Sandown contract and the 'weighting' of the Derby fee. 'Why don't you have a go at your people to put in a bid for Sandown?' inquired the much-decorated air-commodore. I didn't need any encouragement. Commentators are only exceptionally invited to upper-level BBC hospitality. There was an exception in my case that very evening, since the dinner was to mark the appointment of Bryan Cowgill as Director of News and Current Affairs; he and I had worked together for some years on *Sportsview* and *Grandstand*.

In fact in 1973, during an interview with one of the great sports interpreters of all time, Hugh McIlvanney, Bryan, who was given to startling outbursts of extravagant comment, was quoted as saying, 'I've worked with O'Sullevan man and boy for twenty-five years and I've never known the bugger to be wrong. The man's an expert's expert. There are others who have more to say before and after a race, but while the horses are running he is on his own, without a rival. Between the starting-stalls and the winning line Peter is Holy Writ.' I mention this for two reasons: first, because comprehensively unwarranted as I knew it to be, the implicit reassurance was/is irresistible; and second (a poor second) to indicate that we were not on unfavourable terms.

Anyway, during aperitif time in the high altitude of Television Centre I cornered the unfortunate Bryan and received a firm mandate – see your man tomorrow, set up a meeting and we'll go for it; Sandown and very possibly Epsom too. So much for the once every few years Saturday off for the finals at Wimbledon. Brookie and I went over details well before racing on Saturday (the day following the announcement by Victor Matthews that Trafalgar House had acquired Beaverbrook Newspapers) and agreed a session with Bryan Cowgill the next week. My selection, Arctic Tern, ran a disappointing third behind Artaius in the Eclipse. I'd have been better off at Wimbledon, especially after Brookie's call around lunchtime on Monday. No, I hadn't seen the midday editions. 'Better pour yourself a drink before I read you the *Evening Standard* headline,' he advised. It read, in three-inch deep letters, 'COWGILL JOINS ITV.' Surely the fastest Channel crossing ever.

Ironically it was Bryan Cowgill who, two years later, executed the *coup de grâce* which ousted BBC TV from Kempton (where I'd covered every King George VI Chase from 1947 to 1979) and secured Epsom and Sandown as well for ITV. At the United Racecourses Board meeting towards the end of April 1979 a decision was reached to offer exclusive rights to Epsom, Kempton and Sandown as a £1 million package for a three-year-contract. Chairman Evelyn de Rothschild and Managing Director Tim Neligan (appointed in October 1977) were authorized to do the deal. The competitors were agreed on one point – a million was out of the question. Independently, each bid £800,000. Peter Moor, who had slipped in early at Epsom, so that BBC had always been obliged to pay Commercial a fee, was the first to move. He went to £850,000. Auntie went a little pale, but matched him. 'Personally,' admitted Tim ten years later, 'I favoured the BBC as a partner.' If the bidding had ceased at that point the probability is that the 'old firm' would have secured the prize; and, notwithstanding the limitations of its 'commercial' lung, BBC Enterprises, it would have generated considerable overseas income in the process. But Peter went back to his boss, Thames TV's Head of Sport, and Bryan sprang another £50,000, stressing that United Racecourses must be told that £900,000 was as far as they would go. So on a balmy morning in May Mike Dolbear, for thirteen years

BBC contracts manager, who lived nearby, and Head of Outside Broadcasts, Cliff Morgan, met in Tim Neligan's Epsom office just one more time.

Three years earlier, in 1976, Cliff had been involved in contrastingly relaxed negotiations for the Grand National. That year was the first of seven Ladbroke-managed Nationals and – brainchild of John Hughes – the first all-jumping Aintree programme of the era. The international rugger star and the outstanding racing impresario, at whose memorial service on 10 November 1988 Cliff was to pay such warm-hearted tribute, were close friends. The BBC entered into the spirit of the Grand National rescue operation, which was a credit to the Ladbroke team. ITV didn't appear to want to know, so it was a matter of establishing a fair fee. £110,000 was agreed – a sum which would be split fifty–fifty if 'Commercial' decided to exercise their entitlement to cover the only other designated national racing event apart from the Derby. They didn't.

When Cliff, encouraged by Mike, now bid £950,000 for that United Racecourses contract – admitting, years later, in that soft Welsh cadence, 'We were already into £200,000 more than we had to play with' – he was as sure as a man can be, before the number goes in the frame and the blue flag is hoisted, that 'Everything was OK'. Tim Neligan reckoned, 'The BBC was ninety per cent there.'

Peter Moor was at Newmarket when he heard the news, and rang Bryan Cowgill from a coin box. 'Send Neligan a telegram,' the flame-haired Lancastrian told him. 'Say you'll pay £1 million, to include world rights.' In a letter dated 21 May 1979, addressed to ITV's negotiator, Tim Neligan wrote, 'Dear Peter, many thanks for your telegram. My Board intends to accept . . .' The contract between United Racecourses and ITV was officially agreed on 7 July that year. Except for a brief period in 1982, the prospect of BBC cameras returning to Epsom on Derby day were all of 33/1, and poor value at that.

The brief period followed an informal luncheon at Portman Square to which the Senior Steward of the Jockey Club, Captain Johnnie Macdonald-Buchanan, invited five guests who included the Director-General of the BBC, Alasdair Milne, and myself. Talk ranged over a variety of topics, and it was coffee time before I had shuffled my soap box into position and started to launch into the O'Sullevan moan about the BBC's classics profile. Alasdair, obviously well prepared for this one, leaned across the table and said, 'Don't worry, Peter, you'll have your Derby back this year.' I have never enjoyed a glass of port more. 'That was good news,' reflected the Senior Steward after the chief guest had departed.

But as the weeks went by and I seemed to be the only one remotely associated with the BBC who knew we were covering the Derby, a little unease developed. So I put somebody in to discover the SP. They reported that the Director-General had reacted by saying that of course the Corporation was not going to be represented at Epsom. If anyone had gained a contrary impression, it was simply that he had had no intention of getting involved in a dialogue with Peter O'Sullevan about it in front of the Jockey Club.

As well as Bryan Cowgill, another very likeable migratory executive, Michael Grade, who joined the Corporation in September 1984, did the cause of BBC racing no great service before leaving in November 1987 for Channel 4. When I wrote him in May 1986 (after he had endorsed the regrettable forfeiture of the main three-day Chester meeting) expressing dismay over a rumour that the 1986 Arc de Triomphe was to be ditched as well, the reply was hardly reassuring: 'It is on the same afternoon as the World Matchplay and a quick flip to Paris could be feasible.' However, a letter dated 20 June from Sports-Tel (agents for the Société d'Encouragement) to a senior *Grandstand* operative read: 'In response to my question concerning the BBC's intention towards purchasing the Arc de Triomphe, you informed me that the BBC had internally taken a decision not to cover the Arc this year.' Happily the Longchamp victory surge of Dancing Brave, who would have had a lot more to do had it not been for Bering's injury, was not lost to televiewers, as Channel 4 snapped up the prize. And with more than a 'quick flip', which in the late eighties became the pattern of BBC domestic Saturday coverage.

CHAPTER 21

Be Friendly

During the early morning flight from Orly to Heathrow on Monday, 11 April 1960, I was updating my score in twenty-one years of racehorse ownership. Twenty-one horses had carried my colours in 149 races, winning four of them – every one a 'seller'. It read like a blueprint for economic suicide. I'd been reporting the previous day's Prix Greffulhe in Paris and was bound for the less obvious charms of Wolverhampton, where Chinchilla, the little grey filly from whom George Moore had fallen on Derby eve the previous year, was running in a three-years-old maiden handicap.

She not only had the unextravagant burden to which her modest record entitled her, but a top lightweight in Tommy Carter to help her through ground which would have been recorded 4.5 on the penetrometer in France, where the going is measured on the scale of 1 to 5 – from bone dry to heavy. Her best race as a two-year-old had been in similarly holding conditions over the same trip, six furlongs, when fourth of thirty-one in a back-end Lingfield seller. This year, in her only previous race, she'd just got caught and beaten three parts of a length in a seven furlongs selling handicap at Lincoln. I'd rung Wolverhampton for a going report before phoning copy on Sunday and tipped Chinchilla each-way.

An imperturbable girl, she'd travelled from Epsom overnight, had eaten up on arrival, wasn't due to run until the fifth at 3.30, and when I went to see her in the racecourse stables before the first she was lying down having a kip. Within half an hour I'd learnt of three who were sure to beat her; Harry Carr, in particular, insisted, 'Whatever you do, you must save on mine.' Harry's partner was a gelding, Palma Grande, whom *Raceform* had noted finishing strongly as a 20/1 chance when fourth in a thirty-three-runner handicap at Windsor on his seasonal debut. This afternoon he started favourite.

One way and another, there were no grounds for an immoderate punt. Unusually, there would be no auction after the race. I had a score on Palma Grande and £40 each way Chinchilla. Under a caption: PETER O'SULLEVAN QUIZZES A WINNING OWNER, my copy for 12 April 1960 ran:

Well, I never thought Wolverhampton racecourse would appear more attractive than Longchamp. But it certainly did through one pair of binoculars yesterday afternoon, when Chinchilla finally triumphed over fourteen opponents. It seemed an opportunity for an interview at which the usual polite formalities could safely be dispensed with.

'What's the matter with you?' I asked the successful owner. 'Your hair's sticking out under your hat, you're pale as a ghost and you're trembling like a leaf.'

'It's just that I'm rather excited,' he explained, adding: 'You see it's the first time I've ever won a non-seller.'

'I see you tipped it each way,' I said. 'Didn't you KNOW it was going to win?'

'If you're going to ask idiotic questions,' he replied, 'I won't talk to you.'

'All right,' I said. 'How much did you have on it?'

'A quarter as much as when she mislaid her jockey at Epsom last year,' he said. 'And the same amount as when she failed at Alexandra Park, Lingfield, at Epsom again, Salisbury, and more recently at Lincoln.'

'How much did you pay for her,' I then quizzed.

'Eight hundred and twenty-five guineas as a yearling,' he replied.

'So what with training fees, gallops' fees, veterinary bills, entrance and jockeys' fees and travelling costs, etc., how much does she stand you in now?'

With a look of pained resignation, he confessed: 'Around £2400.'

'And yet,' I said, 'having won a race worth £210 you're delighted.'

'That's right,' he said.

'There must be cheaper ways of having fun,' I persisted. 'So why do you go in for owning? Can't you lose enough friends tipping horses every day in the *Express*?'

'Maybe,' he replied. 'But I like it.'

'You must be barmy,' I said. 'Dead raving potty. And you look as though you could do with a drink.'

He could, he said. So I bought him one. And after a couple I swear he was ready to match Chinchilla against Petite Etoile. Oh, well. It takes all sorts.

Cyril Mitchell was marginally less overwhelmed by the merit of my heroine's triumph over maiden contemporaries and, for an encore, proposed a Hurst Park seller, in which we were lucky to get the verdict. Tommy Carter had struck the front a furlong out in an eighteen-runner field, and Chinchilla was beginning to run out of puff inside the last hundred yards when Garnie Bougoure, riding for Chesney Allen (of the Crazy Gang) loomed up, full of running, on Bright and Breezy. As the pair swept by they edged perilously close to the fading grey before racing clear. The manoeuvre was a signal for Tommy to give the impression of having been grossly impeded by accomplishing what Scobie Breasley later referred to as 'a performance of which Laurence Olivier would have been justly proud'.

The injured party returned to the second stall, seething with righteous indignation, insisting that he must object as there was no doubt whatever regarding the outcome. Opinion in the ring was evenly divided, so that you could bet 5/4 on either of them. Personally I had been less than fully convinced by the histrionic talent of Chinchilla's partner and 'saved' on the first past the post. Wrong again. The objection was sustained and Bright and Breezy's trainer, Monty Smyth, who was not best pleased, ran me up to 520 guineas (more than the first-prize money) at the subsequent auction. It was a week before we shared conciliatory refreshment, repeated when Bright and Breezy, without a semblance of infringement, won a seller at Sandown.

The following year, at Newmarket September sales, I fell for a Chinchilla lookalike, with a little more scope, by first-crop sire Quorum, whose most celebrated offspring turned out to be one-time 'plater' and triple Grand National winner Red Rum. Rather than acting on my own meagre judgement I sought reassurance from Etienne Pollet, with whom I was talking as the offering from Irish breeder Willie Madden paraded in the preliminary ring. While the distinguished French trainer conceded that the object of my admiration appeared in no way 'incorrect', he left a clear impression that she did not wholly fulfil his criteria for a potential *classique*. At my self-imposed three-figure limit this was, perhaps, unsurprising. When she was knocked down to me at 820 guineas I rang my absent, silent partner Stephen Raphael and suggested that, while we might not emulate his cousin Walter, the only man to win the Derby with a grey filly (Tagalie in 1912), we should win another seller at least.

It turned out to be a fortuitous bid. Not that Friendly Again (whose immediate unrelated predecessor, Still Friendly, had won us a seller at Epsom) turned out to be any sort of *classique*. Rather far from it. Soon after I'd bought her, Quorum's former trainer Colonel Wilfred Lyde, who won the Free Handicap, Jersey and Queen Anne Stakes, among other races, with the grey son of Vilmorin, kindly wrote to say he was delighted I'd bought one of the new stallion's produce, as 'I never trained a nicer, more honest, genuine, horse.' He was sure he'd get stock in his own image. Well, 'sweet FA', as she inevitably was styled by the least impolite toilers in the yard, inherited all the desirable characteristics of her progenitor except the ability to quicken. In thirty-four outings, on the Flat, over hurdles and fences, between the ages of two and six, she made the frame eighteen times, but the winner's circle only twice. Over distances varying between five furlongs and two miles she finished second no fewer than ten times – taking with her to the stud, aged six, the secret of her favoured trip.

During a BBC TV transmission from Kempton on Saturday, 16 May 1964 I was commentating the 1¼ miles Diadumenos Handicap in which she looked home and hosed, having taken it up half a mile out, before getting caught in the last couple of strides by Sir Winston Churchill's Sun Hat. Ron Hutchinson rode her that day and figured that maybe she needed an extra two furlongs. Reunited over 1½ miles of the same circuit on another TV afternoon, Saturday, 17 April 1965, they were again touched off in the Paragon Selling Handicap. 'What am I going to say now, Pete?' laughed Hutchie.

Next time out we ran her one mile five and a half furlongs in Sandown's Long Distance Apprentices' Selling Handicap. It has to be said that there may never have been a more modest contest staged on what colleagues of an earlier era invariably referred to as 'the slopes of Esher'. So modest that Friendly Again, ridden by stable apprentice Michael Day, started 5/4 on and won by two and a half lengths. In the interim she had been runner-up in the Clive Graham Handicap Hurdle at Cheltenham on 11 April 1964 – the last time her partner, the great Fred Winter, was placed under National Hunt rules – and a short head winner, under a widely acclaimed ride by sixteen-year-old Andy Turnell, of Lingfield's Carewell Hurdle on 19 December. Andy's first ride outside his father Bob's stable, Friendly Again (100/8) was pictured in the *Express* becoming a vital ingredient in a 131/1 O'Sullevan treble at a time when, regretfully, I was phoning copy from bed, owing to being laid up.

I'd have preferred to be absent from Beaverbrook Newspapers day at Cheltenham on 3 April 1965, when she nearly promoted heart failure. I've always found impartial commentary less attainable over hurdles and fences than on the level – especially when one's own are involved. The temptation to focus on fallers and verify survival is irresistible. 'My God, I've killed Stan Mellor,' was my shocked unspoken reaction while calling the 3 o'clock, the Peter O'Sullevan Chase. The mare had schooled well before handling the stiff Kempton fences on her chasing debut, and this was Stan's first ride on her. The pair were going great within a length of the favourite, Pat Taaffe-ridden Cottagebrook, four from home, when I heard myself shout, 'Friendly Again is down.' She was on her feet and galloping within seconds, but Stan lay motionless.

As the leaders jumped the second last, Barrie Edgar, the producer, said through my headset, 'I'm going to give you a shot of the injured jockey.' I looked in the monitor as a St John's Ambulance Brigade volunteer crouched over the prostrate body three-quarters of a mile away, and murmured some banality about Stan Mellor receiving attention. (You get some strange letters. One aggrieved lady viewer wrote afterwards complaining, 'You said a jockey was receiving attention but you didn't say what was the matter with him.') The picture was not very reassuring.

Nor was I happy about the riderless grey's headlong flight in the direction of the lower end of the Members' Enclosure. If she'd jumped the open ditch with the agility she showed when bounding into this hallowed precinct there might have been a different outcome to the third race on the card. As it was, she behaved so impeccably on landing, allowing the first member who offered assistance to lead her towards the unsaddling enclosure, that the Chairman of the Cheltenham Steeplechase Company, Lord Willoughby de Broke, in accepting my apology for unauthorized entry, graciously wrote conferring life membership upon her.

Stan had to forgo the rest of his Saturday rides. But the indestructible, thrice-successive champion who, like such equally fine contemporaries as Fred Winter and Johnnie Gilbert, used skill rather than stick to inspire maximum effort, was back in action at Leicester the following Monday.

Long before she herself was due to enter the marriage stakes, Friendly Again had provided a clue to the possibility that her dam, covered by more of a speed specialist than the admirable Quorum, just could produce a runner equipped with that elusive extra gear. This was how she guided her Skymaster-sired half-brother, Be Friendly, into Cyril Mitchell's stable, and made her contribution to what at Haydock Park shortly after 2.30 p.m. on Saturday 5 November 1966 seemed an extravagant dream.

The dream contained such improbable ingredients as a fine and exuberantly athletic chestnut two-year-old named Be Friendly, carrying my undistinguished black and yellow colours, ridden by an apprentice who could not claim his allowance, striding clear of the season's acknowledged top senior sprinters inside the final furlong – according to my BBC TV commentary – to win the richest all-aged race ever staged in Britain by a comfortable two lengths and to receive a generous ovation in the process. The dream further included such unlikely embellishment as Be Friendly at 15/2 (10/1 to early customers) landing the O'Sullevan nap and becoming the middle leg of a 57/1 *Daily Express* treble completed by another swift-rising young star, Persian War, at Sandown where the gallant Freddie won the Gallaher Gold Cup.

The hazard of tipping is compounded by ownership. Optimism may be unjustified; pessimism misconstrued. Twenty-four hours before post-time for the inaugural Vernon's November Sprint Cup I had intended to make Be Friendly one of my three daily selections – but with a firm each-way proviso. Influenced by the Prix de la Forêt and Prix de l'Abbaye at Longchamp, I believed that at this time of the year two-year-olds of sufficient quality had a great chance at weight-for-age against their elders. Had Be Friendly the necessary quality?

The handsome colt with an unspectacular pedigree, whom Stephen Raphael and I had bought for a then by no means inconsiderable 2800 guineas at the 1965 Newmarket October sales, had been beaten under 8 stone 1 lb in the 10 September Highclere Nursery at Newbury by a rival who was totally unfancied. Sid Dale-trained Early Turn, unsuccessful on his seven previous runs and receiving 12 lb, wasn't even plated. It was the last race and, despite no slight disappointment (BF at 13/2 had been a cautious 'each-way' in the *Express* but I'd plunged win only) I couldn't help laughing at the sight of lifelong friends Sid Dale and Cyril Mitchell standing together in the unsaddling enclosure, awaiting the return of their warriors, hats thrust to the back of their heads, looking as though they'd been pole-axed.

Cyril and I had a marvellous working relationship. A former tough, grafting jump jockey, he took an irreverent view of the 'art' of training, believing that some horses are naturally better than others and that it is the trainer's job 'to see that he doesn't screw up the good ones'. His admiration for jockeys was also kept well under control.

We'd been together as owner and trainer for better (sometimes) or worse (also), in financial sickness and in health, for only a decade when County Limerick-born Be Friendly took up residence in the Burgh Heath stable. The most expensive of his predecessors had cost 820 guineas; we very rarely set our sights above 'sellers' and it was not uncommon to receive a call a few weeks before the opening of the Flat to say, 'I don't know how we're going to win a race with *this* one.' I feared the worst when he rang earlier in the year than usual in 1966, saying, 'It looks as though you've done it this time.' Nice, I thought, remembering that a vet had 'spun' him for a suspect hook (there's always something) at Newmarket.

'Done what?' I inquired anxiously.

'Bought one that can run,' he said, 'and I do mean run.'

It is widely held that if a two-year-old can work with an older horse at a difference of 15 lb around February–March and look him in the eye, then his handler has reasonable grounds for assuming the possibility of settling at least one account to the disadvantage of his bookmaker.

I was staying at Doncaster (which had taken over from Lincoln) for the opening meeting of the season when Cyril called to report that 'himself' had left an older horse for dead at near enough weight-for-age. 'What?' I asked. 'Receiving 15 lb?'

My caller lowered his voice and whispered, 'No, *conceding* 15 lb.' He added, 'The horse he worked with runs at Lingfield tomorrow when you'll be at Aintree. You'd better have a tenner on him – he's called Espeekay.'

Clever. I said it would be reward enough if Espeekay finished in the first ten, and that if he won I'd probably jump off the stands at Liverpool. Luckily I'd finished commentating Lester Piggott winning the 4.10 Liverpool Spring Cup on Patron Saint and had regained ground level before learning the outcome of Lingfield's 4.15 – Espeekay, 'cleverly', at 20/1!

So, in theory anyway, we knew that Be Friendly's lad Tony Boyle was nurturing a potential rocket. Where and when to launch him? The question was quickly resolved by another youngster in the yard.

It is said that accidents only happen to the good ones, and no sooner had our fellow flaunted his ability than he was kicked on the point of the stifle and transformed into a dejected invalid. Recovery was followed by a series of further setbacks which left him as permanently under repair as the M25. So, despite apparent precocity, it wasn't until mid-May that he made his first racecourse appearance. Even then Cyril, unconvinced by a satisfactory blood test, was a little uneasy about him, fearing that a 'bug' which was going the rounds might have taken the 'edge' off him.

The target was Lingfield's Appleblossom Stakes on Saturday, 14 May. I was reporting and BBC TV commentating at Ayr at the time, and found Cyril uncharacteristically dispirited when I phoned him on Friday evening. The two-year-old he'd run at Lingfield that day, Gay Knight, had performed way below par.

'I shan't have a penny on the colt tomorrow,' he said.

The conversation wasn't exactly private. I'd inopportunely elected to forgo Turnberry (where my expense allowance had to be heavily subsidized) in favour of conserving punting resources by lodging in more spartan accommodation in the town centre. Concessions to sybaritic living were minimal, with the only telephone located in a less than tranquil bar. For unconvivial reasons I passed the evening here – updating my *Express* 'copy' and receiving 'urgent' incoming calls from five mostly anxious French owners and trainers; the last of them, Miguel Clément, phoned from a Paris night club at 1.30 a.m.

Immensely popular Miguel (a protégé of François Mathet), whose death in a car crash on 30 August 1978 so shocked the racing world, trained eighty horses in his yard at the avenue de Joinville, Chantilly. He rarely bet, but got the flavour for an occasional punt when serving as pupil/assistant with Humphrey Cottrill at Newmarket. This year he had the right ammunition for a Derby/Oaks double – Nelcius and Phaedra. When I saw the duo in March he said he'd be getting on to me later for a little 'interest' if they came along as expected.

They did. And towards the end of the month, using six accounts, according to my betting book, I speculated singly and in each-way doubles for us both. At 40/1 each it didn't require extravagant outlay to raise the possibility of a handsome return. But we were thwarted by an outbreak of horse-sickness in France, with the result that after a good deal of uncertainty the Ministry of Agriculture and Fisheries banned the Gallic pretenders.

Good friend that he was, Miguel was simply calling me at my hotel that Friday night to make sure that I had the news, saying, 'Never mind, we'll just have to get our money back in the French Derby.' (Nelcius won that, beating the subsequent Arc de Triomphe winner, Bon Mot III, in the process.) Meanwhile part of the 14 May communiqué to my *Express* readers – to employ the plural somewhat loosely – read:

Hope you are not lumbered with as many now very costly-looking ante-post vouchers as your correspondent. Under the circumstances, a bold first effort by Be Friendly in Lingfield's opener today would be particularly welcome.

But while hoping for the best (could Be Hopeful and Be Friendly win in the same week?) even an owner's enthusiasm must be tempered by the reflection that Lady Sliptic's offspring have invariably needed the benefit of experience. A detail somewhat expensively underlined by Be Friendly's gallant half-sister Friendly Again.

I asked Cyril to please tell the pilot on no account to knock him about (who wants any horse knocked about?), but to note I was on each-way.

There were three previous winners in the race and several widely whispered newcomers, including the Duke of Norfolk's Grey Sovereign filly Luciennes, who was rumoured very useful. Nine runners. I positioned the car at the back of the stands for a quick getaway; walked in, dreaming of owning an Ayr Gold Cup winner, with Scottish bookmaker Tommy Marshall; had a 'pony' (£25) each-way with him; likewise with John Joyce as we had a coffee together, and with just about every layer on the rails.

Post time at Lingfield was 2 o'clock, but there was no chance of hearing a blow-by-blow account as this coincided with the off of the first TV race at Ayr, the three miles three furlongs Usher–Vaux Scottish Champion Hunters' Chase. I commentated this – featuring that marvellous old character Baulking Green and my pal George Small – with one eye on the local action and one on the 'away' bookmakers' boards. There was no commentary box – just a vaguely cordoned-off corner of the Members' Stand with an antique black and white monitor, on which images were unidentifiable in daylight, and a sea of cables which made it hard to get 4/1 about being electrocuted if it was raining. It was.

I wasn't worried about the electrocution bit, but concerned that a racegoer in a tam-o'-shanter appeared permanently planted in front of the only 'away' merchant who wrote out the results. When he inclined his head to light up I saw that Luciennes had won and the second began with the letter 'S'. Two down and one to go. I reported Royal Reynard a faller at the fourteenth (and horse and rider, hopefully, all right) and had another peep. There it was – Be Friendly third. Well, he couldn't have run too badly – 25/1 too. Halfway back to London I called Cyril, who reported, 'He hasn't turned a hair, enjoyed himself, and Jimmy Lindley said he'd be better for the race.'

The form looked better later in the month when Luciennes reappeared in Epsom's Caterham Stakes, which she won hard held at 9/2 on before starting favourite for the Queen Mary, in which she was badly hampered in a rough race; while On Your Mark (sixth) trotted up in the Great Surrey at Epsom before winning Royal Ascot's Windsor Castle by six lengths.

'Himself' did not return to action until 6 July. He'd developed sore shins – nature's sign of bone immaturity – and the consequent need to go slow, a procedure with which he co-operated with marked reluctance. Scobie Breasley had ridden him 'work' and been impressed.

As at Lingfield, Kempton's modestly endowed five furlongs Wren Stakes featured unknown quantities, notably Cholo, brother to the high-class speedster Abelia, trained by subsequently knighted Noel Murless and a first ride for the stable for Lester Piggott since a well-publicized 'split' two months earlier. American-bred filly Bloody Mary, out of an unbeaten Molecomb winner, had shown plenty of speed in the Queen Mary. Be Friendly had to be first or second to justify each-way selection in a seven-runner line-up.

Scobie returned full of apology. Through my unsteady binoculars Be Friendly had broken smartly and always seemed to be holding them, despite hanging slightly (drifting to his off) inside the last furlong. The maestro from Wagga Wagga rarely used his stick but to my surprise – and doubtless more so to Be Friendly's – he picked up his whip and gave him a couple. They won by two lengths.

'I must have had a rush of blood to the head being so keen to win for you,' he explained, adding, 'at least the colt took it very well. Didn't seem to resent me at all.'

The *Sporting Chronicle* reported proceedings thus:

The success which undoubtedly gave Scobie most pleasure was the one on Be Friendly in the Wren Stakes which completed the quartet.

Scobie and Be Friendly's owner colleague Peter O'Sullevan, have been close friends for many years but Scobie had never before been successful in Peter's black jacket with yellow cross belts.

After Be Friendly had slammed his rivals I don't know who looked the happiest as Scobie unsaddled this good-looking chestnut colt, who cost 2,800 guineas as a yearling, and would seem to be worth every penny of it.

That Be Friendly bore Scobie no ill-will he made perfectly clear when conveying him to Epsom's winner's circle on 30 July. On the day that England's footballers won the World Cup, the Box Hill Stakes winner's footwork was still less than perfect. Despite the attachment of blinkers he again hung right in the last furlong. As he did so I reflected on the foolhardiness of that morning's comment in the *Express* that 'the chief danger is an earthquake'.

When animals deviate from the norm they are invariably trying to convey something to dumb humans. Even now the penny hadn't dropped – namely that he was ill-at-ease on firm ground.

Scobie, who had survived a horrifying crash at Alexandra Park in 1954, resulting in temporary paralysis and imbalance, was again invalided out for the season after a fall at Newbury in August 1966. He agreed we might as well 'claim' in forthcoming nurseries because BF wasn't a difficult ride. 'You know,' he said one day when I was visiting him, 'you just might find he's even better with a bit of "give" in the ground.'

I'd been quite impressed by Colin Williams, apprenticed to that truly delightful man Jack Leader. Lester said, 'He's all right' (a reincarnation of Fred Archer could not have received higher praise), and when I met Greville Starkey having a coffee break at Norman Cross on the way to a northern meeting and sought his opinion he unhesitatingly plumped for 'young Williams'. I'll always remember Cyril's reaction when I rang to say, 'What about Jack Leader's boy Colin Williams for Newbury?'

'Never bloody heard of him!' was the reply.

When 'young Williams' got beaten in the Highclere Nursery by a rival wearing heavy exercise shoes I naturally expected Cyril to inquire, 'Where did you find *him*?'

So I got in first and said, 'The boy did nothing wrong, did he?'

'Nothing,' said shell-shocked Cyril. 'He'll do any time.'

So he rode him again in the twenty-two runner Wantage Nursery at Newbury on 22 October and, badly drawn (4) in holding going, gave

23 lb to the runner-up, a previous three lengths course winner. Both my readers were 'on' at 7/1.

'He was a different horse in this ground,' pronounced the young man from Cascade, Glamorgan. 'Smashing!'

'Highs' seldom last long in racing. There following a big disappointment when I rang Cyril the next morning to say that, after giving it thought, I very much favoured going for the Vernons at Haydock – a race I wanted to support anyway – where the ground would almost certainly suit us and where we had nothing to lose by flying high. 'Hang on, hang on,' was the reaction. 'We can't do that. When he got beat in the Highclere I thought I'd save you a tenner and took him out.'

So that was that. Until, three days later, Be Friendly's handler rang to say that 'the secretary' (his wife Robbie) had slipped up somehow and the forfeit form had been found, unposted, under the blotter. 'So if you still want to go to Haydock, we can.'

In a way it seemed daft to employ an apprentice who could not claim his allowance – tantamount to putting up 5 lb overweight – especially given the availability of top-liners like my good friends Edward Hide and Ron Hutchinson who could do the required 8 stone. But what a bonus if the two youngsters, horse and rider, could combine to launch each other into the big time.

Cyril fully concurred: 'The boy knows him. He's got confidence in him and he rides all right.'

That settled it. I rang a delighted Jack Leader and booked Colin Williams.

It looked a daunting task ahead with the specialist six furlongs sprinters, Lucasland and Dondeen, principals in the July Cup, and Diadem in the fifteen-runner line-up. Throughout racing at Haydock on the afternoon prior to the big one I was more or less resolved to tip him each-way when I ran into that noted handicap expert Eric Cousins – responsible for four Great Jubilee winners, three Ayr Gold Cups, two Lincolns, the Cambridgeshire, the Victoria Cup . . . you name it; he was to be represented by this season's WD & HO Wills Gold Trophy winner, Kamundu.

'You don't seriously believe Be Friendly's got the remotest chance, do you?' he inquired laughingly.

I did.

Eric, who trained Vernon's chairman Robert Sangster's first winner, had made a particular study of the race and was adamant that none of the two-year-olds – there were five – had any chance whatsoever.

'I guarantee you, Peter,' he insisted, 'they will not be "sighted" against the older horses.'

Well, I thought, if he's half right I'll look just as big a fool tipping each-way as if I put the nap on him.

I went up to the press room where my long-time friend, Quinnie Gilbey, was going through the 'book' before writing his last article after twenty-one years as Kettledrum of the *Sporting Chronicle* and forty-two years in racing. He looked up sharply and, in that rather high-pitched and penetrating voice, shouted across the room, 'Peter, old boy, I'm going to bloody well nap your horse tomorrow. Is there any reason why I shouldn't?'

'None whatsoever,' I replied, with more hope than conviction. 'I'm going to do exactly the same.'

I always preferred to get away from the course to send my 'copy'. So as I was staying just down the road at the Greyhound I went there to phone it over to London, who would transmit to Manchester for the northern edition. Then I set about worrying whether Be Friendly would sleep all right (he'd not been away overnight before); whether I'd handle the commentary without bias; what sort of heading they'd put on my story up north and in London (contrary to widespread misconception, the writer has no part in the caption); whether Colin Williams would turn up early, as requested, to walk the course with Alex Bird and myself (I'd asked Alex, as an exponent of the stratagem of crossing to the stands side, to help explain it); whether we were right to leave the blinkers off; whether we were asking too much of him? It was enough to ensure a sleepless night for the owner, and it did.

Colin and Alex were spot-on for our course walk – it was my second that morning – and although the ploy of crossing the course could cost one and a half lengths BF's young partner was impressed.

I still told him, 'It's entirely your decision. You're riding him, and there'll be no comeback whatever if you'd prefer to take the orthodox route.'

'No way I'll do that, sir,' says Colin. 'The ground is far better here. I *must* come over.'

'Then you'll win,' chimes in Alex. 'No argument.'

'Himself' looked a picture when Tony Boyle led him out for a pick of grass, though I nearly had a fit when he let fly through sheer *joie de vivre* and missed the rails by inches.

The Manchester edition captioned my offering: 'RAVING MAD? WELL LET'S BE FRIENDLY'. London, invariably more prosaic, thus: 'I MAY BE MAD BUT THE NAP'S BE FRIENDLY.'

The tipping tables showed that among the national, provincial and specialist papers thirty-four selectors had forecast Lucasland; ten Dondeen; five Green Park; four Kamundu; three Running Shoes, Potier and Scottie's Coin; and two Go Shell – leaving Quinnie (and I) isolated in our optimistic opinion. By now I just hoped we weren't going to be disgraced.

Alex remained contrastingly confident. He would like, he said, to back him to win £10,000, but didn't want to interfere with my commission. It was a thoughtful gesture but I pointed out that, far from planning a 'commission', I was still dithering whether to have £50 on towards presents in the event of a miracle. He inferred, politely, that I would be certifiable if I didn't. So I did – at 10/1.

The afternoon began with two handicap 'chases – subsequent Grand National winner Red Alligator passing the post first in the second but losing it after a foreseeable objection for interference. BBC *Grandstand* didn't give Clive Graham long in the paddock (surprise, surprise) prior to the big one, but he had time to come on the intercom before handing over to say, 'He looks great, Pedro. Good luck.'

Supposing he gets left, I thought – would Colin still try the planned tactic? That was something we hadn't discussed.

I told viewers not to be surprised if one of the runners, Be Friendly, ran very wide at the turn into the straight and crossed right over to the grandstand rails. That was his rider's intention. Still rather surprised that any sound came out of such a dry throat, I called, 'They're under starter's orders – and they're off.'

Jimmy Lindley had ridden Green Park to all his four victories but, unable to do the weight, was replaced by the talented Aussie Russ Maddock. It was a barrier start and Kamundu, who'd been moving in quite fast at tapesrise, showed early from another fast breaker, Potier. They were quickly overtaken by the youngsters Be Friendly (drawn 8) and Green Park (15) on his outside, who reached the elbow almost stride for stride. Here Colin began his manoeuvre.

'Keep straight, boy!' shouted Russ.

'I'm going across!' yelled Colin. And he did, virtually obliging Green Park to go with him.

When offering congratulations afterwards, and settling his £50 side bet, the latter's handler Jeremy Tree did observe drily, 'I didn't realize we were betting on a game of polo!'

It's difficult to assess relative positions accurately in the Haydock straight because the runners are racing towards the stands and unlike Ascot, for example, there is no intersection to assist judgement. Halfway up the straight, with the field spread wide apart, it looked like Dondeen the leader in the centre from Go Shell, Spanish Sail and Lucasland. But not for long. Be Friendly, who always had the edge over Green Park, began to forge clear in the final quarter, and while hearing myself calling Be Friendly the winner I leaned out of the commentary box, perched high on scaffolding overlooking the Tattersall's crowds, and gave a thumbs-up sign. When I looked down there was a pink sea of upturned faces and the generous roar penetrated my headset.

Oscar Wilde observed that it is easier to sympathize with a friend's failure than to condone his success. All the more welcome the immensely friendly reaction of the pressroom. Long-time colleague Richard Baerlein was quick to pick up and commend in the *Observer* Colin Williams's immediate post-race remark to me: 'Although I've been lucky enough to win the last two races on him, I realize Be Friendly is really Scobie Breasley's ride.' One of the first telegrams to arrive was from Barbados: 'THRILLED BY WONDERFUL NEWS BE FRIENDLY'S GREAT TRIUMPH LOVE TO YOU BOTH FROM US SCOBIE.'

Dear 'Quinnie' was so overjoyed to have signed off with a winning nap that his 'last article' on Saturday, 5 November was followed by another on Monday, 7 November!

No winning nap in my 21 years as Kettledrum has given me quite the thrill I received when Be Friendly, racing as near the stand rails as his apprentice rider Colin Williams could get him, mastered Green Park, racing with him inside the last furlong, and drew away to win by two lengths, with Dondeen, racing wide of them, two lengths away third, at Haydock on Saturday.

It is always a great joy to see a valuable race won by a close friend but Be Friendly's victory in the £5,337 Vernons November Sprint Cup in the colours of Peter O'Sullevan was also a source of personal satisfaction to me as it enabled me to terminate my journalistic career with a winning nap – and what a beauty at 15/2!

When I mentioned to him at the celebration party that I couldn't quite reconcile his Saturday paragraph proclaiming Lucasland to be 'undoubtedly one of the most brilliant sprinting fillies to run in this country for many years' with Monday's dismissive 'I have, all along, considered that this season's sprinters were a non-vintage crop, and I selected Be Friendly to win from another two-year-old, Green Park', he said, 'No wonder the buggers haven't given me a gold watch. They knew I couldn't tell the time of day.'

There was a lovely letter from my old friend Martin Gilliat; a very 'friendly' one from my former Sports Editor, Bob Findlay; generously supportive words by the current incumbent, John Morgan; an approving nod from the *Life*'s columnist everybody reads and pretends not to, Jack (Sir David Llewellyn) Logan; and a great deal of work ahead, following receipt of two sackfuls of mail, for decorative *Express* racing secretary Valerie Frost, who probably had a much less arduous workload when 'doing her two', including the Queen's redoubtable Almeria, at Freemason Lodge. The bright chestnut hero of the first

CLARENCE HOUSE
S.W.1

6ᵗʰ November.
1966.

My Dear Peter.

What a wonderful Triumph for you and all those associated with B.F.

We in the Box at Sandown were all filled with admiration for your "apparent" ice cool outlook when doing the Commentary.

Queen Elizabeth has asked me to let you know how delighted she was and sends her warmest congratulations.

Yours ever.

Martin.

SPORTS ROOM NOTICE BOARD

"What *exactly* did you say when you asked Peter O'Sullevan for a first-person story on the winner of Vernons November Handicap?"

DAILY
SKETCH & DAILY GRAPHIC

NEW CARMELITE HOUSE LONDON E.C.4

Telephone: FLEET STREET 6000

Telegraph: DISKETCH LONDON-EC4

7th November 1966.

Peter O'Sullevan, Esq.,
37 Cranmer Court,
Sloane Avenue,
LONDON, S.W.3.

Dear *Peter*,

What are you trying to do-- put us out of business?

Surely it was enough to own Be Friendly. Did you have to nap him as well? And give so fine a commentary on his performance? And complete a treble for the day?

And to crown it all you kiss my best girl in full view of the public!

All I can say is-- what a performance! It couldn't happen to a nicer chap.

Sincere congratulations on achieving a new Everest in racing.

Yours ever,

Bob

P.S. My love to Pat. She must be very proud of you.
B.

Vernons Sprint Cup had reaffirmed that in the world of racing – both a microcosm of the more complex universe and an escape from it – all dreams are permissible.

There had been some far less memorable occasions before and would be more highlights – and lows – in the future.

CHAPTER 22

Champion of Europe

It remained to be seen how far Be Friendly would stay as a three-year-old. He'd been running on strongly at the end of the sixth furlong at Haydock, so it made sense to go for an early one (like Kempton's seven furlongs 2000 Guineas Trial) to determine whether or not sprinting was to be his game. From a personal point of view, this 25 March race was less than ideal because the BBC was televising at Teesside that afternoon. Although I was not committed to go there, it was no good my whingeing about the Corporation's reduction in coverage if I opted out when it suited me.

More importantly Scobie Breasley, who was to have his first ride that afternoon since his fall at Newbury the previous year and who doubted whether Be Friendly would stay (we'd had an unsatisfactory, inconclusive Sunday workout at Sandown), wanted to ride another in the race, Starboard Watch, on whom he'd also been unbeaten in 1966. He allowed himself to get talked out of that, and his closest jockey pal and fellow countryman, 'Hutchie' (Ron Hutchinson), took over on the John Benstead-trained colt who, as it turned out, had not trained on and failed to win in ten races that season.

Clive, who was at Kempton, arranged to maintain contact with the *Grandstand* studio which would keep me in touch with developments. As luck would have it, the main northern race I was covering and the principal event in the south were 'off' simultaneously, at 3.31. Scobie had been beaten on his first two rides and there was a rumour that his back was proving a problem. Just before I called Forthwith winner of the Roseberry Stakes at Stockton a message came down the line: 'Tell Pedro it's a photo and hellish close. Could be a dead-heat but I don't think he's got beat.' I must be raving mad, I thought to myself, to miss the Kempton race.

It seemed like an eternity before the outcome of the photo was announced. The following day my resolutely independent colleague and friend Richard Baerlein, who achieved two of the major conversions since an incident on the road to Damascus when persuading both the hitherto race-shy *Observer* and *Guardian* to sponsor major events, reported in the former:

Peter O'Sullevan won the last big race of the 1966 season with Be Friendly. And he won the most important race on the opening day of the 1967 Flat racing season with the same horse here this afternoon. Scobie Breasley, returning after a long absence after a bad fall, probably never has ridden a better race than when he landed Be Friendly a short head winner of the 2000 Guineas Trial from Quy. It was feared that Be Friendly would not stay the distance. [I'd explained to readers that I was tipping him each-way on this account], and the son of Skymaster drifted badly in the betting from 5/2 to 7/2. He made practically all the running. This was the third Epsom-trained winner in four races and Cyril Mitchell deserves great credit for the way he has brought the winner along. Be Friendly may easily develop into the champion sprinter, for, in spite of his victory over this seven furlongs, sprinting is most likely to be his game.

Tom Forrest led his lively *Sunday Express* feature:

Scobie Breasley's triumphant return on Be Friendly made yesterday's 2000 Guineas Trial a smash-hit with the first day crowds at Kempton. Breasley hadn't ridden since his crashing fall at Newbury last August 13. For a 52-year-old whose back was still rumoured to be weak, the Australian artist produced a Herculean finish to snatch back the lead from Quy by a shot head.
'Bad back? You hear some right tales, don't you?' laughed Scobie later, 'I didn't feel anything when the other headed mine a few strides out.'

When I raised Scobie on the phone to congratulate him, he gave all the credit to his partner, saying, 'He knew when I needed help and gave it to me. It was his "class" that pulled him through.'

On 5 May 1967, within two days of his fifty-third birthday and five weeks after staging a comeback on Be Friendly, Scobie was floored again in a horrific-looking three-horse pile-up at Ascot where he escaped multiple injuries by a hair's breadth, emerging with severe bruising and a broken collarbone. So Freddy Head took over on our fellow in the five furlongs Prix de Saint-Georges at Longchamp on 18 May. Backed from 15/2 to 5/2 in the eleven-horse field, which featured two fellow challengers from England, Be Friendly took longer to find his stride than several of the stalls-wise locals. Yet by halfway he was cruising in the lead. 'I'd never been so fast in my life,' exclaimed Freddy afterwards, 'but when I let him down he began to hop from one leg to another on the fast ground', and the six-year-old French champion speedster, Yours, caught and beat him half a length, retaining his title in a record time for the race. I had to report, 'Well, I'm afraid it was YOURS instead of OURS at the end of a sizzling sprint for Longchamp's Prix de Saint-Georges . . .'

Scobie was back in action for his next major target, the King's Stand Stakes at Royal Ascot, where, in 1967, the mini-skirt fashion seemed to be exploited by those least suited to exposure. The big sprint which has been won by some of the fastest horses in turf history – notable among them the 1919 scorer Diadem, who is honoured by a race in his memory – was the last race of the meeting. As the sun shone with rare persistence from day one I pestered the long-suffering head groundsman, Hugh Mounsey, morning and evening, to get to work with the sprinklers. But by Thursday, with the going officially changed from 'good' to 'firm', our hopes were fading and Cyril arranged for him to be shod with rubber pads between the soles of his feet and aluminium plates.

If the weather men proved correct, there were good prospects of a break on the fourth day. So I went nap on Be Friendly and chanced further odium by going for Salvo, another who needed 'give' in the ground, to beat the Irish Sweeps Derby and Leger winner Sodium in the Hardwicke. Light drizzle was falling while I watched the French King's Stand challenger, Yours, and others at early morning work. By the first race the going had been changed to 'good'. It was designated 'soft' come mid-afternoon and, as I called home Salvo, half-length conqueror of Sodium with the rest trailing, on TV, the blacksmith was busy removing Be Friendly's additional footwear.

The BBC transmission was ended, so I was free to agonize over the race in silence. The watery paddock felt great underfoot. 'Himself', flaunting the muscle bulk that is the hallmark of the explosive sprinter, looked wet and wonderful. I went back up to the commentary box, which is suspended from the roof above the fifth floor level (the floor had to be lowered after construction, to enable cameramen and commentators to stand up), to watch the action alone through the tripod-mounted long-range binoculars.

Falcon, owned by US millionaire Charlie Engelhard, ridden by Lester Piggott, had been backed down from 100/30 to 2/1 favourite; Be Friendly from 4/1 to 3/1; Yours from 6/1 to 5/1; and, among the seven others, which included another Engelhard hope, Holborn, there was plenty of money around at 8/1 and 10/1 for the Pat Rohan-trained hat-trick-scoring filly Lady Jester. Winners of the two previous races up the straight had come from stalls one and two respectively, and the low-drawn Right Strath, Falcon and Lady Jester were soon well ahead of the remainder. Falcon went on at halfway, with Rose of Tralee and Heavenly Sound in pursuit as Right Strath faded. Two out, Scobie had Lester well in his sights, but Falcon was still running on strongly and Yours improving.

Peter Bromley was in the next box, covering the race for radio. I heard him shout, 'And now Be Friendly is putting in a tremendous challenge.'

He sure was, too. In a matter of strides he had taken Falcon just outside the furlong pole. Now Yours was the danger. I found myself darting anxious glances from the action to the winning line and back. But it was proprietor's funk. As Scobie said afterwards, 'Nothing could come and get him once he'd hit the front the way he was galloping.' Even so Yours, officially beaten half a length, with Falcon one and half lengths away third, ran a fine race from the worst draw, three wide of the winner.

Peter leaned out and gave me a thumbs-up (and later his signed colour chart of the race) as I was running from the box to get down to the unsaddling enclosure. Although it was the last race, and raining, there seemed to be a big crowd to greet the winning duo, and my supportive colleague Len Thomas wrote in the next day's *Sporting Life*:

It was a great end to a great royal meeting when Be Friendly came out a furlong from home in the King's Stand Stakes and beat his French conqueror, Yours, by a thoroughly popular half length. Be Friendly has been a wonderful friend to *Daily Express* racing columnist Peter O'Sullevan. On returning to unsaddle the winning team were accorded a reception which far exceeded in clamour the cheers for the winner of the Hardwicke.

The volume of mail which followed ensured that the *Express*'s blonde racing secretary, Valerie Frost, loyally dressed in black and yellow for the Ascot occasion, was kept fully occupied for several weeks.

But there were no cheers after Newmarket's July Cup, before which Scobie was 'claimed' to ride at Brighton and 'super sub' Bill Williamson reported, 'The way I was travelling I thought he'd pick up the winner as soon as I asked him, but he just couldn't use himself on the firm ground and went from cantering to struggling in a few strides.' It was the first time in twelve outings that Be Friendly had been unplaced.

While the sun shone, we decided to forgo any further attempt on the summer prizes and to wait until shockproof ground made homework enjoyable. The weather 'improved' in mid-September and the Ayr Gold Cup became a clear possibility. To win, Be Friendly would need to overcome the highest weight for a three-year-old since Old Reliance won in 1938, and the biggest field in the history of Britain's richest sprint handicap.

To ask him to do so under anything but suitable conditions would be akin to expecting a mountaineer to scale Everest wearing plimsolls. When I drove up to cover the four-day meeting for BBC TV as well as the *Express*, rain in the lowlands raised hopes of favourable ground. Four days before the big one, the circuit which has been such a credit to the management of the McHarg family for so long walked like a dream – a dream that was soon to become a nightmare as promising clouds gave way to persistent sun. Every time I woke from fitful sleep at Turnberry during the three nights before the Cup it was to the blissful sound of falling water. Every time my spirits soared as I raced to the window, only to be reminded of the fountain in the courtyard below. To add to anxiety over the going, an outbreak of coughing among fellow lodgers in his temporary billet at Bogside necessitated a swift exit.

Scobie had been claimed for Kempton commitments, but Lord Sefton's maganimous release of Geoff Lewis meant that his deputy would be coming up on the night train with Cyril. Geoff was to breeze his first-time partner a couple of furlongs to determine whether we paid the fine for withdrawal and sent him home – or sent him to post. Explaining the morning-of-the-race decision in my column and to my colleagues in the press room, where I had drawn Be Friendly in the half-crown (12½p) sweep, I tipped him each-way and proposed ten-race winner Forlorn River in his absence. The exuberant traveller from Epsom was so full of himself that for a few traumatic strides it was touch and go whether or not he went a lot further than a quarter of a mile – unaccompanied. 'I thought he'd lost me for certain,' confessed Geoff after giving an absolute assurance that there was no way he could come to any harm on the ground as it was.

The next worry was the draw. Barrier position number 4 was generally reckoned a major obstacle in a field of this size. July Cup and Nunthorpe winner, Forlorn River, drawn 27, went off 7/1 favourite. Be Friendly was one of four on the 100/8 mark. As bright sunshine warmed the twenty-two-thousand crowd and I read the runners and riders, Skimp Langley, my assistant, sought to alleviate my anxiety by passing the transcript of a news bulletin which reported two foot of rain in Texas and the wet weather crossing the Atlantic. It had ten minutes to arrive, and it didn't.

I'd rung Scobie in the morning and he'd suggested I impress on Geoff not to be in a hurry early on. Was Geoff overdoing it? They'd gone two furlongs and I couldn't recall having mentioned his name. Those on the stands side, the high numbers, had a very clear advantage. As Geoff told it afterwards, 'The stands side group were beginning to get away from me, so I said, "Come on, old chap, get with them," and in a few strides he was there and I was thinking of Scobie Breasley's advice, "Don't come too soon." I knew I'd done it all wrong, but he didn't bother, just kept going. The best six furlongs sprinter I've ever sat on.' The winning margin was two lengths. 'What would he have done to them in the mud?' a voice in the crowd called cheerfully as I ran down to receive the trophy. After my hastily convened celebration party at Turnberry that evening, one of the guests, Arthur Dickson Wright, the celebrated surgeon who did so much in his lifetime to raise funds for cancer relief, wrote saying, 'I have been racing for many years without ever hearing a winner given such a tumultuous reception.'

Scobie was back on board for his next race, the Prix de l'Abbaye de Longchamp on Arc de Triomphe day when, uncharacteristically, he was left. I'd lunched at the British Embassy – where Christopher and Mary Soames always entertained splendidly before the Arc – as probably the only guest who did not appreciate the warm sunshine in the Embassy garden. But there had been heavy overnight rain and the ground still favoured our chances strongly, I thought. My one concern was whether he might have been affected by an impediment about which I had written earlier in the week on 5 October, which appeared under the heading 'THIS IS NO WAY TO RUN RACING':

Russia's Arc de Triomphe entries Anilin and Actaz are the first foreign arrivals in France for next Sunday's international. As big race runners they will receive V.I.H. (Very Important Horse) treatment. But overseas competitors for supporting events will be less fortunate. For Longchamp's much-vaunted racing plant is bursting at the seams.

'It is regrettable, but in view of the big Arc contingent, we just cannot accommodate other foreign horses here,' revealed stables' director M. Valentin in Paris yesterday. As a result a dozen supplementary week-end raiders will be directed on arrival to the 30 miles distant, cough-plagued region of Chantilly. And after a further trip to Longchamp on Sunday they will have to stand in open stalls instead of boxes. Which, as that most agreeable official M. Valentin said apologetically, is also 'regrettable'. The horses concerned include those representing Staff Ingham, Ryan Jarvis, Cyril Mitchell, Paddy Prendergast, Gordon Smyth, Jeremy Tree, etc.

It is not possible to stable visitors at nearby Saint-Cloud because there is no accommodation there for the lads, revealed the French official. The French Customs, who appear to regard horses as inanimate goods, whose clearance is no matter of urgency, already represent a sufficient hazard. Mr James Peden, whose transport firm is responsible for much cross-Channel equine traffic, was not available for comment yesterday on the latest development – which one trainer concerned described as 'absolutely disgraceful'.

But the owner of Be Friendly (who has Quy as well as Flying By as fellow Prix de l'Abbaye challengers) was available, indignant and talkative:- 'When French horses come to England to run at Newmarket they are stabled at Newmarket. When they come to Epsom they lodge at Epsom. And to Ascot at Ascot. It would be an intolerable imposition to direct an Ascot visitor to Newbury and then hold him for several hours in an open stall at Ascot before his race.

'If the French still want visitors for their non-classic events (and IF is the operative word), they have the much publicised funds and the terrain to provide proper on-the-spot amenities. If overseas challengers are no longer considered desirable, it would be preferable to make this clear rather than impose difficulties which are clearly unfair to the equine traveller.

'Horses like Celtic Song, Le Cordonnier, Quy, Flying By, Be Friendly, etc., will have to be boxed to their despatch airport on Friday. Once disentangled from Le Bourget, reboxed to Chantilly and reloaded to Longchamp on Sunday, they will be without the freedom of a loose box during hours' long wait for action.

'I still fancy one of them surmounting these intolerable hazards, but consider they should not exist.'

In fact no English-trained horse won that day, or finished in the first three in the six-runner Prix de l'Abbaye. French starters are inclined to trigger the stalls mechanism faster than their English counterparts and Scobie, who was renowned for fastidiousness – he was always last to leave the weighing-room after showering and changing at the end of a programme – appeared to be taken by surprise when the gates opened for the sprint. 'The silly old fool was still prettying himself up when the starter let 'em go,' fumed Cyril who, with the future in mind, would have preferred to stick with the younger man, Geoff Lewis.

The 'silly old fool' was booked again for the Vernons Sprint on the last day of the 1967 season, Saturday, 4 November, when the weather was so friendly that I napped Be Friendly at Haydock and went for his younger brother, Stay Friendly, each-way at Lingfield. Scobie had intended to ride at Lingfield on the Friday, but the course was waterlogged and racing abandoned. Geoff Lewis rode at Haydock that day and we stayed together at the Greyhound on the East Lancs Road, dining at an Italian restaurant nearby. There was fog about when we returned to the hotel and, tongue in cheek, Geoff expressed the pious hope that nothing happened to prevent the 'old Scobe' from making the journey in the morning, generously offering to keep the saddle warm for him should the worst occur.

Before the running of the first Vernons the previous year, John Baillie, the owner of automatic favourite Lucasland, told me he'd taken out a £1000 insurance against the race being abandoned 'through any cause beyond the control of the organizers'. The premium had been £100 2s 6d. I'd followed his example for a lesser sum (£250), since abandonment appeared one of the major obstacles to a repeat. Others, which assured a sleepless night, were the two-year-olds Mountain Call and Foggy Bell, who had won ten races between them, and Lester's partner Forlorn River, though he would certainly not be favoured by the ground. In the event the 'silly old fool' arrived on time and not only rode a brilliant tactical race but achieved, in his own words, 'one of my greatest racing thrills'.

It was, I found, an agonizing race to commentate. I'd had the temerity to persuade Scobie to walk the course (which has since been changed into a straight, uncomplicated and far less interesting six furlongs) with me and verify that the position paint-close to the stands rails was the only one to achieve in the straight. One off that rail was the same as a bus-width off.

Scobie's compatriot Russ Maddock, who had ridden the runner-up, Green Park, the previous year and now partnered chief rival Mountain Call, knew this as well as anybody and, as Be Friendly was best 'held up', he was first to the fence. What had started out as a nine-horse race between the quick racing in the 'dead' had turned into a duel with a quarter of a mile to run. Mountain Call was powering along the rail to such effect, with Be Friendly in his wake, that the older horse (conceding 18 lb) was by no means free-wheeling behind him. As I called the horses I was riding with Scobie's dilemma. He wasn't going well enough to come off the fence and challenge. Yet if he didn't do so he'd got no chance – unless Mountain Call finally tired and edged off the rail as he did so. Scobie stayed where he was, knowing he was doing right; knowing he'd get plenty of 'stick' if the ploy failed.

Well inside the final furlong Mountain Call rolled. For several strides the two chestnuts ran head for head. The judge called for a photo. I don't know what I called, because BBC Manchester mislaid the recording they'd intended to send me. I know neither deserved to lose, but the verdict was Be Friendly and Scobie Breasley by a neck.

Mountain Call was no slouch. Never out of a place in eleven runs as a three-year-old, his six successes included Newmarket's Palace House and Challenge Stakes, the Cork and Orrery at the Royal Meeting and Deauville's Maurice de Gheest. We looked like renewing rivalry in the richest sprint handicap in the early part of the 1968 season, the Ladbroke Nottingham, in which Be Friendly was allotted a fairly daunting 10 stone and Mountain Call 8 stone 11 lb. But firm ground delayed our reappearance until 11 May at Kempton.

Scobie had sent me a telegram from Barbados on 30 January: 'CANNOT DECIDE SIR HERBERT OR MINHO STOP VALUE YOUR OPINION.' After giving him a call and intimating preference, I wrote on 2 February:

Scobie Breasley will ride Sir Herbert in the Lincoln. The most significant Spring Double riding engagement to have been made so far means that the 53-year-old maestro will be teaming up with Peter Easterby for a second time in the Doncaster Handicap. The previous occasion was 1965 when the jockey–trainer partnership scored with Old Tom. Further significant details are that before leaving for his Barbados holiday home Scobie had expressed a doubt whether he would return for the opening meeting of 1968 – 'unless there was the chance of a really good ride in the Lincoln,' in which he was also offered the mount on current ante-post favourite Minho . . .

The ink was barely dry on my ante-post voucher when Sir Herbert met with a setback, became a non-runner, and Scobie stayed in the sun until the Ascot April meeting.

I seemed fated to miss Be Friendly's seasonal reappearance. When the ground eased in time for him to run on 11 May at Kempton, where Pay TV was transmitting to a limited London audience, I was due at Newcastle for BBC. *Timeform* assessed the Doug Smith-trained grey speedster Raffingora top; *Raceform*'s private handicap favoured Manacle. There was a good case for three-year-old Porto Bello, winner of six in a row as a youngster, and his most obsessed supporter was not alone in expecting Be Friendly to concede weight all round. I wrote:

Be Friendly (2.30 nap) will be beaten by Manacle in this afternoon's Sceptre Stakes at Kempton IF Jack Watts's opinion of his representative is correct. 'There isn't a horse in England who could give 7 lb to Manacle,' declared Jack recently. Of course he may have just been trying to scare your correspondent. And if he thinks he did – he's darned right! For well-drawn Manacle, who receives 7 lb from our fellow today, has already run twice this season and won in impressive style. Which may well give him another 3 lb fitness advantage . . .

Manacle was a good, tough horse. He won six races during the season and this was one of them. Jack proved his point in a hard-fought photo finish by a head. When the pair met at levels three months later Be Friendly beat his Kempton rival two and a half lengths.

It was Cyril Mitchell's view that when Scobie rode Be Friendly in the Kempton 2000 Guineas Trial the previous year, 'no other jockey in the world would have won on him'. In contrast Cyril felt that the now fifty-four-year-old rider should have won the Sceptre Stakes. Nor was he too happy with the ride he gave our fellow in the Prix du Palais Royal at Longchamp, whence the poor lad had an appalling journey and, in Scobie's words, 'was listless by his normal standards'. The professional racing world has a low tolerance of failure. Scobie, who had a nasty fall at Bath on 23 May, which meant him forgoing the Derby, was by now widely considered to be 'over the hill' – well over it. In fact my friend and neighbour Greville Baylis and I seemed almost isolated in our belief that the old spark was still glowing with sufficient intensity to enable A. Breasley to score on any horse who was entitled to win – as well as a few who weren't.

My immediate fervent hope was to see Scobie and Be Friendly back in the winner's circle after a second successive King's Stand Stakes on 21 June. Given the ground, I reckoned it was just a matter of how much the bookmakers had to lose, but the weather was resolutely on their side. As the Royal Meeting progressed in benign sunshine, with the bars running out of ice before the first and the water from Mr Mounsey's sprinklers drying before it hit the ground, so hope receded.

Then, just as they had the previous year, the met. forecasters suggested that parasols might be replaced by umbrellas on the final day. While resolved to withdraw if there was any fear of injury, we declared him to run and I wrote:

Be Friendly slept (more peacefully, I trust, than his proprietor) in the racecourse stables last night in preparation for a two furlongs 'breeze' over part of the course this morning. But he will only seek to emulate the last winner in successive years, Gold Bridge in 1933–4, if conditions turn in his favour. And if they do I think he WILL win. Under the circumstances D'Urberville (5.30) is proposed as an alternative.

After watching 'himself' in action in the morning, convinced I'd never seen him look better, I drove to Windsor to hire a boat for an hour to unwind. There was still a long day's work ahead, whether he ran or not. I'd been rowing for about twenty minutes when it happened – an authentic cloudburst. It was still bucketting down when I got back to the landing stage and as I returned, soaking wet, along the route to my hotel. After the long dry spell, water was spilling across the road in Windsor Great Park. A new fear surfaced as the windscreen wipers worked overtime: could Ascot be flooded? Hardly. When I reached Swinley Bottom the black, glistening road turned to pale, parched grey. Not a single drop of rain had fallen on the course. Reluctantly we withdrew and accepted the financial penalty for so doing.

What I found less easy to accept was the censure of the Senior Steward, Lord Sefton, who did not always appear to be in close touch with reality. On one occasion, learning that a fellow member of White's had moved from Mayfair to Eaton Square, he exclaimed disapprovingly, 'Good heavens, does the tarmacadam go that far?' On this occasion he gave it as his loftily discharged opinion that by failing to run Be Friendly we were 'playing ducks and drakes with the public'. As my colleagues knew of – and had publicized – our intention, criticism seemed unreasonable. For the irrelevant record, any O'Sullevan follower among the aforementioned public backed a 4/1 winner, D'Urberville.

There was no all-weather gallop at Epsom at this time so that, with the sun on overtime, Be Friendly may have been a fraction 'short' when he went to Newmarket for the July Cup. Anyway he got beat and Scobie reckoned that, just as he was picking 'em off, he 'blew up'. Cyril reckoned, in so many words, that it was all very well for me to indulge the luxury of exercising loyalty to a friend, but in so doing I was prejudicing the livelihood of those who were putting in the work on the horse. It was a point, well put, which I would have appreciated more had I personally considered Scobie at fault.

But the question didn't arise next time because Scobie had a prior claim under his retainer for Sir Gordon Richards on 24 July when we planned a crack at the Prix du Gros-Chêne at Chantilly. Geoff Lewis, who stepped in again, flew over with Cyril and me, and, despite claiming to be suffering from a nervous breakdown after driving with me from Bourget, rode a cracking race.

Drawn in what is considered an impossible position (eleven of twelve) over 1000 metres, in a field which included the highly regarded François Mathet-trained sprinter Rhamnus and Omar Sharif's nice horse Christening, he passed the post in unison with Suzy Volterra's top-class filly Klaizia (drawn four), to whom he was conceding 15 lb. Geoff, riding here for the first time, confessed he'd no idea whether he'd won or lost. Freddy Head, partner of Klaizia (later the dam of Lypheor), was convinced he'd been beaten. After two photo-finish prints and fifteen minutes' suspense, the result was announced. Madame Volterra offered me a white-gloved hand and a sunny smile, declaring herself enchanted with the outcome, a dead-heat. Me too. The pair had come up in a minute dead, a blisteringly fast time for the course, and evidence of the electronic eye left no shadow of doubt that they were indivisible.

Scobie was back on board for York's Nunthorpe, in which Cyril felt he put our fellow in the race too late when beaten half a length by So Blessed. The younger horse, who was on a hat-trick following success in the July Cup and Goodwood's King George, was a top-class sprinter, apparently at his best in midsummer but on occasion a moody customer at home. The duo met five times over a two-year period, scoring 3–2 in Be Friendly's favour.

I had written a 'Farewell to Scobie' piece on 1 August, following the four times champion's long-debated decision to retire at the end of the season, and expressed the hope that on his final day in the saddle, at Haydock on 9 November, he would exit triumphantly by winning the Vernons on Be Friendly. It was a frequently toasted target between us.

In the interim there were, once again, the Ayr Gold Cup and the Abbaye de Longchamp. Scobie had never favoured travelling far from home when there was the chance of an alternative near-at-hand engagement. Kempton was considerably closer to Putney than Ayr, and Gordon Richards had runners there. I happened to know that Gordon would let him off, if requested, but Scobie, who had begun to wind down, probably figured that, under 9 stone 7 lb top weight, the horse had a prodigious task – as well as still being without his required going.

Cyril considered that if Geoff deputized again in Scotland he should also have the ride at Longchamp to avoid any more swopping around. It was time I made a concession, and that seemed perfectly fair. I told Scobie that, while nothing could disturb the Haydock finale, if he forfeited Ayr he'd forgo Longchamp as well.

He stuck to Kempton, and soon looked to have played a winning hand. When John Banks went 7/1 the field I thought it was the hell of a price and took it. I thought the Nunthorpe running showed that my hero was just coming to himself, and any leakage from above would make him a certainty. This desirable support didn't materialize until the day after the race, for which he nevertheless started 5/2 favourite to become the first to win in successive years since Heronslea in 1930–1. But there was more cushion in the ground than the previous year, and they went 100/8 bar. He was so exuberant in the paddock that my principal worry was that he might do himself an injury before he got to the post, where he was drawn twelve in the twenty-one-horse field.

John Joyce, who had laid me £2000–£120 against the double, Be Friendly on Friday and his brother, Stay Friendly, the following afternoon, declared resignedly, 'The public don't want to know about any other horses but yours in the Cup.' These are circumstances under which the patron saint of bookmakers is invariably alert. I was never happy about him from the start of commentary. The closer the field approached, the more obvious it became that, as he ran on into sixth place behind Petite Path, the first filly to win the Queen Mary and Ayr Gold Cup, he was not moving with his usual fluency. Geoff reported that, just before stalls entry, he'd noted the colt's near-fore shoe to be hanging off. With time at a premium, and without on-the-spot equipment, the only expedient was to remove it altogether and leave the favourite to run in three shoes. 'He just could never find his action,' said Geoff, disappointedly.

Co-Clerk of the Course Kit Patterson said, 'We have just about everything available at the start except a blacksmith. Obviously it is something to be considered in the future, because it is clearly a big handicap to run like that.' The Senior Starter, Alec Marsh, added: 'It's like a professional runner trying to perform with one bare foot. In the south my team of handlers includes a qualified blacksmith with the necessary equipment.' As Cyril noted, in commendably restrained terms, this should be common practice. While we were conducting a post-mortem, Scobie was winning for his stable at Kempton on Lady Beaverbrook's Raymali.

The next day Stay Friendly, who had lived so far in the shadow of his senior relative, recovered the double outlay by winning the Craigmore Selling Handicap under Edward Hide, becoming the least likely underwriter of the nine hundred miles round trip, during the return half of which he doubtless had plenty to say to his big brother. On his official twenty-fourth birthday, 1 January 1989, Stay Friendly was still enjoying the care and attention of the understanding guardians of his welfare, Mike and Angela Pelly, at Martin's Farm near Tunbridge Wells.

The spirit of co-operation among competing professionals is one of the many attractive features of the racing game. It accounted for Ian Balding offering Cyril Mitchell the hospitality of Kingsclere's fine peat moss gallop to assist in the preparation of Be Friendly for his Prix de l'Abbaye challenge. He had his last work-out here before travelling to Longchamp where blinkers, to which Skymaster products seemed so well suited and which he had not worn since a solitary occasion as a two-year-old, were to be reapplied.

Because of TV commitment I could not catch a Saturday flight in time to dine in Paris with Cyril and Geoff, but joined them later in the evening at the Grand Veneur for a coffee and brandy before driving them back to the Grand Hotel in the rue Scribe. Geoff was strongly in favour of completing personal preparation for his Sunday assignment with a tour of the place Pigalle. It was not an exercise which I could envisage enhancing Be Friendly's prospects of becoming the first four-year-old to win Europe's richest (£13,000) sprint prize. When I protested, he became so suspiciously compliant that I threatened to sit outside his door all night until we drove out to Longchamp to walk the five-furlongs course at 7 a.m. Sure enough, after twenty minutes a head peered out of a softly opened door: 'You b-b-bastard,' accused Talgarth's most famous son in his engagingly individual stutter before promising to turn in.

We had drawn the ace position (eleven of eleven) in the international field, in which the Aga Khan's versatile seven-race-winning Grey Sovereign colt, Zeddaan, was odds-on in British bookmakers' ante-post lists as well as local forecasts. As we walked the lush green turf on the sprint course, we agreed the marker at which Geoff was to 'let him down', but not before. On the evidence of our soaking feet the going was no problem.

When Geoff came into the unsaddling enclosure after the race and I greeted him hurriedly before running to the Arc de Triomphe commentary point, he said in mock apology, 'I'm s-sorry, mate, I h-haven't let him down yet.' He hadn't either. Even to a hopelessly biased, heart-in-mouth observer there never appeared the faintest requirement for him to hurry. The verdict was that he had beaten the game French two-year-old, A Croquer, two lengths, with Lester Piggott-ridden So Blessed third, ahead of Ireland's Desert Call. Zeddaan was seventh (it should be said he'd only just come back to sprinting after winning the French 2000 Guineas and Prix d'Ispahan); last year's winner from Germany, Pentathlon, eighth; the King's Stand winner D'Urberville ninth; and Klaizia, with whom Be Friendly had dead-heated at Chantilly, last. The only faintly disappointing aspect of the victory was reflected in a paragraph in the following week's *Racehorse* which read: 'Before Be Friendly brought a roar of approval from English throats by winning the Prix de l'Abbaye, the first show was 13/1, and even a hardened professional of our acquaintance was dumbfounded at the final return of 100/30.'

Immediately after the Arc broadcast, during which I made a quick reference to the result of the Abbaye, I hustled to the unsaddling enclosure to interview the associates of the brilliant winner, Vaguely Noble, and was intercepted by Phil Bull, who was in apparently earnest conversation with Bill Hill. 'You know what you should do, don't you?' inquired the boss of *Timeform*, without waiting for a reply. 'You should retire your horse right away and syndicate him for £3000 a share and put William and me at the top of the list. In fact we'll pay you for two shares now if you want.'

The £120,000 capital valuation which this represented is modest by contemporary standards, but in 1968 it was meaningful. To recognize good advice is one thing, to accept it is another. As far as I was concerned, the joy of owning a good horse with a zest for racing was to have him race; while to syndicate was to run the risk of losing control over his destiny, which was to forfeit responsibility. Only fate could obstruct the realization of his next target, a Vernons Sprint hat-trick and a simultaneous dream exit for Scobie Breasley on Saturday, 9 November.

Meanwhile I rang Signor Conti to book his restaurant's private room for an impromptu party that Sunday evening, 6 October, when one of the guests was Robert Elwes, owner of the Ennistown Stud in County Meath, who had been in serious pursuit of Be Friendly as a prospective stallion for over a year. Then I phoned copy, which inevitably began:

In a great triumph for Anglo-Irish breeding, Vaguely Noble, in the mammoth £83,400 first prize Arc de Triomphe, and Be Friendly in the richest international sprint, the £13,000 Prix de l'Abbaye de Longchamp, proved themselves undisputed European champions in their respective categories. And so the 136,000-guineas colt Vaguely Noble, reared, like Be Friendly, on Irish soil, becomes one of the bargain buys of the century despite his record price purchase. For 44-year-old Bill Williamson, sixth individual Australian to win the Arc de Triomphe, there was never an anxious moment from start to finish of the mile and a half all-aged contest. Vaguely Noble started 5/2 favourite and, without a touch from the whip, beat Sir Ivor by three lengths with Camarthen four lengths away third; and the best of her sex, Roseliere, one and a half lengths away fourth, ahead of Epsom Oaks heroine La Lagune. Even reflecting on his four 'Arc' winning partners, Jacko Doyasbère, the only rider to have achieved such a total in Europe's richest race prize, doubted whether any of his partners could have beaten today's magnificent scorer. And, as a further tribute, it was no surprise to hear from Lester Piggott that he considered, 'Sir Ivor ran the best race of his life.' Those of us who doubted Sir Ivor's stamina were surely confounded. For there is little doubt that Raymond Guest's dual classic winner (who'll probably go next for Newmarket's Champion Stakes) got the trip all right without being good enough to handle an utterly exceptional horse. A horse who, in becoming Etienne Pollet's third Arc winner, so fully vindicated his brilliant handler's opinion that he is 'right in the Sea Bird II class'.

It had been a lucky weekend for me, prefaced by my nap, Major Rose, winning Saturday's Cesarewitch at 9/1 after his support had been proposed at more remunerative odds, and reinforced by Sunday selections Vaguely Noble and Be Friendly. Yet, excepting appalling miscalculation on my part, it could have been a far better one.

A year earlier Olga Martin-Montis, mother of Alfonso Marques de Portago and Soledad Marquesa de Moratalla, had asked me during a lunch party in Switzerland, 'Listen, darling, why don't you find me a really good horse, something out of the ordinary, for me to give to Sol?'
   Olga, a stylish horsewoman in her younger days, had bred two horse-mad offspring. Fon, who appears earlier in these pages, was so attached to his horses that he could barely bring himself to administer an encouraging tap during a race. Yet he was France's champion amateur on the Flat and over obstacles in successive years; winning the Grand Prix de Pau and Auteuil's prestigious Prix Montgomery before his twenty-first birthday on his nine-year-old, Garde Toi; scoring on the Flat, over fences and hurdles in the same week on Challenger; and winning a race at the provincial circuit, Mont de Marsan, while handicapped by a broken collarbone. Breeding held less interest for him than riding, so he gave his sister the mare Cassandre from whom Sol bred her Prix du Président de la République hero, Blacklock, who did not run unbacked when he won the big Auteuil prize at nearly 40/1 on 18 April 1965 and helped to finance what was to become the biggest bloodstock enterprise in south-west France.
   A world champion over the Cresta Run, Fon met his last sporting challenge on 12 May 1957, in a race in which he was not even due to compete. As a team driver on the international motor racing circuit, the Mille Miglia was not in his contract. But when another member of the *équipe* was injured Fon rearranged his schedule out of friendship for Enzo Ferrari – with tragically fatal results. Despite Olga's strength of

character, her infectiously humorous outlook on life, the support of her great love, Isidro, and the healing properties of time, I felt that she remained haunted by both the pain and resentment of loss until she died twenty-three years later.

Olga claimed that she married, 'once for money, once for position and once for love'. Her first husband, Frank J. Mackey, US multi-millionaire founder of Household Finance, committed suicide when he learnt he had cancer. Number two was the Marques de Portago de Moratalla e Conde de la Mejorada (this book is long enough already, so I won't be repeating that title), who died in 1940. The exceptionally *simpatico* number three, former Spanish Davis Cup player and keen tennis enthusiast, Isidro Martin-Montis, and Olga divided their time during nearly forty years of married life between their houses in Biarritz – where the Windsors were regular visitors – Lausanne and Gstaad, where our lunch conversation took place. Since Fon's death, ten years earlier, it had been unusual for Olga to 'talk horse'.

'I would like to give Sol something really sensational,' she persisted.

Dealing has positively no appeal to me whatever. At least in the instance of the horse that occurred to me, negotiation would not arise – merely the harmless task of bidding at public auction. I told her about the impending Holliday dispersal sale, in which there was a lot that just might fulfil a horse-fancier's dream but which, I felt, could easily attract an unwarrantably high price. A two-year-old with a good enough pedigree to be anything, he'd won his last two races, including the Observer Gold Cup, with impressive ease, but on both occasions in yielding ground. He was a smashing individual.

What did I think he'd fetch?

Executors' sales invariably inflated prices. Seventy to seventy-five thousand guineas was my estimate.

'What about the Derby?' asked Olga.

That was the big snag, I told her: he hadn't a classic engagement, though there were other highly significant events.

'Darling', she reacted, 'if you are going to be at the sale, will you buy him for me?'

'What if he goes to six figures?' I inquired.

Olga was quite unmoved by the thought. 'If you like him, you buy him,' she said.

Well, I didn't make a bid, did I? When the hammer fell at 136,000 guineas I thought it was madness. He'd have to win the Arc de Triomphe and everything *en route*, and then some, to justify that . . .

But I'd been suspecting for a while now that I'd done it all wrong. On 9 June 1968, when I went to Chantilly to report the French Derby, I knew it and led my copy with: 'Vaguely Noble is a potent threat to

Sir Ivor. Make no mistake about that. For, even on French Derby day, the 136,000-guineas colt completely stole the show with an electrifying eight-lengths triumph in a minor supporting event, the Prix du Lys.' When the subsequently notable stallion retired after winning the Arc, he did so having recovered most of his purchase price in prize money and with a capital valuation of £2 million. My miscalculation was that Olga Martin-Montis, to whom 136,000 guineas was peanuts, could just as easily have bought the son of Vienna out of Noble Lassie as Dr Franklyn. Probably more easily. I'm surprised Sol Moratalla still speaks to me.

Ten years later, during our annual stay at the chalet in Gstaad, Olga repeated the proposal of an equine present for her daughter. The only two-year-old I knew of who might be bought was the 1977 Gimcrack winner, Tumbledownwind, owned in partnership by my colleague Julian Wilson and two ladies who were friends of the colt's trainer, Bruce Hobbs. Not very big, but strong and well put together, he ought to get a mile all right and, given decent ground – which was normal at Newmarket – could be ideally suited by the 2000 Guineas.

I rang Julian and he consulted his partners. They wanted £175,000. The original cost (he'd been a shrewd Bruce Hobbs yearling purchase at 4800 guineas) was irrelevant, but I thought £150,000 was right. Less, maybe, but certainly no more. They came down to £165,000, then £160,000. Personally I'd rather spend a day in the greatly over-rated Kasbah in Marrakesh than haggle. I told Sol and she said, 'If you like it, don't lose it!' Julian reported that if they reduced to £150,000 his partners would not be prepared to pay a penny commission. I said the question of any commission did not arise. At £150,000, subject to the normal veterinary exam, it was a deal. Julian nevertheless generously sent me a case of Louis Roederer Crystal champagne and Sol insisted on giving me 10 per cent of the cracking little colt who, I firmly believe, granted ordinary fortune, would have won the 2000 Guineas in 1978.

As it was, he had to be withdrawn from his intended Ascot preliminary owing to a cough. He appeared to bounce back so exuberantly that the 50/1 advertised looked irresistible. The weather seemed set fair, so Sol and I had a good bet, each-way, between us. Two days before the race the rain began, and reached such intensity on the eve of the classic that we gave serious thought to withdrawal. Geoff Baxter was asked on no account to be hard on him. One hundred and fifty yards out they were still leading when the combination of unfavourable ground and lack of a previous run found him out. And, like so many good each-way bets, he finished fourth, three lengths off the winner.

As the last day of the 1968 season approached, the stage seemed set for a perfect ending to Scobie Breasley's great career. In what appeared the increasingly unlikely event of Be Friendly being 'turned over' in the six-runner Vernons Sprint Cup, Lester Piggott had arranged for his old rival to take over on the apparent 'good thing', Harbour Flower, for which he'd been booked in the last. I had been in touch with the insurance brokers with whom I had dealt the previous year and forwarded the £35 premium for a policy which would require the underwriters to pay £500 in the event 'of the race aforementioned being abandoned through any cause beyond the control of the race organizers'.

The going was soft, and Be Friendly was odds-on in ante-post betting to confirm Longchamp placings with So Blessed. When I drove to the course at 7 o'clock on the morning of the race, the East Lancs Road was clear but there were patches of fog swirling round the grandstand. As Tony Boyle led out the Vernons favourite, I remarked to him apprehensively, 'I hope this fog doesn't get any thicker.'

Be Friendly's lad gave his horse an affectionate pat on the neck. 'It's the only thing that could beat him,' he said. 'There's nothing else will.'

I went back to the Greyhound and tried to enjoy breakfast. On the short return trip at nine o'clock the sun was shining. That was better. But half a mile short of the track there was this sudden blanket. John Hughes, the Clerk of the Course, who was expecting a record crowd for the Scobie Breasley finale, paced the weighing-room precinct anxiously. He had sent a car to Warrington station to collect his wife, Susie, and mine from the London train. Pat had rarely seen Be Friendly run and had never been to Haydock. The met. forecasters reckoned it would clear by midday. If they were wrong she wasn't going to see a lot of either horse or course.

I rang *Grandstand* to warn them. John had wanted to stage the programme a week earlier, but he could not get TV coverage then and it was essential for the sponsorship. Readmission tickets for any future meeting were issued when the gates were opened at noon. In the hospitality box, presided over by Robert Sangster's father Vernon (chairman of Vernon's) and mother, guests watched Sandown's jumping programme on TV. But they couldn't see the first fence at Haydock and, following postponement, both chases were abandoned.

The stewards had the jockeys weigh out in colours for the Vernons so that the start could be effected with all speed if and when the fog lifted. Looking down on the ring from my commentary point, I noted the bookmakers offering an ungenerous-looking 6/4 Be Friendly, 'all in – race or not'. And, appreciating that all my sympathy should have been focused on Scobie, I cast a mercenary thought to my £1000–£100 voucher Be Friendly for a Vernons hat-trick, struck with John Banks these many months ago.

By three o'clock I would have laid a shade of odds that the *Racehorse*'s best bet of the week was going to return to Epsom without getting his feet wet. And that is what happened. At some stage the waiting had to end, and in a curious way it was almost a relief when the officials were finally obliged to terminate the suspense. I went down to console Tony with a small share of the insurance money. *Grandstand* said they wanted an interview between Scobie and me on the paddock camera. I asked if we could not use the finish camera on the roof to avoid what I always found the excruciating embarrassment of an audience. Permission was granted, but when we got there they didn't want it after all. Little changes. In less than two miles from the course I switched off the Jag's fog lights. The visibility was perfect.

Those who entrusted themselves to my care were driven straight to the Bon Accueil in Chelsea. Shortly after dinner there was a long-distance call to the flat. 'How f-far did he win, Pete?' inquired the voice on the other end. Geoff Lewis was phoning from Calcutta where he and Tommy Carter had flown, two days before the end of the local season, to fulfil winter contracts. 'The g-good l-lord looks after bookmakers,' reacted Geoff when I told him.

Insurance interests appear to be well protected, too. As the £500 hadn't arrived a month after the non-event, I rang the broker, who promised that I would receive a 'claim form'. Once the insurance jargon had been translated – to the degree that this is possible – it transpired that I was permitted to claim actual, as opposed to notional, out-of-pocket expenses up to the sum of £500. It might have been helpful of the broker to have indicated this circumstance at the outset so that I would at least have been aware that the premium was unlikely to be recoverable. There had, of course, been no previous reference to 'out-of-pocket expenses', which in fact amounted to Scobie's riding fee, since the jockeys had weighed out, totalling £7 7s. And I was only responsible for half of that. There would have been a bill for 'himself's' transport but Stanley Wootton, controller of the horsebox company involved, was so upset on behalf of Scobie and me that he refused to issue an account. So I didn't receive the 'monkey'. And no personal/household possession of mine has ever been insured since.

CHAPTER 23

Percy's Progress

I felt that, at four years of age, Be Friendly was better than ever. His run at Longchamp endorsed Geoff Lewis's enthusiastically expressed contention that 'When he's right and conditions are in his favour – he's unbeatable.' He was in the prime of equine life, still relishing competition. Why the hell should he retire? OK, I had received the knowledge that this was the time to 'cash in', and had rejected, as politely as possible, the extravagant Japanese offer (without indicating that there were not enough yen in circulation to buy him) before consultation with my partner. Praise be for an indulgent associate. Stephen willingly agreed that we should continue to campaign our hero, but he would like to protect his investment by selling one of his two legs now as a prospective stallion. Among all the propositions (my friend Robert Elwes, with whom we eventually 'stood' him in County Meath, had offered half the Ennistown Stud in exchange for half of the horse) this was probably the soundest. We each sold a 'leg' (for £22,000) to Robert Sangster – it was the first stallion in whom he bought a share – and Jeremy Hindley respectively.

Perversely, Be Friendly's last season coincided with one of those summers to which England was still susceptible. As if he regarded the boring bromide 'A good horse goes on any ground' as a personal affront, he reappeared at Kempton on 5 April, 'undisputed sprint champion of Europe' (*Daily Mail*), 'looking magnificent' (*Observer*), 'on ground very much too firm for him' (*Evening News*), and 'ran his heart out in his usual game fashion to take the Sceptre Stakes by a head' (*Sunday Telegraph*). While the proprietors of sunbed parlours were going bankrupt, Be Friendly's exercise was limited to a roll in the private sandpit created for him in the centre of the Downs House yard. Could he be 'straight' enough for his next assignment, Newmarket's Palace House Stakes?

'Better sprinters than Be Friendly are seldom seen,' wrote my perceptive colleague, Michael Phillips, in *The Times* on Wednesday, 30 April, 'but today he is faced with the formidable task of having to give 10 lb more than the weight for age allowance to the three-year-old Acquit, who, earlier this month, won a competitive handicap at Ascot by five lengths without coming off the bit'. In the following day's *Sporting Chronicle* Peter Willett, who was to make such a significant contribution to the sport, reported, 'Be Friendly, whose courage never flags, restored some sanity to top-class form by giving his usual impeccable performance, running on gamely as ever to hold off the challenge of his old rival, So Blessed, with the Irish horse, Excessive, third, in front of the three-year-old Acquit.'

He could not be expected to maintain this level of performance, on ground unsuited to him, indefinitely. So news of the dark clouds in the north, where the Duke of York Stakes on 15 May looked a likely target, was especially welcome. Unfortunately, when the rain came it was so excessive that Chester had to be abandoned because the track was waterlogged. Likewise Teesside, Newcastle and Pontefract. At York a mechanical digger was employed to excavate a 'monsoon trench' in a bid to drain the soggy Knavesmire. This initiative by the course's dynamic impresario, Major Leslie Petch, enabled the three-day meeting to open on time, when this anxious observer (we were not due to run until the last day) reported:

Squelching slow motion through the black Knavesmire mud, non-classic colt Activator outslogged eleven Derby hopes in yesterday's Dante Stakes. The time was a record – more than 100 lengths slower than average for this extended ten furlongs. As a classic trial it was a good endurance test in conditions described by one competitor, Jimmy Lindley, as 'the worst I've ever ridden in' . . . The two-year-old, Fast Track, covered the five furlongs Zetland Stakes in nearly eleven seconds (or over fifty lengths) slower than average time.

In the following day's Musidora Stakes more than forty lengths separated the first six home, and the official view was that further significant rain would wash out Thursday's card. I was staying at the Feathers at nearby Pocklington where, around midnight, it resumed, torrentially, and was maintained throughout most of the night. Remarkably, the course still survived early-morning inspection and, under the caption 'GROUND IS JUST RIGHT FOR HIM – BE FRIENDLY CAN CONFIRM KEMPTON FORM', the *Sporting Life*'s Augur predicted:

With ground conditions in his favour, top sprinter Be Friendly looks a good thing to gain his third win off the reel this season in the Duke of York Stakes (4.30) this afternoon. The Epsom five-year-old is in cracking form. At Kempton last month he gained a narrow win over Star and Garter and Great Bear, and followed up with a fluent victory from So Blessed in the Palace House Stakes at Newmarket on 2000 Guineas day.

Great Bear, who again opposes Be Friendly – and on similar terms to the
Kempton race – won at Ascot next time out from the smart Raffingora. But I
cannot see him reversing placings with Be Friendly.

Milesius and Marton Lady, who make up the field, are useful, but must be
ruled out in this company.

Even allowing for apprehension which accompanies the approach of a
race, that reflected my thoughts, though in view of limited odds appeal
I went along with 'Alvaro (3.15 nap) to complete a five-timer for us in
the City Bowl Handicap at Salisbury.'

Back on 25 April, under the heading '196/1 TREBLE FOR O'SULLEVAN',
the *Express* front page had quoted a William Hill spokesman: 'It cost
us at least £30,000 . . . and that is a conservative estimate because we
still have cash letter bets to work out.' One of the ingredients of the
threesome was 6/1 chance Alvaro, in connection with whom I wrote:
' "Frenchie" Nicholson, responsible for the tutorship of Paul Cook and
Tony Murray, among others, has another clearly very bright pupil in
17-year-old Pat Eddery, who handled his first winner Alvaro, with
exemplary sang-froid. Pat is a son of Jimmy Eddery, who won the Irish
Derby on Panaslipper.' The combination of Alvaro and Pat Eddery,
champion apprentice in 1971 and champion jockey for the first time in
1974, obliged any O'Sullevan followers on five successive occasions.

To my horror, Be Friendly was never at ease in the Knavesmire muck.
While he and Geoff Lewis were ploughing a laborious furrow along the
rails, Hutchie had Great Bear lobbing in the wake of the 9/4 on
favourite. Approaching the sixth and final furlong the pursuers eased
out and sailed by like a powerboat passing a paddle streamer. The
winning distance was five lengths, with a similar margin between second
and third, and eighteen lengths between first and last. Shaking his head
ruefully, Geoff said, 'He just couldn't get any sort of grip on the ground.'
And I immediately recalled the remark, made the previous day, by one
of Be Friendly's staunchest admirers, Sandy Barclay: 'You wouldn't
want to be too disappointed if you were beaten on this going,' offered
the quiet-voiced young Scot. 'Under these conditions the greatest horse
in the world could lose.'

Teddy Lambton, who was just about to saddle the last-race favourite,
Lyrical, backed from 9/4 to 7/4, said, 'Hard luck. If you've left any
money behind, this filly will love the ground.' Because of the odds I
hadn't had a bet in the Duke of York, but I did so now. Bidding for a
hat-trick, Lyrical, who had already won in going officially described as
soft, looked well treated in this mile three-year-old handicap. But she
wasn't just beaten when becoming the fifth vanquished York favourite
– she finished a good furlong behind the winner. Mud on the

Knavesmire, scene of public executions before bookmakers took over to execute the punters, is a very special variety.

Be Friendly returned to Epsom with very sore heels, which were treated with cortisone, and an obviously unimpaired appetite for his favourite Polo mints. Thereafter he never found anything but firm, unyielding terrain wherever we went. In the week before his presence at Newmarket ensured round-the-clock sunshine over the Heath, Geoff collected a four-day suspension from the Longchamp stewards for involvement in a traffic problem while riding Critérium favourite, Gyr. So Lester Piggott deputized. Cyril had always insisted that 'Lester wouldn't ride one side of this horse'. I found this opinion incomprehensible, since I could not believe that a horse had been foaled that Lester could not ride one side of. 'He won't ride this one – you'll see,' insisted Be Friendly's handler.

In the sizzling sprint for the six-furlongs Challenge Stakes, our fellow led to the top of the hill, but began to change legs on the descent into the dip. The talented three-year-olds Burglar and Tudor Music picked him off and York rival Burglar grabbed third spot from him on the line. Lester returned to the appropriate area, removed the saddle, gave his partner a perfunctory pat, turned and, with the economy of verbiage for which he is renowned, pronounced judgement: 'He's gone,' said Lester, striding into the weighing-room from which he would shortly emerge to guide Nijinsky to victory in the £10,576 Dewhurst Stakes.

'I told you he wouldn't ride one side of him,' said Cyril. 'He came up there like a crab – he was never galloping.' Surely, I wrote after Newmarket, the ground would have to ease before the final curtain at Haydock on 1 November. But it didn't. During the week before the race I received a supply of good luck talismans – four-leaf clover, heather, mini-horseshoes and so on. A group from Halifax wrote to say their vehicle would be placarded 'Members of the Be Friendly Supporters' Club'. He was to be driven up from Epsom by his 'lucky box driver', Charlie Kingsley, who was at the wheel in 1966–7, but not last year when the programme was fogged off.

Under the circumstances, which prompted me to quote Bert at the garage, 'If he's no good at stud you can always flog him to Fred Pontin to keep the sun shining over his holiday camps,' I made him 'a more hopeful than confident nap'. Aubrey Renwick wrote in the *Sporting Life*: 'I would dearly like to see Be Friendly end up his brilliant racing career on a successful note,' adding prophetically, 'but the going seems unlikely to be soft enough for him.'

It wasn't. Despite the freak, unfavourable weather he was backed down to 100/30 second favourite to Tudor Music (11/4) in the eleven-horse field. For a few strides at the quarter-mile pole he raised hopes of a glorious exit, but, as the slow motion TV re-run showed, he changed his legs repeatedly as soon as effort was required.

Cyril Mitchell reckoned, 'He was only able to have one gallop at Epsom all year which he really enjoyed.' He still left the course with the European prize earnings record (£44,000) for a sprinter, after winning twelve races and being placed ten times in twenty-nine races. And, apart from one disapproving correspondent, he received as big a fan mail in failure as he did after success. The exception wrote, 'It was obvious from the excitement in your voice that you backed the winner, Tudor Music, and that your horse was blatantly stopped.' Later in the month Be Friendly flew off to the Ennistown Stud – where his half-sister, Friendly Again, was already a matron – accompanied by Tony Boyle, who stayed for a few days in case he was homesick. And I went to the December sales to buy him a bride.

It was 9.45 a.m. on 3 December 1969 when lot 608 entered Tattersall's arena at Newmarket. My daily concern – finding a 'lead' story for the following day's 'copy' – had already been satisfied. Forty-six-year-old Melbourne wizard Bill Williamson was to be signed up to ride the potentially brilliant Gyr in all his races next year. Now I could concentrate on the loose-limbed young mare who had been so appealing when she circled the preliminary ring.

Once in the main arena she surveyed the calculating ringsiders with fierce pride, as if defying the auctioneer to make reference to her modest public achievement (success in a three-year-old maiden at Edinburgh). In deference he simply described her as 'a winner'. At 5500 guineas I had already passed the sum represented by my annual earnings from the *Daily Express*. At 6500 I was beginning to weaken. I thought she looked better and better, but I evidently wasn't the only one. At 7000 guineas Peter Nugent, one of Tattersall's brilliant men on the rostrum, swept the assembly with his gavel and inquired, 'For the last time, then, is there no advance for this well-turned mare from a very successful family, believed in foal to the Italian Derby winner Appiani II? I nodded, and at 7100 guineas El Galgo was mine.

She was the first brood mare I had ever bought and it was a little disconcerting when, within moments of the hammer falling, that noted authority and friend Alec Head, inquired with an air of incredulity, 'Have you bought that mare for yourself?' I had – and what was wrong with her? I reacted nervously. 'Nothing that I can see,' said Alec. 'She's a very, very nice mare. The incredible thing is I have just bought a yearling filly in Saratoga who is almost as close to her in blood as you can get. So if she's any good I'll be putting value on your mare.'

The yearling (who cost $15,000) turned out be none other than the illustrious Pistol Packer – one of the best fillies to race in France since the war and a six-race winner of over £200,000, including the French Oaks, in her first two seasons. So far so good. But when El Galgo foaled her first-born, a colt, at 02.30 hours on 26 March 1970, the portents were not particularly favourable. A 'friend', who visited the Ennistown Stud before I was able to get over to Ireland, reported back, 'If only he grows a bit you could have one big enough to run at the White City.' He did grow, but not entirely in the right direction. His feet turned outwards, Charlie Chaplin-like, and his upper jaw exceeded the development of the lower, giving him a parrot mouth. Otherwise, apart from being narrow as an arrow, he was a perfect physical specimen with a bold, bright and inquisitive eye.

In the sympathetic hands of Robert Elwes and his splendid head stud man, Jack Murphy, his personality, if not his physique, developed conspicuously. Right up to the time he was due to leave the quiet countryside around the village of Kilmessan to be groomed for stardom at Epsom by Cyril Mitchell he had never put a misshapen foot wrong. Immediately after foaling I had got on to Weatherby's in the hope of reserving the name Amigo, both to maintain the 'Friendly' link and to incorporate Appiani II and El Galgo. The Jockey Club secretariat confirmed Amigo available and reserved. However, when it came to registration those sticklers for other people's accuracy were unable to grant the name. Pat suggested Attivo (active or busy in Italian) to take account of his Latin father and lively temperament.

Young stock are usually the most amenable air travellers, but Attivo was a near-fatal exception. He became so agitated on the flight to England that, in the interest of the safety of fellow passengers, he received a series of tranquillizing shots. Although groggy with drugs on landing, he came to sufficiently in the horsebox transporting him from Heathrow to Downs House stables to set about full-scale demolition of the vehicle. So when the poor little lad tottered down the ramp into the yard he looked as if he'd been attacked by a maniac with a knife.

It is very unusual for a thoroughbred who has undergone such a traumatic experience to tackle a meal. Attivo didn't know that. On a 1000/1 off-chance he was given a light snack. In less time than it takes to say 'hot mash' he licked out his manger and made it abundantly clear that he was unaccustomed to a starvation diet. An admiring audience watched 'Percy' – as he was nicknamed for no reason that anyone can account for – wade into a substantial evening feed.

Generously described by *Raceform*'s expert commentators as 'unfurnished', Attivo made an unspectacular racecourse debut at Windsor's evening meeting of 19 June 1972. Returning to the same circuit the following month, he at least beat four of his eleven opponents before running fourth of thirteen a fortnight later in a Goodwood seller. He had been running on so strongly in the sixth and final furlong that it looked as though he'd appreciate a mile. Early one morning he went to Kempton for a trial over the trip with a fairly useful stable companion, two from Brian Swift's and three from the yard of that great perfectionist, Staff Ingham. The work was a revelation. Always in the first two, Attivo drew clear in the straight and left the others for dead. Staff, who had included two he regarded far superior to plating class, gave it as his opinion (always worth noting): 'There is no one-mile selling race for two-year-olds in the calendar that Attivo would not win.' He added that, whatever the selected target, he would like to be included in the stable commission for 'the maximum'. His request was echoed by Brian Swift.

We aimed for the eight-furlongs Barrow Selling Plate at Newmarket on 26 October, in which, on all public evidence, his four opponents appeared to be exceptionally mediocre. Having contacted the interested parties, I arranged to meet Victor Chandler (father of the present principal) for a coffee in Fortnum's to place the commission in his hands. I remember telling him, 'It'll probably end in disaster, but if things work out as they should he'll win from here to the Ritz.' It was the first time I'd had £1000 on a horse. While the cash was being 'invested', at all rates from 5/2 down to 11/8 on, the object of feverish market activity was shuffling round the freezing paddock, clearly discomfited by the chill for which the region is renowned, and showing alarming lack of concern for his imminent responsibilities.

In the event Attivo and his partner, Brian Jago, opted for conflicting tactics. 'Percy' felt he should jump off and go from the outset. Brian favoured conserving energy until the vital stages of the contest. By the time they settled their differences the gamble of the day had forfeited either his vitality or his interest – or both. The 2 o'clock favourite finished third, five lengths behind the winner.

He 'ran' once more that year, at the end of the season, when, allowed to stride on from the start, he showed ahead for five of the seven furlongs of Haydock's Vernons Finance Nursery before beating a hasty retreat into ninth place. The outlook was not promising.

Nor was it brightened in March the following year when that renowned raconteur, Geoff Lewis, took over the reins in the Waterdale Selling Handicap at Doncaster. We sold ourselves the proposition that Attivo had strengthened immeasurably (or, as Cyril put it, 'He looks a little bit less like a Spanish chicken') during the months when frost gripped the Downs, and backed him from 7/1 to 3/1 favourite to support the illusion. He beat quite a few home, but there were still four ahead of him at the place that matters. 'He's a right little m-monkey,' reported

Geoff, adding, 'I couldn't ride one side of him.' Nor was a return excursion to Newmarket, where he was apprentice-ridden in another three-year-old selling handicap, any more productive.

The first of the Tote Roll-Up series was due on 7 April at Ascot. Anxious to support the innovation, I asked Cyril to nominate 'Percy' for every one of the sixteen-runner televised Saturday handicaps in which (5p per entry) the punter sought to name the first six.

The Tiercé, a 1, 2, 3 forecast pool on selected races, had boosted the prosperity of French racing to a dramatic extent, so that their prize money far outstripped that in Britain. There had to be a means of harnessing the pools firms expertise to the advantage of British racing and its immense following, particularly during the football close season. Robert Sangster and I had discussed the possibility at length during the Western Meeting at Ayr in 1970. The following year, when I was inflicted on the Gimcrack dinner audience at York, where Prince Charles made a first public speech that was both impressive and witty, I suggested that a 1, 2, 3 forecast on a £10,000 sponsored handicap which could be seen every Saturday, during the period when the customers of the top two pools firms were reduced from seven to four million, would surely have more appeal than betting on Australian football.

It was thanks to Robert's initiative with the Pools Promoters' Association that – to the extent it did – the enterprise ever got off the ground. It was run by the pools in conjunction with the Tote, whose ability to leave the ground, commercially, at this time appeared zero. The launch, or 'leak', as Clive Graham pertinently described it, was a calamitous exercise in public relations. Sponsorship was refused; the prize money was paltry; and, although Weatherby's operated a computer to arrange horses in merit order in all handicaps with guaranteed prize money of £4000 or more, the Roll-Up did not qualify. So, before the system was finally modified on 23 July, haphazard balloting introduced a further complication for punters seeking to name six finishers in correct order – a task involving 5,765,760 permutations for full cover in a sixteen-horse field. And yet by curtain fall, despite multiple impediments, some substantial dividends had been paid, and the scheme, which merits further consideration, had really started to run.

After the inaugural event the *Sunday Times* reported, 'BBC commentator Peter O'Sullevan had to smother ironic disappointment during yesterday's Roll-Up start. His horse, Attivo, was the only one of twenty-one entries (every runner receives £100 appearance money and each of the four reserves on standby £150) balloted out of an event he helped to set up.' Thereafter the Italian Derby winner's slimmest son received a season ticket for the Roll-Up and took up more or less permanent residence in a horsebox.

In a six-furlongs handicap at Newmarket on 5 May, his burden reduced to 6½ stone by apprentice Chris Leonard's 7 lb claim, he came home well to run sixth and collect £30 prize money. A week later the Lingfield round was over one and a quarter miles. First and second were Willie Carson and Lester Piggott respectively – not far behind in third, little old Attivo collected £180. Returning to a shorter distance (seven furlongs) but a longer trip from his Epsom base to Thirsk on 2 June, he slipped back to fourth. After journeying home for such rest as he could ever be persuaded to take, the Roll-Up regular had only to stroll across the famous Downs from his stable adjacent to the Derby start to compete over seven furlongs on 9 June. He finished out of the first ten. And a subsequent 'run' over the course in April 1976 (last of four) confirmed Chris Leonard's impression that 'He just seems to look on this place as his playground and doesn't want to know about racing over it'.

If ever a lad deserved to have the object of his care and devotion come good it was Derek Wilmot. In the hands of a less tolerant stableman, 'Percy' might well have turned nasty. For in between employing his teeth for their principal purpose, his chief pleasure was striking, thumping and nipping his faithful attendant. 'It's only fun,' insisted black and blue Derek, lightly dismissing the handiwork of his equine tattooist. On Saturday, 30 June, when I was commentating at The Curragh, Attivo and his lad came within a length of ending up in the winner's circle at Lingfield after a first attempt over one and a half miles. The following month a run over the same trip yielded a creditable third at Newmarket. Attivo had clearly developed spirited enthusiasm for competition in 1973. It was the year in which, ignoring wiser counsel, I made the worst decision of my life.

CHAPTER 24

I Bogged It Alright

Max Aitken had lately appointed Jocelyn Stevens troubleshooter-in-chief to Beaverbrook Newspapers. 'Old' Max's legacy of over-manning, coupled with his antipathy to TV involvement, had left the *Express* bedevilled by high production costs and unsupported by outside interests. Now circulation was falling and overhead costs rising as the price of newsprint quadrupled. On New Year's Day 1969 Max had called in Jocelyn to save the ailing *Evening Standard*. A conspicuously successful rescue operation was effected by a resolute manager combining with a purposeful Editor, in the civilized persona of Charles Wintour, to lead a skilled team. Max's brief to his new managing director was to adapt the formula to the *Daily Express*; to exercise his persuasive charm on the unions and to blow away expendable elements. To have command of the enterprise, Jocelyn recalls, was 'like trying to run a restaurant with a chef who couldn't cook'.

The London Editor at the time, Ian McColl, had achieved considerable success in Glasgow, where circulation increased during his tenure, but appeared less effective in London. After Jocelyn had breezed into the Manchester office, where he took a favourable view of the local Editor, John McDonald, news of his requirements filtered through to the power-hungry in the region and staff changes followed in London, whence a member of the northern personnel was imported in the guise of Sports Editor. The new incumbent may not have been the character type the author had in mind when writing *Sense and Sensibility*. Referred to as 'Hitler' by the more civil among those under his authority, he was reputed to have low regard for the journalists he had inherited and neither attachment to horse racing nor any comprehension of it.

I guess I had been spoilt during twenty-three years with scarce a restriction on movement or expression. In 1963, when the proprietor himself decided to run a campaign to abolish bookmaking, he invited Clive and me to dinner at Arlington House to discuss it. When neither of us favoured the project, Lord Beaverbrook chuckled, 'I guess you boys just enjoy the whole racket', and that was the end of it. Not long afterwards, on 8 April 1964, he wrote, out of the blue, from Cherkley: 'Dear Peter, I have asked Mr Blackburn to add £15 a week to your income – telling him to apply it as you wish. He can apply it as (1) salary, (2) expenses or (3) insurance money. Alternatively you may wish to split it up. We have got the best racing team in London and we should be among the first to recognize it. Yours sincerely, Beaverbrook.'

The atmosphere had changed somewhat lately. Now copy was subject to 'approval', and specific articles were demanded. While Clive shared my unease, he took the temperate view that the new man was simply establishing his authority and that he would settle down in due course. When we discussed this with Max, he was sure that was the case. Maybe.

The degree and range of power which a section head may exercise over his department on a newspaper is considerable. Our man appeared driven by a compulsion to overturn established order. Clive and I, suspecting the 'divide and rule' syndrome, found ourselves competing for ever-diminishing space. When I suggested to him that, under these circumstances, we'd be better writing on alternate days, he did not think there was a chance of this being acceptable 'upstairs'.

I have never responded favourably to aggressive authority or an abrasive manner, and relations with my 'superior' were short of harmonious when a trivial incident widened the breach. I was due to go to Ireland to report the Oaks at The Curragh on 21 July, and intended to incorporate a quick drive down to Tipperary on the eve of the classic to see Vincent O'Brien. When I was collecting tickets from the *Express* travel organizer, Derek Stark, he said, 'The Sports Editor has changed your usual booking to the lowest category of self-drive.' It was because of the provision of fast transport that I overlooked my low level of pay, relative to the going rate. When I remonstrated with the Sports Editor on the grounds that I drove an XJ12 in England, he reacted by saying, 'You are very lucky to do so,' adding, 'I doubt if even *I* will receive a Jaguar.' My instant response, 'I'll be bloody well amazed if you do,' would probably have been best unsaid.

I rented a swift means of locomotion on my own account, and we had no further contact until the following Tuesday. After phoning copy from Folkestone that day I stopped on the way home to check whether there were any queries, and learnt from the long-suffering and ever-supportive Racing Editor, Reg Bailey, that 'you-know-who' wanted the intro changed and two paragraphs deleted. I could foresee nothing but 'needle' ahead. I drove straight to the office, wrote a short note of resignation and returned home. If it was a foolhardy act to jettison my pension prospects after twenty-three years, I felt nothing but relief. I wondered how Pat would react. 'We've lived on little money before,' she said, 'and if we have to I am sure we can again.'

Like rumour on a racecourse, trivial news travels fast in Fleet Street. Bob Findlay, my admirable and considerate Sports Editor for eight years on the *Express* and now head of *Daily Mail* sport, rang on Wednesday evening to inquire if the stories were true. We had a drink the next day and he set up an immediate meeting with the *Mail* Editor, David English (knighted in 1982), at the Berkeley. David, former Foreign Editor and later Associate Editor of the *Express*, had made a tremendous impact on the *Mail* since its merger with the *Daily Sketch* in 1971. He was sorry to learn of my problems at the *Express* and proposed a stunning contract which, by comparison with my current situation, read like the difference between servitude and freedom.

Written confirmation dated 27 July 1973 was hand-delivered that evening to the flat. It offered me the job of *Daily Mail* Chief Racing Correspondent at a salary of £12,000 – more than double my present £5500 remuneration – 'to appear on average four days a week with maximum projection'. In addition it offered £2500 a year fixed general expenses; plus £11 raceday allowance; first-class travel and accommodation worldwide; a fully maintained and serviced Jaguar XJ12; and eleven weeks' holiday per annum. It also promised me unrestricted freedom to undertake television work and gave the assurance that 'The layout of your copy would be subject to your approval as well as the headline writing', and 'Your copy would not be edited except by senior executives, and should we desire to make any alterations or cuts, this would be done in consultation with you.' David said my appointment would not result in any job loss on the paper, where he was sure I would be very happy. And, unlike one of his predecessors who had offered me a job nearly twenty years ago, he appreciated that I would want a little while to think about it.

Max had instructed his right-hand man, John Coote, to 'sort everything out'; we met in the Royal Court Hotel that evening, but without getting very far. The Chairman now called on Jocelyn Stevens to handle the situation as a matter of urgency.

He, the Editor and I assembled in the Editor's office on Monday morning. I reiterated my major concern, which was, as politely as I could express it, that the Sports Editor be removed from my back. It wasn't my only concern, but without this assurance it was pointless to proceed further. The Editor felt that a talk from him should resolve that issue. I was far from convinced. Nor, I gathered, was Jocelyn, who was later to go on record as saying, 'In my opinion the engagement of the Sports Editor was not a successful appointment.' But at this juncture he said he didn't see how we could officially undermine the Sports Editor's authority.

The next day, when I got through to the office from Goodwood, there was an urgent message to ring Jocelyn. Max had told him and John Coote, 'You boys have screwed it up. I *must* see Peter.' I was staying at Bailiffscourt, near Littlehampton, for the meeting, during which there were twenty-three TV races in the five days and a load of homework every evening. It just wasn't 'on' to return to London – and for what purpose? Max rang the hotel later and proposed sending a car for me so that I could work while travelling. I said I'd drive myself to his flat in the morning, provided he had Jocelyn there as well. This would be the final meeting, and I wanted to be as certain as possible that there was no misunderstanding.

When I told Pat, she said, 'I hope you'll go to the *Mail*. I have a feeling you'll never be happy with the *Express* Sports Editor.'

We met on Wednesday, 1 August at 9.30 a.m. at Marsham Court. Like his old man, Max had been good to work for. Typical was an incident in 1960. I had received a letter dated 2 February from David Brown, Chairman and Managing Director of the David Brown Corporation, in which he wrote: 'Dear Mr O'Sullivan, I was interested to read about "Linwell" in this morning's *Daily Express* and that he belongs to a Mr David BARNES. This, of course, is completely incorrect as the animal belongs to me. Copy to Mr Max Aitken.' I had never met the engineering tycoon and, regarding the 'Copy to' as a gratuitous attempt to get a reporter into trouble, replied:

Dear Mr Brown

I write regarding the 'completely incorrect' interpretation of your name in my *Daily Express* column on 2 February. I have had frequent cause to be grateful to your excellent horse Linwell, particularly when napping him to win the 1957 Cheltenham Gold Cup. On each occasion his owner's name has been correctly identified both in print and, when applicable, on television. I would have thought this instance to be a fairly obvious error in transmission for which I nevertheless apologise. I hope you will not have any further cause for complaint. In the event that you do, perhaps you would note that the correct spelling of my name is Yours sincerely Peter O'Sullevan.

Copy to the Hon. Max Aitken.

I wasn't altogether surprised when there was a call from Max's secretary within a few days to say he'd like to see me the next time I was in the office. I thought I'd been a bit brusque. The following morning I called in before racing and Max said, 'It's about that letter from David Brown.'

'I thought it might be,' I reacted.

'Yes, old boy,' grinned Max. 'I just wanted to tell you I thought it was a bloody good reply. What a shit!'

I am a sucker for supportive attitudes. Max now kicked off our meeting with 7 lb in hand. He pleaded that, at this delicate stage in the paper's history, it would be a crippling, even mortal, blow, to lose me to their principal rival. (If I'd believe that I'd believe anything.) There was, he lamented, no way that the *Express* could match the *Mail*'s financial offer. But wasn't loyalty more important? Hadn't we been together for more than a quarter of a century? 'Even our wives know each other,' threw in Max. And I remember wondering at this point what the hell that had to do with anything.

But I was already hooked on the best act of persuasion since Lester kidded Ribero into winning the 1968 St Leger. Max would give his personal, absolute guarantee of editorial freedom. He would raise my salary (and Clive's) from £5500 a year to £9000 from this day; guarantee 'no less than £12,000 by 1978' and immediately increase our individual expenses allowance from £1560 a year to £2500. He would also endorse the proposition that Clive and I write on a rota basis, except on big race days, when we would both appear in the paper.

Uncertain whether Clive was truly sold on the latter idea, I asked Max to confirm his agreement. The Chairman favoured doing this at a personal meeting, but I urged that we clear everything up now. So he went into the next room to phone the Richmond Arms, and emerged laughing. Clive's reaction had been: 'What sort of a nut case do you think I am to turn down twice the money for half the work?'

We shook hands and I returned to Goodwood, pausing at Downs House, Epsom, to slip Attivo a Polo mint. I'd cut it a bit fine, and on reaching the commentary box the producer, Dennis Monger, said through my headset, 'We're on air in three minutes. Clive wants a quick word on your intercom.' The Scout said, 'Well done, Pedro,' adding, 'I've got an old frigidaire at home. It's been broken for a few years now and I was wondering if you could sell it to the Eskimos?'

In the evening a dispatch rider from the *Express* delivered confirmation of the morning agreement to Bailiffscourt Hotel. I rang Bob Findlay and he later wrote me a charming letter. I could not get out of my head the only seven consecutive lines of Shakespeare I know by heart:

> There is a tide in the affairs of men,
> Which, taken at the flood, leads on to fortune;
> Omitted, all the voyage of their life
> Is bound in shallows and in miseries.
> On such a full sea are we now afloat;
> And we must take the current when it serves,
> Or lose our ventures.

'Shallows and miseries' were a bit strong. But I had bogged it alright. Although he had not thought of it at the time, the guarantor of freedom was soon to sell Beaverbrook Newspapers. And while the Editor's chair was subject to impermanent tenancy, the leader of the Sports Department survived every putsch. As far as I was concerned, it was like trying to play in an orchestra under a hostile conductor who was tone deaf.

On 1 September 1973, while I was lying by an Algarve pool dreaming of Attivo nipping round an extended one and a half miles of Chester's tight circuit and sprinting clear to win the £1600 Roll-Up, he was doing just that. Well, not exactly nipping round. He ran into a traffic problem at every other turn and twice appeared irredeemably hampered. But setbacks only served to rekindle his zest, and the ITV video of the twenty-second Tote Roll-Up, which Brough Scott kindly sent me, remains one of my favourite recordings.

Clive had tipped the 8/1 winner in that morning's *Express* when writing, 'I am inspired to think that colleague Peter O'Sullevan's Attivo (2.45) will meet his deserved reward at long last. Trainer Cyril Mitchell remarked at Kempton yesterday: "This could be the day".' When I called Cyril afterwards, he reported that Percy was immensely pleased with himself. 'We'll go back and win the Cup next year,' I suggested, not too seriously.

Meanwhile, having started the season running over six and seven furlongs, we made his next ambitious target Sandown's one mile six furlongs, all-aged, Sportsman Club Handicap, worth more than £4000 to the winner. Chris Leonard, who had got on so well with him, could now claim only 5 lb allowance. So featherweight Harry Ballantine was called in to ease the burden off one of the narrowest backs in the business by the full 7 lb. Eleven of his thirteen opponents were seniors and, among the unofficial assessors, *Raceform Private Handicap* estimated that they would all finish ahead of him. Marginally less disheartening, *Timeform* placed the restless resident of Downs House tenth. If the *Racing Post* had been published at this time it is doubtful whether that powerful aid in the punters' armoury, 'Pricewise', would have counselled readers to dive in, even at the 50/1 rate offered by Hill's. Having personally tipped him each-way, in the slow-dawning expectation that distance running was his forte, I couldn't resist £50 to win and a 'pony' a place at the ante-post odds.

Unlike many racecourses which have undergone modernization, Sandown remains an aficionado's delight where, granted moderate sobriety, the action may be followed clearly from any vantage point. I watched this one from the press stand parapet, to which one of racing's heroes, Bob Champion, was a temporary visitor. Standing between Bob and my long-time colleague Len Thomas of the *Sporting Life*, I watched the little demon ease himself to the front six furlongs out. At the quarter-mile pole the leader was still going strong, no one was sitting in behind with a double handful, and Bob was nudging my already shaky binoculars, saying, 'You'll win, you'll win.' By the furlong marker Harry and Percy had beaten off three successive challenges and Len, loyally abandoning his own selection, was bellowing for Attivo. In the last fifty yards the four-year-old Pamroy ridden by Tommy Carter, meeting us at 9 lb better than weight-for-age, was beginning to get up. They went past the line together in a photo.

'Did you win?' quizzed Len.

'Just beat,' I reacted. 'But wasn't he terrific?' It's a funny angle at Sandown, and down in the unsaddling enclosure some thought Attivo had held on. But I was already congratulating the winning trainer, my old ally Scobie Breasley, when the verdict was announced: Pamroy first – by a neck, too.

Shortly afterwards we decided that Percy must accept a break, after which he might have a pop over a hurdle or two to give him a new interest and help sustain his abundant zest. It was a ploy much more widely practised in France than in England. As a former successful jump jockey, Cyril had wide experience of both riding and training some very useful winter performers. Experience had taught him to exercise caution in his judgement, but there was no trace of reservation in his enthusiastic tone when he telephoned to report: 'This little fellow's brilliant! Come down and watch him "school".' There was no doubt about either his talent or his barely containable enthusiasm – talk about jumping for joy!

The Daily Express Triumph (Britain's richest four years old hurdles prize) was jokily proposed as his objective. In a way it was tantamount to dreaming of Derby prospects with an unsuccessful selling plater. But the only similarity between the Flat and the jumping game is that both activities involve horses. As frost modified our launch programme, I wondered whether a suggestion I had made at the 1963 National Sporting League's annual dinner that 'A £1 million all-weather racecourse, situated off the M1, accessible to stables north and south, incorporating a general sports complex, could be a great asset to the industry' might ever be realized.

Attivo had a choice of engagements on the 1974 New Year programme at Cheltenham. He could either tackle the well-established Evesham Four Years Old Hurdle, featuring the impressive Newbury and Chepstow winner Fighting Kate as well as hat-trick seeker Park Lawn. Or he could take on fellow novices the following afternoon. Cyril outlined the options realistically: 'If he runs in the novices' you can have a bet, and if he does it half as well "out" as he does at home you'll be unlucky to leave it behind. Or you can avoid the greater risk of injury in a big field and see how he goes against the best.'

Be Friendly (Colin Williams) wins the inaugural Vernons Sprint, 1966

Trophy presenter Sandie Shaw is friendly (*left*) and *Express* racing secretary Valerie Frost surveys the generous response (*above*)

Top: Be Friendly (Scobie Breasley) wins the second running by a neck from Mountain Call (Russ Maddock), and (*above*) the King's Stand Stakes

Top: Be Friendly hacked up in the Prix de l'Abbaye de Longchamp with Geoff Lewis, who also won the Ayr Gold Cup, Palace House Stakes, etc., aboard. But (*above*) when Pat and Pucci came to see Be Friendly win a third successive Vernons fog foiled a brilliant exit for Pucci's handler, Scobie Breasley

Attivo wins his first Tote Roll-up at Chester

My first born agrees ...
to try a few steps

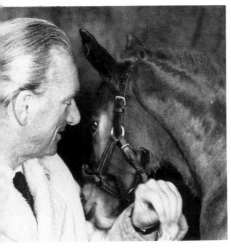

It was tempting to start the New Year with a successful punt and winning nap, but he could easily get buffeted in a big field. The Evesham Hurdle it was. At least the already notable achievements of his two principal rivals meant that they must concede him 10 lb. When I reached the course early, frost was still gripping parts of the famed jumping arena and there was to be a stewards' inspection. Local sage 'Frenchie' Nicholson, handler of Fighting Kate, forecast that racing would be 'on'. His meteorological prediction was more reassuring to this owner/commentator than the rider to the effect that 'Kate will not get beat'.

Racing was 'on', but two intended runners in the Evesham dropped out, leaving seven. So to justify advice to readers to back him each-way Percy would have to beat one of the 'good things', if not two. The last time I'd commentated a race featuring this afternoon's 2/1 on favourite, Park Lawn, who had won his last two hurdles races by an aggregate of seventeen lengths, was when he led the field for a great part of the way in the Irish Sweeps Derby. The more I thought about it, the more foolhardy the selection appeared. Fighting Kate was 3/1, Attivo 8/1 (from 10s) and it was 12/1 bar three.

By post time, at 1.15, I had abandoned hopes of glory and was simply willing the duo to return in one piece. Cyril came up to the commentary box to watch it with me. While the riders of the 'big two' – each instructed to employ waiting tactics – played cat and mouse with each other, young Robert Hughes, claiming the 5 lb allowance to which inexperience entitled him, let Attivo bowl along. He loved it. At halfway, a mile from home, Cyril whispered in between my commentary, 'They'll have a job to catch him now.' They would indeed. And they didn't. The judge posted the winning margin 'a distance' – which is to say more than thirty lengths. The widespread professional verdict was that it had been a fluke. 'As far as I am concerned,' Percy seemed to be saying, as he returned with an unmistakable swagger, 'they can think what they like.'

The view that the race for the Evesham Hurdle was 'a complete nonsense' – to quote the opinion of that notable and forthright judge of racing merit, Mercy Rimell, whose late husband, Fred, was the trainer of Park Lawn – would be put to the test, in so far as opinion may be appraised in the light of subsequent events, at Newbury in one of the acknowledged Triumph graduations, the Stroud Green Hurdle, on Saturday, 8 February.

Cyril's son Philip, who was later to assume responsibility for Percy's destiny, handled my modest commission while I paced the limpid shore (prior to the invasion of parasitic developers) between Dickenson Bay, along Buccaneer Cove to the idyllic Runaway Bay, in Antigua. The incompletely dependable local gazette had omitted Attivo's name from the list of runners in the 3 o'clock at Newbury. That evening, while awaiting the cable in the bar of the Spanish Main, the unique colonial-style establishment run by Bob and Janice Brancker – he of the corncrake voice from Harlem, she with the musical lilt of the neighbouring island of Barbuda – I envisaged every conceivable permutation of disaster. The supply of grappa was running low by the time the economically expressed message arrived. It read 'Twenty lengths no problem.' The 'fluke' theory, advanced five weeks earlier, had gained sufficient support for the winner to ease from 2/1 to 7/2 in the market, in which he was replaced as favourite by Bird's Nest (subsequently runner-up in the 1976 Champion Hurdle), whom he beat by twenty-one lengths into third place.

One of his keenest observers, the redoubtable Ryan Price, who promptly decided to re-route his stable's intended Triumph Hurdle runner, Chocolate King, pronounced on my return, 'You missed one hell of a performance by your little star. I've always said you shouldn't go away in February!' Ryan was referring to the traumatic aftermath of the Schweppes Gold Trophy in both 1964 and 1967. On the former occasion I was on holiday in Switzerland when the *Racing Calendar* of 20 February carried the announcement that: 'The stewards found no satisfactory explanation for the reversal in form of Rosyth between his previous races of the current season and the Schweppes Gold Trophy . . . They therefore withdrew Price's licence to train until the end of the current season and declared him a "disqualified person".' On receiving the news I rang Clive at the office. I knew that Ryan regarded Rosyth as a 'spring horse' – that the colt had a tendency to break blood vessels, as his former handler, Ryan Jarvis, would confirm – and that Ryan Price would for sure have offered little defence, since he had a naive belief that a clear conscience was sufficient to establish innocence. Clive wasn't over-impressed and suggested that if I felt strongly about it I should file copy, which I did. It appeared on 22 February under the caption 'TALENT WE CAN'T AFFORD TO LOSE' and read:

THE official sentence on Ryan Price raises the question as to how good at his job a trainer can afford to be.

Ireland's top two, Vincent O'Brien and Paddy Prendergast, have each endured suspension for periods which, happily for the prestige of Irish blood-stock, were not prolonged indefinitely.

Among Price's achievements, surely one of the most remarkable was to win £14,733 with little Beaver II.

A £150 horse bought in France – where his trainer returned with him to collect the £9,551 four-year-old hurdling championship on June 17, 1962.

Rare talent

Rare are home-based trainers with the Price-Walwyn type initiative and talent to reverse the usual Anglo-French race-prize traffic.

It is a talent which cannot lightly be dispensed with. And the N.H. stewards, guardians of the essential good name of racing, will not have lightly reached their grim decision.

The facts need little recapitulation. Rosyth, a six-year-old with a tendency confirmed by veterinary evidence to breaking blood vessels, ran sixth at Sandown on January 11.

And five weeks later – meeting three of his conquerors on worse terms, and one, Salmon Spray, 4 lb better – reversed those placings.

I didn't see either race. So why open my big mouth. This is why . . .

On November 29 at Newbury I inquired of the trainer of Britain's largest N.H. team why he repeatedly ran two horses with apparently similar chances in the same race – like Rosyth and Brocade Slipper, who were due to appear in the Berkshire Handicap the following day.

And why not?

"Why the hell not?" 51-year-old ex-commander Captain Ryan Price, M.C., replied.

"They are in different ownership, and they are both doing their level best," he declared vehemently.

I said I didn't doubt that. But maintained that although their respective partners, Josh Gifford and Fred Winter, would also be aware of it (which made four of us) – for every four who believed there would be 40 who wouldn't.

"My conscience is absolutely clear and that is all that matters," continued Ryan, adding: "In fact, I am worried about both these horses and at the moment can't see either of them coming back." (Coming back to form.)

They performed moderately and Brocade Slipper ran only once more.

I saw Rosyth run in this Newbury race and subsequently at Kempton. And anyone who says he wasn't trying wasn't looking.

Later at Sandown, last year's evidently progressing Schweppes winner obviously ran his best 1963 race.

In the five weeks' interim, he had progressed sufficiently to reverse placings with White Park Bay (who appears to have "gone"), disappointing Greektown, Oedipe (who has had some very hard races this season), and Salmon Spray, whom he met on only 4 lb better terms.

Certainly

Grounds for an inquiry by vigilant stewards? Certainly. But this same Salmon Spray has been in peak form for quite a while – ever since he beat Ryan Price-trained Invader by nine lengths at level weights after being beaten 28 lengths by the same Invader on 1 lb different terms on his first outing of the season.

"The Captain," whose respect for authority is in striking contrast to his deep affection for his horses, may not have been his best advocate.

And one wonders whether certain bookmakers' lamentations over last Saturday's Schweppes winner would have been as vociferous had not the trainer concerned previously declared himself in favour of a Tote monopoly.

In a letter posted two days before the Cavendish-square "trial" Ryan affirmed: "It is a very distasteful

business, but my conscience is absolutely clear."
    I for one do not doubt that, and
firmly hope that the authorities will
set a limit on the suspension of a
trainer whose talent we can ill afford
to do without.

Ryan Price was a brilliant horse conditioner. No weights and measures
man, he had a gypsy instinct, as it were, for producing a horse at its
peak on the appointed day. It was a talent that made him vulnerable,
not crooked. Whenever Ryan was preparing one for a specific occasion
it was worth taking note.
    The 1966 Cesarewitch was a case in point. Here he was preparing an
eight-year-old ex-invalid, Persian Lancer, who had not won a race for
five years, to win one of the most arduous handicaps on the level – and
firmly expecting him to do so. Even allowing for the master of Findon's
natural enthusiasm, I wrote after seeing the old lad run at Kempton on
17 September, 'I can foresee Ladbroke's being well accommodated after
knocking out Persian Lancer from 16/1 to 33/1 for next month's
Cesarewitch.' Soon shortened to 20/1, he started 100/7 on the day and
justified selection cleverly. Afterwards Cyril Stein sent a telegram to the
Express: 'We were well and truly accommodated.'
    There was no recrimination after this one, but the fourth Price
triumph in the Schweppes, via the enigmatic Hill House, became a *cause
célèbre* and transformed disciplinary procedures. The horse was a bit of
a head case, as his earlier handler, Bernard van Cutsem, confirmed, but
if Ryan was right he was coming on-song at the *moment critique*. Before
leaving for a holiday, I took a little 10/1 and advised readers to be sure
to have him on their side. The telegram I received from Ryan's mercurial
secretary, Bill Scrimgeour, read: 'URGENT O'SULLEVAN GRECIAN HOTEL
FAMAGUSTA HILL HOUSE BY TWELVE LENGTHS ALL HELL LET LOOSE HOPE
YOU ARE RETURNING SOON BILL.' I was moving on that day to Beirut
for a short stay at the Hotel St Georges – one of the attractions in this
subsequently tragic city was a seaboard restaurant, La Grotte aux
Pigeons – but delayed departure to compose and despatch to Clive a
detailed summary of Hill House's background, as Ryan had outlined it
to me.
    But Clive was no Price fan, and his reaction provoked one of our rare
firm disagreements. 'I find it difficult to gild the halo you propose,' he
replied, sniffily, 'and question whether racing can afford the image
created by Captain Ryan Price,' adding, 'Even George Todd described
it as the act of a very stupid man.'
    I replied, in part, 'I am a great admirer of George, but since he is
capable of refrigerating a potential winner for a couple of years, I
consider his comment singularly inappropriate. And your reference to

it akin to acknowledging the testimony of Jack the Ripper as a witness for the prosecution.'

The Hill House affair was complicated by the detail that no sooner had a case been prepared to show that the horse had not made abnormal improvement than the result of a dope test was declared positive. The question was whether the level of Cortisol to which Hill House reacted was self-created or administered. Its resolution resulted in probably the most exhaustive tests ever carried out on a racehorse. I saw Ryan quite frequently during this period and had no doubt whatever that he was completely innocent. The inquiry raised two pertinent questions: what would have happened to a trainer less able to sustain the cost of legal representation over a long period; and was it acceptable to exclude the defendant's counsel from the room in which the hearing took place?

Over lunch one day, at what turned out to be half-time in the case, three months after the event, Ryan, who was apt to fix one with a penetrating stare and raise his voice an octave or two when about to make a point, inquired loudly, 'Do you know what I think of the Committee?' I didn't, but I could guess, and hoped there were not too many Jockey Club members within earshot. 'They're a bright lot of buggers,' he thundered. 'Make no mistake about that, and scrupulously fair. That's what gives me hope. Plenty of it.' He was full of surprises, was the Captain.

Tucked away at the foot of my column, to avoid making a meal of it, on 9 May 1967 I suggested: 'The latest tests on Hill House at Newmarket are likely to confirm the findings of one eminent diagnostician. Namely that the elements traced in the horse are part of his natural organism.' But it wasn't until 9 August that, along with my colleagues on other papers, I was able to report the closing chapter. Under the caption 'ALL CLEAR – AFTER SIX MONTHS' ORDEAL' I wrote:

The Hill House case which finally closed yesterday – with complete honourable discharge for all concerned – may both revolutionise the method of racehorse dope testing and alert trainers as a body to the need for legal representation. After Lord Willoughby de Broke had informed Ryan Price and all concerned with the 18 February Schweppes Gold Trophy winner that they left yesterday's hearing 'without a stain on their characters.' And after Ryan had affirmed, 'it is an ordeal I would not like to have to undergo again,' Lord Willoughby looked towards his fellow stewards Lord Leverhulme and Captain Miles Gosling and assured the Hill House connections: 'I can guarantee that goes for us too.'

The duration of the nearly six months' inquiry underlines the extent to which the unpaid administrators of the Turf are determined to safeguard the good name of the sport. Allegations of irregularity in running were dismissed by the investigators following detailed scrutiny of filmed evidence of the races which led up to the sensationally easy success of Len Coville's horse in the £6,706 prize . . .

Jockey Club procedures were modified within eighteen months, and full legal representation approved.

As for the central character in the Hill House story, he was sent to Doncaster sales 'to dissolve a partnership' and bought by Scottish bookmaker John Banks for 12,700 guineas. So Dublin-born Malton trainer Frank Carr took over the eight-year-old, who continued to attract as much attention on the sports pages as Arkle in his heyday.

On 18 January 1968 I drove through the night from London to Newcastle to obtain what my Manchester *Daily Express* colleague, Tom Dawson, generously referred to as 'A magnificent Hill House scoop right under our northern noses!' The report 'revealed' (as we love to say) that:

Shrouded in the Newcastle dawn damp the best kept secret of the season – the secret racecourse gallop of Hill House – materialised yesterday. The most controversial horse in the race game arrived at the course on the eve of his test – to sleep in a security guarded box. Driving up the 210 miles from his Shropshire home in the dark, jockey Jimmy Morrissey was met at dawn on the course by John Banks who, after getting up at a time 'when I am normally going to bed', looked more like a forlorn punter wondering where his next haggis was coming from than the prosperous proprietor of the sensational 1967 Schweppes Gold Trophy winner.

The workout by the 'galloping dope factory', whose immediate target was the 1968 Schweppes renewal, underlined the problem that lay ahead for his new handler. For although, as I mentioned, he 'blew enough steam afterwards to power an old fashioned engine from Newcastle to John Banks' native Glasgow', it had been very much touch and go whether he ever set off.

In fact he featured in further drama when refusing to start at Ayr, when he was again dope-tested ('It's me they should have ordered the test on', I quoted the owner) and again in the big one at Newbury. John passed him on to Harvey Smith as a potential showjumper. But HH didn't want to know about that either, and he ended his days back with Ryan among the Findon heroes: old campaigners like Kilmore, What A Myth, Major Rose, Charlie Worcester, Persian Lancer, Le Vermentois and so on, for whom the trainer's care and concern was, and remains, an example to all. When, for whatever reason, their time had come (Hill House lived until 1980), they were put down at home among familiar surroundings.

CHAPTER 25

The Bomb was a Hoax

Anyone who spends a lifetime associated with the racing game inevitably develops certain hang-ups. I had long since promised myself that, in the highly unlikely event of ever becoming so lucky as to own a horse good enough to run at the incomparable National Hunt Festival, I would ensure that he went there fresh. The normal progression towards the Daily Express Triumph on 14 March was via the Yellow Pages Hurdle at Kempton on 23 February. A less magnanimous trainer might have protested vigorously when I indicated a firm preference for giving Kempton a miss and keeping the lad fresh for the big date. All Cyril said was, 'The race is worth well over three grand to the winner and it would only be an exercise canter for him', adding gently, 'but if you can afford to act the millionaire it's OK by me.' I couldn't, but did. And Attivo's twenty-lengths Newbury victim won the Yellow Pages.

Instead of the 'exercise canter' we took 'himself' to Sandown Park one Sunday morning, where he jumped three flights down the back stretch quite brilliantly and almost wrenched poor Robert's arms out of their sockets before he could be pulled up. For all save the principal, the build-up to 'the day' was fraught with anxiety. To begin with, there was the spectre of the ballot coming into operation. I was on my annual stables tour (terminated the following year) in France when Clive, with his unerring nose for the topic of the moment, wrote on 6 March:

Attivo, hot favourite for the Daily Express Triumph Hurdle, could be balloted out of the big race at Cheltenham tomorrow week. If that sounds ludicrous – it is! There can be few more urgent problems facing racing at the moment than this situation. It has caused concern in the past, may well bring new fury at Cheltenham, and could even affect the Derby. Balloting out comes for safety reasons when too many horses are entered for a race that cannot be split into two divisions (how could you have two divisions of the Derby!). Rule of Racing 123 makes no distinction in the ballot between those with reasonable chances and no-hopers. And, inevitably, too many no-hopers swell big race fields for the gratification of owners. There can be no doubt that something must be done. Obviously the paramount factor must remain consideration for horses and jockeys. Equally, it would be unthinkable to call on sponsors for a double handout, let alone divide prestige races. Yet a system must be devised whereby the candidates for such events are graded by handicappers who feed data into racing's new computer. 'It won't be easy,' a Weatherby's spokesman told me yesterday. 'In races such as the Derby we would have to take into account the form of foreign entries.' Maybe. But can there be any argument that the no-form horses should be the first to go? Of course not. Just look at the facts. Recently a well-backed horse – Golden Thorn in Kempton's Yellow Pages Hurdle – was balloted out while other lesser entries ran. In eight days' time, Peter O'Sullevan's Attivo will have an awful lot of ante-post money riding on it in the Triumph . . . *if it runs*. Attivo is current favourite at 7/4 for the Cheltenham race, with Irish challenger Davy Lad second choice at sevens, having been backed down from 100/1. Yet, with 64 horses still in the race and a safety limit of 30, both could be balloted out. Owners, trainers, jockeys – and punters? – are entitled to a better deal.

Ballot hazard apart, the course was snow-covered and, granted the predicted thaw, flooding would be a significant threat. And yet, despite the possibility of the favourite's glory day being frustrated, I received a staggering offer for him. This was one decision that posed no problem. He was as much for sale as our poodle; and money couldn't buy her, either.

Now, as the soggy Gloucestershire arena narrowly survived a stewards' inspection on the eve of the meeting, another thought began to nag me. The 1974 Festival was to mark the retirement of one of the county's most celebrated and popular sons, thrice champion Terry Biddlecombe. The tall blonde laughing cavalier of the weighing-room, whose bravery and panache had brought such colour to the sport for more than a decade, appeared to have very little chance of bowing out with a winner.

Although I still found it nigh impossible to believe that little old Attivo represented one of the soundest prospects at the three-day fixture which unites the best in the world, the form book, for what it is worth, was conclusive. His very presence had removed the ballot threat, reducing the field below the safety limit to twenty-one, among whom the second favourite was Supreme Halo – a horse he had beaten out of sight at Newbury. On the one hand the 1974 Daily Express Triumph Hurdle could provide Terry with the means of a glorious exit which would delight his countless fans, among whom I was one. On the other it could launch a young rider, Robert Hughes, who was on the threshold of his career, but who had everything before him, into the big time. Robert, who was apprenticed to Cyril, had ridden Attivo impeccably in his two races. Now he would be unable to claim the 3 lb allowance to which he was entitled because of the value of the Triumph. Even so, would it be fair to deprive him of this great opportunity?

I rang Cyril and arranged to meet him on the course before the BBC TV transmission began on the Tuesday, two days before our race. It would be his decision. I'd barely started to ask him what he thought of putting up Terry when he chipped in with, 'No, no you can't do that,' and the conversation changed to Attivo's travelling arrangements.

Cyril retired to live in Majorca at the end of the year, handing over to his son, Philip, and it wasn't until fifteen years later that I asked him what had prompted his swift negative reaction to my proposal regarding Terry Biddlecombe. He recalled instantly:

I remember thinking, 'Wherever is he going to sit?' Terry was a big fellow and there simply wasn't room on top. I'm not saying that he wouldn't have ridden him. Terry Biddlecombe was a very good horseman, but Percy needed knowing. He was very easy to unbalance, even at home, and he was used to doing things his way. If he'd been corrected at a hurdle he might easily have said, 'Right, if you know all about it, go and do it yourself.'

On the rota basis the Wednesday of Triumph eve wasn't a writing day for me, so I phoned selections, including Attivo (nap), early and left the course hurriedly so as to get down to learning the next day's colours. Back at the hotel there was a terse message: 'Up to seven hundred words requested soonest Attivo's chances.' So I phoned a piece recalling the favourite's unpromising beginnings, and, pursuing the dream theme, ended:

Four nights ago Attivo and Robert Hughes galloped gaily up the final Cheltenham hill on which so many dreams have foundered, followed remotely by a pack of vain pursuers. Then I woke up. More recently he has fallen, faded out of contention, or (apologies to Robert) taken the wrong course. Last night fog caused the abandonment of the race. As a result I was called into the office of the chairman of Beaverbrook Newspapers. 'Look Peter,' smiled Sir Max Aitken benevolently, 'I am sure Attivo would have won. So I want you to accept this cheque for the £9,030.50 first prize by way of consolation.' Then I knew I was ruddy well dreaming!

At early morning exercise on race day Percy's lad, Derek Wilmot, was more colourfully tattooed than ever after a playful doing-over on the overnight trip from Epsom; while his 'pet' was so exuberant I feared a self-inflicted injury. Later in the day I told Frenchie Nicholson that, whatever the outcome of the Triumph, we'd be wanting one of his boys who could claim 7 lb for the Chester Cup. He had, he said, the ideal young man.

Now, as the field for the Daily Express Triumph went to post I was no longer thinking of winning – just praying that Attivo and Hughes would return unscathed. Clive's voice came over the intercom, 'Good luck, Pedro.' Julian Wilson gave me the thumbs-up sign across the commentary box. And they were off!

The young rider who was out there now, competing against the most seasoned and best jump jockeys riding in England and Ireland, pursuing the richest four years old hurdling prize in either country, had received one uncomplicated instruction from Cyril: 'Ride your own race as you find him but, whatever you do, NEVER take your finger out of the neck strap.' Percy had a launch mechanism to match anything at Cape Canaveral. They set off in front, without overdoing the pace, and flew the first three of the nine flights before I remember commenting, 'A mistake there at the fourth by Attivo.' Others were crowding him soon after halfway, and I thought he wasn't going that well – though John Hislop, who had been watching him carefully, assured me afterwards that the clever little monkey had just been giving himself a 'breather'.

Running down to the second last, the redoubtable Tommy Carberry was almost upsides on the impressive Leopardstown winner, Gleaming Silver, and going ominously well. Then, all of a sudden, as the field swept round the home turn, Attivo simply detached himself from the remainder, as if roused by the recollection of his previous visit here. Two lengths clear, four, six, eight. One leap between himself and triumph. The crowds were already roaring for him. Now he would really show them what he could do. The excitement communicated through Attivo's muscles to young Robert momentarily overcame him. All instructions were forgotten. Out came his finger. Into the hurdle went the odds-on favourite. Into it and through it – coming to a virtual standstill in the process. Robert soared skywards. My heart plummeted. More by luck than judgement Robert came down where Attivo was. Meanwhile 'Big Ron' Barry and burly Banlieu, achieving a contrastingly fluent leap, were almost on terms.

But not for long. Summoning further well-camouflaged reserves, the young duo sprinted up that uncompromising hill to win by an officially judged four lengths, with the Yellow Pages winner, Supreme Halo, a further three lengths back. Below the commentary box on the open roof, which provided such a marvellous vantage point in the pre-private box era, the crowds looked up and waved and cheered.

I ran down and out into the car park, through which the horses were led back at that time, and met up with my heroes. Robert said he was worried when he made the mistake at the fourth because he'd never known him do such a thing, but otherwise he was just looking for company and fooling around. Derek made to pass me the leading rein. I couldn't think of anything more inappropriate. The lad grooms him, sponges his eyes, wipes his nose, feeds him, rides him . . . he is the one to lead 'his' horse into the winner's circle, as he did, to tumultuous applause, while I walked in behind him. Vi Aitken presented me with the fine Jean Walwyn-sculpted bronze challenge trophy – uninsured during my year of tenancy – and I did a quick radio interview with John Dunn before returning to the commentary point. It was sad to have to call the next 'good thing' on the floor when odds-on Pendil was brought down three out in the Gold Cup. But the emotional level was sustained by Bobby Beasley staging a fairy-tale comeback, riding for my long-time friend Pat Taaffe on Captain Christy.

It was a slight anti-climax when I pulled up at a coin box in Northleach to phone copy and discovered I had lost my voice. For two days everyone was spared talk of Attivo – but I have made up for it since. In a few weeks' time Frenchie Nicholson's wife Di ferried one of the stable's young riders, Roger Wernham, to Epsom to meet his prospective Ladbroke Chester Cup partner. They got on fine, which was more than I did when trying to get on the combination, ante-post, for the 8 May prize.

The bookmakers, like many of my friends no doubt, had heard enough of Attivo by now. For a horse who had carried 7 stone 9 lb when winning a modest Roll-Up, the allocation of 7 stone 12 lb in the richest prize (£6428) for the historic Cup scarcely gave him the appearance of a handicap good thing. No wonder Joe Mercer exclaimed, 'This'll take some beating in the "Cup",' on dismounting from Kambalda, who had just won a two-miles Nottingham handicap with his head in his chest under 9 stone 1 lb and incurred no penalty for Chester, where he had 7 stone 13 lb, in the process. That was five weeks before the big one, by which time several others among the large entry had already won their prep races. Yet Percy continued to inspire extravagant respect among the leviathans of shop and ring. The nearest I got to relieving one of them, Heathorns of 93 Newman Street, London W1, of two grand was a month before the contest, when their intrepid ante-post manager wrote a voucher (timed 5.56 p.m., dated 8 April 1974) '£2000–£160 Attivo to win Chester Cup'. And just below: 'Less than twelve runners no bet.'

There were twenty-one acceptors at the final forfeit on 25 April, but only seven runners on the day when the pride of Downs House forfeited his advantage to Kambalda half a mile from home on the Roodee, and looked like being 'taken' by Lester Piggott-partnered Cumbernauld as well. That was when he put to the test the theory that the winter game had strengthened him both physically and morally. The commentary point on the course with the longest history of any circuit in England is well before the line. As Attivo stretched his head and fought back, he and Kambalda, David and Goliath, flashed past the line together. As I called, 'It's a photo', I just didn't know whether he'd got up or not. John Hanmer nodded across the box encouragingly and I switched off sound for an instant to say, 'Evens Attivo'. John said, 'Even pony' and I indicated he was 'on'. My readers in the south missed out because there was an 'industrial dispute', but Manchester published and any northern follower was on a 6/1 winning nap, by a short head.

Roger Wernham's claim was down to 5 lb by the time the pair set off for Newcastle at the end of June in a bid to emulate Elizabetta, the last to complete the Chester Cup–Northumberland Plate double sixty-four years earlier. As I was committed to Irish Sweeps Derby commentary, Pat went north in case the little lad should inspire acceptance of a further sponsor's prize.

Irish TV had thoughtfully installed at the commentary point on the grandstand rooftop a small black and white monitor on which I might follow ITV's relay. The picture wasn't too clear, but I thought he had just about won when the set packed up. The London studio confirmed down the line that Attivo was first past the post but there had been an objection. Then Michael O'Hehir leaned across and inquired quietly, 'Did you hear that announcement?' It was the Garda requesting the public to clear the stands as quickly and in as orderly a fashion as possible, because a bomb might have been planted. But there was no question of either of us quitting the site, since Michael was describing the scene to Irish viewers and the link with England was continuing. 'Nice thing,' I said. 'I may go without ever knowing whether he's won the Northumberland Plate.'

The bomb was a hoax. Attivo had won. The objection concerned second and third, whose placings were transposed. Both horse and handler, Cyril Mitchell, took a well-deserved break – the former for six months, the latter for good.

Attivo never took kindly to rest and he didn't do his new handler any favours when undergoing a series of setbacks before returning to action in the Fighting Fifth Hurdle at Newcastle with a below-par effort behind the formidable Comedy Of Errors. Once again I had to view his race on television, as it clashed with BBC coverage of the Mackeson at Cheltenham. Two and a half lengths' defeat by the dual champion was no disgrace in itself, but I was disturbed by his apparent lack of enthusiasm, which prompted Comedy's trainer, Fred Rimell, to tell young Philip Mitchell, with uncharacteristic asperity, 'You've lost him, boy.'

Fred didn't miss much. A month later they met in the Cheltenham Trial and, once again, the old fire was missing. Comedy Of Errors (after whom I suggested the ill-sited new racecourse restaurant should be named) beat him by twenty-one lengths and Robert Hughes suggested a change of pilot, saying, 'Percy doesn't seem to want to go for me any more.' So stylish Johnnie Haine replaced him in the SGB Hurdle at Ascot, where the little horse was very edgy. He set off at an unsustainable gallop and faded quickly, to finish more than a hurdle behind one of his Triumph victims, Supreme Halo.

There were those who reckoned that Attivo could do with a change of scenery, but such a course was unthinkable at this stage of his trainer's career. After my colleagues had generously nominated the ex-selling plater's lucky proprietor the Horserace Writers' and Reporters' Association Owner of the Year (prompting the dry aside from the *Sun*'s Claude Duval, 'That shows what a little wine and cheese can do!'), John Hislop, breeder of Brigadier Gerard, cabled:

> An honour well deserved, it's clear
> That you are owner of the year.
> This glory shone on the *Express*
> Deserves a bonus – nothing less.

To which he received the reply:

> An accolade from such a source
> Would turn the head of any horse
> (For of course, I realize
> It was Attivo won the prize)
> He hopes we'll plan his whole career
> Just like you did the Brigadier
> Tackling any competition
> As long as he's in top condition.
> (But keeping a little in reserve
> To benefit the girls he'll serve!)

Unhappily, he was never to serve those girls after all. Exhaustive post-Ascot tests resulted in the veterinary diagnosis that, during effort, a testicle was becoming withdrawn – causing him discomfort – so that he would have to be gelded. No sooner had he recovered from an operation that is taken in its stride nowadays than a fit of exuberance landed him with self-inflicted disability.

Restored by painstaking treatment, he'd been out of action for a year before returning to Ascot on 13 December, when Robert Hughes's mission was to persuade him to settle. After granting limited concession to his partner's demands, Attivo ran on very encouragingly – and again at Windsor on New Year's Day. As a result a polite inquiry apropos the Schweppes was sufficient to inspire a *Sporting Life* report that 'Attivo, subject of a massive ante-post gamble, is a top-priced 10/1 with Corals, Ladbrokes and Mecca.'

In the interim he was to run in the Oteley Hurdle at Sandown on 7 February, before which Richard Baerlein wrote in the *Guardian*, 'Attivo has the worst of the weights with all other runners, but if he gives the slightest suggestion that he is back to his form of two years

ago, he will start hot favourite for the Schweppes.' I was in Tobago
when I received a telegram on 1 February: 'PERCY OKAY PLEASE RING
TONIGHT WAIT PROBLEM PHILIP'. The 'wait' problem was that the
weights looked like being raised in the Schweppes. Philip knew that if
they went above 11 stone I would want to claim. I suggested booking
Pat Taylor's 7 lb claimer, Tony Carroll.

Percy seemed to be as well known in the betting shop in Scarborough,
Tobago, as he was in Chelsea. The proprietor kindly arranged for me
to receive the 'live' Exchange Telegraph commentary by phone, via
Trinidad, in his office. So I listened to Percy's progress while watching
a ruby topaz hummingbird collecting nectar just outside the window.
In the background brown boobys were diving into the shimmering
harbour for their daily fish.

Another 'bird', Sea Pigeon, who was to feature in a series of
memorable Champion Hurdle encounters with Monksfield, won the
Oteley Hurdle with what sounded like impressive ease. My Schweppes
hope had faded out of contention, and Philip's cable read: 'PERCY OKAY
FINISHED SIXTH SLOW RUN RACE BEATEN FOR FOOT HAVE BOOKED
CARROLL PHILIP.' The 'Percy OK' preface was a legacy from an
understanding with Philip's father that whenever he rang about Be
Friendly, or whatever, he began by saying: 'The horse is OK' (provided
he was) to limit the suspense between polite introduction and the
anticipation of disaster.

Philip's capacity for positive thinking was not readily suspended. He
was buoyantly confident that the Sandown race had been just what he
needed, was delighted with Tony Carroll's handling of him during their
first association at exercise on 12 February, and reckoned that every
drop of rain that fell (several programmes had been lost through
waterlogging) increased Percy's already outstanding prospects. Richard
Baerlein's post-Oteley view was: 'Bookmakers are still keeping Attivo
among the favourites because he is one of their heaviest losers, but even
allowing for the hold-up in his work it now looks as if his comeback is
unlikely this season.'

I was back in microphone harness for the eleventh running of the
Schweppes on 14 February when, on the assumption that restraint
disappointed him, Attivo was allowed to take up his favoured
prominent position from the outset. But, once again, he went an
unsustainable gallop and faded in the straight behind runaway winner
Irish Fashion. Then, returning to the course a month later, conceding
nearly 2 stone to an admittedly unlucky runner-up, Space Project, he
fought his way back into the winner's circle for the first time in twenty
months. But the *Sporting Life*'s Len Thomas reflected the general
opinion when, after loyally pronouncing that, 'It was great to see Peter

O'Sullevan's Attivo back in the winner's enclosure again after the Eastleigh Handicap Hurdle at Newbury yesterday,' and after awarding 'full marks to trainer Philip Mitchell for coaxing the horse back to winning form,' he wrote, 'To me Attivo is but a shadow of his former self.'

A damp squib would have sparkled with more fire than our hero on his next sortie on the level in the four-horse Great Metropolitan at Epsom on 20 April. With apprentice Wally Wharton claiming 7 lb, the 3/1 second favourite (the shame of it) appeared to keep his adjacent stable in his sights as he toured the Downs in the lead for twelve of the eighteen furlongs, at which point he forfeited further interest and ambled home twenty-eight lengths behind the winner.

An appointment with 'Doctor' Syd Mercer was arranged forthwith. When they were faced with a difficult problem, Syd was the man to whom such as Dick Hern, Barry Hills and Ryan Price turned for diagnosis and treatment. Now eighty-six and with a recently broken leg, the ex-trainer, who had learned his equine physiology when handling thousands of horses in the remounts during World War I, was less than fully mobile. So Bob McCreery organized the collection of the Warwick-based guru while we delivered the patient to Bob's Moreton Paddox Stud. Syd, to whom the fine stayer Trelawny owed his life after breaking a cannon bone in the 1960 Goodwood Cup, and who treated Rheingold for five weeks before his Arc de Triomphe victory in 1973, rolled back Percy's eyelid and shook his head solemnly.

'He's sick,' pronounced Syd as his patient seemed to shrink further in the eyes of the anxious assembly. 'His liver and kidneys are wrong and he's anaemic.' Before the catalogue was extended, I interrupted to inquire, 'Does that mean his ration of draught Guinness [which he was mad about] must be reduced?'

'On the contrary, double it,' reacted the lively octogenarian.

This was the doctor for me. Did I remember, he asked, the horse he'd made me have a 'touch' on in the Hunt Cup? Very well, I told him, recalling the 1958 winner, Amos, whom Syd had transformed from a selling plater into a multi-handicap winner. It was the losers that memory disposed of. 'Well,' said Syd, 'he was like this before I gave him the powders which I will send to Philip Mitchell.' While Attivo was taking his homeopathic remedies, among which comfrey featured prominently, I was becoming increasingly exercised about treatment of an altogether different nature.

CHAPTER 26

Dope

I believe that man, as a *soi-disant* superior animal, has a responsibility towards lesser breeds in the scheme of life, and that to drug a horse, other than with the intention of effecting a permanent cure for an ailment, is an indefensible abuse. In George Lambton's classic mirror of the Turf, *Men and Horses I Have Known*, first published in 1924, the author tells of his earliest experience of a doped horse, Damsel II, a chestnut mare whom he bought for £450 after she had beaten a useful plater he trained, East Sheen, at the First October Meeting at Newmarket in 1896. 'She was pouring with sweat, looked very bad, and I thought I could probably improve her,' he wrote, continuing: 'That evening, when I went to my stables my head man remarked that the mare I had bought was a wild brute, and had been running around her box like a mad thing ever since she came home. I went to look at her and she certainly was a miserable object, with eyes starting out of her head and flanks heaving.' After a long rest Damsel II recovered somewhat physically, but she was no good for racing purposes and, sent to stud, produced a dead foal.

'There is no doubt,' wrote the great trainer, who won every English classic, 'that the Americans started the practice of doping, though it must not be supposed that they all doped their horses.' Among those who came over to train in Britain at the turn of the century there were men who deplored the use of dope after seeing its effects on horses in their own country, and whose more natural treatment of horses transformed the attitude of the locals during a period when opening doors and windows was unheard of.

Doping was not unlawful – anywhere. Its origin in the USA, George Lambton learnt, was due to the fact that,

They used to race eight or nine days in one particular place, and would then move on to some other district, where the same thing would take place. The consequence was that towards the end of these meetings most of the horses had run several times and would be played out . . . every dodge and device was used to keep the poor devils up to the mark, and some man hit on the marvellous properties of cocaine for the jaded horse.

By 1903 the Hon. George Lambton referred to the 'horrible practice of doping' having become a scandal, and wrote:

One constantly saw horses who were notorious rogues running and winning as though they were possessed of the devil, with eyes starting out of their heads and the sweat pouring off them. These horses being mostly platers, and running in low class races, did not attract a very great deal of attention, but three veterinary surgeons told me that the practice was increasing very much, that it would be the ruin of horse-breeding and ought to be stopped. Then there occurred a case when a horse, after winning a race, dashed madly into a stone wall and killed itself.

Lord Derby's trainer became seriously concerned. Accustomed to tales of larceny, which were, are and presumably always will be part of the oxygen of the sport, the stewards were sceptical – until the fifth son of the second Earl of Durham gave notice that he was going to dope five of the stable's unsuccessful residents who were distinguished only for their antipathy towards exertion. Four won; the fifth ran second. 'The effect was astonishing,' said George Lambton. The stewards did not delay. At the Jockey Club meeting of 15 October 1903 at Newmarket a resolution was passed to the effect that any person administering or causing to be administered drugs or stimulants for the purpose of affecting the speed of a horse should be warned off.

Doping continued for more than a quarter of a century in the USA through the use of digitalis, glycerol trinitrate, cola nut and heroin among other substances. At one period in the 1930s – before the State of Florida became the first to take preventive measures against the abuse – the drugs squad made over one hundred arrests for offences against the narcotic laws.

In England August 1930 featured the most dramatic confrontation since the introduction of the Jockey Club's anti-dope edict. Don Pat, the winner of Kempton's High Weight Handicap, was tested positive and at a subsequent inquiry the stewards told the young trainer, Charles Chapman, 'We have come to the conclusion that Don Pat was doped and he is disqualified for life. We consider you, as trainer, were directly responsible for the care of the horse. Your licence to train is revoked and you are warned off Newmarket Heath.' The words appeared to imply that he had been in breach of his duty to ensure the safety of the horse in his care. There was no inference of guilt in respect of doping. However the words in the *Racing Calendar* read: 'The stewards of the Jockey Club satisfied themselves that a drug had been administered to the horse for the purpose of the race in question. They disqualified the horse for this race and for all future races under their rules and warned Mr Chapman, the trainer of the horse, off Newmarket Heath.'

The *Calendar* statement was picked up by *The Times* under the heading ANOTHER TRAINER WARNED OFF. THE DOPING OF DON PAT. That day's noon and evening papers left little room for doubt in the public mind that the former amateur rider, for whom Gordon Richards had a 100 per cent record on the Sussex stable's horses, was a doper. The Duke of Richmond and Gordon, who was both a patron and supporter of Mr Chapman, wrote to the stewards on his behalf pointing out that he had been hitherto a young man of unblemished character, and asking them to make clear to the press that he had been warned off for negligence and not for actual doping. The stewards found this unnecessary.

Determined to clear his name, the disgraced trainer ignored contrary advice – since the stewards had acted entirely within their powers under the Rules – and decided to bring an action for libel against them for their publication in the *Racing Calendar*; against *The Times* for their alleged libellous statement; and against Messrs Weatherby's, printers and publishers of the *Calendar*. The trial, before Mr Justice Horridge, hypnotized the racing world. Best of the odds 3/1 Chapman, 1/5 stewards. According to one report, Chapman, the first witness on his own behalf, was a good-looking young man who gave evidence with great moderation and self-restraint. He accepted that the horse must have been doped, though how or by whom he had not the remotest idea. Although he considered he had taken every possible precaution, he accepted full responsibility for the horse's safety. As for the hearing before the stewards, he acknowledged that he had been treated with every courtesy and consideration, and that the inquiry had been fairly conducted. His only complaint was over the misleading words by which, he maintained, the actual decision had been wrongly conveyed to the public.

Norman Birkett, counsel for the defendants (Lords Ellesmere, Harewood and Rosebery), submitted that there was no case to answer. But the judge said that the words were capable, in law, of a defamatory meaning and he asked the jury to decide an important question of fact: did the words complained of mean that the plaintiff was a party to the doping of Don Pat, or did they mean, as the stewards maintained, that he was warned off because he had failed to prevent Don Pat being doped? The sixth Earl of Rosebery, Senior Steward from 1932 to 1948 and captain of Surrey from 1905 to 1907, may seldom have faced tougher bowling than he did from the plaintiff's counsel, Patrick Hastings.

'Do you realize,' began Hastings, 'that the decisions of the stewards of the Jockey Club may bear the gravest consequences?'

'Yes,' said Lord Rosebery.

'A trainer who is warned off will be ruined socially and professionally?'

Lord Rosebery agreed.

'In a case like this,' continued Hastings, 'where a trainer has had nothing to do with the doping of a horse, you convict him of carelessness?'

The defendant demurred: 'I think it is more than carelessness. I should call it a grave dereliction of duty.'

Hastings nodded and continued, 'Do you realize that, in the eyes of fair-minded persons, there must be all the difference in the world between a man who has doped a horse and a young trainer at the beginning of his career who is guilty of dereliction of duty?'

'Yes,' reacted Lord Rosebery.

'If the wording of the notice sent out by the stewards conveyed to ordinary people that Mr Chapman had been warned off the Turf for doping, a grave injustice would have been done him, would it not?'

Lord Rosebery paused before replying, 'It would be an injustice.'

Hastings bristled and inquired sharply, 'The answer is "yes", isn't it?'

Lord Rosebery answered in the affirmative, and from that moment, if not before, another odds-on chance was heading for defeat. It was an experience which Albert Edward Harry Meyer Archibald Primrose, 6th Earl of Rosebery, did not greatly relish and was not lightly to forget. The jury not only returned a verdict in favour of Mr Chapman, but awarded him the then enormous damages of £16,000 – £13,000 against the stewards and Messrs Weatherby, as publishers of the *Calendar*, and £3000 against *The Times*.

Barely had the court risen than there was an objection. An appeal was lodged on the basis that the wording in the *Calendar* was, in a strict sense, actually true, and that the stewards were completely protected by privilege. And, further, that the damages were too high. Briefly, the appeal judges upheld the objection, dismissing the case against the defendants, except *The Times*, against which a new trial (which never took place: the matter was settled out of court) was ordered.

The plaintiff had cleared his name, and ruined himself in the process. The case resulted in extra caution being exercised in future wording in the *Calendar*, as well as discontinuation, for a long period, of the practice whereby local stewards communicated their findings to the press. Nearly a quarter of a century later Sir Patrick Hastings, recalling the case, reflected: 'It left a strange feeling that there is a defect in our legal system when a completely innocent person may have to suffer from the public belief that he is guilty, and there exists no means of proving his innocence, except by bringing an action he cannot win.'

Almost another twenty-five years on I received a letter, written in a very shaky hand, at the end of which only the Christian name was faintly decipherable. The writer, who was virtually housebound by arthritis, explained that, as a fervent follower of racing, he had known me for more than a quarter of a century through the *Express* and TV, and hoped that I might be able to call in for a drink or a coffee on any day during Goodwood – as he and his wife lived within three miles of the course.

In an endeavour to keep pace with correspondence I responded by phone whenever practicable. 'Charles' answered when I rang. And later, as I walked into the garden of Shifnal Cottage, Lavant, he stood, a tall, bent figure in the doorway. 'Peter,' he said, 'how lovely to see you. I am Charles – Charles Chapman.'

It was the first of many fleeting visits to a man for whom the withdrawal of contact with horses had been like an amputation, yet in whom there was not the mildest trace of bitterness. His mother had taught the Duke of Richmond's children to ride in Hyde Park, and through the family's support – sustained during his 'trial' and throughout the years that followed – he had fulfilled a childhood ambition to become involved in racing. After the Don Pat affair and the dispersal of the horses he kept on the yard for as long as he was able, hoping one day for the restoration of his licence, and stabling ex-colleagues' horses for the Goodwood Summer Meeting – among them those of Staff Ingham, whom he taught to swim at nearby Bognor. He employed a series of private investigators, who got as far as discovering that an Ashton-in-Makerfield chemist had supplied a prohibited substance to a 'lad' at a time when the Chapman stable had a runner at Haydock. But when the Chapman staff were laid off, the lad left racing and was not traced again. Charles invested his remaining funds in a lorry and drove a daily delivery run to London for local farmers. In 1934, four years after his sentence, by which time he was employing four men as a haulage contractor, the *Racing Calendar* carried an announcement that the warning-off notice on C. Chapman had been withdrawn. As he had in 1932, with more optimism than hope; now, with more hope than optimism, he reapplied for a licence. On each occasion he was supported by the Duke of Richmond, and on each occasion the application was declined.

He joined up at the outbreak of war and was posted to the frozen wastes of East Anglia, where, through his unsoldierly bearing, he became the *bête noire* of a particularly officious commanding officer. During the phoney war period his superior became very excited by the prospect of imminent review by the General and instructed Chapman: 'For God's sake smarten yourself up and try not to let the side down.'

The camaraderie of the Turf would sustain him for much of his life. 'I'll never forget the expression on the CO's face,' he recalled delightedly nearly forty years later, 'when General Lumsden [a former rival amateur under NH Rules] strode across this bleak hall with outstretched hand to inquire, "Good God, Charles, what the hell are you doing here?" '

At the end of the war, in 1945, Charles Chapman's application for renewal of a licence to train was supported not only by the Duke of Richmond but by his compassionate neighbour the Duke of Norfolk as well. But, while Lord Rosebery was a good friend, he was an implacable foe. It was reported back to the applicant that he had reacted by saying, in so many words, that man took us on – he shall not come back. As Jockey Club records show, the trainer of Don Pat had one more go in 1952. 'Although I did so with the encouragement of my former sponsors,' he recalled, 'I made an independent application, as I felt that a further refusal would be an embarrassment to them.'

Charles Chapman became a market gardener until his back gave out and arthritis set in. Brigadier Roscoe Harvey, the most enlightened stipendiary steward of his era, and Sir Gordon Richards were two of his regular visitors over the years during Goodwood week. When I spoke to Gordon about him at the last jockeys' dinner the great champion attended in 1985, before his death the following year, he said, 'Charles Chapman is a lovely man. He would be no more capable of doping a horse than you or I would be of swimming the Channel.'

In 1961, five years after Charles Chapman's final application, the Duke of Norfolk's exhaustive and carefully reasoned report on doping suggested that the old rules placing absolute responsibility on trainers were 'very harsh', and that a trainer should not be warned off if 'he used all due diligence to prevent the occurrence and. . . the substance was administered without his consent, connivance or default.' Charles Chapman was born too early but, as he pointed out with remarkable detachment, the situation at the turn of the century when the stewards framed their anti-dope laws demanded draconian methods. Even so, the Chapman story may not be seen as the most creditable in the history of the Jockey Club.

There was an uneasy feeling in the early seventies that the practice of doping, imported to Europe from the USA at the turn of the century and subsequently outlawed, had now leaked back in a more sophisticated form. It had leaked back to France – not, for heaven's sake, because the *indigènes* were more venal than the *Britanniques*, but because their set-up was more prosperous, and consequently more attractive to the relatively *nouveau* American proprietors.

The prosperity of horse-racing in any country is dependent, in the simplest terms, on the return to the sport from betting. In this respect England fares badly – approximately seven times worse than France where ownership is, consequently, a 70 per cent less suicidal venture. Whether it is more fun is a matter of taste. Personally I don't think so.

In 1974 François Mathet had just returned from a February stud visit in Brazil and I was lunching with him at Gouvieux. It is commonplace for the less successful to attribute dubious methods to the more advantaged, but François could scarcely be rated unsuccessful, having finished top of his profession for the seventeenth time in 1973, winning over £800,000 in prize money – a total which exceeded the top six trainers in England by more than £100,000. He was, nevertheless, preoccupied to the point of obsession with the biochemist's seemingly irremediable advantage over the analyst.

Since we were talking off the record, he named, and fulminated over, a big race winner during the previous season (trained by a non-French national) which, he strenuously maintained, could not conceivably have been prepared to win other than by artificial means. There would, he insisted, come a time when the breed simply had to be protected. '*C'est indiscutable*' (a favourite word *chez* Mathet), he proclaimed. 'When a horse needs treatment he is unwell and therefore not racing. When he is in good health and active he needs natural nourishment and no treatment.'

On the one hand I was receiving persistent, highly disturbing information that active horses were receiving irregular treatment. On the other I had this nagging and optimistic thought that professional jealousy, a regrettably ever-present ingredient in an intensely competitive activity, was distorting reality. Still, the mention of treatment in Gallic racing circles bestowed the silence evoked by a cat passing an aviary. More than two years on, the respected French racing journalist Michel Morice wrote a piece which appeared in *Le Figaro* on 21 July 1976, under the caption ' "TRAITEMENT" EN FRANCE = "DOPING" EN ANGLETERRE', in which he questioned the validity of the French anti-doping code in the light of contemporary training methods practised at Chantilly.

On Saturday 24 July 1976 there was an unusual development following the King George VI and Queen Elizabeth Stakes, won by Daniel Wildenstein's dual Oaks scorer Pawneese, so I left Ascot for Paris, knowing that if nothing of great account occurred at Maisons-Laffitte I already had a 'lead' for Monday's paper. The Aga Khan's nice colt Blushing Groom, very well bought by Keith Freeman at 16,500 guineas on the owner's behalf as a December Sales foal, won the big two-year-old prize, the Prix Robert Papin, after which Karim said, 'I know the "Boss" [as he referred to François Mathet] wants to have a word with you.'

Some while previously, when he was not getting on well with Mathet, Karim had asked me to lunch and sought suggestions for a replacement. I could well imagine his trainer not being easy, but strongly advised resolving differences. It was one time, I hope the subsequently brilliantly successful owner–breeder agrees, when I gave good advice.

Now the 'Boss' looked far more preoccupied than elated by victory. He led me into a corner of the weighing-room and launched into a tirade about '*traitements*', declaring that the time had come to speak out. There had been a recent positive test on a French-trained winner in England and, although he did not allude to it, this as well as Michel Morice's article, appeared to have acted as a catalyst. It was courageous for a man in his position to go on record thus.

I drove to Orly airport to phone copy, offering a prayer that the Sports Editor might be having a rare Sunday off. If not, there was the dreaded prospect of such copy being resited on the back page. It would then be rewritten for the enlightenment of non-racing readership and all potential benefit forfeited in the process. The Sports Editor was, unfortunately, a committed worker, but exceptionally he acceded to my request. Copy appeared under the caption ' "DOPERS" OF CHANTILLY ARE SLAMMED BY MATHET' and all hell was let loose. It read:

Immediately after Pawneese had established herself undisputed Queen of Europe in the King George VI and Queen Elizabeth Diamond Stakes, the Ascot stewards took an unprecedented step following a major English prize. The chief official, Major-General Sir Randle Feilden declared: 'We've ordered the whole field to be "tested".'

And 24 hours later after winning the first of France's big two-year-old prizes – the £22,000 Prix Robert Papin with the Aga Khan's strikingly handsome Blushing Groom – François Mathet added fuel to racing's most emotive topic. 'Horses are being "doped" throughout Chantilly. I know what is used and how it is being done. When we have the opportunity of a full discussion away from the racecourse, I am prepared to tell you everything in the interests of the future of racing,' was his shattering comment. France's all-time record-breaking trainer affirmed: 'The practice of so-called "treatment" of horses in Chantilly is widespread. French racing law is unequivocal,' says Mathet, 'inhibiting as it does the use of any preparation to alter the natural function of a horse's organism. Yet,' he continues, 'the law is being flouted totally by a number of individuals every day. In so far as racing is concerned with improving the breed, this means that artificially prepared horses are being used for the purpose, and the public is being cheated. It is imperative that what is happening should be widely understood.' Meantime the French racing authorities are expected to receive samples of recent tests taken in England . . .

The phone started early on Monday morning and continued, with little interruption, until I had to leave for Goodwood the following day. Most disturbing of the communications was a long cable from Mathet, claiming both that he considered our conversation private and that his words had been distorted. Indeed they were, in the sense that I had toned them down in case they were actionable. What I did not know at the time of our discussion at Maisons was that he had already written to Michel Morice in response to his article and referred to the miscreants, as he saw them, in a published letter, as 'Bandits, assassins and gangsters who operate the law of the jungle.'

When phoning copy from Goodwood on Wednesday I led with three hundred words on the day's racing and followed:

Meantime the French Trainers' Association have convened an urgent meeting to discuss the implications of comment I understood François Mathet to have made to me at Maisons-Laffitte last Sunday, and which was the subject of an article the following day. In a subsequent statement they declared: 'It is not for us to say whether M. Mathet was accurately reported, but, as they are, the words constitute an unacceptable, calumnious and defamatory attack against the profession, and against the centre of Chantilly in particular.' Their reaction is not surprising since the number of individuals reputedly associated with artificial treatment of racehorses constitutes a probable minority. More surprising to me is a subsequent declaration of France's longtime record breaking trainer that he both considered the conversation to be a private one, and further that he considered his words distorted.

Maybe it is accounted for by my imperfect interpretation of the nuances of the French language. However, I note that in a letter to *Figaro*'s correspondent Michel Morice, who appears to be conducting a lone campaign to bring to notice certain irregularities, François refers to 'a certain number of individuals who violate the code every day,' suggests that 'it seems they are more strict in Montreal than in Paris' and concludes that ' "Treatment" equals doping in every country of the world.' It is disappointing that a highly responsible individual with the courage to speak out should be constrained to withdraw. For, in what I believe to be a very serious situation, it is rare to discover a responsible source prepared to be quoted. An internationally renowned professional with regular practical access to horses in French and English stables puts it to me: 'The practice of "treating" with techniques largely imported from America and involving blood transfusions, "dope", and the administration of agents which mask the dope, is a routine feature in some French yards. It gives them a big advantage, and if it spreads English horses will have no chance with the French.' What I would like to know from the largely highly reputable and dedicated horsemasters in the French Trainers' Association, among whom I count many personal friends, is how they feel about the instances of 'Treatment' and what action they favour?

Alec Head and Roland de Chambure, who represented the French breeders, rang me that morning at Lythe Hill Hotel, Haslemere, where I was staying for Goodwood, and I promised an airing of their views in Friday's paper. It was a promise I had to break. When I made a check call to the office, half an hour after putting over copy, the sub reported he'd had to take out the first six paragraphs. 'The Führer's decreed there is to be no reference to anything to do with dope in your stuff.' The next day was my last before holiday when I would meet my friends, or ex-friends, at Deauville. It had been a lucky meeting for the selections, which might help, so I tried again.

The 'leader' was off duty but his deputy, a contrastingly *sympathique* guy, Norman Dixon, regretted he'd been left instructions. Thankfully my colleagues John Oaksey (*Sunday Telegraph*), Brough Scott (*Sunday Times*) and Desmond Stoneham (*Irish Field*) – to name only three – were immensely supportive. Relations were seemingly unimpaired with my friends in France. François Mathet wrote ('*Mon cher ami*') that he regretted any misunderstanding, and reacted with enthusiasm to my report on 4 January 1977: 'A new chapter for 35,000 racehorses is imminent – hopefully. For, with only 355 doping days to Christmas, the top equine forensic experts of England, France and Ireland meet in London today in a bid to reach agreement on the emotive questions of "treatment" and analysis . . .'

I reported the outcome on 29 March:

Britain has secured a new charter for racehorses in at least 16 countries. This is the welcome sequel to an International conference on doping, at which delegates firmly resolved to protect the horse against malpractice. Blood transfusions, administration of anabolic steroids and forms of 'treatment' are now totally outlawed throughout several continents. England introduces new laws on 12 April, after which it will virtually be an offence to be found with a syringe, and horses may be officially examined before a race for which they have been declared . . .

The future may not have been quite as rosy as that, but the air was a lot clearer and less polluted.

CHAPTER 27

A State of Shock

Attivo, refreshed by six months' absence, restored by Syd Mercer's magic powders and reunited with Roger Wernham, returned to action at Sandown on 19 October 1976 in the one mile six furlongs Coombe Handicap. A ring-rusty 20/1 outsider with 9 stone aboard – gone were the days when handicappers padded his weight cloth with feathers – he attacked the home straight with much of the old familiar zest, failing by a photographed head to achieve third prize in a competitive ten-horse handicap.

Twelve days later the young hurdling star of 1974 returned to Esher for a very private work-out. The light of battle rekindled in his observant eye, flaunting his rediscovered power, he flew three hurdles in the back stretch and was restrained to keep company with two talented gallop companions – whom he evidently regarded as seriously defective in the speed department – only under vigorous protest. We had a modest enough target in view and I was already beginning to feel sorry for the bookmakers. When Robert Hughes hopped off him he reckoned that Percy was not just back to himself, but stronger and better than ever.

There had been a sharp overnight frost and it was a cold morning. As Derek Wilmot walked his horse round the tarmac stable precinct Percy exhaled little puffs of warm air and I watched and marvelled at the talent within that slight frame. Then, all of a sudden, a breath was cut off. There was a look of horror in his eye as Derek turned him; his near-hind lost its footing and he fell on the point of his hip. He leapt up, as animals will if they can, however badly injured, and stood in a state of shock – refusing my well-intentioned offer of a Polo mint as if this were a rather insensitive gesture in a time of crisis. He boarded the horsebox diffidently for Downs House, Epsom, where his attentive veterinary surgeon, Michael Simons, was already waiting to examine him.

He had broken his hip and suffered severe bruising. There was little

315

thought of him running again, but every chance of sufficient recovery to enable him to enjoy a quieter life. I didn't want him to be 'slung', feeling him so temperamentally unsuited to such rigid inactivity. He just had to be kept as quiet as possible and was, in fact, a pretty good patient – though, as his transporters had discovered when he was a yearling, he had such high tolerance of anaesthetic that a double dose was needed at Newmarket's Equine Research Station to knock him out. On his second visit, six months at grass was prescribed, followed by regular swimming. So he enrolled at Ron Hutchinson's Health Farm at Reigate. He drank so much draught Guinness *en route* to recovery that it became a question of which would give out first, his liver or my pocket. Happily both survived and, after a little over a year, he not only passed his medical but it was suggested that he went back in work before his natural exuberance cost him further injury.

Following more than fourteen months' absence he returned, a 20/1 forgotten horse, in Newbury's L'Oréal Handicap Hurdle to run a very respectable third, beaten only a short head for second prize. In July that year I asked Lester Piggott if he'd ride him at Lingfield. 'Why?' he reacted sharply. 'Has he "gone"?'

I hoped not, I said, asking what prompted the question.

'You only want me when they've "gone",' he grinned, recalling his previous appearance in my colours nine years and nine weeks earlier on Be Friendly, when the old horse was seemingly over the top.

While we were driving to Lingfield I impressed on him the need to be careful of Percy because of his hip fracture, and I remember Lester inquiring, 'What do you think I am, some sort of butcher or something?' He added, 'Don't worry, I'll look after him.'

Just over a furlong out in the two-miles Ferrendons Handicap, Attivo, who had to concede plenty of weight all round, was very much in contention without appearing to be giving his partner maximum assistance. At a critical phase Lester gave him one, in the correct stride, in the correct place. Until that day the outraged eight-year-old had mostly been ridden by claimers whose exercise of the whip may have escaped his notice. Now he reminded me of my greyhound Slim when he brushed against an electrified fence on the Berkshire Downs and I feared I'd never see him again. Percy's eyes popped, as if inquiring, 'What the hell was that?' He stretched his neck and the photograph showed him a head to the good.

'He's a bit of a monkey,' said Lester, giving him a pat in the unsaddling enclosure. 'He doesn't do a lot more than he wants to.' Far from leaving a little of his evening feed, as horses tend to do after a race, the 3 o'clock winner returned home in high spirits and licked out his manger with relish.

When Lester renewed the partnership over the same course a fortnight later he pronounced him a 'different horse', after they'd cruised round to lead from start to finish, conceding 10 lb to their three-lengths-distant nearest pursuer. If I'd listened to Lester, who advised, 'Let him run while he's well. I'll ride him again next week and he'll win,' instead of opting for a break, he'd have avoided another serious self-inflicted injury. Although sedated before being turned out for a summer holiday, he still had enough bounce to go spare in his paddock and give himself a nasty leg.

It was some performance on Philip's part to produce him, after another five months' absence, fit enough to defy 12 stone 5 lb at Fakenham and, under a stylish ride by subsequent Official Starter Brian Reilly, to beat off fourteen rivals to whom he was conceding up to near 3 stone in the Tom Caxton Home Brew Handicap Hurdle. It was two days before Christmas and the sporting holiday crowd gave him an enthusiastic reception.

All being well, Brian Reilly, who claimed 4 lb, would be riding him again at Newbury when he had another crack at the L'Oréal Hurdle. But was all well? Ever since the hip break there had been a faint irregularity in his gait. Throughout the foggy drive back to London on icy roads I could not dispel the impression that, as Derek led him from the unsaddling enclosure, it had been more pronounced than usual. The next day he was hopping lame and the poor lad was back under repair for twelve more long months.

Ultimately retuned by extensive roadwork and introduced to his first schooling fence, Percy, who had always favoured a challenge, made it abundantly clear that this was for him. Aimed at a medium-sized haystack, he'd have tried to jump it. Returning to Fakenham on 15 February 1980 for his first public demonstration of how to make the big ones look like doll's brooms, he all but bolted with his new partner, Chris Kinane, on the way to the start. Cautiously restrained on that account, he still achieved a creditable third. There followed a flamboyant round at Ascot, ridden by the incomparable John Francome, and a third over the same distinguished circuit in the valuable Pierce Duff Novices' Handicap Chase, in which he gave weight to the first two.

He was clever, like another former selling plater, Red Rum, and to such an extent a proven sorcerer when it came to converting dreams into reality that even a crack at Aintree was not entirely out of the question. Not, that is, until irrepressible spirits inspired him to cart Derek Wilmot on an unscheduled, headlong gallop which ended in 'final' breakdown.

After yet another period of confinement, Attivo's long-time faithful physician, Michael Simons, built him a special shoe so that Percy could hobble away his days in minimum discomfort. But hobbling is anathema to Attivo. Maybe green pastures represent Elysian fields to some; to him flies are poor company and heaven is attained by jumping there over a regulation fence. It was a tribute to all who lavished tender care upon his slender person that – in defiance of all medical prediction – he was able to return to the arena for which he seemed to pine for a last 'go', at Fontwell on 2 May 1983.

After a spell of rehabilitation at Richard and Meg Bower's Elms Stud, where Be Friendly enjoyed such outstanding care to the end of his days, Attivo moved to Mike and Angela Pelly's farm at Frant, near Tunbridge Wells, so that he might benefit from the company of another equine OAP, Stay Friendly. The pair became instant friends, and in 1989 at the age of twenty-four Be Friendly's brother was still enjoying an active and pampered life there.

But in 1981 Percy resented that, while his fellow resident went out riding, he didn't. However, the ebullient Celt, Mike Doyle, creator of the electric impulse machine, Magnetopulse, treated him so successfully that the 'leg', although an imperfect match with its neighbour, became a cool, dependable limb. Valerie Frost, who had answered several thousand letters about Be Friendly and Attivo during her years at the *Express*, started to ride Percy daily in lovely Eridge Park – on a long rein too. In time, after negotiating all available obstacles in the area, he appeared restless for further challenge. Unhesitatingly granted an MOT certificate, he moved to the south coast to enjoy the advantage of sea water training under Jeff Davies near Worthing.

From here, just along the road, he made that final sortie in a race which I anticipated with far more apprehension than the Daily Express Triumph Hurdle nine years earlier. In a wise bid to protect him from his own exuberance, Robert Earnshaw only succeeded in disappointing his partner and sensibly pulled him up when he tired before the end of the Fontwell Novices' Handicap Chase. Robert, who had won the previous year's Gold Cup on Silver Buck, said he'd like to ride him up with the pace from the outset next time.

The 4.30 at Fontwell on this bright May afternoon was Attivo's fifty-first race, of which twenty-one had been over hurdles and fences, and thirty on the Flat. He'd won ten races (five in each sphere) and been placed in thirteen more, earning £32,000 in first prize money. The only horse ever to have been nominated in the *Directory of the Turf* as 'Best Horse Ridden' by three jockeys (Robert Hughes, Chris Leonard and Roger Wernham), he had made more comebacks than Frank Sinatra. Now, although he had never fallen – except in Sandown's stables precinct when he broke his hip – there were signs that the thirteen-year-old's battle-scarred limbs could no longer be expected to sustain his ambitions. He could stay in training, since he preferred stable routine to an outdoor life, and he did until, out of the goodness of his heart, Ron Sheather took him on as a hack at Newmarket. When Chief Singer's handler decided on a sabbatical, Percy returned 'home' to Downs House, Epsom. More relaxed now, he is content to share his corn with pheasants in the paddock, looking out over the course which has generated more emotion than any other in the world of horse racing.

CHAPTER 28

Excessive Use

On 7 November 1979 I wrote an article the theme of which was to evoke a chilling reaction at Cheltenham four months later. For years now I had been concerned over the growing practice, both Flat and jumping, of habitual misuse of the whip in a manner which was invariably unnecessary, generally unproductive, and visually offensive. Cruelty is relative. In Britain – where 90 per cent of eggs on sale ('fresh from the farm') are the produce of battery hens, two million of which die annually in cages with less floor space than a sheet of typing paper and without ever having stretched their wings, perched, or seen the sun or a blade of grass; where inhumane factory farming has led, inevitably, to consumer poisoning; where Battersea Dogs Home alone admits 430 discarded pets every week of the year – the racehorse is probably the most pampered animal around. When fit and properly ridden it may not be unreasonable for him to receive a crack, or two, to induce maximum effort. When 'a crack or two' develops into what is ambivalently termed 'a good hiding' it becomes wholly unacceptable from every aspect. Callous behaviour brutalizes and is habit-forming. There was daily evidence that a gratuitous, often misdirected, striping, had become accepted as the norm, summer and winter. It was a situation which had to be questioned. How best to do so had been worrying me for years; until Sunday 30 September 1979 when an afternoon's racing in Stockholm suggested the answer.

None of the top visiting jockeys, who included four past, present and future champions of England, appeared in the least restricted in the exercise of their skills through adhering to firm local rules regarding minimal use of the whip. None of the 10,000 crowd, among whom teeny-blonde fans were clearly captivated by the young American, Steve Cauthen, saw any violence. None of the riders with whom I discussed the day at the cheery post-racing dinner felt that a result would have been altered granted freedom to employ more ruthless pressure.

Champion Willie Carson was entitled to feel less benevolent than usual towards the equine race in general, since his partner in the fifth event not only gave him an appalling ride but added injury to insult by putting his full weight on Willie's right big toe in the unsaddling enclosure. As the offending horse was wearing calkins (steel flanges which are screwed into the aluminium shoe to prevent slipping) the needle-like pressure rendered the normally exuberant Scot almost unconscious.

But when fully recovered that evening and reflecting on the day's action, Willie gave it as his opinion that some sort of whip limitation might not be out of order back home. Before endeavouring to write about it, I sounded further opinion in England; without doubt my concern was widely shared. Hopefully the subject would not be considered unacceptable. But prohibitions included a ban on reference to Be Friendly in my column since October 1978. So, by way of precaution, I awaited a day when the Sports Editor was absent before kicking off with a piece which was headlined 'YOU CAN'T BEAT 'EM' and which read:

Backed any "beaten" horses lately? I was afraid you'd say yes.

Well they haven't in Sweden – or Norway, come to that. Horses may not be "beaten" in either country – that's in the rules. These rules do not necessarily protect the punter. But they sure spare the horse. And happily, my postbag suggests that you regard the latter consideration to be significantly important.

The maximum total length of whip possible in Sweden is 50 centimetres, which includes a 30 centimetre shaft and two three-centrimetre-wide leather flaps.

CARRIED

There is no restriction on the length of whip carried in England (a 65 centimetre–75 centimetre fibreglass whip is "normal") and no restriction upon its use, except that "excessive use of the whip" is regarded as "improper riding".

Some horses may feel that rules 153 and 15 provide inadequate protection.

Not so the firm instruction of the Swedish Jockey Club who insist that the restricted whip may only be used to drive a horse "exceptionally" (if he has a chance of gaining a prominent place) and that if a new stroke is to be given the rider must have ridden him with his hands, holding the reins in both hands, before doing so.

Norwegian rules are even more protective. There a rider may not remove his hands from the reins other than to correct a horse who is hanging.

SPARINGLY

A personal view is that the whip should be employed sparingly as an instrument of encouragement rather than chastisement.

Televiewers and racegoers are becoming increasingly dissatisfied with its use. Or am I wrong?

Your views would be welcome.

Meanwhile, the opinion of England's new champion, Joe Mercer, who stresses that a jockey's actions invariably reflect the instructions of owners and trainers: "I certainly would not be against the introduction of a shorter, more harmless whip. It could be greatly to the benefit of two-year-olds."

And Ryan Price's characteristically forthright postscript: "In 25 years I never had a jumper return with a whip mark. Now I see two-year-olds with stripes that last for weeks. And I don't like it."

No objection was raised internally to the article – to be fair, I did not expect there to be one – which elicited a massive response.

'As of now,' I was writing four days later, 'the reaction has been 100 per cent in favour of the introduction of limitation in either the whip's size or use – or both. But against a background of general indignation the new champion, Joe Mercer, is singled out for "his sheer artistry and gentleness". A northern fan expresses the hope that, in view of the results he has achieved without using the whip, "other jockeys may follow his example". As our interest will now be focused on the jumping scene I draw attention to the reaction of that former fine jockey Johnnie Gilbert, now General Manager of the Apprentice School: "I always tell them [apprentices] that if they learn to wave a whip correctly they will get the same from a horse as they do when they try to hit him hard . . . the terrible thing one sees at Fontwell and jumping tracks in general are 10 stone men hitting horses down the stifle as they have never been taught where the whip should land".'

The avalanche of mail showed no sign of slackening. On 14 November I wrote: 'WANTED: A sponsor for a special race. Many readers, distressed by repeated evidence of apparent excessive whipping, propose a race "in which whips may not be carried".' Both racegoers and televiewers appealed for official action to limit use of the stick, particularly in respect of two-year-olds who, in Joe Mercer's view, would greatly benefit from the introduction of the Scandinavian-style short whip. While Tim Molony, five-times champion jump jockey, reported: 'As soon as I found I marked horses with a long whip I shortened it to 25 inches maximum – and never marked a horse after that.' Trainer Tim added: 'Every boy who rides for me is told to slap a horse down the shoulder. And, if he has to pick up his whip, to make sure he hits a horse in the right place – not down the stifle or ribs.'

I packaged a selection of the letters and delivered them to Portman Square. The Senior Steward of the Jockey Club, Captain Johnnie Macdonald-Buchanan, acknowledged receipt on 17 December, expressing sympathy with many readers' views and leaving no room for doubt that the issue would be carefully considered.

On 17 January 1980 I was reporting, under a caption WHIPS – A WARNING: 'The Jockey Club issued a directive yesterday banning "beaten" favourites. Nor will they tolerate any horse being beaten in future. Particularly good news for horses – and indirectly for punters. Improper use of the whip can only result in the development of "dodgy" or ungenuine horses, who are poor allies of form students. In their general instruction to all local stewards on the use of the whip yesterday, racing's disciplinary authority expressed extreme concern "with the apparent increase in the misuse of whips in races" and expressed a wish that stewards exercise more fully their powers in the matter. It was pointed out that veterinary evidence of a horse being marked was not required as an essential before a rider may be penalized. So, in future a jockey may be fined up to £275 or suspended for seven days, or both, if in the stewards' view he has used his whip excessively, and is consequently guilty of improper riding . . .

'Captain Macdonald-Buchanan has further directed that the stewards of meetings are to be particularly vigilant in cases where horses which have no chance of being placed in the first four are urged on under the whip unnecessarily. And further that, when dealing with apprentices and conditional jockeys, officialdom takes account of the trainer's responsibility – and acts against any trainer as they consider necessary.

'Hopefully, the next measure will be an official limitation of the length and weight of whips. As Michael Dickinson observed to me recently: "Apart from the important humanitarian aspect, this can only be to the advantage of owners (whose horses will last longer) and trainers, who will have less ungenuine horses to handle".'

There appeared to be a salutary reaction. On 20 January 1980 Richard Baerlein devoted his *Observer* column to the subject, leading with the question, 'Have you noticed on your TV screens recently a sudden change in the way National Hunt jockeys ride out their mounts in a finish? Seldom nowadays is the whip used as an instrument of chastisement.' For this regrettably short-lived respite he generously suggested, 'Horses and viewers have to thank Peter O'Sullevan. On 8 November last Peter began a campaign in which he was strongly supported by the champion Flat jockey, Joe Mercer, to try and get the use and the length of the whip limited by official action . . . the campaign grew rapidly with support coming in from all sides, particularly from trainers . . .'

Richard went on to quote my criticism of Tommy Carmody's harsh handling of Deep Gale in the Irish Sweeps Hurdle, after which I wrote: 'If the normally quiet and outstandingly effective Irish rider studies the video, he may agree that his use of the whip achieved little other than setting a poor example.' And later he reprinted a letter on the same subject addresssed to the *Sporting Life* by Alex Bird, who expressed himself rather more forcefully when referring to the rider's 'barbaric exhibition'. Alex ruffled an emerald feather or two in the process and, since no whip stricture had been issued in Ireland, where, it has to be said, the stick had become even more of a winter habit than in England, the prospect of conflict beyond the normal level of competition at the 1980 Cheltenham Festival was regrettably predictable.

During an interview with John Francome at the outset of the best three days' racing of the year the champion jockey, who made riding over obstacles an artform, expressed a doubt whether 'more than one horse in a hundred runs faster for the whip'. Evidence during the Festival suggested that John's opinion was not widely shared by his fellow riders. The meeting ended with Ireland's champion jockey Joe Byrne, who had been fined £50 at Haydock on 1 March for 'excessive use', being reported to the stewards of the Jockey Club – a sequel to veterinary examination of his Daily Express Triumph Hurdle partner Batista – as well as his compatriot Tommy Ryan, who had been charged £50 for his treatment of Mountrivers on the opening day, and who was sent on to Portman Square after his Sun Alliance Hurdle victory on Drumlargan. This featured what I mildly referred to as 'one of the least stylish and effective exhibitions it has been this viewer's displeasure to observe'.

Describing the incident in the following day's *Daily Telegraph* John Oaksey reported: 'It was hardly surprising that the stewards took a poor view of his [Tommy Ryan's] antics on Drumlargan. Coming to the last alongside Farmer with the race apparently at his mercy, Drumlargan hit it very hard and landed on the flat with balance and momentum gone. What he badly needed was pulling together; what he got was a shower of blows down the neck and along the flank, including at least one after he had passed the post . . .'

Monty Court digested what he saw as best he could and wrote in the *Sunday Mirror*: 'Racing can do without the artless brutality of Tommy Ryan . . . If I never see him in action on a racecourse again I shall deem it as a prayer that has been answered. In fact, I don't think racing would survive many performances by the likes of this twenty-eight-year-old Tipperary jockey whose whipping made me physically ill.'

As the two riders referred to London (and disqualified for three months) were both visitors, accusations of prejudice inevitably fuelled bar debate. But on the morning after the Drumlargan affair, on 13 March 1980, I reported that, 'I found Irish press room colleagues firmly sharing the hope that Irish stewards would take the lead from their English counterparts, and act to reduce employment of the whip, before the support of a great part of the racing public is forfeited.'

In his own defence Tommy Ryan related that he had recently been taken to task by Irish officialdom for being too easy on a horse. 'They told me I should have used the stick,' he said, adding: 'Anyway, with the money our lads had on this one, I'd have been lynched if we'd got beat.' Up on the course, in the early hours of the morning after, during an exchange of views with Drumlargan's trainer, Edward O'Grady, who was fully supportive of his jockey's riding, I inquired how he thought Fred Winter would have handled similar circumstances. 'There are not many Fred Winters around,' reacted Edward. That was one point on which we were agreed. 'How will there ever be,' I asked, 'if a leading trainer, whose jockey has just given an unappealing impersonation of a demented carpet-beater, claps him on the back and offers congratulations on a great job?'

It was then that the riders' dilemma was highlighted by what I considered the most chilling comment since misuse of the whip was first mooted, when one of the Tipperary trainer's compatriots interrupted the exchange to inform the sparse assembly: 'If my jockey doesn't pick up his stick two out, I want to know why.' Frank Byrne, former correspondent of *The Times*, took up this aspect of the problem in the immediate issue of *Country Life*, in which he wrote: 'We have seen some savage use of the whip this year . . . since there is a course of conduct to be seen in some riders, it must be right to bring in the owner and trainer on every occasion to explain to the stewards if this is the way they want their horses ridden.'

Valentine Lamb wrote in the *Irish Field*, 'It is somewhat odd that while both [Byrne and Ryan] ride in the same way in Ireland, they have not upset the Irish stewards.' In most areas of innovation on the Turf Ireland has moved in advance of England. Exceptionally, Gaelic officialdom followed English initiative when in January 1981 the Turf Club issued guidelines in relation to use of the whip which they prefaced with a statement: 'The stewards consider that over a period of time there has been a growing tendency for some riders to become dependent on the use of the whip as the only aid to obtaining maximum performance from horses. This tendency is deplored because it is unnecessary and in fact could be construed as cruelty. In this context the stewards urge riders concerned to give serious consideration to their application of the whip and to consider the possibility of using other aids, i.e. use of hands and heels, in the obtaining of maximum performance from their mounts. The stewards emphasize that trainers . . . have a responsibility to ensure that the whip is not used excessively, unnecessarily, or as the only aid.'

The comprehensive directive included an order that from 1 March 1981 whips would need to conform with a prescribed maximum length and width. As it had in England, the directive promised a wind of change. But attitudes are not transformed by proclamation. For as long as vigorous application of the whip was regarded as a macho and indispensable expression of determination then rules circumscribing its incontinent employ would invite no more respect than unrealistic speed limits. To this observer, whose personal level of expertise did not include ability to switch the whip hand in a single deft movement, there was precious little evidence of horses having benefited from the well-intentioned instruction. Now, in the era of the video recorder, just as every commentary error was embarrassingly perpetuated so, more significantly, was each blow with the stick repeated *ad nauseam*.

Five years after the start of the campaign, letters of protest over alleged misuse of the whip remained a regular feature of my office mail, with the jumping scene attracting most attention. Typical of the complaints I received after weekend commentating at Haydock on 5, 7 May 1984 was the reaction of a Great Sutton, Wirral schoolmaster, Gordon Linnell, who wrote: 'It has just been my misfortune to observe the appalling slogging match between Messrs Scudamore and Knight over the final quarter mile of the Tia Maria Hurdle at Haydock Park. To my mind, and particularly in the case of Scudamore, this has been the worst example of whip abuse since the infamous Cheltenham of a few years ago when T. J. Ryan and J. P. Byrne were suspended for a long period. In my view both riders in today's race deserve heavy punishment, especially Scudamore . . . I used to be a regular racegoer (from 1959 until 1982) but now I no longer go to race meetings. However, if the Norwegian restrictions on whipping were to be brought into effect here, I would be glad to go again.'

A fine, stylish horseman and a delight to watch as, with sensitive hands, he settles his partner and plots the shortest route, Peter Scudamore's compelling determination continued to make him a target for criticism even during his record-shattering 1988/89 season. In the latter year Bryan Marshall, champion in 1948 and one of the most outstanding and least whip-reliant jump jockeys it has been my privilege to see, gave it as his always carefully considered opinion that, granted 'Scu's' flair and unprecedented scoring rate, he 'still doesn't get down behind a horse enough and push with his bottom to help him. Instead he lets his enthusiasm run away with him and he brings his whip down from too high and uses it too fast.'

Bryan reckoned Jeff King, the professionals' professional, to have been the most faultless jump jockey of his time. Significantly Jeff – the winter game's equivalent of Joe Mercer on the level – expressed the view in 1989 that the majority of jump jockeys hit horses 'to compensate for their inability to push and shove'. And apropos the whip he rated some 'so desperate', exempting 'Scu' and Richard Dunwoody, that 'something just had to be done'.

Both Fred Winter and Stan Mellor, who monopolized the championship for eight of the ten years from 1953 to 1962, used the impulse of their own bodies to inspire their partners. Stan, whose method had an affinity with five-times title winner on the Flat, Willie Carson, and who entered the winner's circle 1034 times, used his whip less in one month than some of those who followed him fifteen years later would do in a single afternoon. 'Instead of hitting horses,' says Stan simply, 'jockeys should ride properly.'

A man who did both was Lester Piggott, the bravura of whose Derby finishes on Roberto (1972) and The Minstrel (1977) defied imitation. While a tiring jumper often requires help and support in the closing stages, a horse on the Flat may need motivation. Seven of the nine Piggott Derby winners won by a minimum of one and a half lengths, receiving the guidance of a genius and the equivalent pressure of a flick from a feather duster in the process. Roberto and The Minstrel, on the other hand, may have suspected their pilot of harbouring a more coercive aid to propulsion. It was acknowledged that when Lester struck, he hit a horse in the correct place, in the right rhythm, persuading his partner to lengthen stride. But how to account for the rapid-fire salvos, in double or treble time, just before the line? 'It was against all logic,' he agrees, 'but both those horses were very lazy. Roberto [who beat Rheingold a short head] didn't do much for me as it was. You don't really hurt them when they're galloping at that speed,' he adds, 'it all happens so quickly. Both of them ate up clean that night and, as you know, they both improved. Roberto went on to beat Brigadier Gerard at York and the chestnut horse won the Irish Derby and King George.' We were discussing the emotive topic after he had withstood the humiliation of prison, from which he appeared to have emerged with a broadened outlook on life and certainly with more dignity than some sections of the media.

Major Michael Pope, twenty-five years a successful trainer under both codes and for fifteen years President of the National Trainers' Federation, had castigated jump jockeys in particular on several occasions ('sickened by the cruel and unnecessary abuse applied to tired and beaten horses already doing their utmost and incapable of going any faster'), and in 1989 he called for a month of whipless racing to cover both jumping and the Flat. As a man who won on twenty of his fifty-six hurdles mounts, what did Lester think of the current riding standard over obstacles? 'I suppose,' he reflected reluctantly, 'three-quarters of them are not that good – they just have a bump around.'

Edward Hide expressed the view in his both entertaining and instructive autobiography *Nothing to Hide* that 'those who commentate on TV and report races for newspapers are responsible for encouraging jockeys to use the whip. When they say, as they frequently do, that a horse wins "under hands and heels" they give the unfortunate impression that if the jockey had hit his mount it would have run even faster or won by a greater margin. This is seldom the case. Many free-running horses will find virtually nothing under the whip; indeed quite often will do the opposite and "curl up". Racegoers often don't realize this and a jockey always has it at the back of his mind that if he is beaten and is not seen to be riding a strong finish and using his stick some people will blame him for not doing enough on the horse. Maybe,' he continued, 'if racing writers more frequently publicized the "stopping" effect the whip can have, jockeys would feel less compelled to use the stick to keep the connections happy.'

In 1958 a horse was severely lacerated by the spurs of an over-enthusiastic rider, prompting the National Hunt stewards to immediately prohibit further use of either sharp spurs or those fitted with rowels. An additional restriction was introduced in 1972 when spurs which were angled (upward or inward) were disallowed. Otherwise, except in races confined to conditional or apprentice jockeys, spurs are permitted (1989) and must be included in a rider's weight. But they are very rarely worn. Because spurs are no longer regarded either as a macho extension of a jockey's equipment or as an acceptable aid, they have been virtually outlawed. When routine application of the whip is more widely looked upon as an uncouth substitute for talent it will be employed with far less frequency.

I have never asked him, but I believe the perennial Irish champion amateur, Mr TM Walsh, may not wholly disagree. One of the best amateur riders in my time, or any other, Ted had a fine record aboard a useful hurdler, Daring Run, upon whom he tended to rain a farrago of blows down the shoulder in the latter stages of a race. Neither Daring Run nor his supporters appeared to reap any benefit from this unmerited onslaught and finally, resisting the impulse to interrupt commentary by yelling 'Put that —— stick down', I suggested in print, somewhat forcefully, that the rider's tactics were particularly superfluous on a willing horse.

A short while later, on Grand National day, 4 April 1981, I had just commentated a tenderly ridden Daring Run winning the Sun Templegate Hurdle under his regular partner and had hurried to the weighing-room for a last anxious view of the thirty-nine big race riders in colours when Ted Walsh, whom I had not seen since criticizing his conduct, strode across the weighing-room towards me. As the nearest I ever got to achieving official status in the saddle was being elected an honorary life member of the Jockeys Association of Great Britain in 1970, the then eight-times champion may have felt entitled to question my critical qualifications. What he said was: 'You were right, Pete. There's no need to be hard on that horse. It's a poor man who can't take advice and learn from his mistakes.'

Nothing could have put me in a better frame of mind to 'call' one of the great fairytale results to steeplechasing's spectacular, in which Bob Champion, who had fought such a courageous battle against cancer, triumphed on another ex-invalid, Aldaniti, at the expense of gallant fifty-four-year-old John Thorne and Spartan Missile. The winner's trainer, Josh Gifford, who had been so supportive throughout his jockey's long ordeal, took a clairvoyant view of the outcome. In my horse-by-horse guide on the day I quoted him affirming, 'In my opinion there are only three runners – Aldaniti, Spartan Missile and Royal Mail.' 1,2,3!

CHAPTER 29

Satellite Hostage

It sounded like a straightforward enough brief. The New York Racing Association was to combine with the International Racing Bureau and Ladbrokes to screen 'live' via satellite, direct to London, the fourth running of the 1½ miles $300,000 Turf Classic at Aqueduct, twelve miles from New York, on Saturday, 25 October 1980. Britain's first direct transmission of racing in America was to be beamed to an invited audience of one hundred and fifty – including European Turf administrators, owners, trainers, press and so on – at the Clive Hotel, north London, where the guests would see two introductory races during the first four courses of their dinner and the 'big one' while sustained by coffee, port and liqueurs.

I was to fly Concorde to Kennedy Airport (take-off 09.30; scheduled arrival 08.29) on the morning of transmission; take part in the pre-race 'build-up'; commentate the Turf Classic; interview the winning jockey; phone copy in the early hours New York time on Sunday (for Monday's paper), having stayed overnight; and then return. The Classic at Big A, race number eight, was due off at 5 p.m. local time, which was 10 p.m. in London where former BBC *Grandstand* boss Mike Murphy was in charge of production and Brough Scott was presenting. I would hear Mike in my 'deaf-aid' (in theory) but he could be over-ridden by the US producer, Lou Tyrrell.

Despite conditions which were later to place in jeopardy the entire satellite innovation, the remarkable Concorde sped to earth in a gale-force wind without a ruffled feather. The IRB's smoothly efficient managing director, Nick Clarke, was on the spot for an airport briefing and to handle a personal problem. I had been troubled by arthritis lately and the previous morning, before televising at Newbury, needed to pay an emergency call on my osteopath saviour Grania Stewart-Smith. My neck had somehow locked so that I could only look straight ahead, and the pain was difficult to ignore. Unrenowed for doom-laden forecasts, Miss Stewart-Smith insisted that flight, under such circumstances, was fraught with peril; a surgical collar must be worn for the duration of

330

the handicap and no weight lifted heavier than a toothpick. Would they have a straw on Concorde, I wondered, to facilitate access to Dom Pérignon? They did and, on arrival, the attentive steward handed over to Nick my briefcase and collar (I wasn't going to turn up at the track wearing that).

Our cab driver glanced nervously in the mirror with resigned dismay when invited to convey his fares through the tempest to Aqueduct. A moat appeared to separate the 204-acre area (80 of them allocated for the parking of sixteen thousand cars) where we were greeted in the presidential suite with the news that the international equine Olympics, which were scheduled to open the day's action at 11 a.m., had already been abandoned. No one at the mammoth plant which provided seating for 32,332 of its ninety thousand potential customers was voicing a doubt concerning racing – not yet, anyway. But it could not be said that the 10 a.m. production meeting was charged with an atmosphere of unbridled enthusiasm.

By post time (one o'clock) for the first race a record low attendance for a Classic – 10,129 in their soaking wet feet – were gathered around the eighty-four closed-circuit TV screens. The jocks were discussing the feasibility of operating in a cyclone. One of the uniformed guards patted the holster which circled his 220lb frame and announced to any interested parties, 'You couldn't make me go out in that on a horse for a million bucks.'

Yet at 1.15 p.m., in defiance of the elements and operating for a somewhat less substantial reward, the intrepid little men made it. And James P. Heffernan, President of the New York Racing Association, who was in London to address the Clive Hotel assembly, mopped his brow gratefully. His relief was short-lived. All horses are known to run fast passing trees. Here we had trees passing horses, and after the volatile Laffit Pincay (who on this track exactly twelve months earlier had become the first rider in thoroughbred history to ride purse earners of more than $7 million in a year) had been all but blown out of the saddle in race two, the wise boss man of the storm-lashed circuit, 'Dinny' Phipps, prudently called a halt.

Ordinarily the faithful would have been issued 'emergency admission tickets' and – their dreams of achieving a sequence of Daily Doubles, Exactas and Quinellas intact – released into the more hostile outside world to return on the day of their choice, like tomorrow. For Sunday racing had been introduced to Big A in 1976, the year in which a young phenomenon, Steve Cauthen, had his first Aqueduct ride and his winning partner, Illiterate, paid $61.20. But this was no ordinary *réunion*. The satellite saga apart, there were three French challengers on hand for the big one, including the redoubtable 1979 Arc de Triomphe heroine Three Troikas. Mr Phipps was gambling on the meteorological forecast that by 3 p.m. the wind velocity would be reduced to less than 30 m.p.h. By this time the Clive customers would be approaching the filet de sole bonne femme and Pinot Chardonnay from California. My neck was killing me. A friendly medic supplied additional painkillers and offered a 'shot' – without specifying bullet or syringe – in the event of further deterioration.

In contrast to most racecourse predictions the met. man's assurance was partially fulfilled and, with no slight misgiving, we were 'off'; the red light glowed on the camera in the subterranean studio and I was introducing fellow presenters Frank Wright, who doubled working for CBS with being a successful trainer, and a slick female interviewer, Charlsie Cantey. Ace track announcer Marshall Cassidy called the two events which coincided with the rack of lamb accompanied by Pinot noir (with any luck they'd be paralytic by the time it came to my turn) and the fresh pineapple and lemon sorbet.

The 'dirt' course was a sea of glistening slop which rendered all but the temporary leader instantly unidentifiable. As I took the elevator to the 110 foot-high top tier of the stand I was still mumbling 'Match the Hatch'. I just couldn't get into my head whether the wearer of saddle cloth number one in the Classic was Match the Hatch or Hatch the Match. Commentary can do without undigested detail. The heavy-weight 10+80 tripod-mounted ex-submarine binoculars which I normally used for TV were required at Newbury, so Peter Bromley kindly arranged for me to borrow the BBC radio pair and Nick Clarke had organized their outward journey and emplacement. There were only eight runners competing round a nine furlongs oval, so I should have been capable of saving everybody concerned a lot of trouble, but I hate trying to hold binoculars while spieling and, as it turned out, I couldn't have done so anyway. I remember muttering to myself, 'Just relax for a change. You've got a maximum audience of one hundred and fifty and well lubricated at that.' But there was still such a gale at roof-top level it was hard to be heard talking to yourself. The ornamental lake in the in-field looked like the intro to *Hawaii Five-O*. The monitor was on the blink.

Three Troikas, tail tucked tight between her legs, abject as a Cairo cab horse, was the last to be installed – and the first to pack it in. The local turf hero and market leader, John Henry, who cost his original owner under £500 and after being passed on, unwanted, on four occasions, had already won over £500,000, made the early play. Anifa, the unconsidered 44/1 outsider of the field, happy as a hippo in the mud, followed the favourite three lengths back, with Temperance Hill, bidding to beat Spectacular Bid's single season's earnings, close up.

Racing out of the back stretch Alfred Gibert, who had lately won the 2½ miles Prix Gladiateur on Anifa in heavy ground, eased her towards the leader. John Henry had no answer whatever. Three lengths she won, with Golden Act beating the long-time leader five lengths for second spot.

While successful owner Mahmoud Fustok (eldest of nine children of Palestine origin who became Saudi citizens) greeted his heroine, brother Moustapha and friends, who had flown to London to see the satellite transmission, cheered her in the Clive Hotel. The waiting lift whisked me to studio level whither the victorious jockey had been hustled for interview.

For a man who had just underwritten a year's housekeeping for two minutes forty-three seconds' work 'Freddo' appeared inappropriately distracted.

'Peter,' he said, breathlessly, 'I need your help.'

The continuity girl shrilled, 'You're on in thirty seconds – tell him to take his shirt off. The colours are green, same as the background.'

I told the surprised but compliant ex-champion jockey of France, 'She wants you stripped.'

While unbuttoning the damp Fustok silks he hissed, 'I am a hostage,' adding, 'please don't question me in English, I won't understand a word.' The brief exchange completed, the interviewee explained. 'My flight check-in is in thirty-five minutes; the valet's got all my *affaires*, including passport and tickets, and he won't hand them over until I pay him five per cent.'

As the victorious reinsman's 'cut' amounted to $18,000 the guy responsible for his tack and turnout was understandably disinclined to forego his entitlement. Rich men never carry money and none of the successful entourage appeared to have the wherewithal. 'I've been in promise land before,' complained the jockey's aide, who had some very dirty tack to clean and prepare for the morrow, 'and all I ever got was the promise.' It was near take-off time before a cheque was grudgingly accepted and the hostage released.

I led with the hostage incident when phoning copy from my hotel on Lexington at 6 a.m. the following day. Sleep was difficult because I had to sit up in the surgical collar, and when I discarded it and took a cab out to the track later that Sunday morning I thought my head would fall off every time we went over a bump. Once in the presence of equine action, however, such minor inconvenience was forgotton. Repairs were still in progress at Big A after the previous day's devastation. Yet, amazingly, the going on the dirt circuit was officially designated 'fast'.

Assisted by such favourably disposed luminaries as Angel Penna, who had an impressive barnload of talent in his care; Sammy Renick, former top US contract rider who became a telecast pioneer; and that urbane chronicler of the American racing scene, Joe Hirsch, I backed some fast horses. Not unusually, however, their opponents proved faster still. Joe, my excellent host at dinner that evening, laughed politely at the hostage story. 'You'll have that on your own tomorrow,' he predicted.

We had little news in New York of the reaction to the satellite programme. The International Racing Bureau had arranged for the reports in Monday's English papers to be enlarged, poster-style, and displayed at Aqueduct. Like a 'bit' player waiting for the reviews, I went to bed fearing the worst. As well I might. In the early morning, New York time, Pat telephoned to enquire, 'Are you all right?' She had just received the Express in which, apparently, a bland account of the transmission, written from the London end of the operation, made no reference to my participation. And there was no article from me. I called the office to learn that the Sports Editor had both 'spiked' my copy and invited a further contribution for Tuesday's paper. Duly submitted, it also ended up on the reject prong – in the south, anyway. Either less selective or more supportive, Manchester printed in full.

As a tailpiece I had written:

The vice-president at the 35 million dollars Big A complex is former successful Canadian jockey David Stevenson. One of the highly paid New York stewards is skilled ex-jockey John Rotz. Another State steward is noted ex-reinsman Sam Boulmetis. Prompting the thought, do we in England make sufficient use of the experience gained within racing among those no longer able to fulfil more strenuous participation?

Considering what a short time elapsed before a former professional rider was to be elected a member of the Jockey Club, and others were appointed to paid official duties such as starters, course inspectors and clerks of courses, it was surprising that the response of letter writers was wholly reactionary.

From a personal standpoint the Aqueduct excursion had fallen somewhat short of journalistic success; but, more relevantly, the overall reaction to the telecast was warmly enthusiastic. The *Life* led their Monday, 27 October 1980 edition with a comprehensive account of 'an historic occasion and a memorable breakthrough', generously acknowledging the contribution of all those involved, and claiming that everyone present in London was excited by the 'quality, efficiency and purpose of the production'. Most of the dailies, heavy and light, were similarly charitable – though, after chivalrous reference to the 'compelling' race-call, the *Daily Telegraph*'s Howard Wright did express a legitimate note of regret that my post-race interview with M. Gibert (who described the weather as the worst he'd ever known, let alone ridden in) had been 'conducted in quickfire French which baffled all but a few'.

The *Sun*'s Claude Duval wrote that, 'Not even 100 mph [the *Sun* doesn't mess around when it comes to figures] winds and a rain-lashed track could wreck the excitement and professionalism of the venture,' and predicted: 'It could take a photo-finish to decide which comes first in England. . . . Sunday racing or live coverage of races all over the world on TV in betting shops.' While, significantly, in view of the bookmakers' firm initiative over Satellite Information Services eight years later, Joe Ward Hill, chairman of BOLA (Betting Office Licensees' Association), suggested that satellite racing coverage 'could provide a big source of revenue'. Bill Hill's younger brother didn't specify for whom.

The new era of international racing which, among public broadcasting interests, Channel 4 was to embrace with greater fervour than the BBC, was imminent. Channel 4 Racing's commitment, which developed over the decade, reflected a healthy disinclination to share most programmers' uncritical acceptance of researchers' evidence: namely that horse racing takes low precedence among TV sportswatchers. This conclusion was partly accounted for by the surprising detail that, towards the end of 1989, none of the major survey bureaux had yet taken account of a single viewer in any one of more than ten thousand betting shops in England alone.

Still, irrespective of survey data, professional association with the world of the racing horse, in no matter how modest a capacity, remained a passport to friends in high, and low, places. Right now I was on my way to John F. Kennedy Airport and an unexpected rendezvous with friends in very high places. For British Airways Concorde captain Colin Morris, and most of the crew of that morning flight, turned out to be followers of the sport which had brought me to the Big Apple. A consequent invitation to the flight deck during take-off, landing and much of the swift-passing period in between was a memorable unearned bonus which increased personal indebtedness to the horse and effaced petty preoccupation with my journalistic upset.

The next time I saw the failed Turf Classic favourite, John Henry, he was a dollar millionaire twice over and had been named US Champion Grass Horse of 1980. For a six-year-old gelding who had once reacted to competition in claiming races with overwhelming indifference, this achievement underlined the fact that some horses are capable of writing more improbable scripts than most humans. In three days' time, on Sunday, 30 August 1981, he was scheduled to run 1¼ miles over Arlington Park turf against top US specialists as well as challengers from

England and France who had flown to Chicago's O'Hare Airport to compete in the first million-dollar thoroughbred horse race.

The event had attracted an assembly which included the senior handicappers from leading racing countries, who were to discuss the feasibility of compiling an international classification of merit. Their conference appeared likely to take place without a contribution from the French delegate when M. Maze-Sencier presented a visa-less passport at immigration. The principal airport of the second biggest city in the USA was clearly not the ideal point of entry for a European unequipped with obligatory documentation. While the dapper, courteous Gallic official in no wise resembled one of Italy's less creditable sons, who chose St Valentine's Day 1929 to reduce the population of the capital of Illinois, he would have been regarded with no deeper suspicion if decorated with a badge proclaiming: 'I love Al Capone.' As a fellow passenger I sought to interpret to Immigration, who had consigned him to a specific area for questioning, and I probably prolonged his restraint in the process. Throughout, the senior French handicapper exercised the two essential ingredients of his profession – patience and a sense of humour.

I was on leave from the *Express* at the time, so freed from any concern over copy; though the BBC did indicate that, as I was there, they might be prepared to take commentary. In the end they weren't. It was probably just as well since, before the photo was printed, I never heard of more than one among the forty thousand present who thought the winner might have won – and he was sitting on the horse.

During the build-up to the Arlington Million horsemen gathered at the track for breakfast and told tales as tall as the nearby Sears Roebuck Tower which, at 1454 feet, is the world's tallest building. Bookmakers, who only operate here in between holidays at the state's expense, took careful note that the renowned Charlie Whittingham, who so rarely leaves California, was on hand to supervise Kilijaro; that Maurice Zilber-trained Argument looked as good as when winning the Washington DC International; and that the appearance of the filly Madam Gay, responsible for a 13,000 miles round trip by her rider, Lester Piggott, was a credit to her Newmarket entourage. And yet with eight more solid contenders to reckon with, they offered no more than 7/5 against the combination of the oldest horse and the senior jock in the twelve-horse line-up – six-year-old John Henry and William Lee Shoemaker, the world's winningmost reinsman, who reached his half century that month.

At the 'off' Key to Content, in Paul Mellon's Rokeby Farm colours, set a fast gallop ahead of The Bart, Match the Hatch, Super Moment (who was bracketed at 11/10 in the betting with John Henry), P'tite Tête and Madam Gay; while, in the manner characterized by Scobie Breasley in Europe, Bill Shoemaker had John Henry lobbing, relaxed, just off the pace in eighth place. There wasn't much change until running out of the back stretch when Madam Gay moved up third with John H. improving into fifth. The Bart took over from Key to Content as they straightened up for home, and I remembered having called him a clear leader three furlongs out in Troy's 1979 Irish Sweeps Derby. Now there were no signs of weakening, whereas Key to Content could give no more and Madam Gay was struggling – courageously, but struggling none the less. If ever a trainer was entitled to anticipate the judge and reflect on a horse short of star status well prepared, and a mammoth prize landed, it was 40/1 outsider The Bart's soft-spoken ex-Irish handler John Sullivan.

.Then, in a deft movement which a blink would have obscured, Bill Shoemaker changed his sensitive hands. John H. got the message and it was a photo. It wasn't until breakfast next morning in the Arlington Hilton that I located the only man who thought there was a chance of the electronic eye adjudicating in favour of the old firm. As it did – by an officially designated 'nose'. In response to my inadequate congratulation the trim four-feet-eleven-inch Texan conceded, 'He ran real good for me.' Then, since I had made reference to his economical use of the whip, he momentarily studied his well-polished size two and a half shoes and articulated a thought which might usefully be inscribed over the entrance to many an apprentice academy. 'I reckon,' he said, 'more horses are whipped out of the money than into it.'

Acting on the best tip I'd received all week, I called in at the Chicago Art Institute (a marvellous collection of Impressionists here) before flying to New York. While racing at Belmont, which features John Skeaping's fine bronze of Secretariat in the centre of the paddock, I asked one of the officials, from whose eyrie I had been invited to view the action, 'Do you often have reason to speak to jockeys regarding use of the whip?' The question was prompted by what appeared to me to be its severe, unsparing employment even when all chance of success had passed. Talk about being divided by a common language: the question was simply not understood, and evoked the response, 'We don't have any trouble with these boys, they all hit pretty good!'

When I related the conversation to John Gosden, who trained with such notable success from a Los Angeles base between 1980 and 1988, averaging seventy-five winners a year, he was not in the least surprised. 'Even if they are finishing ninth of ten,' said John, 'the young riders will give them a good whack to impress the stewards.' It was the trainer's experience that the better the rider the less reliant he was on the stick. When Laffit Pincay first arrived from Panama he was, John considered, a savage whip rider. Yet on 4 July 1987, when he won the American Handicap at Hollywood Park by a short head on Gosden-trained Clever Song, breaking the track record in the process, he never touched the horse. By now the second winningmost jockey in world standings, Pincay commented after a hard-fought finish, 'He was doing everything he could, so why hit him?'

That fine jockey Chris McCarron, who rode a staggering 546 winners in 1974 during his last rookie season, was another who could be relied on to divine when force was superfluous. But for horses who misguidedly developed a reputation for responding to raw pressure ('He's a good stick horse') there seemed little protection – apart from hair. Take the 1986 Travers Stakes, for example. Entering the home stretch in the prestigious Saratoga prize, which is run over 1¼ miles in August, Wise Times, ridden by Jerry Bailey, was around four lengths off the lead. Sammy Renick, writing afterwards in *The Blood-Horse*, quoted the Texas-born jock, 'I yanked him [Wise Times] out for a clear run to the finish line. He is an excellent stick horse. I hit him four or five times on the left side. He responded. Then I switched to the right and hit him every place but the bottoms of his feet. We just got up to beat Broad Brush and Angel Cordero by a nose.' Wise Times may have considered hair to be inadequate protection.

CHAPTER 30

Still Accumulating Debt

I had a melancholy piece to write on 22 October 1981. It began:

Be Friendly has eaten his last polo mint, covered his last mare. The life of the brave champion sprinter of his era – so familiar to *Daily Express* readers – ended yesterday. It ended painlessly among those he knew and trusted after sudden and distressing illness . . . At the last count by the official Statistical Abstract the super-fertile chestnut had sired winners of 325 races valued at more than £550,000 worldwide. And already 30 of his daughters have themselves produced winners . . . The great heart was beating regularly yesterday but the flesh was becoming heart-breakingly weak. After several days of agonising deliberation – with 'himself' the sole consideration – Be Friendly's sympathetic vet Bob Bainbridge regretfully pronounced the only course of action. Thanks be for partners who care – or he might well have been in Japan. And sympathy for the 'lass' whom he plainly idolised, and vice versa, Maureen Caddick. She will be viewing the Be Friendly foals at The Elms Stud through misty eyes for a few days to come.

Following the death of Robert Elwes, who had originally 'stood' the old horse at Ennistown, Be Friendly moved to Frank Hillman's Old Fairyhouse Stud until its sale in the late seventies. It was then that he returned to England and the welcoming, outstandingly run Northamptonshire stud of Richard and Meg Bowers. He had developed a little lung trouble some while before repatriation. Now, at seventeen, it was worsening rapidly and no longer responding to drugs.

On the day the deed was done the horse whom Scobie Breasley described as 'the greatest sprinter I ever sat on' was led into his paddock by Maureen and his gentle executioner. While they made a fuss of him the deep, rasping cough disturbed a cock pheasant. He pricked his ears as the bird scuttled across his line of vision. And it was all over. It had been a harrowing but correct decision. When Bob Bainbridge carried out a post-mortem he found the lungs completely collapsed, and a heart which he described as 'twice as big as normal'. In the words of Timeform's imperishable *Racehorses Annual* Be Friendly had been 'a fine, handsome, consistent performer, a great battler, smashing sprinter and deservedly one of the most popular to have raced in this country for many years'. Among worldwide comments David Mollett referred in South Africa's *Rand Daily Mail* to the death of 'the punters' darling whose popularity in British racing in the sixties was on a par with footballer Bobby Charlton. . . .' Letters flowed into the office on an emotional tide which reflected the infinite variety among whom the horse strikes a responsive chord – from the kind-hearted to the coroneted. As Henrietta Tavistock, who gracefully fulfilled both categories, put it, 'There really is nothing quite like a horse, is there?'

Five weeks later I was still responding to mail when I received a note containing a photocopy of a 'Private and Confidential' memo which the Sports Editor had sent to the current Editor, Christopher Ward. The paper became much more readable during Christopher's brief authority (1981–3), but circulation continued to fall; while, to me, the atmosphere in the sports department retained all the charm of a police state. The sender of the memo explained that, in view of the discord between the Sports Editor and myself, it seemed proper that I should be aware of 'what he is doing now'.

If I had any grounds for developing a swollen head (and I hadn't), the contents of the missive, dated 2 December 1981, would have been the perfect antidote. 'May we please have words about Peter O'Sullevan,' it read. 'He is due to retire in approximately 15 months and I believe he should do so. I think the days are gone when Fleet Street would fall over itself to hire him. I don't think we would lose a single copy if his name appeared in another paper. And, anyway, his contribution to us is fairly minimal. . . .'

Well, no one could complain that the writer left any scope for misinterpretation. It is difficult for a journalist to evaluate his own worth, and there was the disturbing thought that the departmental head's unflattering assessment might be well founded. It hadn't occurred to me until then to retire from racing journalism at sixty-five. Regular opportunity to comment on the sport becomes addictive and, irrespective of impediment, allegiance to a paper with which I had been associated for more than thirty years was inevitable. As I wasn't supposed to have seen the memo, I dismissed thought of it, as far as possible, and awaited developments.

If Victor (Lord) Matthews had been tainted with a trace of self-importance – the galloping companion of so many successful self-made businessmen – we could have easily got off on the wrong foot when he took over Express Newspapers in 1977. Knowing him as a fellow racegoer and blithely unaware that a few hours earlier he had become my boss, I wrote him after a particularly moderate dinner at the

Cambridgeshire Hotel to complain that the establishment which was part of his conglomerate was 'rapidly acquiring a well-earned reputation for serving the only authentic motorway cuisine obtainable outside a service area'. A less unaffected managing director and deputy chairman of Trafalgar House might have justifiably suggested that if I didn't like the hotel at Barr Hill I should stay elsewhere for Newmarket. Typically, Victor took it up with the manager, Bob Marconi, and wrote a charming letter of explanation and apology. The next time I visited there were enough flowers and varieties of fruit in my room to furnish a Carribean carnival float. And the kitchen had perked up, too.

As a newspaper proprietor, Victor Collin Matthews made swift impact on the industry by becoming the first to tackle restrictive practices in Fleet Street with firm resolution. His pragmatic approach to the business led him to hire and fire more editors than Dorothy Paget sacked trainers – though, like Aly Khan and his girlfriends, he invariably remained on good terms with them. Realistic appraisal of the market led him to create the *Daily Star* while admitting that he wouldn't have the paper in his house. Wary of 'experts' and convinced that 'the *Daily Express*'s greatest disaster was going tabloid', as it did on 24 January 1977, he strongly resisted pressure to change the format of the *Sunday Express*.

There is a certain *esprit de corps* among those who volunteer for the pain and pleasure of racehorse ownership, which the 1978 Royal Commission on gambling perceptively referred to as 'seldom a rational pursuit'. Allied in irrationality, we got on well and I found Victor good to work for. He made some bizarre judgements at times and in 1985, after the outfit had changed proprietorship again, Jocelyn Stevens, who had been sacked four years earlier, wrote a highly entertaining piece in the *UK Press Gazette* which was captioned: 'Where Victor went wrong'. Since the subject left office with a peerage and more than £8 million in petty cash he may have found the areas of failure endurable.

Lord Matthew's reaction to the question of my retirement had been (I learned later) unequivocal, and a new contract, whereby I was to continue to give three selections daily and write a weekly column on Friday for Saturday, was mutually agreed with his managing director, Mike J. Murphy. The extension of association did little to promote greater harmony between my Sports Editor and his contributor. In an Irish sort of way there was something about our relationship which reminded me of a winter morning at Windsor in the late forties. As the PA representative I had just rung the office to report, 'Racing abandoned', and I was surveying the watery scene with the irrepressible Clerk of the Course, John Knight. The adjacent river had exceeded its normal bounds to the extent that several fences were barely distinguishable above the waterline. The tide lapped the third and final step to the stewards' luncheon room while three pairs of mallard swam round the paddock. 'It's a shame,' pronounced John solemnly, 'because underneath all that the going is perfect.' Similarly I felt that no more than a fathom below the surface of disagreement between my mentor and me there was potential for understanding; but it was never adequately explored. Nor did writing once a week significantly reduce conflict over the content of my copy.

There were areas of concern to me which I could not expect to voice within the confined space of a tabloid racing column. For the past few years I had been in correspondence with some of the brave, unacknowledged ladies who seek to alleviate equine hardship. So in July 1983, when invited by the *Sporting Life* to fulfil the role of guest columnist one Friday, I sought permission from the *Express* and wrote:

Forgive me for raising the subject but did you ever find out where that horse you were following finished up?

Mrs Eileen Bezet, 69, might be able to help. She follows horses – and cattle too. She has followed them from Channel ports through the long misery of their fodder-free journey across Europe. She's had her camera smashed and been knocked down by ungallant transporters too.

Mrs B bravely opposes a very lucrative trade. One described by her spirited colleague Mrs Hilda Allen as 'a degrading and indefensible activity in which the faceless and powerful men who operate on an international scale are protected by the claptrap emanating from Whitehall'.

You might catch up with the horse who once carried your hopes in, for example, Egypt. But don't expect to recognise him.

Mrs Pamela Blenman-Bull, whose mother Dorothy Brooke founded the Brooke Hospital in Cairo in 1934, has discouraging evidence to prove the impossibility.

It takes the form of documentation and photographs including the sickening print of a skeleton barely supported by two broken legs – prompting Mrs B-B to lament with marvellously suppressed anger: 'It is not a question of cruelty but of an entirely different attitude.'

Once an animal has lost its value, in some Middle East areas (where British interests boast large contracts for delivery of bloodstock) he will be sold on without delay 'finding no mercy from the poor and ignorant.'

It is widely considered very unlucky to put a horse down, so unless the Brooke Hospital can rescue them, slow painful death in intense heat is the only release.

'I've seen and photographed horrendous sights in Egypt,' reports *Riding Magazine* production editor Mrs Judy Payne, adding: 'I love the archaeological treasures but could never face up to returning there and the prospect of seeing the horses again.'

She has high regard for the persistent endeavour of renowned horse traveller Miss Chris Larter who was collecting some of the fine Royal mews inmates last week to deliver them to their ceremonial duty location.

Chris has been 'revolted' by what she has seen while ferrying the top jumping horses worldwide. Including the spectacle in May of thousands of horses from both Russia and Uruguay waiting to be unladen at the Italian port of Bari where after a 24-day sea journey the Uruguay shipment was not unloaded for four days owing to a holiday. But as an official observed, they were only due to become *charcuterie* anyway.

It was at Bari in 1979 that a French TV crew bravely ran the gauntlet of the Mafia-controlled horse traffic between Greece and Italy and shot film of horses being wilfully maimed to qualify them as consumption potential.

Miss Larter insists that far tighter scrutiny – as opposed to scant surveillance – should be exercised in England over dealers' lorries.

'They don't care how horses are packed in,' she says, 'and they excuse themselves on the grounds that they are going to be 'topped' anyway.'

The horse meat trade from Britain is now big business. From worldwide sources, Italy receives 350,000 per year; France 300,000 followed by Belgium, Holland and West Germany.

Russia and Poland between them supply 240,000 to Italy, 160,000 to France, 24,000 to Belgium, 20,000 to Holland.

British carcass exports alone now account for £10 million per annum. Last year, reports Peter Hunt, secretary of the National Equine Welfare Committee, one slaughterer alone bought 2,000 horses and ponies in a week.

No wonder the pallid 'meat' men – their calculating eyes assessing the weight of a mare in foal – are regular attenders at all bloodstock sales.

So that when long-serving Migelitto (11 years) was reported in the *Life* having been knocked down for 420gns at Doncaster on June 22, this sometimes sad observer of the racing scene feared the worst.

For the record, Migelitto has run 115 races under Rules winning eight of his 80 Flat races and being placed in another 27. He's won at Ayr, Beverley, the Curragh, Galway, Gowran Park, Lanark, Newcastle and Phoenix Park. He's been in the frame at Royal Ascot in both the Queen Alexandra and Ascot Stakes and also competed for 25 hurdle races (placed nine) and ten chases (placed once), earning £24,345.

But neither long service nor earnings qualify a racehorse for individual or collective responsibility. Nor is Migelitto any stranger to the sales ring. His first introduction to the equine mart was on October 16, 1973, at Newmarket where, submitted as an Aston Upthorpe Stud yearling, he was bought by the BBA for 13,500gns.

Two years later he was back in the same arena, sent over from the Rosewell House Stables in Ireland, and sold for 1,000gns.

After 13 months, offered as 'the property of a gentleman.' Migelitto was parading before the assembly at Ascot Sales where his commercial value slumped to three figures (900gns).

Back at Ascot on May 5, 1981 – as the property of Westwood Garages Ltd – his stock rose to 1,100gns. Come August 11, 1982 at Doncaster however, the son of 1970 Champion Stakes winner Lorenzaccio, submitted by Manor House Stables, entered the danger zone for the first time – 480gns.

His future looked bleaker still when three weeks ago the hammer fell at the aforementioned 420gns.

Happily, research yielded the news that Migelitto was neither bound for the abattoir or one of the more sinister collecting areas.

His purchaser Michael Clarke, who served his time in stables with Eric Cousins and Bob Ward and now runs a riding centre near Stratford-on-Avon, related: 'I just wanted a good home for him. He's a super ride and jumps well. If he'd turned out to be unsound when I got him home he'd have been put down on the place.'

That, I suggest, is a proper attitude. The privilege of owning a horse involves obligation. It is incumbent upon owners to take every precaution to ensure that the animal for which they have assumed responsibility is, ultimately, despatched with the minimum discomfort.

It is the collective responsibility of those whose pleasure and profit is derived from the breed to defend their interest.

It is an abysmal reflection on the multi-million pound horse racing industry in Britain, and elsewhere, that the equine condition should be solely dependent upon the unemotional, generally unacknowledged, initiative of a handful of compassionate ladies.

As the law stands, a posse of carriageless horses may be driven through it. 'Who,' asks Eileen Bezet, one time member of the Ministry of Agriculture Advisory Committee, 'is going to be so silly as to write 'slaughter' on their export licence when all they have to indicate is 'riding, breeding or showing.'?'

The Brooke Hospital's Mrs Blenman-Bull says: 'A racehorse is a status symbol in Egypt. I appeal urgently to sellers to realise that in the end most of them follow the long miserable downward path between shafts.'

Mrs Stella Baum, of the International League for the Protection of Horses, reflects regretfully that the last racing professional to take an active interest in the League's work was the gentle and charming Freddie Fox who rode two Derby winners and pipped Sir Gordon by one for the 1930 title.

Mrs Baum's chief concern in the regrettable absence in so many countries of slaughter on the spot, is the alleviation of suffering in transit.

A persistent campaign has resulted in reduction of the makeshift transport whereby horses are ferried across Europe with 'legs sticking through the floor and dragging along the road,' to quote the League's tireless inspector Mr Roger Macchia.

She is striving to end the agonising 24-day sea ordeal between the Americas and Italy. Since although the US is squeamish about this, South America has less scruples – resulting in horses being herded from the North to begin their final nightmare.

That the Horserace Betting Levy Board makes no contribution to any equine welfare organisation such as the International League for the Protection of Horses (PO Box No 166, 67A, Camden High Street. NW1 7JL for annual report) or Brooke Hospital (1 Regent Street, SW1Y 4PA) represents a situation which surely most contributors would wish to be redressed. Quickly.

Fellow members of the Horserace Writers' and Reporters' Association, who had generously supported an auction in favour of Stoke Mandeville Hospital at our annual luncheon in 1980, now agreed, at our December

1983 renewal, to back a similar initiative on behalf of both the International League for the Protection of Horses and the Brooke Hospital.

Since visiting Morocco I had been haunted by the condition of working animals and particularly by the plight of Arab ponies provided for tourists along the nine kilometres beach at Agadir. I reckon that any patient reader who has survived this marathon so far has already given evidence of greater stamina and endurance than Brown Jack did in winning six successive Queen Alexandra Stakes, and does not deserve to be harrowed by grisly detail. Suffice to say that the guardians of the sad subjects who stood, rusty bits in sore mouths, shifting their meagre weight painfully from one unsound limb to another, insisted that no veterinary attention was available to them. As ever, the Queen Mother graciously provided a key auction item from her private collection. The audience responded nobly to my pleas, and at the end of the luncheon there was £36,883.18 to divide between the two charities.

It was a great credit to the ILPH that already by September 1985 a clinic had been built and equipped, and was being officially opened by the governor of Agadir. The League's man on the spot, Andrew Faulds, gained the confidence of the local authorities to such an extent that handlers of the beach ponies, as well as those responsible for haulage animals, were required to pass clinical examination and to report on a regular basis. If I hadn't returned and seen the ponies equipped with new bits, their feet having been tended by Newmarket farrier John Goode, and former lifeless coats exchanged for a healthy sheen, I would not have believed the evidence of the photographs I took at the time. When problems developed later I wrote hopefully, but vainly, to seek the intervention of the king's sister Princess Lalla Amina, a horse enthusiast. Happily, a subsequent letter from Clarence House was contrastingly productive!

A residual benefit from the HWRA auction was that both charities gained wider recognition in the racing world, receiving as a result regular and substantial support from the Ritz Club Charity Trophy series and the Timeform Organization. Three weeks before the fundraising event I met Sheikh Mohammed in Tokyo, where his filly High Hawk was favourite for the third running of the Japanese Racing Association's star attraction, the £200,000-to-the-winner Japan Cup. He fully endorsed the principle of supporting equine welfare, and promptly gave me a nomination to Jalmood to auction as well as making a donation. Easy when you've got it, some may think. But those who have it don't necessarily part with it. Government-controlled racing and betting (tote only) in Japan is organized with authoritarian efficiency and the invitational 'Cup' is promoted with ceremony and panache. The

immensely wealthy sport, which generated a turnover exceeding £9
billion in 1988, is seen as a significant element in overseas trade and
international relations. Yet, somehow, a feeling for the horse (*sense du
cheval*, as the French put it) seems to be missing. When I expressed this
thought to Sheikh Mohammed he reflected that, unlike in other
continents, the horse had not been a part of the country's evolution. 'To
us in the desert,' he said, 'the horse, like our saluki and our hawk, has
been an essential part of our lives for centuries.'

It was as well that no lives depended on the performance of England's
Arab-owned representative, High Hawk, at Fuchu racecourse on
Sunday, 27 November 1983. On that sunny afternoon a hundred
thousand packed the stands to see seven home defenders bid to uphold
local honour against challengers from eight nations – including two
from the USA – over 1½ miles. I write 'to see' advisedly. For, unlike
football followers, punters do not attend a stadium in order to register
parochial or national pride. They are properly indifferent to the area or
country of origin of their selection. They form an orderly queue at the
tote in the extravagant hope of purchasing a ticket which may afford
them grounds for joining another – slimmer – line after the race. In the
interim they look forward to an exciting contest.

The punters who set an Eastern Hemisphere record by wagering £15
million on the national showpiece made France's Esprit du Nord second
favourite and the Irish-trained mare Stanerra third choice. During the
big race build-up, when horsemen gathered for early breakfast and to
work their horses at the track, Frank Dunne's amazing mare Stanerra
attracted even more incredulous attention than Channel 4's flam-
boyantly attired John McCririck, who makes rather less concession to
sartorial convention than the late Prince Monolulu. Earlier in the year
at Royal Ascot, where the second day's TV coverage was 'blacked' by
a dispute, Stanerra had not only won the ten furlongs' Prince of Wales
on the Tuesday but, three days later, turned out to lower Grundy's 1½
miles record in scintillating style in the Hardwicke.

But, with four days to the 'off', it looked all of a barrel of saké to a
cup of green tea that the 5000 punts bargain would never make the line-
up. Flown out ten days previously on the twenty-hour-plus journey, she
had 'tied up' hopelessly and strode out with little more freedom than a
hobbled donkey. Her owner–trainer, already renowned for his unorthodox methods, telephoned from Dublin his daily instructions which
included six hours' walking *per diem*. While America's Half Iced (the
1982 winner) and Erin's Isle breezed 1200 metres together; England's
Premio Roma winner, High Hawk, and France's imposing Esprit du
Nord cantered a course circuit; Italy's Celio Rufo sprinted alongside
German hope Tombos, with Canada's Canadian Factor following; and

New Zealand's zestful little horse McGinty – so slight in stature he'd need to stand on tiptoe to see over a well-grown bonsai tree – galloped a fast mile, Stanerra, like Felix the cat, just kept on walking. Round and round the stable yard she went as former Irish champion jockey Wally Swinburn and his wife Doreen took it in turns to give the mare's attendant, Chris Ryan, a spell.

As zero hour approached there was no doubting the fitness of Stanerra's entourage. It remained to be seen how she reacted when her regular pilot, Brian Rouse, arrived from Hong Kong to test the prospects of achieving his biggest-ever pay day. For as well as a five-figure sterling percentage, the winning jockey would receive a Mitsubishi 1800 saloon – not bad for the London-born reinsman who once found the going so tough that he quit the game for several years to become an electrician.

While TV cameras and interviewers sought enlightment from the visitors on behalf of Japanese punters, irrepressible New Zealand race commentator, auctioneer and one-time hairdresser Keith Haub was eloquent on behalf of little fairy-tale horse McGinty. Withdrawn from the yearling sales through injury (he'd run a stake into his chest), the son of obscure English import, One Pound Sterling, had been bought by Keith ('I mortgaged the house without letting on to the wife') for £900. Pint-sized McGinty's grooming for stardom imposed such a strain on Mr Haub's capacity to nourish both horse and family that he sold a half share to Irishman Barney McCahill who had arrived in New Zealand with a pick and a shovel in 1951 and by 1965 had become a millionaire contractor. More fraternal than some Protestants and Catholics, they registered their colours green and orange.

'Wonder Mac's' progress to head the classification of his generation as both a two and three-year-old was dramatic – despite suffering a three-inch cannonbone fracture which looked like ending his career in 1982. After nine months in plaster and devoted attention from Auckland handler Colin Jillings ('McGinty's got one owner who is a millionaire and one who thinks he is!' says the trainer drily) the now twelve-race winner of US$247,000 was back and bouncing and Haub – due to 'call' the Jap classic 'live' to New Zealand and Australia – had not only turned down an offer of US$1½ million but made it known that, 'Ten wouldn't buy him either.' The one reservation about McGinty, ideally suited by the firm ground, was whether he'd stay the 2400 metres over which he'd never won.

When Stanerra, reunited with Brian Rouse, was finally permitted to break out of a walk, no auditioning dancer's footwork was ever more widely studied than the action of the daughter of Guillaume Tell. In pre-race interviews I had hazarded the view, 'Stanerra is a total freak. If she's "right" she's capable of anything', wondering how the interpreter would handle that. Now, as the forty-three-year-old rider vaulted down after circling the fifty thousand plastic roses in the infield and coming a nice half speed on the roughish ground along the back stretch, he proclaimed, 'She'll do.' But I got the impression that, secretly, he wasn't totally convinced. Me – I was here as a director of the International Racing Bureau (which had a contract with the JRA), but hoping that both a preview and sequel to an event which had the ingredients of an exciting 'international' would yield acceptable *Express* copy. I filed on Friday for Saturday's paper and, having done so, was relieved to see Stanerra move with perceptibly greater freedom in her final work-out.

Willie Carson, who had flown in to partner High Hawk, appeared less than his usual exuberant self on big-race morning, a circumstance which he blamed on the person (apologies, Willie) who introduced him to marc de Bourgogne at the end of a splendid dinner given by John Dunlop at Maxim's of Tokyo the previous evening. But it had no connection with the demise of the favourite, who was slowly away and never in contention, having come in season at an inopportune moment.

At the 'off' local speedster Hagino Kamui set a blistering pace from Germany's Tombos, with McGinty bravely bidding to overcome the handicap of an outside draw by sprinting across to the best ground on the 'inner'. Esprit du Nord and Amber Shadai moved up close as the sixteen-horse field sped towards the final turn where Hagino Kamui finally cracked, hampering Tombos as he faded abruptly, and Gary Moore hit the front on Esprit du Nord. While Amber Shadai fought to sustain Jap hopes, young Kiwi Bob Vance was getting a great run up the rail on McGinty, and Keith Haub was simultaneously calling the race and giving him powerful vocal encouragement. But to no avail. 'Wonder Mac's' early effort had taken its toll.

As he faltered, Keith looked like lapsing into shock and I shouted at him: 'Stanerra.' Kyoei Promise, a 30/1 outsider, had suddenly loomed on the scene, but Stanerra was cruising in his slipstream. When Brian eased her out into the centre of the course she simply took off. Officially it was a photo finish, but before the print was flashed on to a hundred closed-circuit screens there was no doubt that Frank Dunne, who checked in that Sunday morning, had arrived in time to see his mare from the bargain basement realize his, hers and Brian Rouse's outstanding racing attainment.

As one of the hundred thousand in the stands watching the presentation ceremony in the centre of the course, I suspected that maybe the proudest of all was the tall young man standing whisper-close to the mare's near-side ear. Chris Ryan had continually fed her Polos, in between more substantial snacks, to alleviate the monotony when she stood – as horses do in flight – throughout the arduous journey. Then, after she had tottered hesitantly down the aircraft ramp, he had begun the walking marathon, round and round the sand-cushioned stable area for hours and hours on end. The ceremonial completed, the dewy look of mutual admiration between Chris Ryan and Stanerra as they wandered back to the stables precinct was worth travelling a long way to see.

The nine-hour time difference meant that the big race went off just after 6 a.m. GMT, so there was plenty of time to send copy, which I did at 7 p.m. (or 11 a.m. in Fleet Street). Whether a horse race which has taken place some six thousand miles away from the nearest British betting shop, on a Sunday at that, is of sufficient interest to warrant allocation of space – especially in the not unlikely event of there having been disagreement on the terraces of a more adjacent football ground – was a matter of editorial judgement, against which there was no appeal. If Stanerra had met with an accident (Japanese Race Sensation – Dual Royal Ascot Winner Breaks Leg. Owner threatens, 'I will sue'. Full Story Back Page.) that would have been different. But all she had done was win. The more I thought about it, the more I figured that just wasn't good enough. In the improbable event that it was, I had a good quote from Frank Dunne to add. I rang room service for a large vodka and called the office again at 9 p.m. Reg Bailey, the Racing Editor, knew I wouldn't be overjoyed. 'I'm sorry, mate,' he said gently. 'When I came in your story was already on the spike,' adding, 'I'm afraid Friday's went too.'

Unconcerned by tabloid neglect, Stanerra returned ultimately to the pastures of County Meath where her first three sons and daughters – by Seattle Song, Shadeed and Caerleon respectively – had no mean family reputation to sustain. I wrote my last column in the *Express* on Saturday, 19 January 1985. Frost and snow had taken its toll of the jumping game and there had been no racing in England for a fortnight. The Jockey Club handicapper was to receive the Grand National entries that morning and, after conjecturing on the Aintree weights, I reported; 'Lester Piggot ended all speculation regarding his future in the saddle yesterday when revealing. "I will definitely pack up at the end of the year and start training."' He and Susan had left for Los Angeles the previous day and, since I'd had flu and felt like a break, I was going to fly to the West Coast on Sunday, pick up a car and drive down the Gulf of Mexico.

Irrespective of the contemporary climate at the *Express*, the split was still a wrench after thirty-five years. In fact Victor Matthews wanted me to continue tipping for another year as well as giving the *Express* first refusal on anything I wrote in the period, and a generous contract was agreed. But I knew I wouldn't volunteer for pruning or spiking again, and that I'd written my last piece in the paper.

Little did I realize what a stir it would create. I'd barely checked into my first hotel after a smooth Pan-Am flight via Washington (which was gripped by a blizzard) when BBC radio, who'd got my number from Pat, were on to know if I would do an interview on the furore over the Lester Piggott retirement story. What furore? I asked, innocently. It was explained that other newspapers, as well as TV and radio, had followed up my Saturday story, and now Lester and his wife had issued categorical denials from California. I said I'd answer any questions that were put to me and, during the course of the interview, related that Lester had suggested, 'You'd better raid your piggy bank and we'll have a horse together.' I was asleep when the caller rang. Now the penny dropped. Lester was under contract to the *Daily Star*.

On Tuesday, 22 January, under a caption: 'Piggott Fury – I am not going yet', the *Daily Star* reported:

The world's champion jockey Lester Piggott was furious last night at stories that he had announced his retirement. And he has asked the *Daily Star* to put the record straight. His anger follows stories in other British newspapers and on TV and radio yesterday that he would quit riding at the end of the coming British Flat season. . . . The *Daily Star* columnist has not yet made up his mind when he will retire. . . . Family, friends and racing associates all greeted reports . . . with a mixture of dismay and disbelief.

Four days later, writing in the *Irish Field*, Jonathan Powell, who had generously sent me a note ('Nice one, Peter, what a way to sign off') after my valedictory piece, wrote, 'It should not be forgotten that the *Star*, in its wisdom, pays Lester a massive retainer for his exclusive views. Could it just be that the vehemence of the *Star*'s rebuttal of the retirement story was fuelled by their dismay and embarrassment at reading of it in a rival newspaper in the same group?'

Later in the year, on 5 July 1985, in a 'STAR WORLD EXCLUSIVE', Lester announced: 'I can reveal exclusively to *Star* readers I'm hanging up my riding boots at the end of the season.' In a letter commenting on the *Daily Star*'s directional change, Geoffrey Levy, the outstanding *Express* reporter and feature writer who was to move on to the *Mail*, wrote, 'I don't think anything has given me a better laugh in years of reading cuttings.'

On return from my brief transatlantic trip I was amazed and touched by the volume and range of response to my farewell article. At a professional level the Manchester Sports Editor, Mike Dempsey, and his team had a presentation copy of it printed and framed in my black and yellow racing colours to accompany a generous letter. Alan Thompson, executive sports columnist, made a significant observation when offering enthusiastic congratulation on the maintenance of high standards to the end, writing, 'I just don't know how you have done it in face of the "direction from above" to which we have been subjected over the last decade.'

Six months later Manchester's Deputy Sports Editor, Len Gould, wrote to inquire if I might be interested in writing again. He was to become Sports Editor of *Today*, which would be launched in March 1986 as Britain's first national daily printed in colour. I didn't want to revert to daily reporting, so the invitation to write 'whenever you pleased' had clear appeal. And it was a challenge. My extended contract with the *Express* would end in January. In the interim a different outfit had taken over, and it seemed only courteous to learn their intentions before entering negotiations. This proved a trying and wholly superfluous exercise.

So on 18 January 1986, in what the *Sporting Life Weekender* referred to as a 'brief, terse, rather sad conclusion', the London editions reported that I was giving my last three selections that day. With the best intentions, but to my ultimate embarrassment, dear old Manchester went to town on the announcement. Under the caption, 'Bye, bye Peter . . . Last tip from the top' they wrote:

Peter O'Sullevan, the man the bookies feared for 36 years, tips for the last time in the *Daily Express* today. Peter, crowned King of the Naps by the racing world, retired from writing last year and today signs off after a career unparalleled in racing journalism. His naps have shown a profit in 46 of the last 71 Flat and National Hunt seasons. His best sequence being 22 out of 24 over jumps in 1965–66. We will miss him. We will never forget his famous sprinter Be Friendly: We will never forget his brilliant little hurdler Attivo. But above all we will remember. . . .

At the end of the full treatment readers were reminded that, 'Peter's last tips are in the Top Tips box in column 6.' No need to tell you what happened. Before I'd commentated the defeat of ill-fated Forgive 'N Forget in Haydock's 1.30 Dunkirk had fallen at Kempton. Two down, one to go – and fifteen minutes later Whiskey Eyes 'also ran'. In fact, with the regrettable exception of the day that mattered, the stratagem of tipping without writing had been successful to the extent that, in the somewhat unlikely event of my becoming a newspaper proprietor, I would employ a student of the 'book', essentially one who backed his own judgement, to go racing six or seven days a week, to make three selections daily, without further responsibility.

As it was, I signed up for a year with *Today*, and it was the best move I had made since buying Attivo's dam. Pedigrees are important to a racing writer – none more so than the pedigree of his Sports Editor.

There wasn't a man, or woman, on the paper who was not a delight to work with. The disasters with the new technology were seemingly unending, but the enthusiasm unlimited. Len Gould was an immensely supportive departmental head, while if ever a racing journalist was responsible for sustaining the momentum of a sometimes faltering national daily it was my friend and colleague Fred Shawcross.

I wrote my first piece in the launch issue, on 4 March 1986, after a visit to Manton, Britain's biggest private training complex, where the record-breaking thirty-six-year-old jumping trainer Michael Dickinson was introducing American-style horse handling to one of Europe's most historic stables. Instead of lads both 'doing' and riding the horses for which they were responsible, eighteen grooms were employed to care for the current complement of forty-six horses, and fifteen work riders were there to exercise them.

The general level of reward for racing's most essential workforce was, and remains, a problem. In 1977, in response to a Jockey Club-commissioned report, the Economist Intelligence Unit expressed the view, in so many words, that higher basic wages could and should be paid and that the recruitment and retention of labour would benefit owners, racegoers and punters by increasing the quality of horse care. The experiment, in Robert Sangster's privately owned stable, might not commend itself to less affluent yards, but it would be keenly monitored.

Michael's track record, which included turning out twelve jumping winners in a day and the first five home in the Cheltenham Gold cup, encouraged Ladbrokes to make him 2/1 on to produce more winners than another first season trainer, Lester Piggott (6/4). It occurred to me that the combination of newly laid terrain and backward youngsters would confer no obvious advantage on the former amateur champion. And – how sharp the memory for winning bets! – after visiting Newmarket a fortnight later I took £300–£200 Lester.

The ultimate scores (MD 4; LP 30) had no bearing upon the end-of-season split between owner and trainer, after which Michael took the full force of the racing world's perverse capacity to relish the discomfort of its heroes. But that is another story. This one, like its author, is well into extra time. It is more than sixty years since Fairy and I shared an excursion round Tattenham Corner – a long while to have been accumulating debt to the horse. Although Be Friendly and Attivo each underlined the knowledge that, in racing, all dreams are permissible, I guess I've left it a bit late now to ride a winner. But hopefully, and gratefully, there may still be a few more opportunities to experience the blend of apprehension and excitement which precedes . . . calling the horses.

INDEX